DEAN CLOSE SCHOOL

LIBRARY

This book must be returned by the latest date stamped below.

THE EVERYMAN
LIBRARY

*The Everyman Library was founded by J. M. Dent
in 1906. He chose the name Everyman because he wanted
to make available the best books ever written in every
field to the greatest number of people at the cheapest possible
price. He began with Boswell's 'Life of Johnson';
his one-thousandth title was Aristotle's 'Metaphysics',
by which time sales exceeded forty million.*

*Today Everyman paperbacks remain true to
J. M. Dent's aims and high standards, with a wide range
of titles at affordable prices in editions which address
the needs of today's readers. Each new text is reset to give
a clear, elegant page and to incorporate the latest thinking
and scholarship. Each book carries the pilgrim logo,
the character in 'Everyman', a medieval mystery play,
a proud link between Everyman
past and present.*

Joyce Cary

THE MOONLIGHT

EVERYMAN

J. M. DENT · LONDON
CHARLES E. TUTTLE
VERMONT

Critical apparatus © J. M. Dent 1995

Chronology and bibliography compiled by Douglas Matthews

The Moonlight © J. L. A. Cary Estate 1946
First published in Everyman 1995

J. M. Dent
Orion Publishing Group
Orion House
5 Upper St Martin's Lane
London WC2H 9EA
and
Charles E. Tuttle Co. Inc.
28 South Main Street
Rutland, Vermont 05701, USA

Typeset by CentraCet Ltd, Cambridge
Printed in Great Britain by
The Guernsey Press Co. Ltd, Guernsey, C.I.

British Library Cataloguing-in-Publication Data is
available upon request.

ISBN 0 460 87585 X

CONTENTS

NOTE ON THE AUTHOR

JOYCE CARY was born Arthur Joyce Lunel Cary in Londonderry, Northern Ireland, in 1888. He studied art in Edinburgh and Paris before going to Trinity College, Oxford. In 1912–13 he fought, and served in the Red Cross, in the Balkan War. In 1913 he joined the Nigerian political service. During the First World War he served in the Nigerian Regiment and was wounded at Mora Mountain. After the war he returned to political duty as a magistrate and executive officer and was sent to Borgu. His health never recovered from his time in active service and he was advised to retire from tropical Africa. Upon retirement he started writing. His first novel, *Aissa Saved* appeared in 1932. *Herself Surprised*, the first volume in a trilogy, was published in 1941, and was followed by *To be a Pilgrim* in 1942 and *The Horse's Mouth* in 1944. His other books include *An American Visitor* (1933), *Mister Johnson* (1939), *Charley is My Darling* (1940), *A House of Children* (1941), which won the James Tait Black Memorial Prize in 1942, *A Fearful Joy* (1949), the trilogy comprising *A Prisoner of Grace* (1952), *Except the Lord* (1953) and *Not Honour More* (1955), *The Captive and the Free* (1959) and *Spring Song and Other Stories* (1960). Cary also produced three volumes of verse and a number of political tracts. He died in March 1957.

CHRONOLOGY OF CARY'S LIFE

Year	Age	Life
1888		7 December, birth of Arthur Joyce Lunel Cary in Londonderry, son of Arthur Pitt Chambers Cary and Charlotte Louisa Cary (*née* Joyce)
1892	4	28 January, birth of brother John

CHRONOLOGY OF HIS TIMES

Year	Literary Context	Historical Events
1888	Zola, *La Terre* Wilde, *The Happy Prince* Birth of T. S. Eliot	Wilhelm II succeeds as German Emperor; Jack the Ripper murders in London
1889	Jerome K. Jerome, *Three Men in a Boat* Stevenson, *The Master of Ballantrae*	Suicide of Crown Prince Rudolf at Mayerling; birth of Adolf Hitler
1890	Wilde, *The Picture of Dorian Gray* Tolstoy, *The Kreutzer Sonata*	Bismarck dismissed; first underground railway in London; Forth Bridge opens
1891	Hardy, *Tess of the d'Urbervilles* Shaw, *Quintessence of Ibsenism*	Triple Alliance renewed; Young Turk movement founded; Pan-Germany League founded
1892	Wilde, *Lady Windermere's Fan* Shaw, *Mrs Warren's Profession*	Keir Hardy first Labour MP; birth of Tito and Haile Selassie; Grover Cleveland US President
1893	Wilde, *A Woman of No Importance* Pinero, *The Second Mrs Tanqueray* Death of Maupassant	Second Irish Home Rule Bill passed; Hawaii becomes a republic; Nansen sets out for North Pole
1894	Kipling, *The First Jungle Book* Shaw, *Arms and the Man* G. & W. Grossmith, *The Diary of a Nobody*	Dreyfus arrested and convicted; Nicholas II succeeds as Tsar; births of Macmillan and Khrushchev
1895	Conrad, *Almayer's Folly* Wells, *The Time Machine* Wilde, *The Importance of Being Earnest*	Jameson raid into Transvaal; Marconi invents wireless telegraphy; Armenians massacred in Turkey
1896	Chekhov, *The Seagull* Housman, *A Shropshire Lad*	Klondike goldrush; Madagascar annexed by French; Abyssinians defeat Italians at Adowa

Year   Age   Life

1898	10	28 January, death of mother
1900	12	Father remarries (cousin Dora Stevenson); family moves to Chiswick, West London; Cary enters prep school (Hurstleigh, Tunbridge Wells)
1902	14	30 October, birth of half brother Anthony
1903	15	Begins at Clifton College
1904	16	15 January, birth of half sister Sheila; 8 May, stepmother dies; brother John enters Royal Naval College, Dartmouth; Normandy sketching holiday; confirmed into Church of England
1906	18	Leaves school; studies art in Paris

Year	Literary Context	Historical Events
1897	Conrad, *The Nigger of the Narcissus* Strindberg, *Inferno* Mary Kingsley, *Travels in West Africa*	Russia occupies Port Arthur; Queen Victoria's Diamond Jubilee; Zionist Congress, Basle
1898	James, *The Turn of the Screw* Wilde, *The Ballad of Reading Gaol* Birth of C. S. Lewis Death of Lewis Carroll	Battle of Omdurman; radium discovered by Curies; deaths of Bismarck and Gladstone
1899	Tolstoy, *Resurrection* Pinero, *Trelawney of the Wells*	Boer War begins; first Hague Peace Conference; Philippines claim independence from USA
1900	Conrad, *Lord Jim* Chekhov, *Uncle Vanya* Death of Oscar Wilde	Boxer rising in China; Umberto I of Italy assassinated; Australian Commonwealth founded
1901	Kipling, *Kim* Mann, *Buddenbrooks* Butler, *Erewhon Revisited*	Death of Queen Victoria; Boxer rising ends; first Australian PM inaugurated (Edmund Barton)
1902	Conrad, *Youth* Doyle, *The Hound of the Baskervilles* Kipling, *Just-so Stories*	Boer War ends; Balfour becomes PM; Aswan Dam opens; death of Cecil Rhodes
1903	James, *The Ambassadors* Shaw, *Man and Superman* Butler, *The Way of All Flesh* Birth of Evelyn Waugh	'Entente Cordiale' established; Britain completes conquest of Northern Nigeria; Wright brothers make first powered flight
1904	Chekhov, *The Cherry Orchard* James, *The Golden Bowl* Death of Chekhov	Russo-Japanese War begins; Theodore Roosevelt wins US Presidency; British drink licensing laws introduced
1905	Wharton, *The House of Mirth* Wilde, *De Profundis* Orczy, *The Scarlet Pimpernel*	Russo-Japanese War ends; Norway separated from Sweden; Sinn Fein founded
1906	Everyman's Library begins Galsworthy, *The Man of Property* Birth of Beckett Death of Ibsen	France and Spain given control of Morocco; Dreyfus rehabilitated; San Francisco earthquake

Year	Age	Life
1907	19	Enters Edinburgh School of Art; father marries for third time (Mary Agar); family moves to Gunnersbury, near Kew
1908	20	First published volume by 'Arthur Cary', *Verse*, privately printed, Edinburgh
1909	21	Enters Trinity College, Oxford University
1910	22	Visits Paris with John Middleton Murry
1912	24	Leaves Oxford University; lives in Store Street, London; in Antivari, Montenegro (1 November); joins Red Cross; writes 'Memoir of the Bobotes' (published 1954)
1913	25	Returns to England; awarded Oxford law degree; joins Irish Agricultural Organization (Plunkett's Co-operative Movement), but leaves; applies to Northern Nigerian Political Service
1914	26	Appointed Assistant District officer, Bauchi, Northern Nigeria
1915	27	Serves in West African Field Force; wounded in action (Mora Mountain, Cameroons)
1916	28	Home leave in England; 1 June, marries Gertrude Margaret Ogilvie; returns to Lagos

Year	Literary Context	Historical Events
1907	Conrad, *The Secret Agent* Cambridge History of English Literature (–1927) Births of Louis MacNeice and Auden	Hague Peace Conference; Lenin leaves Russia; Boy Scout movement founded; New Zealand achieves dominion status
1908	Bennett, *The Old Wives' Tale* Forster, *A Room with a View* Birth of Ian Fleming	Asquith becomes PM; Congo transferred by Leopold II to Belgium; Union of South Africa established
1909	Wells, *Tono Bungay* Maeterlinck, *L'Oiseau bleu* Birth of Spender Death of Swinburne	Girl Guides established in UK; Selfridge's store opens; Bethmann-Hollweg becomes German Chancellor
1910	Bennett, *Clayhanger* Forster, *Howard's End* Wells, *Mr Polly* Deaths of Mark Twain and Tolstoy	Mann Act passed (USA); Montenegro proclaimed kingdom; deaths of Edward VII and Florence Nightingale
1911	Beerbohm, *Zuleika Dobson* Rupert Brooke, *Poems* D. H. Lawrence, *The White Peacock* Death of W. S. Gilbert	Mexican Civil War ends; Lloyd George's National Insurance Bill; Agadir crisis; Amundsen reaches South Pole
1912	Synge, *Playboy of the Western World* E. C. Bentley, *Trent's Last Case* Death of Strindberg	Woodrow Wilson wins US Presidential election; Kuomintang founded by Sun Yat-sen; *Titanic* sinks
1913	D. H. Lawrence, *Sons and Lovers* Proust, *Du côté de chez Swann* Shaw, *Pygmalion*	Poincaré elected President of France; Balkan War; Schweitzer opens Lambaréné hospital; *New Statesman* founded
1914	Joyce, *Dubliners* Burroughs, *Tarzan of the Apes* Births of Mistral and Tennessee Williams	Northern and Southern Nigeria united; outbreak of First World War; Panama Canal opens
1915	Buchan, *The Thirty-Nine Steps* Lawrence, *The Rainbow* Maugham, *Of Human Bondage* Death of Rupert Brooke	Second Battle of Ypres; Haig becomes British C. in C.; death of Keir Hardie and W. G. Grace
1916	Joyce, *Portrait of the Artist as a Young Man* Death of Henry James	Battle of Verdun; Roger Casement executed; death of Kitchener; Lloyd George becomes PM

Year	Age	Life
1917	29	3 April, birth of first son (Arthur Lucius) Michael
1918	30	Further leave in England; tour of Borgu; 9 December, son Peter born
1919	31	Ends tour of Borgu and submits report
1920	32	Retires from Nigerian service; buys Oxford house (12 Park Road); writes for magazines as 'Thomas Joyce'
1922	34	Visit to Hungary
1924	36	Begins *Cock Jarvis* (unfinished novel; published 1974)
1925	37	14 May, birth of third son, Tristram

Year	Literary Context	Historical Events
1917	Norman Douglas, *South Wind* T. S. Eliot, *Prufrock* Alec Waugh, *The Loom of Youth*	USA declares war on Germany; Balfour Declaration on Palestine; Treaty of Brest- Litovsk; Bolshevik October Revolution
1918	Cather, *My Antonia* Hopkins, *Poems* (posth.) Joyce, *Exiles* Deaths of Wilfred Owen and Apollinaire	Armistice ends First World War; Yugoslavia formed; Russian royal family killed; Polish Republic proclaimed
1919	Maugham, *The Moon and Sixpence* Mencken, *The American Language* Lofting, first 'Dr Doolittle' story	Treaty of Versailles; German fleet scuttled; Alcock and Brown make first non-stop transatlantic flight; Civil War in Russia
1920	Colette, *Chéri* Hasek, *Good Soldier Schweik* Wharton, *The Age of Innocence*	League of Nations formed; US women given vote; Government of Ireland Act; Sacco and Vanzetti arrested
1921	A. Huxley, *Crome Yellow* Lawrence, *Women in Love* O'Neill, *Anna Christie* Pound, *Poems* Shaw, *Heartbreak House*	Northern Ireland Parliament inaugurated; Imperial Conference, London; Washington Disarmament Conference
1922	Eliot, *The Waste Land* Joyce, *Ulysses* Lawrence, *Aaron's Rod* Woolf, *Jacob's Room* PEN Club founded	Poincaré becomes French PM; Treaty of Rapallo; Mussolini forms government; Irish Free State proclaimed; Bonar Law becomes PM
1923	Svevo, *The Confessions of Zeno* Wodehouse, *The Inimitable Jeeves* Death of Katharine Mansfield	Earthquake destroys Tokyo and Yokohama; Hitler's 'Beer Hall Putsch' fails; *Radio Times* founded
1924	Forster, *A Passage to India* Mann, *The Magic Mountain*	Greece becomes republic; Hoover appointed Director of Federal Bureau of Investigation; British Empire Exhibition; deaths of Lenin and Woodrow Wilson
1925	Coward, *Hay Fever* Fitzgerald, *The Great Gatsby* *New Yorker* magazine begins	Locarno Conference; deaths of Sun Yat-sen and Lord Curzon; Reza Khan becomes Shah; Hitler publishes *Mein Kampf*, Vol. 1

Year	Age	Life
1926	38	Works as docker in General Strike at Hays Wharf, London
1927	39	12 August, birth of fourth son, George
1932	44	*Aissa Saved*, first published novel (US publication 1962)
1933	45	*An American Visitor* (US publication 1961)

Year	Literary Context	Historical Events
1926	T. E. Lawrence, *Seven Pillars of Wisdom* Faulkner, *Soldier's Pay* Kafka, *The Castle* A. A. Milne, *Winnie the Pooh*	Germany joins League of Nations; General Strike in Britain; birth of Queen Elizabeth II; Hirohito accedes to throne of Japan
1927	Cather, *Death Comes for the Archbishop* Woolf, *To the Lighthouse*	Allied military control of Germany ends; Sacco and Vanzetti executed; Lindbergh flies Atlantic solo
1928	Radclyffe Hall, *The Well of Loneliness* D. H. Lawrence, *Lady Chatterley's Lover* Waugh, *Decline and Fall* Sholokhov, *Quiet Flows the Don*	Chiang Kai-shek elected President of China; women's suffrage in Britain lowered to age 21; deaths of Haig and Asquith
1929	Hemingway, *A Farewell to Arms* R. Hughes, *A High Wind in Jamaica* R. Graves, *Goodbye to All That*	Yugoslav constitution suppressed under Alexander; Kellogg-Briand Pact; Trotsky expelled from USSR; St Valentine's Day massacre (Chicago)
1930	Coward, *Private Lives* Eliot, *Ash Wednesday* Hammett, *The Maltese Falcon* Waugh, *Vile Bodies*	Haile Selassie becomes Emperor of Ethiopia; Allied troops finally leave Rhineland; death of Balfour
1931	Faulkner, *Sanctuary* O'Neill, *Mourning Becomes Electra* Bridie, *The Anatomist* Death of Arnold Bennett	Mosley founds New Party; Alfonso XIII of Spain exiled; Invergordon mutiny; Al Capone jailed; Statute of Westminster
1932	G. Greene, *Stamboul Train* A. Huxley, *Brave New World* Morgan, *The Fountain* Deaths of Lytton Strachey and Edgar Wallace	Hindenburg elected German President; Nazis win majority in Reichstag; F. D. Roosevelt wins Presidential election
1933	Caldwell, *God's Little Acre* Orwell, *Down and Out in Paris and London* Mann, *Joseph and his Brethren* (–1943)	Hitler appointed Chancellor; Reichstag fire; Japan quits League of Nations; USA recognises USSR

Year Age Life

1936 48 *The African Witch* (simultaneous US publication)

1937 49 23 November, death of father

1938 50 *Castle Corner* (US publication 1963)

1939 51 *Power in Men* (US publication 1963); *Mister Johnson* (US publication 1951); joins ARP (Civil Defence) as air-raid warden (–1945)

1940 52 *Charley is my Darling* (US publication 1960)

1941 53 *A House of Children* (awarded James Tait Black Memorial Prize; US publication 1956); *The Case for African Freedom* (revised and enlarged 1944; US publication 1962); *Herself Surprised* (Part 1 of First Trilogy; US publication 1948)

1942 54 *To Be a Pilgrim* (Part 2 of First Trilogy; US publication 1949); delivers Edinburgh University lecture: 'Tolstoy on Art and Morals'

1943 55 Visits Africa to write screenplay of *Men of Two Worlds* (director Thorold Dickinson); *Process of Real Freedom*

Year	Literary Context	Historical Events
1934	Fitzgerald, *Tender is the Night* Graves, *I, Claudius* and *Claudius the God*	Dollfuss assassinated (Austria); Kirov executed (USSR); Japan renounces naval treaties; Dionne quintuplets born
1935	Compton-Burnett, *A House and Its Head* Eliot, *Murder in the Cathedral* Left Book Club founded	German Nuremberg laws against Jews; Italy invades Abyssinia; British Council founded; Beneš becomes Czech President
1936	Dylan Thomas, *Twenty-five Poems* Mitchell, *Gone with the Wind*	Death of George V; Edward VIII succeeds and abdicates; Spanish Civil War begins; Roosevelt re-elected
1937	Auden/Isherwood, *The Ascent of F6* Hemingway, *To Have and Have Not* Steinbeck, *Of Mice and Men*	Moscow show trials and purges; George VI crowned; Neville Chamberlain becomes PM; US Neutrality Act; Duke of Windsor marries Mrs Simpson
1938	Greene, *Brighton Rock* Wilder, *Our Town*	Munich agreement; Germany occupies Sudetenland; *Queen Elizabeth* launched; WVS founded
1939	Joyce, *Finnegan's Wake* Llewellyn, *How Green Was My Valley* Steinbeck, *The Grapes of Wrath* Death of Yeats	Second World War begins; Spanish Civil War ends; Italy invades Albania; Britain introduces conscription
1940	Greene, *The Power and the Glory* Hemingway, *For Whom the Bell Tolls* Chandler, *Farewell My Lovely*	Fall of France; Dunkirk evacuation; Battle of Britain; Trotsky assassinated; Roosevelt elected for third term
1941	Brecht, *Mother Courage* Coward, *Blithe Spirit* Deaths of Joyce, Woolf and R. Tagore	Germans invade Russia; Japanese attack Pearl Harbor; BBC Brains Trust begins; death of Baden-Powell
1942	Camus, *L'Etranger* Anouilh, *Antigone* Douglas, *The Robe*	Battles of Alamein and Midway; Singapore falls; North African landings; Oxfam founded
1943	Balchin, *The Small Back Room* Thurber, *Men, Women and Dogs* Saroyan, *The Human Comedy*	Casablanca Conference; Battle of Stalingrad; Italy surrenders and declares war on Germany; Bengal famine

Year	Age	Life
1944	56	*The Horse's Mouth* (Part 3 of First Trilogy; US publication 1950)
1945	57	*Marching Soldier* (poem); final revision of *Men of Two Worlds* screenplay
1946	58	Indian tour with Thorold Dickinson; *The Moonlight* (US publication 1947); *Britain and West Africa*
1947	59	*The Drunken Sailor* (poem)
1948	60	Wife has operation for cancer; holidays with her in Switzerland
1949	61	*A Fearful Joy* (US publication 1950); 13 December, death of wife
1950	62	Publishes prefaces to *Herself Surprised*, *To Be a Pilgrim* and *The Horse's Mouth* in *Adam International*
1951	63	Lecture tour of USA; Prefatory Essays to *A House of Children*, *Charley is my Darling* and *The African Witch*

Year	Literary Context	Historical Events
1944	Eliot, *Four Quartets* Maugham, *The Razor's Edge* K. Winsor, *Forever Amber* Camus, *Caligula* R. Lehmann, *The Ballad and the Source*	D-Day landings in Normandy; Warsaw uprising; First V-2 rockets on Britain; July Plot on Hitler's life; Roosevelt elected for fourth term
1945	Carlo Levi, *Christ Stopped at Eboli* Orwell, *Animal Farm* Waugh, *Brideshead Revisited*	Atom bombs used against Japan; end of Second World War; Mussolini killed; death of Roosevelt; Labour government elected in Britain
1946	O'Neill, *The Iceman Cometh* E. Wilson, *Memoirs of Hecate County* Arthur Miller, *All My Sons* Death of Gertrude Stein	UN Assembly holds first session; Perón elected President of Argentina; Nuremberg trial verdicts; London Airport opens
1947	Camus, *The Plague* Anne Frank's *Diary* Mann, *Doktor Faustus* Mackenzie, *Whisky Galore*	British coal nationalised; Marshall Plan inaugurated; Peace treaties signed; marriage of Princess Elizabeth; Indian independence
1948	Greene, *The Heart of the Matter* Paton, *Cry, the Beloved Country* Waugh, *The Loved One* Sartre, *Les Mains sales*	State of Israel founded; Truman wins US Presidential election; Gandhi assassinated; British railways nationalised; Berlin blockade
1949	Algren, *The Man with the Golden Arm* Nancy Mitford, *Love in a Cold Climate*	Republic of Ireland proclaimed; German Federal Republic formed; apartheid established; Berlin airlift ends
1950	Hemingway, *Across the River and Into the Trees* Snow, *The Masters* Fry, *Venus Observed* Waugh, *Helena* Death of Shaw	Senator McCarthy begins persecutions; London dock strike; Alger Hiss sentenced; Korean War begins
1951	Monsarrat, *The Cruel Sea* J. Jones, *From Here to Eternity* Tennessee Williams, *The Rose Tattoo* Carson, *The Sea Around Us*	Abdullah of Jordan assassinated; MacArthur relieved of Korean command; Burgess and Maclean escape to USSR; Rosenbergs sentenced to death

Year	Age	Life
1952	64	Prefatory Essays to *Aissa Saved, Mister Johnson, A Fearful Joy, Castle Corner* and *The Moonlight; Prisoner of Grace* (Part 1 of Second Trilogy; US publication 1952)
1953	65	8 January, death of son George; awarded honorary degree, University of Edinburgh; lecture tour of USA; *Except the Lord* (Part 2 of Second Trilogy; US publication 1953)
1954	66	Lecture tours in Italy (March), Germany (June–July), Scandinavia (Nov.–Dec.); also at British Institute, Paris (27 October); *Paris Review* 'Interview with Joyce Cary'
1955	67	Unhurt when plane crashes on take-off; lecture tour of Greece and Cyprus (Jan.–Feb.); beginnings of paralysis in leg; *Not Honour More* (Part 3 of Second Trilogy; US publication 1955)
1956	68	Clark Lectures, Cambridge, read by nephew Robert Ogilvie because of Cary's physical deterioration
1957	69	29 March, dies in his sleep; funeral and burial in Oxford
1958		*Art and Reality* (Clark lectures); *First Trilogy* (as one volume)
1959		*The Captive and the Free*
1960		*Spring Song and Other Stories*
1974		*Cock Jarvis*
1976		*Selected Essays*, ed. A. G. Bishop

Year	Literary Context	Historical Events
1952	Hemingway, *The Old Man and the Sea* Leavis, *The Common Pursuit* Doris Lessing, *Martha Quest* A. Wilson, *Hemlock and After* Beckett, *Waiting for Godot*	Death of George VI; Queen Elizabeth II succeeds; Eisenhower elected US President; Mau Mau emergency in Kenya; London trams cease service
1953	Ian Fleming, *Casino Royale* Miller, *The Crucible* Williams, *Camino Real* Deaths of Dylan Thomas, O'Neill and Belloc	Tito visits London; Korean armistice; Rosenbergs executed; death of Stalin
1954	Rattigan, *Separate Tables* Thomas, *Under Milk Wood* Sagan, *Bonjour Tristesse* Tolkien, *The Lord of the Rings* (–1955)	Nasser takes over in Egypt; Dien Bien Phu falls; Senator McCarthy censured; US rules against school segregation by colour; Independent Television Authority established in UK
1955	Waugh, *Officers and Gentlemen* Greene, *The Quiet American* Miller, *A View from the Bridge* O'Hara, *Ten North Frederick*	Eden succeeds Churchill as PM; Germany joins NATO; European Union founded; Duke of Edinburgh awards inaugurated
1956	Osborne, *Look Back in Anger* Lampedusa, *The Leopard*	Khrushchev denounces Stalin; Hungary invaded; Suez crisis and war; first Aldermaston march
1957	Shute, *On the Beach* Kerouac, *On the Road* Murdoch, *The Sandcastle* Osborne, *The Entertainer* Braine, *Room at the Top*	Macmillan succeeds Eden as PM; Bermuda Conference; Treaty of Rome; Wolfenden Report

THE MOONLIGHT

PREFACE

The essential characters in this book are three women: Rose, left by her mother's death to bring up her sisters; Ella, the youngest, most dependent, and also most rebellious; and Amanda, Ella's daughter.

Each belongs at once to her sex with its nature and relations, and to a period, with its temporary answer to that everlasting problem.

I was surprised that critics and correspondents almost all looked upon Rose as a 'typical Victorian tyrant'; instead of the woman of character and unselfish goodness, who had sacrificed her own happiness to her duty. They read into my book what was not there, but which had been floating about in popular notions for a long time – that any Victorian parent who attempted to bring up children to be (according to contemporary standards) good women, good husbands and citizens, was a tyrant.

It showed me more immediately than I expected how profound are the roots of that injustice, that cruelty of judgment which poisons every age, and especially our own.

In this case, the judgment was that Rose was wicked because she tried to manage her sisters' lives. But every parent and guardian has to manage the lives of children, to take responsibility for teaching them, that is, forming their character. They may leave the job to some schoolmaster, but they are still responsible for his acts. And children insist on being managed. They ask to be taught, for their own peace.

I also saw how difficult it is to make oneself understood, for Rose's tragedy was stated in the book. I went even further than I liked in underlining it.

The see-saw of fashion which makes so much tragedy in art is also at work in ethics. But again, after the first reactions of fashion against a ruling generation, one begins to distinguish good and bad by standards that have nothing to do with fashion. One begins to say of morals, as of art, this was a great time, this was a small one.

And the test of greatness is the response of the time to some fundamental and eternal character of being. We say of women's fashions – the style of 1820, with its short waist and thin clinging folds – the opposite style of 1860, with its long waist and crinolines – that both are beautiful, and always will be beautiful because they emphasize character that belongs to women by nature. The style of 1926–7, once so chic, will always be hideous (though it may be chic again) because it arose from a denial of that nature.

So, the Victorian's answer to the eternal problem of sex will always have greatness and dignity. It said: 'Woman's chastity and refinement of sentiment are so precious to civilization, and to her own responsibility as wife, as mother, that they must be guarded from every contamination.' It concentrated, that is, on woman's central importance to family life; and it saw that the family is a fundamental character of civilization, not a construction, but from nature itself; that it is to all civilization what love is to religion, the original state of affairs from which, should every idea of existing civilization be abolished, a new one will instantly begin to grow.

There are, however, an infinite number of possible growths from this seed. A great number exist at this moment. Malinowski has told us of family organization and the rights, duties, and education of women among 'savages'. The modern young woman, brought up in a completely different moral climate from her grandmother (and often her mother – many Victorian households existed in full force until 1914), has almost complete sexual freedom, but, with it (or so I think, but I am, of course, too near the facts to be very sure of their relative significance), a sense of responsibility and integrity which, in this completely different situation, has value and distinction possibly greater than the other.

For she has *chosen* (whatever else she may do) family life, she has brought children upon herself, it lies upon her honour to make a success both as housewife and mother. The anxious sense of duty, of a typical modern wife, not only towards her family but often towards society, is very noticeable. Ask any doctor about the nervous pressure that comes of it. And this enlarged conscience, arising directly from enfranchisement, is a mark of the period.

Yet this period too is, no doubt, only another climate of the moon (to use the title of a French translation which is perhaps more descriptive than 'the moonlight'), it will be repudiated by another time, perhaps one of decadence, like the '20's (the one-child marriage, the good time) when the moral idea, as well as the fashion, was trumpery; or more likely by a return towards more austere standards. A young woman said to me the other day, 'All that promiscuity before the war was rather unnecessary. I suppose D. H. Lawrence started the idea.' Her tone despised a foolish generation which could be influenced by 'an idea'. Her own idea which seemed to her not an idea at all but tne 'natural thing', was to take a certain part-time job which would not tie her to fixed hours, so that she could marry and have four children at least. In obedience to that mysterious idea of the period which she would not even acknowledge, she was choosing a life of extremely hard work and great self-sacrifice.

And the idea itself is, I suppose, a powerful reaction against that of the twenties, when college girls were told that it was a crime against their sex in its battle for freedom, to have any children at all. Their duty was to fight their way into men's careers.

That age is now even more rejected than the Victorian. A modern business woman, herself with both a career and a family, asked what all the fuss was about, and described those pioneers of her freedom as a 'lot of hysterics'. This is extreme injustice. That period was actually an interregnum, the time of confusion which follows every successful revolution, when the slogans necessary to rouse passions begin to show their real character as battle cries, and like battle cries after a battle begin to disgust. It was a time when the women's leaders, like every junta, brought together only by a common revolutionary purpose, began to quarrel among themselves, and the mass of their followers began to discover, like all rank and file, that life for them individually had not lost any of its old problems, but rather acquired new ones.

The Victorian idea had been blown away, but nothing took its place, for the modern idea to combine career and family; experiments to show how it can be done; aids to the doing of it (creches, canteens) and, above all, the modern acceptance of the question, as one to be solved by each woman according to her own circumstances, had not yet appeared. Woman was still told from both sides, the old conservative and the new feminist, that she could not have both, that she must choose; and that the family, marriage itself, her own fulfilment as a woman, was at stake. The first said, 'Destroy the family and you destroy civilization and your own importance.' The second said, 'Let the family go – see what Russia is doing for women – free yourself for ever from these man-made bonds.'

Of course, for the majority, this advice merely perplexed. They fell in love, they married and had children, or at least (sometimes with apologies) one child. They suffered chiefly in confusion of mind and feeling; in uncertainty of purpose and achievement. But this means that they were deprived of happiness which consists in the certainty of values, that life is being well used. Perhaps the furious pursuit of pleasure, the pessimism of the writers (Huxley, Waugh), the perversity of dress (women dressed like little girls, or pederasts) were symptoms of that frustration which will not be seen again.

For the revolution, in its main victory, is an old story, its wreckage has been cleared away. Women are essentially free, and, as I say, the interesting thing to see is how they are tackling a life infinitely more difficult and complex for them, more responsible, than that of the average Victorian girl. Their freedom, in short, like all freedom, means work and suffering, insecurity and the endless anxiety of moral choice; and yet it is the most precious thing they have. It is the soul of their dignity as modern women.

The book, as a book, sprang from two quite different sources: first, a violent reaction against the Kreutzer Sonata which seemed so ludicrously wrong-headed about the whole matter of sex. In that book, you remember, a murderer tells how he killed his wife, out of jealousy; and blames the education of women 'for the marriage market'. It is penetrated throughout with Tolstoy's obsession with sex which ruled his senses and filled him with loathing, which gave him (as Gorki tells us) so foul a tongue about women, and so acute a need, which he savagely resented, for their flesh.

Horror of sex is not altogether, as some people think, a mere neurotic invention of monks, imposed on the Christian world. Modesty is a fundamental instinct, jealousy is certainly so, pride is a definition of the person. Malinowski shows that among people who enjoy before marriage the utmost sexual freedom, the married must use the strictest decorum. And such rules, founded on instinct, can very quickly become oppressive or hysterical, in the hands of a ruling clique which consists necessarily of persons who like power and think themselves therefore chosen by God (or votes, or Marx, or any other excuse) to make over the world to suit their own obsessions.

Tolstoy wanted to abolish sexual attraction and ball dresses because they excited his lust. But sexual attraction cannot be abolished; it can only be civilized; it can only be taught, like any other primæval force, to give more joy to the world and less pain. And to accuse a young girl of manhunting, of lust, because she makes the best of herself for her first ball, is false as well as mean. She obeys a hundred impulses, as well as her mother, social conventions, a sense of duty, even a sense of modesty, which denies her the right to behave differently from others. And what if the mother wishes her to attract partners, is it not of the most vital importance for her to have a choice of partners, to be admired, to make friends among men?

Tolstoy's bias was so detestable to me that I began at once to write a counter book, which was to be called (as answer to *The Kreutzer*) *The Moonlight*. It was to be the exact reverse of *The Kreutzer*. An old woman in a railway carriage (instead of Tolstoy's old man) was to tell how she had murdered her sister for preventing her daughter's marriage. And in the course of the story, she would give the true case for women as a sex, the real dilemma of a girl who is held by nature in so firm a grip; to whom, as it were, nature says, 'You are so necessary to me in my creation of society, that I shall mark you for my own. You shall be set apart like a dynastic clan. You shall have the privilege of the blood and also its pain. If you try to escape into triviality and decadence, you shall be condemned to frustration, for you were born to deal, generation after generation, with great issues, the primal issues of creation, love and birth, the first education. But you shall suffer also, like a dynastic house, the burden of inescapable duty, the constriction of power. And so I seal you with my mark.'

This first version of *The Moonlight* was written at speed, but after five or six chapters it was laid aside. I don't remember why, perhaps because of some interruption or counter attraction, and I forgot all about it.

Years later I was interested by the story of an elder sister left in charge of a family, who brought them up at the cost of her own happiness (she refused her lover) and was rewarded by being feared and detested. This injustice risked by everyone who takes responsibility for government of any kind, was a fascinating theme, and I had begun to sketch it for some future book when all at once I remembered *The Moonlight*. My wife had carefully stored away that manuscript and promptly brought it out. But when I began to read it I felt at once (I may have been wrong) that it was no good to me. I wanted to show the different sexual ideas of two or three generations in their relation with each other and with the final shape of things, the nature of sex itself, of the woman who serves, the woman who rebels (every set up, every regime has its rebels; for all regimes, dealing in general rules, cause special injustice) and the woman who is taught to conform, for her own good. I needed a big scene, a contemplative mood, and the classical third person not centred in one mind but entering into all the characters. And so I planned. As for the old version of *The Moonlight*, it was so powerful, it had such drive, that I dared not read beyond the first few pages. I was afraid it would seduce me from my now determined plan. So I tied it up again, and it is buried somewhere in the rattantoo which fills the darkest and dustiest corner of the attics.

J.C.

CHAPTER I

Miss Ella Venn, aged seventy-four, coming downstairs just before dinner, saw her niece Amanda in the arms of a young farmer called Harry Dawbarn, who had just entered the house by way of the garden. The sight gave her such pleasure that she ran back to her room. 'Oh, thank God!' she said to herself. She was tearful with joy.

Harry Dawbarn and Amanda were old friends and Harry had paid many visits to the house in the last year, but Ella had almost given up hope of an engagement. She had almost given up hope of seeing Amanda married, for the girl was thirty-two, and showed to all men the same friendly but detached kindness. She had been handsome in a classical style, with regular features, a well-shaped head. She wore her fair hair long, and it was dressed in the classical manner, parted and drawn back into a coil. But now she had begun to stoop, her eyes had a short-sighted look, her forehead showed the wrinkles of thought, and her hair had lost its lustre; slight changes which in ten years had altered a Venus, rather solid and tranquil, but of a grand presence, into a faded young woman whose only attraction was a good-natured expression.

Ella could not stay in her bedroom. Her other guests had arrived. But her excitement was still plain when at last she came down to welcome them and send them into dinner. She chattered, and her eyes despite herself, flew every moment to Amanda or young Harry. 'Did you see that the Duchess of Kent has had another baby? Isn't it nice? I am so glad for her.' Her talk, as usual, followed her mind; to the mild embarrassment of Amanda, and the amusement of the guests, who had been asking each other for a year past if Miss Ella would succeed in marrying Amanda to the young Dawbarn.

Amanda herself, though an absent-minded young woman, perceived a certain intention in her aunt's manœuvres. And this evening when after dinner Ella, lingering behind the two other ladies, suddenly kissed her and said 'Darling, I feel so happy!' she answered with a smile more of patience than of sympathy, 'Why, Aunty?'

'Because of you and Harry. I saw – I could not help seeing – when he came in.'

Amanda looked down at the excited little woman, whose big dark eyes, set in a face like that of a French pug, were the only relic of a reputed beauty, and felt a deep sigh rising in her breast. She answered with a mild reproachfulness, 'But Aunty, I didn't kiss Harry, he kissed me. And you know that doesn't mean very much. Harry is rather a flirt.'

'He loves you, darling, anyone could see it.'

'You mustn't judge by a kiss. Everyone kisses nowadays. We seem to be going back to the old English tradition.'

'Oh dear, oh dear, you will always make things so historical.'

'Come, Aunty, they're waiting for us.'

'You won't analyse, darling, will you?'

'No, Aunty, I won't analyse anything,' said Amanda, careful not to smile. 'I'm much too lazy. I want to sleep in a nice armchair, while you play to us.'

Ella, when the men appeared, consented under general demand to play to the party. But Amanda was not allowed to sleep. Harry was sent for her coat in order that he might take her for a walk in the garden. It was so warm for March, Ella said, and the view was so lovely, even under cloud, across the Longwater below.

Amanda protested, 'Oh, Aunty, I did want peace tonight.'

'Darling, that's not very kind to Harry.'

'I'm sorry, Aunty, I'll be good.'

'You are good, my blessing – and I so long to see you as happy as you deserve.'

Harry arrived with the coat and Amanda submitted to her fate. No sooner was she alone with Harry in the garden than she felt his hand on her waist, and creeping already towards her left breast. She clipped down her left elbow to protect herself, but sighed again. For she was a good-natured girl who hated to refuse anybody anything, especially to show unkindness to an old friend like Harry.

She had known Harry since their childhood when they had played together about his father's stooks and her aunt's garden. She was three years older, but that maturity, in a nature so intelligent and friendly, had made their friendship the closer. They had grown up in the easy unjealous friendship of a mutual admiration, with local gossip as a common interest. Their only difference had appeared in the last few weeks when Harry had begun to make love.

'What is that your Aunty is playing?' said Harry, working his fingers a little more beneath Amanda's elbow.

'The Moonlight sonata – you must have heard it before. It is one of Aunty's favourites.'

'Yes,' said Harry. 'It's nice: nice and tuneful.'

'It's supposed to be very romantic and passionate,' said Amanda, pressing down still harder with her protective arm.

'But you don't feel it like that, Amanda?'

He was a tall, thin young man of twenty-eight, with a long thin face, a long thin nose, a long back. With this figure, with his small fair moustache, and with a certain habitual expression as of one whose attention is fixed in the immediate present, and on patent facts, Harry might have been taken for a cavalry officer. But his walk, a slow long stride with a forward inclination from the hips and a perceptible roll, at once betrayed the farmer.

Harry's arms were also singularly long. Amanda now felt his hand pass beyond her elbow and curl down towards her chest from outside. She sighed and murmured 'No, not exactly.'

'Ah,' said Harry, 'there was a lot thought about love and marrying in those days.' His hand was now encircling Amanda's breast. She reflected, 'Really Harry is too much of an expert in female flesh – altogether too technical.'

'I like the tune,' said Harry. 'Your Aunty can play and no mistake.'

Amanda was reflecting on a certain disturbance in her pulses; a kind of dance which had begun in every part of her body and was growing wilder. 'It's most annoying,' she reflected, 'that Harry's scientific approach does have an effect. You press the button and the wheels go round.'

She adjusted her coat, raising her elbow in such a way that Harry had to release his clasp. She murmured in excuse, 'How hot it is. No, I'm not musical, I'm afraid, not like Aunt Ella. She studied for years.'

'They say at Pinmouth Fair,' Harry said thoughtfully, 'the band is worse than the cider for getting the girls into trouble. No,' he continued, smiling at Amanda, 'you're not supposed to look in the ditches after Pinmouth Fair, in case you might see people you know where they wouldn't want to be seen. It's awkward for a girl in the country, when so many know her without even getting sight of her shape.'

'Have you been in the ditch, Harry?'

'Aman-da.' But he was pleased by this question, which, in the country, was appropriate to courtship. He pressed closer, and said in an affectionate tone, 'You've never been to Pinmouth Fair, have you?'

'No, Aunt Rose doesn't approve of the Fair.'

She was preoccupied. Her mind was examining, with a calm gentle disgust, the picture drawn by Harry of sweating country couples heated to lust by a pounding brass band. But she thought, 'I mustn't be disgusted. That's so dangerous.' Amanda had that critical attitude towards her own mind which is the virtue of scholarship, and which destroys so many scholars. While Harry spoke of the coming Fair, she was reflecting, 'and I mustn't be prejudiced by Aunty's schemes. The great thing. I suppose, is not to get flurried. If that's at all possible. At least one must try not to get flurried.'

Harry was saying, 'And if your Aunty was afraid of the crowding and pushing, I could take you there by myself. I should like that very much.'

'And would you lead me to the ditch, Harry?' she murmured.

'Amanda dearr, what a thing to say.' Harry was shocked. He withdrew his hand from her waist. Amanda was ashamed. 'Of course, Harry, I know you wouldn't—'

'Why, I want to marry you, you know that.'

'Oh, but I didn't quite—'

'Haven't I been courting you this last year?'

'Have you? Was that courting? I'm sorry, Harry, I feel so sleepy tonight. Yes, I must go to bed. Goodnight."

'But Amanda, aren't you going to say—' Suddenly she was seized and pressed in Harry's arms, which seemed to go round her several times. 'Amanda dearr, tell me—'

'I can't think, Harry, while you squeeze me so tight.'

'If you love me.'

'Oh, Harry, please – I'll tell you tomorrow, perhaps.'

Harry, surprised by her urgent tone, released the girl, who suddenly retreated into the darkness. But a moment later her voice said to him, 'I'm sorry, Harry, but it's your own fault: you know too much about the female sex.'

'Now what does that mean?' said Harry.

But Amanda had gone. On a second reflection, the bemused Harry said to himself, 'She was quite upset. Amanda! And I thought her so oncoming, too.'

Amanda was hastening to her own rooms at the end of the long east corridor. She entered with relief and delight, as into sanctuary. Indeed, the sitting-room, furnished by herself, with its light brown carpet, cream distempered walls, white book shelves, steel-framed chairs upholstered in earth-coloured corduroy, a typewriting table, with a typist's spring seat, had a cool restful air which contrasted strongly with the rest of the Victorian house.

Amanda fell into her armchair, so deceitfully luxurious in spite of its angular form, and lit a long and thick cigarette. 'How lovely to be by oneself.'

But as she relaxed among the hygienic cushions, of sponge rubber, a little sense of guilt started up. Was she, after all, an escapist? Amanda had a great contempt for escapism. She reflected with careful but impartial concentration.

'No, I didn't run away from Harry. Of course, I don't quite like being stirred up like that, it's rather humiliating. It's so mechanical. It makes one feel like one of Pavlov's dogs. Harry *scatters* one so frightfully. And I must get on with my work.'

She went to her table, squared her chest like a soldier coming on parade. A typed memorandum lay before her.

The Primitive Market.

'Robson's report on the ceremonial market at Atta-Atta seems to show that it was not merely a protected market for intertribal exchange but had a religious significance from the beginning.'

Beneath was a pencil note, 'Dear Miss Groom, I think Robson is bogus, but what do you say? It's your beat more than mine. Yours. B.L.M.'

Amanda smiled. 'How Moss hates anything not purely statistical. He knows as well as I do how religion affects primitive economics – it leaks into everything.'

She began to read the report, but found after a page that she had gathered nothing. The dance was still whirling in her head, a chain dance of which the first member, with a foolish face, asked, 'Should I like it?' and the next cried, 'I might loathe it,' which led on, 'I like my job,' which drew, 'But am I using it to dodge something?' and then came a panic-struck creature begging, 'What on earth shall I tell Harry?'

Amanda stared. 'Really, it's too humiliating.' She set herself firmly to work. And by midnight she was able to sum up a careful judgment, 'The problem is thus one of all science, definition within a complex; assessment of the values for analysis on the one hand, economic or material motives, on the other, moral ideas.'

Amanda laid down her pen. Her head was splitting, but as she read her work over, she enjoyed a small triumph over the enemies of reason. Suddenly in mid-text, a phrase moved and began to dance, twisting its snake-like limbs in a long African chain, jerking, swaying in monotonous lechery 'complexsexsexment of values'.

Amanda turned slowly red. She was extremely startled. Then she stooped down her tired eyes. The words at once ceased to move, the esses and exs fell demurely apart.

Amanda brushed her eyes with her hand. 'But I really thought they were wriggling – in a horrible sort of magic. It only shows how tricky it is to – as Robson says – but really I'm too tired – too frightfully tired.'

Ella paused after the first movement, and little Colonel Hicks, who, at seventy-six, preserved the youthful manners of the eighties, cried repeatedly, with enthusiasm, 'Delightful – delightful – oh, charming. Do please give us something else.' But Ella did not seem to hear. She had once been trained for a professional pianist, and she had still something of the professional aloofness.

And on this night she was more than usually absorbed; her old fashioned style, indeed, with its exaggerated rubato, her swayings, murmurings, tosses of the head, might have amused or disgusted a modern audience. But for her they were a part of her execution. She had been taught to regard music as a poetry of the elemental feelings in which, while she performed. she was required, like a poet, to lose herself. Thus Colonel Hicks interrupted for her a kind of trance in which emotions of tenderness, excited by thoughts of Amanda, were mixed with sensations of exaltations, sacrifice, danger, mortality and pride, all that belongs, in the minds of old ladies like Ella, to a woman's fate as bride, wife and mother; a confused and cloudy world of large vague impressions which in a modern brain could have been instantly brought down to very commonplace physical events, no more than enough to fill out half an hour's gossip at elevenses.

A bell rang in the hall. The music stopped and Ella rose from her stool so abruptly that she seemed to have been jerked upwards on a string. She was out of the room before the bell had ceased.

This bell, a temporary fitting, came from Miss Rose, the eldest of the Venn sisters, who for more than a year had been lying ill of heart disease. Since she could not climb stairs she had been placed on the ground floor, where Ella could watch over her.

Ella flew now across the hall into a large room, the house's largest, which was called the library. Three of its high walls were fitted with open book shelves in pale oak, and the fourth served to display between two long plush-curtained windows a row of Venn portraits, including two full lengths, of their grandmother in crinoline and their grandfather in nankeen trousers, brown frock coat and high black stock. An astronomical telescope, of which the brass gleamed in the lamplight, stood on its tripod in one corner. Elsewhere among the formal library chairs one saw reading tables, a double music stand, an immense roll-top desk, and two of those high flat-sided cases used for the storage and display of prints.

The room was lit by a standard electric lamp close to the great desk at the far end, and by a reading lamp, with a green shade, on a small table at the bedside. The bed, a plain servant's bed, of black iron, set, with all its belongings of night cupboard, washstand and towel rail, in the middle of the room, opposite the great fireplace with its black marble clock and French bronzes, had an incongruous appearance, and, perhaps because of that appearance, the air of possessing and even intimidating the room.

This bed seemed to be empty. Its white quilt lay hollow. It was only on approaching closely that one saw above the smooth fold-over of the sheet a minute thin face, resembling that of a famine child about ten years old, which, with its livid fallen cheeks and hollow eye-sockets, lay motionless at the bottom of the flat pillow.

Ella gave an exclamation, darted to the bedside and snatched up from the night table a bottle from which she poured drops into a glass of water. But as she put her hand beneath the old woman's back, to raise it, the head was slowly shaken, the eyes opened, and a voice, like rustling leaves, whispered, 'No, no, never mind.'

'But you must take your drops, Rose.'

'No, no, I don't need them.'

'You were fainting, and the doctor said you mustn't be allowed to faint.'

Rose made no answer. The two sisters gazed at each other. Ella, glass in hand, rose slightly on her toes, in a ferment of anxiety, affection and of some sense which always preoccupied her when she was in Rose's presence, even when she was aware of Rose anywhere in the house – of nervous tension. It was that complex feeling which always obtains between two people, especially two women, who have lived together all their lives, who have a thousand reasons both to love and to hate each other; and who have perpetually to keep the love in repair, recreate it, regild it; and perpetually to suppress all motions of hatred, crush them, hide them, transform them into something else. Ella did not remember the time when she had not felt that strain of family love, sisterly criticism. It pervaded for her every room in Florence Villa. She raised herself to the very tips of her toes, opened her large eyes still wider, and said in a coaxing, affectionate voice, 'You felt yourself fainting when you rang?'

The question was not only affectionate, it contained an accusation. It meant, 'If you were not fainting, why did you ring, and if you are fainting, why do you refuse the medicine.'

'You had a party?' Rose whispered.

'No dear. I told you that I was asking Mr Sangster and the Hickses to dinner.'

Rose opened her eyes and looked at her sister. Ella turned slowly pink. At last, in a high nervous voice she exclaimed, 'And Harry Dawbarn came in, just at the last minute.'

'Ah!' breathed Rose, and no one could have told whether she had known this fact before, or had drawn it forth.

'Is that why you rang?' said Ella. But this was a tactical mistake, especially as Rose and Ella had long differed about Harry Dawbarn. For Rose he was not only an ill-educated country oaf, he was a loose and untrustworthy young man who was already under suspicion of seducing a girl in the village; for Ella, he was charming, handsome, good-natured, the patient victim of circumstance.

Ella's remark, therefore, since the sisters were at variance, was an act of war. It accused Rose of prejudice, of tyranny, even of double dealing. For if Rose had rung for information, she should have asked for it at once.

'I should like to see him,' said Rose.

'Oh dear, I think he's gone,' said Ella.

'No, I can hear him in the drawing-room, and so can you. Go and fetch him, Ella.'

Ella gazed at her sister with rage and despair.

'Amanda will be very hurt if you are unkind to him,' she muttered.

'Don't be absurd, Ella. Amanda is not such a fool. Go and fetch the young man, or must I ring for Mrs Hendy?' Rose's voice grew sharp as she jerked herself up on the pillow.

Ella trembled all over and clasped her small strong hands together. She thought, 'No, I mustn't argue, I mustn't. She might fall dead and think how dreadful that would be. Anything but that.' And she exclaimed in a low voice, 'Rose, if you insult him and drive him away, I'll – I'll never forgive you.'

'That's your business,' said the other, and fury gave her the look almost of health. She reached for the bell, but it was three inches beyond her hand.

'And you yourself tried to find a husband for Amanda. You asked Professor Moss to stay just—'

'Professor Moss is not a vulgar young man of the worst possible character.'

'No, but he was sixty, and Amanda never cared for him in that way. And she likes Harry and Harry likes her. And Harry is not uneducated. He went to Queensport Grammar School, which is quite a good school.'

'You know the man's character and you take every chance of leaving him alone with Amanda. My dear Ella, one would think you wanted to see the child compromised.'

'Oh, Rose!' Ella was scarlet. 'How could you?'

'My dear Ella, what is the good of looking so shocked. No doubt you think I exaggerate. But how often have you deceived yourself about your own intentions – even as a child you were famous for saying one thing and doing another. But what is the good of argument.' Rose made a sudden leap in bed and struck the bell, which gave a single trill in the hall.

Ella turned and flew towards the door. She was so enraged that she almost ran into the chairs and the screen. She thought, 'But how unfair, how wicked, she knows I daren't stand against her in her illness.'

She shut the library door quickly behind her just as Mrs Hendy, the night nurse, came from the little back parlour. 'Thank you, Mrs Hendy,' she said smiling, 'I answered the bell, you needn't trouble.'

Mrs Hendy went back into the parlour, Ella into the drawing-room. She was breathless with excitement. She thought defiantly, as she had thought as a child of six, defying the same sister, 'She can't kill me.'

In the drawing-room Harry was talking to the rest of the party – Sangster, the retired banker; Mrs Sangster and Colonel Hicks, about the betting for the Grand National.

Ella threw herself boldly into the talk. 'But which was the horse that won the Derby? Isn't he still the best? There, you're laughing at me. I don't really understand races. I'm really rather afraid of racehorses. They're so delicate looking. What I love are your horses at Brook, Harry: real horses, so big and – and monumental. Really noble—'

The bell was ringing in the hall, and suddenly she exclaimed,

'Oh dear, I'm afraid my sister is not so well. Yes – I'm so dreadfully afraid . . .' She rose and put out her hand. The guests came to their feet. They had already the apologetic look of those who intrude. In a moment they were in the outer hall, and Ella and the parlour maid flitted round them with coats. The bell, still ringing, urged every one to haste.

Mrs Hendy passed into the library; the bell stopped. As the front door closed at last, behind Harry, she came out again with a perplexed air and called urgently to Ella. But Ella was rushing upstairs as if pursued.

'Miss Ella.'

Ella flew round the corner and disappeared. The nurse, startled, went back to tell her patient that Mr Dawbarn had left the house and Miss Ella had gone to bed.

But Ella had not gone to bed. She could not go to bed. She stood in her room, almost cataleptic in terror, waiting for Mrs Hendy to tell her that Rose was dead, when the bell stopped. 'And I killed her,' she thought. 'I murdered her – oh, I deserved this! I have been a bad sister all my life. Ungrateful, cruel. Perhaps I wanted her to die, perhaps I argued with her on purpose. Yes, Rose was right when she said I had an evil will – it is evil – right down inside – the true me – is evil – evil.'

The tension had relaxed. She sat down on the bed. 'Yes, evil, selfish.'

She gave a long tearful sigh and raised her legs upon the quilt, 'selfish, scheming.' She fell back on the pillow. 'I am a wicked woman, I always was. Yes, and so cunning, that's what makes me so hopeless, hopeless.' Her eyes closed on her thin old woman's tears. In a moment she was asleep.

CHAPTER 3

Amanda was composing a letter to Harry explaining why she could not marry him, when Ella appeared before her in mackintosh and boots. 'Oh dear, I mustn't interrupt you – though I'm sure you are working too hard. If only you don't ruin your eyes. They are quite sunk in.'

'I didn't sleep very well,' said Amanda, who had not slept at all. 'Do you want me?'

'Oh no. I was just going for a little walk to the village, but don't you move. No, please.'

'Of course I'll come, Aunty.' Amanda, with a sigh, abandoned her letter and put on her own mackintosh. Ella meanwhile protested against the waste of her time. 'I shouldn't have interrupted you, I'm always interrupting you.'

'Did you say the village, Aunty?' For Ella was leading the way through the garden and paddock towards the fields.

'Yes, yes, we'll go round, it's so nice this way.'

'It will be rather wet in the grass.'

'Oh no, darling – yes, perhaps a little wet, but it's cleared up now.'

In fact a shower was falling as the two ladies passed through the paddock towards the field gate. 'How beautiful,' Ella cried, tilting her small face to the sky. 'This fine rain is a real pleasure. Amanda, do you think I am a very deceitful person?'

'No, Aunty, of course not.'

'Your Aunt Rose thinks so, she has always thought so. She says I am always pretending to do one thing while I am really doing something else.'

'I haven't noticed it,' said Amanda, who had noticed it very often.

'No, because it isn't true. That is, it's partly true. Yes, I'm afraid so. For instance, your Aunt Rose says I've been trying to marry you to Harry Dawbarn, and yes, I did think you might be happy with Harry.'

'But you mustn't blame yourself, Aunty. I've always liked Harry.'

'No, no, it doesn't matter now when you and Harry are so devoted.'

'Hardly devoted, Aunty. We're old friends, of course.'

'Oh dear, I shouldn't have told you.' Ella touched Amanda's arm. 'Now you'll begin to wonder and ask yourself questions.'

'No, Aunty, but I don't want you to think—'

'You mustn't ask yourself questions, darling.' Ella spoke urgently. 'Happiness is so easy to spoil, especially when you are happy. Oh yes, I've seen it so often. just when a girl is going to be married – yes; just because she *is* so happy, so full of love, she begins to examine her feelings, and then she begins to wonder if they are real feelings, and then she gets frightened and all at once her happiness is gone.'

Ella glanced at Amanda in alarm. 'Yes, gone for ever. All at once she is in despair – just empty and wretched. Go on being happy, darling, that is such a precious thing. Oh dear, what a lovely day it is – yes, it's like a blessing. The rain makes it even nicer.'

Ella, noticing that Amanda was a little thoughtful, threw herself into the enjoyment of the day. She was a great enjoyer of weather, as part of nature, which she had learnt to enjoy from her very earliest years, when her nurses and especially her sister Rose, had called upon her to admire the beauties of hedge, flowers, trees, sunrises, cattle, shepherds or thatched cottages. 'Look at the sun, how lovely it is after rain, but of course the air is washed so clean, of every *minutest* particle of dust. And how wonderful the drops are on the grass, and the leaves. Like little lenses, all shooting different sparkles at you.'

'If we are going to the village, Aunty.'

'Oh dear, I have taken the wrong path. But it is only a little longer through Brook.'

Ella, by taking the left hand path instead of the right, had come out above Brook farm, which now lay below them on the right, displayed to its greatest advantage.

The whole of Brook's three hundred acres lay in one long shallow valley, like a pie-dish, sloping from north to south; a stream, dammed in several places to form pools for stock, flowed down the middle; and the house, a long building in grey stone, was set by one of the larger pools at an obtuse angle to the stream. It stood thus cornerwise to the slope so that it was at one end, next the water, two stories high; at the other, the east end, only one storey. Barns and byres, in a double quadrangle, climbed up the hill behind, so that an insignificant tool shed at the top north-east corner by the stack-yard had all the importance of a watch tower overlooking a fortress.

There was no garden or hedge along the bare front of the house, and the front door, never used except by summer visitors, opened direct upon the farm road, a mere track across the open meadow.

At the moment when the two ladies came over the hill from the villa, another sea shower was passing across the vale; that is to say, something too light to be called rain and not substantial enough to appear as mist. It seemed as if parts of the middle air, over the vale, had lost some of their transparency and acquired instead an inner light of their own, a greenish radiance which threw a similar shade on everything below, so that the grey winter grass appeared almost spring-like, the blue slates on Brook roof seemed like stone tiles, and the pool beyond became olive.

'How charming it is,' said Ella.

'It's quite time,' said Amanda, 'that somebody mended these tracks, they're a disgrace.'

'But what is happening over there?' said Ella, stopping. 'I do believe lambing has started.'

Amanda had already noticed, on an upper field, gradually appearing through the shower, like a piece of landscape through a wet windowpane, sheep, a waggon full of straw, and several active figures very busy on some construction. She recognized Harry, waving his long arms in the direction of the work. His long white mackintosh was conspicuous against the bush and hedge, still black with winter, which made the horizon on that side of the vale.

'Isn't that dear Harry?' said Ella.

'He won't want to be interrupted.'

'No, we mustn't go near him.' Ella turned to cross the field towards the group of workers. 'Only I must ask him about the eggs.'

Nearer approach showed that a new lambing fold was being built in the midst of a field of kale.

'You can't go in there, Aunty,' said Amanda. 'You'll be soaked.'

But Ella had already lifted her skirts, showing her old-fashioned lace boots, and was picking her way among the wet plants.

The fold was only half-built. It consisted at present of three walls of straw, about twenty pens complete with roofs, for ewes with new-born lambs, and piles of straw, wheat reeds, hurdles, stakes, with which one very old man and three children were putting up a fourth wall, and knocking in hurdles to make the pens and divide the fold into two parts.

'What luck,' said Ella, 'to catch them at the beginning.'

'We mustn't stay,' said Amanda.

Harry, appearing from behind the further wall of the pen, now caught sight of the ladies and waved to them with what looked like a long blue and white scarf, of which one dangled from each hand. A second glance showed these scarves to be two new-born lambs, held by the fore feet.

'Well-come,' cried Harry, smiling and touching his hat with a lamb. 'Now that's a good sight, Miss Ella, to see you.'

'It's a delightful surprise to see your lambing has started – at least, I did hear something from the milk-boy. I do hope you will have a good lambing, Harry.'

'Twenty-four dropped since yesterday morning, and three triplets. There's a lot of bottle-work due to somebody – wait a minute till I put these down.' He entered the fold and put down the lambs, with a deft swing which laid them neatly stretched on their sides, in one of the small pens. An old woman was dragging straw into this fold; and a young one, in spite of one arm in plaster, was constructing the eastern range of pens with the help of a boy so small that he was rather shorter than the hurdles. The child's duty was to tie the hurdle to the stakes supporting the roof, after the girl with the broken arm had set it in place.

This gathering of workers, very old or very young, crippled or merely casual, did not strike either Amanda or Harry as worth remark. For one thing, it was common enough at a time of crisis, folding, singling, harvest, to see almost the whole population of a small village like Brook at work; so that one might say that in this purely farming valley, all were neighbours not only of one another, but of the processes of nature; of the sheep and cattle, the crops and the weather; for another, old Dawbarn was accustomed to employ all the year round, labour so casual that it could hardly be reckoned even as casual labour in the ordinary sense of the word. He would hire a tramp off the road to clean a ditch for a shilling, a schoolboy to lime-wash apple trees at a farthing a tree, or induce a sailor on leave to drive a horse and waggon to Queensport, to fetch coal, for a quart of cider and the fun of the thing.

But to Ella, this very quality of Brook, its improvisation, was delightful. The girl with a broken arm seemed to her a heroine, the old twisted workers, especially the old man, called Uncle Bobby, who was Dawbarn's man of all work, as servants of God, crippled in service to nature, to growth. 'Oh, Harry, we must help you. Why didn't you send for us, Amanda is so good with lambs. Amanda, dearest, I'm sure you will help Harry.'

'Well,' said Harry, 'Wilson being laid up—'

'What, the new shepherd?'

'Well, Miss Ella, he's not so new. Eighty-four, I should say, and not too good for his age. So we're a bit behind. But if Amanda could give a hand.'

'Of course she will, so will I.'

'Here's the milk,' said Harry, 'and that one over there is waiting for it, born this morning.'

A schoolgirl, neat and prim, had appeared at the gate hurdle. She was carrying a whisky bottle full of milk. She took a baby's feeding-bottle out of her satchel and handed it to Amanda. 'If you'd be so kind, Miss Amanda, I really haven't time, I got such a turble lot of prep.'

Amanda poured the milk into the feeder and put it through the bars of the pen. A small grey lamb, sitting by itself with a stunned air, looked at the bottle, and rose a little way upon its clumsy legs. But the legs collapsed under it, a failure which it seemed to accept as a natural event belonging to its new world of experience. For it folded itself up and settled once more to contemplation.

'You'll have to go in,' said Ella eagerly, 'the poor little thing is too weak. Harry will show you.'

Harry was already opening the outer hurdle for Amanda, and now lifted the lamb, laid its nose against the bottle and cried out sharply, 'Kak kak kak-puss,' which was his standard encouragement to young lambs learning to suck.

'What a pity,' said Ella, who had remained outside the pen. 'What a pity that you can't have a farm of your own, Amanda. You are so good with animals. I think I must buy you a farm – yes, I shall buy you a farm, and then you must marry a farmer.'

'Ah, she'd do well at it, too,' said Harry. 'Kak-kak-kak-p-u-s-s – go on, you.' The lamb slightly raised its tail and Amanda, who felt herself, to her indignation, going red, said, 'It's getting the idea.'

'So it ought to,' said Harry. 'Ah, a real motherly hand with the bottle.'

'Yes, I shall buy you a farm. Perhaps I could buy Brook. If your father wants to give it up, Harry. Yes, what a good idea. But, dear me that poor girl.'

Ella, having closed the hurdle to shut in the young couple, hastened to the furthest corner of the fold to offer her help to the girl with the broken arm.

'Buy Brook,' said Harry. 'Well, it is a good idea. Wouldn't cost so much either, with the debts.'

'Aunty doesn't mean half she says.'

'She means that all right, she's said it before. It's a good deal on her mind, that idea.'

Amanda felt a slight warmth across her back which she perceived to be Harry's sleeve. He was not clasping her, but resting his hand on the hurdle, in a position to clasp her.

'I don't know how it is,' said Harry, 'but I had an idea the other night that you were getting more into the notion of marrying.'

'Oh lord!' Amanda sighed to herself. 'He's starting again, and then I'll start again.'

'It's not such a bad idea,' said Harry. 'I mean of the old lady's. For she told me I should have to keep on old Hannah for the housekeeping. That would save you all those chores. And you know, Amanda, you'd find it nice and quiet at Brook for writing.'

'I knew it,' reflected Amanda sadly. 'There's the old dance again. How I do wish my heart wouldn't go on in this extraordinary way whenever Harry approaches me with intent. Because I'm not a bit excited, far from it.'

'Yes, my dearr, taking a fair view, I don't think the old lady is so stupid. Look at it yourself. I should be out most of the day in the fields, and I'm not too particular about meals, and for all that, I'm a domestic sort of man. I'd be a fond husband to you, my dearr, indeed I should. It's the way I'm made.'

'You know how much I appreciate – ' Amanda began, fearful of being embraced.

'I wouldn't hurry you,' said Harry. 'Easy does it. Only if your Aunty did want to take up the lease of Brook, she'd have to see the bank before Lady Day. And to tell you the truth, Amanda, I'm worried about the bank. We're a bit behind with 'em.'

'Are they annoying you?'

'Not me. But Father's gone to bed again. That has a bad look. And he's talking of retiring, which is worse.'

'But would it matter to the bank so much if he retired? I should have thought the bank would have preferred you.'

This was a reasonable view, for Dawbarn was reputed one of the worst farmers in the Brook district. Amanda knew him as a little thin crow-faced man with a stooping back, who spoke always with great deliberation, and the air of a sage. He had the name of being a hard bargainer and something of a miser, who, at the same time, was never ready for his season and always missing his market.

'You make most of the income as it is, don't you?' said Amanda. 'On hire jobs and the stock.'

'You never know with a bank.' Harry spoke as if banks were creatures of very erratic temper. 'But my idea is this one wouldn't stand for being owed such a heap of money by anyone but an old client like father. They're used to him owing 'em money, he's owed it twenty years now. But any change might frighten 'em. Banks don't like a change with old debts – it gives 'em a shock.'

'It wouldn't even pay them to turn you out?'

'No, but it might make a better tale for the Head Office. So that's what I say, Amanda, if changes are coming, it mid be a good thing to have 'em on both sides.' He paused and plainly waited for an answer. Amanda, stooping over the lamb, said at last in mild and reasonable voice, 'I quite see your point, Harry. The only thing is, that it's a little unexpected.' She stood up and shook the feeder. 'I thought so – the milk isn't going through the teat, there isn't enough of it. I must fill up.'

Amanda, on this excuse, left the pen with dignity. 'Really,' she thought, as she looked round for the schoolgirl with the milk, 'Aunty is rather trying – offering me a farm. Things were bad enough as it was. Though I suppose the real trouble is in myself. I've been getting a little detached.' Ella had disappeared. The schoolgirl with the milk was also out of sight. But the very small boy, who seemed to know, at fifteen yards distance, exactly what she wanted, shouted, 'She'm behind yere,' pointing at the pens, and then running across the fold yard to show her the way. He carried his arm still at the point, so that in turning the corners of the outer gate hurdle, and the lambing fold itself, it described a quarter circle. At this corner the boy stopped and the arm pointed directly at the schoolgirl who was seated on a truss of straw knitting her brows at a primer.

Amanda thanked him warmly, for she was glad to be able to take a decisive line.

'Of course,' she thought, 'if I did think of a husband at any time in the next few years, simply to get the thing settled and done with,

Harry would be quite a good choice. Yes.' She examined her feelings. 'It's not only that I like him, but he's so matter of fact, so unsentimental. Marriage with Harry would be almost – surgical.'

She approached the schoolgirl with a calm, decisive air. The whisky bottle, half full of milk, stood beside the child, and Amanda began carefully to refill her feeder.

The small boy meanwhile had put his hands in his pockets and was looking suspiciously at a black-faced ewe leaning against the straw fence. The creature was panting and straining. It had been in labour for some time. The small boy, who wore a man's cap hung rather than placed on his head, watched attentively and then set up a cry. Harry's voice was heard in urgency. 'Ah, is that the long tail?' He appeared and joined the small boy. They seemed to agree at once upon the gravity of the case. 'I thought there'd be trouble with her.' He approached the ewe, which jumped up and tried to run off. He caught her with a tiger pounce, turned her over, and stooped down.

After a moment he began to call, 'Bobby, where's Bobby?' The small boy ran up but was sent away. 'You call Bobby, that's who I want.'

Amanda was meanwhile filling her bottle with great care, while the girl, frowning at the disturbance, repeated in a soft but irritated voice, 'The products of Africa *are* – cocoa, *ground* nuts, *palm* oil, gold and – and . . .' She gave Amanda an angry look as if to say 'Do go away.'

Amanda would have liked to go away if her path back to the fold had not lain past Harry. She felt a disinclination to see what he was doing. But like everyone who tries not to look in a certain direction, her head and eyes turned that way as if of themselves. She glanced suddenly, quickly, at the ewe. Harry also raised his head, looking for help, caught her eye and passed over her. He shouted loudly, 'Bobby.' His hands, as Amanda saw, were red to the wrist. The ewe, under Amanda's fascinated glance, licked her lips exactly like a human being in pain. And suddenly, as if dragged by the rope of her own reluctance, she walked up to Harry and said, 'Can I help?'

'Ah, thank you, Amanda. Just hold these two hind legs, and don't let her kick you. She'd cut your eye out.'

Amanda grasped the legs and shut her eyes. Harry operated, muttering, 'Ah, a dead one. I thought so.'

'Who would be a female?' said Amanda.

'Let her go.'

Amanda released the ewe, who jumped up and trotted away.

'Head her off,' said Harry, 'there's another to come.'

Together they drove the ewe into a pen and shut her up behind a hurdle. Harry wiped his hands upon a convenient sheep and turned to speak. Amanda, to her own surprise, exclaimed, 'Heavens, five o'clock. I must fly.'

But Harry placed himself in her way. 'Amanda, dearr, there's only one thing.'

'Yes, Harry?'

'You're not against marrying in a general way?'

'What do you mean, Harry?'

'Well, some girls don't fancy the idea – and I thought just now when you were helping me with the long tail – perhaps you might have your own feelings against matrimony.'

'What nonsense,' said Amanda. She was as angry as she could be with anybody. 'If you believe that, you believe anything.'

But already another figure had joined the dance, a strange gibbering ghost with an umbrella and elastic-sided boots.

Harry was apologizing. 'I'm sorry', dearr, you have a right to be cross at me. But as I am a marrying man, you see—'

'What about Nelly Raft, Harry?'

Nelly Raft was the village girl reputed to be pregnant by Harry. But Harry would never discuss this subject with Amanda. He seemed to regard it as his own very particular business; his silence was a comment on intrusion.

'I'm sorry, Harry, perhaps I shouldn't—'

'What I mean is, Amanda,' said Harry severely, 'that I'm a marrying man *now*, and to you. I'm twenty-eight and I need a wife. And you know, Amanda,' he added in the view of one honestly exposing all sides of a transaction, 'you needn't be afraid I'll go running after girls. I'll be a good husband to you, my dearr, because I'm made for peace. I like things comfortable at home, as you do yourself.'

'And are you sure about me, Harry?'

'I should say, my dearr, you were the nicest girl for marrying within ten miles. It's not only the way you're built, it's your nature. Yes, a really kindly girl, that's why I'm so set on marrying you.'

'You want a comfortable woman and a nice farm.'

'Now, Amanda, that's not fair. It's true, and why not. But it's

not fair – not the way you put it. But there, you don't like the idea.'
Harry's voice showed a slight despondency.

'What idea?' – Amanda was indignant.

'Well, marrying is a queer idea, especially for a young lady. Every nice girl hangs back a little at the first go off: it's natural. Yes, I didn't blame you when you ran off the other night.'

'But I didn't run away from – I don't mind marrying.' Amanda gave a deep quivering sigh and said, to her own surprise, 'In fact, I never said I wouldn't marry you, Harry.'

'My dear Amanda,' said Harry, 'that's the best thing I ever heard. But come in behind the pen, just a moment.'

'No, Harry dear, please.'

'I see. Well, sweetheart, I don't know what to say.'

'And you mustn't tell anyone. Not just yet.'

'Not a word, my dearr. So long as you'll be getting on getting used to the idea. Because you know the best time to get married is after lambing and before the hay. I wouldn't hurry you, Amanda, but after lambing is the best time except about Christmas, and that's too long to wait.'

'Thank you, Harry, I'll remember – but heavens, it must be frightfully late, and where's Aunty?' Amanda hastened to seek her aunt. Ella had hidden herself with some skill, but she was found at last behind the waggon. She was conversing with the housekeeper, an old friend, though no one could conceive how either understood the other's words, and it was generally supposed that they did not, but conveyed only general feelings of a negative or positive character.

'Hi – heehoo – haw,' the old woman was saying. She had a cleft palate and no teeth. Dawbarn had hired her, at the age of ten, on account of her defect, for two shillings a week, paid when he chose, less fines, and she had spent forty years at Brook. She was invariably cheerful and would sing to herself, at her work, songs which resembled the cries of the herring gulls which, in bad weather, would fly over the farm house.

'Aunty, oughtn't we to go, it's past five.'

'Good gracious, I'd no idea! I was just asking Hannah about Susan. You'll tell me, Hannah, when you hear from Sukey?'

Sukey was an illegitimate daughter born to Hannah thirty years before, now a prosperous farmer's wife in Australia.

'Hoohee,' said Hannah. 'Huh hees ho hoo hoo hee – hee hehe ha.'

'She says Sukey's no good to her,' said Harry. 'She's a silly girl.'

'Oh no, Hannah,' said Ella; 'She's a very nice girl. Goodbye, Hannah, dear. Look after Master Harry.'

'He – ha – hoy – hee – ho – hee ayhee,' said Hannah, much excited.

'She says I'm a bad boy, I don't eat anywhere.'

'Ha – hee – ho,' said Hannah, with a fierce snort. 'Ha.'

'Yes, you're quite right, Hannah, dear,' said Ella, and walking across the fields with Amanda, she exclaimed, 'How good old Hannah is, a devoted servant. But what devotion there is everywhere in the country – old Bobby there, he would die for Harry.'

'I suppose neither Hannah nor Bobby get their wages very often. It's a shame the way they're treated.'

'Oh, but Hannah is so happy. She wouldn't be anywhere else.'

'She's not fit for anything else after forty years at Brook. Why do you want to marry me off, Aunty? Marriages aren't always happy.'

'No, no.' Ella was much agitated. 'But there, I suppose – it's nature's intention for us women – for most of us. And nature is so wise. Yes,' glancing round at the fields, as if for support.

'Was she wise when she made that half-wit woman at Ancombe have an illegitimate half-wit last year?'

'Oh dear, oh dear! Yes, it's so – difficult.' Any suggestion that marriage was not necessarily a happy state always threw Ella into confusion. She looked at Amanda with alarm, and as they reached the house, uttered several deep sighs. 'Yes, it's all very hard to understand. But you will be happy, dear. Oh, I'm quite sure. With God's blessing. At least, you will never be sorry – you won't want it not to have happened. But I must go to Rose.'

She hastened away as if from an unlucky scene.

Amanda went upstairs to work. She would not even wait for tea, but sent for it to be brought to her desk. She was eager to enjoy the peace of decision. But to her surprise she found that the dance began again as soon as she opened her book; not the old dance, but one in which she could not even distinguish the figures. Harry, the mad spinster, had been replaced by dark forms, revolving in such a deep recess of the mind that she could not distinguish one from another, or even guess at their sense.

'I suppose,' she said, laying down her pen, 'that I'm not going to have any peace until I'm married – married at least a month, and bored with the whole thing. Yes, I can see why long engagements are a mistake.'

CHAPTER 4

Two days later Ella, in uncertain and fluttering spirits, was taking
Rose her evening cup of tea at ten o'clock. But the old woman lay
still gazing at the ceiling and seemed not to notice Ella's presence.

'Your tea, dear.'

But Rose did not move. Her black eyes were fixed upwards in a
mournful stare.

Ella, alarmed, bent over her. 'Are you ill? Shall I fetch the drops?'

Rose's lips parted and she said in a slow voice, 'Did you promise
young Dawbarn to buy him a farm if he would marry Amanda?'

Ella started back. 'No dear, of course not.'

'Is that true?' And after a short pause, Ella said faintly, 'I only
said it would be nice for Amanda to have a place of her own, a
quiet place to write in.'

'And how were you going to buy this farm?' said Rose, suddenly
twisting her eyes towards Ella. 'You haven't any money.'

'I don't know, Rose. I didn't think of how – I thought—'

'You thought that I should die soon, and then you would buy
this farm and Dawbarn would marry Amanda.'

'No, no, Rose – how could I calculate – on your death?'

'Of course, of course you were,' cried Rose, sitting up in her bed
with an energy terrifying in so worn out a frame. 'I've always
known that you hated me, I've always been in your way. I'm in
your way now.'

'Oh, Rose, not in my way; but perhaps we think differently
about Amanda's happiness.'

'Rubbish! What do you care about her happiness? You only
want to thrust her into the arms of some man, any man.'

'It's not true,' cried Ella. 'Oh, how wicked – but of course, how
can you understand, you have never even been in love.'

Rose fell back on the pillow and muttered, 'Yes, you would like
to kill me.' Her eyes closed.

Ella, in sudden terror, fell on her knees beside the bed and caught
her sister's hand. 'Oh, Rose, I didn't mean – oh, Rose, isn't it

enough for me to want anything for you to say it's wrong and bad
– you would rather spoil Amanda's happiness – her only chance of
happiness – than *not* contradict me. Yes, you want Amanda to be
an old maid.'

Rose merely looked at Ella, who, feeling her guilt, pressed Rose's
hand to her cheek. 'Oh, I didn't mean – yes, I did mean – I don't
know what I meant.' She cried out like a child, and the elder sister
said in a voice full of mournful resignation, 'Yes, darling, I
understand.'

And Ella, kneeling still, clasping the hand as if she were clinging
to her only salvation, thought as always, 'No, she doesn't understand. She never, never understands. She doesn't try,' and instantly
cast this wicked thought out of her heart. In penitence for it, she
passionately kissed Rose's hand.

Rose, disengaging her fingers, whispered, 'No dear, you mustn't,
you mustn't get so excited.' She was gasping, her hand fell back.
Ella struggled to her feet and seized the medicine glass. The old
woman drank, sighed and lay still. Ella bent over her, but even in
this maternal pose she had the air, not of the nurse, but of the
servant. She seemed not to take a responsibility, but to await a
command.

'Can I do anything – would you like tea?'

'No, no.' Rose opened her eyes and looked at her sister. 'You
must forgive me, dear. I have to do – what I think right.'

'Please don't excite yourself, Rose. You know what the doctor
said.'

'I have prayed,' said Rose, 'but it is so difficult to decide for
others, especially when they are so dear to me as you and Amanda
are.'

'Oh dear, I must – I must – get you some more water.' Ella
snatched up the carafe from the washstand and almost ran from
the room.

'Yes,' she thought, 'she means to stop the marriage. She's quite
determined, but I mustn't be angry with her. It's because she's so
hard, so much of an old maid. Because she was disappointed in
love, because she had to give up her lover, because she suffered so
terribly and wouldn't admit it. She has always deceived herself. But
it's no good trying to make her see anything, anything. One could
kill her and she wouldn't give way. Oh,' cried the little old woman,
rushing into the butler's pantry, 'how I' – she was going to say
'hate her,' but she changed the phrase into 'hate it all.'

This hatred between the sisters had a very long history; almost as long as their devotion. Indeed, both were a legend since the time when Ella, at five years old, had set Rose's bed on fire. Rose, at thirteen, accustomed already during her mother's long absences abroad, to act as mother to the younger children, had prevented Ella from going upon a water party. The brother Theo, one year younger than Rose, had made a pet of Ella that summer, and it was he who invited her and brought her to the landing stage.

But Rose, arriving with the other sisters, seven-year-old Florence and six-year-old Bessie, at once cried, 'Oh, Theo, why ever did you bring Ella?'

'Why not?' said Theo languidly, raising his long lashes and giving Rose a haughty glance. Theo was a delicate boy, fair and blue-eyed like his father, spoilt and pleasure-loving. He was taught at home by his sister's governesses, and had something of a girl's susceptibilities.

'You know she can't swim,' cried Rose. 'You know the rule.'

'Oh yes, yes I can,' cried Ella, a very small fair child, who was renowned for every kind of mischief. Her eyes were fixed upon the lake now glittering in the afternoon sun, whose rays, reflected at all angles from the dimpling surface of the water, formed over it a kind of active brilliance, an aerial electricity of sparkles, which enchanted her. She could scarcely believe, as she clung to the hand of her benefactor Theo, that in another moment or so she would be carried into this magical, this sparkling world. Even the green fields and dark trees of the opposite shore, so familiar to her from her nursery windows, now seemed of extraordinary fascination. They were to be approached only across the wonderful lake, and were therefore part of its wonder. A picnic, Ella felt, eaten under those trees, would be a pleasure quite beyond imagination. So now she cried desperately, 'But I can swim. I swum in my bath.'

'I shan't let her fall in,' said Theo. 'Don't fuss, Rose.'

'Theo, how can you be so thoughtless. Suppose we capsized? And, besides, we promised Mama – we're *responsible* for her.'

Ella was already preparing to cry. She was an accomplished and formidable crier. Even Theo was alarmed out of his languid dignity by the threat of Ella's tears. He hastily squatted down. 'Don't cry, Ella, it's all right, you're going to come.'

'No, Theo, she can't, you know she can't. It would be absolutely *wicked*, when poor Mama has to go away so much and depends on us.'

'I *shall* go. I *can* swim – wah – ' Ella gave a roar. Rose knelt down and took her in her arms. 'Darling, but think, you might be drowned, drowned! And then what would poor Mama feel, and poor Papa, and poor Theo and me, and Bessie. And really it's not a bit fun on the water.'

'Wah-wah-wah-eh,' shrieked Ella, struggling to escape from their hands. She wanted to throw herself on the ground, to kick, to hurt herself.

'Oh, do shut up, Ella,' said Theo. 'Do be *reasonable*, or I'll be sorry I brought you.'

'Ah-oo-woo-wah.' Ella struck out so furiously that Rose could hardly hold her.

'Oh, very well,' said Theo, 'I *am* sorry I brought you, but it's your fault, Rose.'

Rose, with a great effort, lifted the kicking shrieking Ella from the grownd. 'Please, Ella,' she implored, 'be good, don't spoil everything. Catch her legs, Theo, she's kicking me.'

'Dash it, there's a carriage coming down the road,' said Theo, who hated to attract public attention. 'Do shut up, Ella. Jesus won't love you if you go on like that.'

Theo was not of a religious turn, but he quite understood the value of religion in the nursery, especially for younger sisters. 'Jesus won't love you, and you won't get any jam for tea either.'

But Ella still howled and fought. It was only by enormous and exhausting efforts that Rose and Theo managed to bring her back to the house and hand her over to the nurse. And Ella, as soon as nurse's back was turned, had gone to Rose's private doll drawer, taken out her very best wax doll, and carried it to Rose's bed in the night nursery. Then she took the forbidden matches off the mantelpiece.

'I'll bub-burn her,' she blubbered.

She did not, however, dare to light the precious doll. She put the burning matches on the bed, which would not take fire. It only charred and smoked until at last a smouldering edge of sheet touched the gauze dress, and in a moment the whole doll was in flames.

Five minutes later, when a gardener saw smoke pouring from the windows and ran in, the woodwork was burning. Ella, with blackened face and burns on her fingers, was found in the new rustic summerhouse, still sticky with varnish, opening and shutting the windows. 'It's a boat,' she said, 'a big boat,' and there were more howls when she was taken away to be washed.

The nurse and nursemaid, the whole staff, were horrified by this anti-social crime. 'It's the last of that limb's tantrums,' the nurse declared, 'or I'll give in my notice.' Ella, by popular vote, was locked up in a bedroom until her parents should come from their dinner party. Even the kitchen maid. usually a friend to all rebels, insisted that Ella must be whipped; even Venn, when he came home at half-past eleven, was obliged to be disturbed.

'Really,' he cried, 'that child is impossible. No, it's too much, she must have a lesson.'

Still in full evening dress, but suffering from that special discouragement which follows two hours after a dinner party, when the champagne has evaporated, and the prettiest eyes and shoulders seem like trivial decorations upon a base of tedium, he stood protesting in the hall. At thirty-seven, rich, spoilt, successful in every way, even in the luck, which, during the Austro-Prussian war of a year before, had persuaded him to gamble on a German victory, merely because of his liberal prejudice against Austrian power in Italy, he was a man who hated discomfort.

And he ascended indignantly to his wife's room. 'My dear, have you heard about this latest prank of Ella's? She might have burnt down the house.'

Mrs Venn, small, shrewd, already too fat, coarsened by childbearing and good living, gave her husband a quick glance to judge his mood. 'She will have to be punished. I'm afraid she ought to be beaten.'

'There's nothing else for it.'

'I think the back of a clothes brush.'

'That will do very well, only take her well away. I never knew such a child for screaming.'

'But my dear John, you don't propose that I should do the beating.'

'Certainly, she is your daughter. Surely it's a mother's part to beat the girls.'

Mrs Venn gave her husband another glance. She understood completely this charming, selfish, sensitive husband, whose hypocrisies were so carelessly assumed that they sat on him like an additional grace.

'My dear, you made me slap Theo when he was rude to the Vicar.'

'That was quite another thing.' Venn let himself fall into a chair and stretched out his little legs and ladies' boots. 'Religious instruction, I should have thought, was in your province, at least while the children are in the nursery.'

'I'm afraid we must do something, my dear, or nurse will give notice,' with a nervous glance at the man who now, in the sulky drawl of a spoilt beauty, said, 'Oh, if you're going to take that tone, there's no more to be said. I'll go and deal with the child.'

This meant, 'Put me out at your peril,' and Margaret Venn at once gave way. She was quite as selfish and pleasure loving as her husband, equally intelligent in balancing one good against another, and choosing the least troublesome; but also she was in a weaker position. John could sulk, at least in the privacy of their lives together, like a child, that is to say, he was not afraid to use such methods in order to get his way. In extremity he would recollect business in London and disappear for a month. Whereas Margaret could not sulk on pain of such a retort, and could not use the retort herself on pain of forfeiting her self respect as a mother and her position as a mistress. Public opinion, of which she was a part, did not allow wives the privilege of the strike, while it paid her well to keep John in a good temper. John, pleased, took as much pains to be charming as, cross, he was careful to get full profit from that onerous policy.

'Oh,' she cried. 'Of course, darling, I only meant that you might want – to do it yourself, it would have so much more effect.'

And John, not quite mollified, but in a tone that promised mollification in a few moments, under proper treatment, answered, 'No, my dear, I can't agree. I hate to punish the children, and so I do it badly. If you like, I'll talk to the child. Does she say her prayers yet?'

'Oh yes.'

'Quite regularly. That's so important. The habit.'

'I've given instructions to that effect, and nurse is very Scotch.'

'Very well, if you will beat her, I shall talk to her,' rising from his chair with a heroic look and adjusting his curls in the glass.

Ella, now brought by terror and solitude to a state of quivering imbecility, received three gentle slaps on her behind, which set free at once sobs of relief and therefore of penitence, and afterwards, sitting on her father's knee, in a delicious smell of eau de cologne, held tightly to his hand as it clasped her body and heard his awful but beloved voice tell her that she must not be a bad girl or no one would love her.

'But I knew, my darling, that you did not mean to be so wicked. Poor Rose was crying all the evening over her doll. No, you didn't mean to hurt your darling sister, who loves you so much, or darling Mama, or me. You just forgot, didn't you?'

Ella gave a sob of mingled exhaustion and propriety. 'You couldn't be so wicked, could you?'

'No, Pa-pa-pa,' with a sob in the middle.

'Now you must say your prayers like a good girl, and go to bed.'

And Ella, sobbing now more freely, in the delightful sense of comfort, of return to grace, knelt down and hastily mentioned the names of God, Papa, Mama, Rose, Theo, and Jesus, all her deities, before climbing into bed, and receiving what she valued most, her papa's kiss and blessing. She clung to his neck then with all her power and cried, 'Oh, papa, I will be good, darling, darling papa.' She adored her father then, for he had brought her the assurance that still, in spite of all her wickedness, she was loved. And in a moment she was asleep.

Nurse did not give notice, but she, and all the staff, were greatly offended by this leniency on the part of the Venn parents, of which the cause was judged by Nurse.

'Things are not what they were in my young days. My father'd have taken my skin off for a deed like that. But there's no real God-fearing religion in this house.'

The judgment of the old nurse may have been true of her master and mistress, it was not true of the girls, who had a thorough evangelical grounding. The Venns indeed set great store by education, and John Venn, preoccupied as he was with his pleasure, would himself instruct them in the fine arts, in English composition, and the proper way to begin and end their letters.

He was, in short, like many of his generation, among rich and liberal men of business, proud to be enlightened. While Lord Slapton, grandson of a celebrated amateur of the Regency, would show off his ancestor's collection of Greek sculpture as 'some of the fancy from Rome, I believe, to judge by their noses', and hung his Wilson landscapes in the gun-room, Venn, whose grandfather had been a farmer-brewer, was an authority on the Italian primitives, and an excellent 'cello player. Slapton had gone from Eton into the foot guards, Venn had taken a double first; Slapton's guests at Slapton Old Court were racing men and politicians, neither of the first rank; Venn at Florence Villa entertained artists, scientists, all the celebrities whom he could catch. True, they were also, for the most part, of the second rank. Queensport was a little too remote for the Tennysons and Brownings. But Rose had sat on Coventry Patmore's knee, and attended, with a number of Queensport little girls, to Ruskin, while he instructed them in the morals of beauty and the beauty of morals.

The men were old friends, brother magistrates, liberals of the Gladstone school, and strong low churchmen. But Slapton and his guests would condescend genially to Florence Villa as to a business man's show place full of gimcrack and eccentrics; Venn's guests condescended politely but without geniality to Slapton's friends as to savages and boors. Indeed, there was an awkward moment on one occasion when young Professor Groom at the Villa remarked loudly at the luncheon table, in the presence of Slapton himself and a racing friend, come to enjoy the best food in the county, that all racing men were thieves and blackguards.

'You've been unlucky in your friends, Venn,' said Slapton.

'To bet is a double crime,' said Groom, who was a tall dark young man with a large nose, large jaw, large mouth. He was visibly full of arrogance and youthful success. 'It debases both parties.'

'I quite agree with you,' said Slapton. 'I never bet, I only race.'

Groom was naively surprised that any man should race horses for the pleasure, and in that naivety Slapton and his friend, with a grin to each other, forgave him.

This Groom was Venn's latest capture. He was a Pinmouth boy, son of a fisherman, who had educated himself, made some of the earliest researches into the action of light, and afterwards founded in London, the Groom Academy of Sciences, for both research and teaching. This had had a great success, and lately Groom had suddenly been made known to the public by a speech in Parliament on technical education. A minister had called him 'Doctor Groom, whom we all delight to honour, and whose advice we are so glad to seek'; *The Times* had printed an article on the Academy, and the public, very uneasy, at that time, after German victories, under the idea that Britain was falling behind in scientific education, had made a hero of him. He was now on a lecture tour, gathering funds for the permanent endowment of his Academy.

Groom, still in his early thirties, still a little surprised by his fame, had the startled uncouth manners of a colt. He stalked about on his long, heavy-jointed legs with a grand air, but continually knocked things down. He waved his long arms and enormous hairy hands, and was always making speeches. Even to young ladies he gestured and orated. Then he would suddenly become embarrassed, look round nervously, and scowl, as if at enemies. But he had great pride. After luncheon he approached Slapton, and stretching out his arms in an attitude which resembled that of a railway signal, exclaimed gruffly, 'My Lord, I have to apologize to you.'

'Not at all, Professor – not at all,' said old Slapton, much taken aback.

'It is my duty,' said the other with a tremendous air. 'As a man of science I should have taken the trouble to know my facts.'

Slapton wagged his bald old cabman's head, screwed up his eyes, and muttered with a grin, 'Not at all, not at all.' And as he shook hands with Groom, he looked round to catch his friend's eye, as if to say, 'Good enough for *Punch*. What?'

This scene took place in the garden, and was observed with close interest by Rose, who had a fancy for Groom. And the great man, catching the child's black eyes, fixed on him with such sympathetic interest, turned aside to her and said, 'I made a fool of myself, did I not? How easy that is when one forgets the first principles.'

'But what happened, Professor Groom?'

Groom explained the circumstances and remarked with emphasis, 'To know the facts – that is the fundamental law. Oh, how different the world could be if everyone obeyed it.'

And Rose, stretching her legs to keep up with her Professor, warmly agreed that the world ought to be different. Groom was much attracted by this handsome and serious child, who so frankly offered him her worship.

Rose was now fifteen, and though still technically in the schoolroom, she had great freedom in the house. Theo's absence at school, and the great gap of six years between herself and the next daughter, left her in a position which would have been solitary if the Venn parents had not given her that freedom. She came down to all but formal meals and was presented to all guests. Thus with her excellent education by governesses, and her habit of being among grown-ups, she was a mixture of precocity in mind and manner, of childishness in idea and feeling, not uncommon among home-bred girls.

Rose was not allowed to speak at table, unless spoken to, but she attended closely to every word. After breakfast two mornings later she approached Groom in the library and said, 'Professor Groom, do you truly believe that Mr Darwin is a benefactor of humanity?'

'Most certainly,' said Groom, amused. He looked down at Rose, who, being small and fragile, seemed younger than her years, and said, 'You don't agree with me, Miss Rose.'

'Oh no, I couldn't – Mr Darwin is an atheist.'

'I beg your pardon – he is most regular in his attendance at church.'

'I'm glad to hear that – but – may I ask you something?'

'Anything you like.'

'You won't think me impertinent?'

'No, no. That would be impossible for Miss Venn,' with a little smirk which would have offended Rose if she had not been so much in earnest.

'Are *you* an atheist, Mr Groom?'

'I should not like to say that – call me rather an agnostic. I agree with Mr Spencer that the ultimate source of activity is unknowable.'

'Oh dear,' cried Rose. 'Oh, what a pity. Oh, *what* a pity.'

This exclamation did not make Groom smile. He was a serious man. He said, 'I should like to believe if I could – but I can't do so with honesty.'

'Oh dear,' said Rose again, 'I am so sorry.' She made a hasty step as if to run away.

'You think it easy to believe in a divine providence?'

'How can anyone help it? God is so good. He sends us so many good things, love and beauty and nature.' This was the disciple of Ruskin speaking.

'There is much suffering in the world.'

'But that is because people *won't* believe. Because they are so wicked.'

'In Africa, many poor savages have never heard of our God.'

'But we send missionaries to them.'

'For thousands of years they have suffered every kind of oppression and misery – but providence did not help them. Neither did providence prevent terrible religious wars in Europe.'

'But men *are* wicked, Mr Groom. I never said men were not wicked.'

'I must think their chief vice is ignorance – you have a beautiful garden here.'

'Would you like to see it? Oh yes, do come.'

And the pair strolled then along the garden paths, discussing providence, the problem of evil, and education as the hope of the world, especially scientific education.

Groom was quite as impassioned as Rose in his belief, and as he delighted in her earnestness, so she felt an eager response in him. Both, indeed, were pure evangelical spirits, for whom the form of their creed was not so important as the object, which was the salvation of humanity. Thus while they argued they forgot their difference of age. In mind there was perhaps not very much difference. The little girl, accustomed to look after the younger children, had already a woman's sense of responsibility. She looked forward to being the head of a household, and unconsciously took from her mother the feeling and tone of one to whom matters of conduct and belief were of the weightiest importance.

Groom stayed a week, and long before the end of the week it was understood that Rose was in love with the man; and he, for his part, was charmed by the child. The Venns saw no harm in the affair. They considered that it could do Rose nothing but good. They were pleased when Groom asked leave of Mr Venn to correspond with his daughter.

This correspondence went on for two years. During this period Rose met Groom only once, in London, when, for the first time, he saw that the girl's love for him was more than the ordinary friendship of sentiment common enough between enthusiastic girls and men of character. He was alarmed and consulted Mrs Venn, who said to him: 'Rose is a good girl of very strong character. She is much in love with you and I don't think that she will change. She would make a splendid wife to any man, and you are just the husband to suit her, a man of real distinction and one who knows his own mind. She will be able to respect you as well as to love you, and Mr Venn and I both feel that this is what Rose especially needs for her happiness.'

Groom at once declared his own willingness. It was agreed that he could propose, and that the couple could consider themselves privately engaged until, in another year, Rose was eighteen and old enough for marriage. They were left together. Groom took the girl's hand and began to speak, but she flew into his arms and exclaimed, 'Oh, you know, you know – why need you say anything.' The man perceived all at once what passion was hidden behind the sedate manners and formal speech of the child. In fact, the engagement, though not announced, could hardly be private. Rose might be a woman in thought and responsibility, but she was a child in dissimulation. She proclaimed her love in every glance and movement, in her colour, her voice, her eyes, and she fretted so much at her return to the West, that Mrs Venn began to think of shortening the time of waiting.

'She's seventeen and a half – why wait another six months?'

'No, my dear – eighteen is quite young enough. We have to consider the child's health.' Venn was firm. He had great regard for all questions of health.

And four months later, Mrs Venn died suddenly and unexpectedly from a stroke, followed by pneumonia.

Venn took a housekeeper, but he was at once uncomfortable. He complained that his table was not properly served, the accounts were mismanaged, his rooms dusty or untidy, the servants noisy and careless. He was, in short, a spoilt man who could not bear the least disturbance to his comforts. Rose, who had always worshipped her kind, clever, affectionate father, asked to be put in charge. The experiment had to be tried because the housekeeper, unable to bear Venn's captious temper, gave notice. Rose at seventeen became housekeeper until another could be found, and proved so successful that her father joyfully confirmed her in the post.

Indeed, Rose would have been deeply mortified by any other result. For she had set herself, with all her powers of will and character, to take her mother's place in the household.

The announcement of her engagement, her marriage to Groom, had already been put off. Venn now persuaded the girl to wait another year until he could find an efficient housekeeper. But the year became two, and one day Groom said to Rose, 'Unless you insist on freedom, you will never get it and we shall never be married.'

'Oh, James,' said Rose, 'only wait a little. You can see Papa is not fit to be left just now.'

And this could not be denied. Venn, in short, on his wife's sudden death had become careless and, it might be said, confused. He drank too much, and though never drunk, was, even at home, often excited and unsteady. He began to be known in the neighbouring towns as a member of the set, found in every county capital, which frequents expensive fast young women. He showed, that is, all the symptoms of the hedonist who begins, in his forties, to think that the forms of propriety are, after all, an unnecessary waste of the vital energy that remains.

He even brought one of his favourites, a clever, ugly young woman whose husband was in India, to the Villa. But though Rose knew nothing of her character, she instantly divined, with her honest and simple feelings, that it was ambiguous. She refused to be charmed by all her graces, and when Venn asked her afterwards, 'How did you like Mrs Carron? Isn't she a delightful person?' she coloured up to the eyes, a deep, painful flush, and said, 'But Papa—'

Venn also coloured. He was for a moment almost equally embarrassed by this mysterious influence, this spirit of the air which gave an inexperienced girl of twenty the power, in his own household, of passing moral judgment on his guests.

He recovered himself at once, smiled, kissed Rose's still rounded cheek, and said, 'You don't like her, my darling. I shan't ask her again. She is, however, perfectly respectable.'

'Oh, Papa, I didn't mean – ' Rose cried out under this imputation of criticising her father; tears rose to her lashes.

'But perhaps you are right,' said Venn, with his perfect taste. 'She mightn't be good for Florence and Bessie and Ella. She is a little – what shall I say – Londony.'

'Oh yes, Papa, and her hat.' Rose blushed again as if ashamed of this impulsive criticism.

'Her hat – bless me!' He was delighted. 'Was it the wrong kind of hat? Fancy, I didn't know you would notice hats.' And for days he told friends the story, adding, 'My little puritan, you see, is all the same a woman. Really the older one grows the more one realizes the truth of the old tag, "There is only one woman in the world, and she is a woman still."'

But he never again brought to the villa any woman not of the completest respectability. He also began to accord to Rose a new respect and distinction. He asked her advice, he urged the younger sisters to look up to her. He was a fastidious man, and perhaps on consideration he had perceived the value to his own self respect of a Villa uncontaminated even by his wittiest mistresses.

Rose had some right to consider herself necessary to her father, as well as her sisters. But it cost her her lover. A few months later, in 1880, Groom presented an ultimatum. She must marry him or he would break off the engagement. Rose begged for a little while until she could find a better governess for the children.

But Groom had waited five years. He asked if Rose was always to put her father's convenience before his. And this question, so reasonable to his rough mind, was brutal to Rose. It brought in ideas of competition, of rights, detestable to her warm feelings. There was a sharp quarrel and the engagement was broken off.

Probably Rose and Groom would never have met again if it had not been for Venn, who did not see why he should lose his lion. He kept in touch with Groom, and when, four years later, Groom happened to be lecturing in the neighbourhood, he managed to bring him once more to stay at the Villa.

The Professor had greatly changed in these years. Nothing changes a man so quickly as success or failure, and Groom was now established in reputation, indispensable on boards and councils. His figure was stouter, his clothes of the best fit and quality; his large gestures were smooth, confident; his speeches had no longer a defiant note. On the other hand, his lack of humour was more noticeable. Nothing saved him from being a pompous bore, but his sincerity and vitality, set off by his imposing presence and his name. What is pompous in an unknown person may seem like natural dignity in a famous one, and Groom, except perhaps to Venn, was now a great man. There was quite a stir in Queensport when his visit was expected, and his reception at the station, by Rose and some other friends, was like that of a minor royalty. He sustained the character even better than minor royalties, as he moved down the platform.

He found a changed household. Venn was recovering from an illness and kept to the house. He was still frail, and seemed in his conversation more sensitive, more delicate of wit. He spent his time between reading French novels, playing the piano, and conversation with a stream of visitors whom Rose entertained for him. Upon Rose his dependence seemed complete. At every moment it was, 'Ask Rose. Where's Rose? Rose, my dearest, where have you been?' And Rose served him with quick devotion.

Rose at twenty-six looked thirty, a mature woman, handsome, stouter, more reserved, and already with a look which could subdue the most impudent. A woman who had suffered and upon whom the world had begun to grow ominous and monstrous.

She was absolute mistress of the house. Theo, the son, had gone from Oxford to Paris, with the declared intention of studying art. But he was said to be an idle waster. The second girl, Florence, was dead of consumption. The third, Bessie, was nineteen, and had come out. Bessie had all the fire of the young Rose, with much more recklessness. She was a declared flirt. But even Bessie accorded to Rose respect which was both deeper than that appropriate to a daughter, and little less affectionate. For Rose was passionately devoted to her young sisters.

CHAPTER 6

Bessie Venn, it was agreed in Queensport, was not so handsome as
Rose, so pretty and accomplished as the youngest girl, Ella. She
exaggerated the Venn defects, her nose was not merely short, it
was snub; her mouth was not merely generous, it was large; her
eyes were not merely large and bright, they slightly protruded. But
she was so attractive that she had the name already of a breaker of
hearts. 'She's a tonic, that child,' Lord Slapton declared, who was
her god father and had always loved to have her, as a little girl, sit
upon his knee and pull his whiskers.

'And really she was a darling. Yes, with all her spoilt careless
ways, she was a darling. How I loved her.'

Ella, in the butler's pantry, under the high ceiling of the narrow
room, turned on the brass tap and filled her jug. Then remembering
Rose's old instruction that the first water out of a metal tap should
never be used, she threw it away, and again held up the jug. 'Why
was it that everyone admired Bessie, even Rose. She wasn't clever
or even very kind. She used to say sharp things. And she hadn't a
very good temper either – she would fly out. But she was sorry at
once – and it was almost worth being abused by her just to have
her come flying with apologies – no, not apologies, that is much
too small a word. She simply overwhelmed herself with reproaches
– she was furious with herself. And afterwards it was so delightful,
it was like spring after a storm, like a new life. I suppose that was
the truth of it,' Ella mused, as she refilled the jug. 'She brought life
to everything and everybody. She wasn't clever herself, but she
made everyone feel clever. She took such interest in people and
their ideas. And that, of course, is just why James Groom fell so
madly in love with her. She opened her eyes at him and said, 'Oh,
Mr Groom, how wise that is, how true that is,' and he felt wise
and true. Bessie made him feel like a great man, a tremendous man,
and he went and asked Papa for her. And Papa consulted Rose.
Papa left everything to Rose – everything that bothered him.'

Ella seldom permitted herself the smallest criticism of her father.

But in the last months during her long battle with Rose, she had begun to fall into that sincerity of desperation which is willing to admit all truth but the last. 'Papa was not really a selfish man,' she said to herself, 'but he could not bear worry. And he was forgetful. He forgot that it was hardly fair to Rose to ask her to decide a case like that – nor to Bessie. But no one could blame Papa for not understanding the situation. How could he know that Rose was still in love with James, and what an agony it was for her to have him in the house and to see him so attracted by Bessie. And then to be asked for her advice.

'Oh, what a stupid thing,' said Ella, nearly dropping the jug in her agitation for an event nearly sixty years old, 'and how stupidly things happen. Why did Mama die – why was Rose so, so good – yes, it was goodness – oh, how can one blame anyone so good and generous?'

For in fact, as Ella saw, it had been Rose's Christian feeling, the exaltation of a young woman ardent for loving sacrifice, which had made her go to Bessie and say, 'My dear, I have very good news. James, Mr Groom, has asked Papa if he may propose to you. As you realize, or perhaps you don't realize, that's a very great honour.'

But Bessie was shocked, astonished. What an extraordinary idea; why, Mr Groom was at least fifty. And a fearful bore. His whiskers were absurd, quite grotesque.

Thrusting one hand into the breast of her bodice, and planting her feet apart, she lifted her absurd nose and imitated Groom. 'Of course, for my part, I cannot agree with Mr Gladstone. As a man of science, I am opposed to any measure intended to strengthen the forces of obscurantism. It is a most elementary duty.'

'Oh, Bessie.' Rose tried to look severe.

'And I bet anyone a pair of gloves – sixteen buttoners – that his knees knock,' cried Bessie, excited to recklessness by her own audacity.

'Mr Groom is not fifty, he's barely forty-two or – three, and you know very well he's worth ten of those silly young men who flirt with you at the hunt balls. Bessie, surely you realize – the difference. You ought to be proud that such a man needs you.'

'Needs me!' cried Bessie. 'What good should I be to him? I can't teach his inky students how to make bad smells. And why doesn't he marry you? I thought he was your beau.'

This remark, more cruel perhaps than Bessie had intended, made

Rose tremble with pain. 'Oh, Bessie, I'm ashamed of you – yes, I'm ashamed – isn't it enough that he doesn't want me?' She flew away.

And ten minutes later Bessie was hunting for her, full of remorse. The sisters embraced, cried together, and Bessie admitted that she was indeed small-minded, a spoilt girl. 'But oh, Rose, don't make me marry James Groom, I really can't bear even the idea of him – he is so knobby.'

And Rose, sighing from her soul, murmured, 'Oh, my darling, you are incorrigible. But I know you don't mean it.'

'But I do – I *do* mean it. Oh, I know it's not fair, but if you could only plane him—'

'Bessie, how can you – he is one of the most distinguished men in England.'

'There, I know you're determined to make me marry him.'

'I can't make you do anything, Bessie, not even to keep your drawers tidy. I wish I could.'

'Yes, you always make me do things; you make everybody do things. Everybody who loves you. You have terrible power, darling, because you are so unselfish.'

'I'm not going to force you into marriage, Bessie.'

'Yes, you are,' Bessie answered. 'You're forcing me now—'

'I shan't say another word about poor James.'

'But you'll go on feeling and thinking. You'll lie awake feeling how petty I am – what a small, cheap girl. And I'll feel you feeling it. That's what I can't bear.'

And in fact eight months later Bessie agreed to go to the altar with James Groom. This is the right phrase, for, as it soon appeared, the girl did not allow her mind to go beyond the altar.

Her decision was made suddenly. She wrote to James a note of four lines: 'Dear Mr Groom, – If you still wish to marry me, I am willing to do so. I know very well that this is a great honour for a stupid girl as I am, and I hope you are sure that you have counted the cost of a stupid wife. – Yours affectionately, Elizabeth Venn.'

Perhaps she hoped that this letter would prove discouraging. But she had not reckoned on the passion of one whom she still imagined, as a great man, to be above passion. He wrote instantly to declare his unaltered love, his gratitude. And the marriage was fixed to be within three weeks, as soon as the banns had been read.

CHAPTER 7

Bessie did not reason upon causes. She lived from day to day. And she was not vain. She shed some tears on her wedding day, but she was firmly convinced that she was silly and perhaps wicked to cry; that she was making a most enviable and distinguished marriage.

She had begged for Ella to come with her on the honeymoon. as a *dame d'honneur*. This practice was not completely abandoned in that neighbourhood, though it was used only by such conservatives as the farmers. But Groom, as a Londoner, was startled by a suggestion which seemed to him actually indecent. And Bessie did not insist.

The couple, however, by Bessie's choice, did not go for their honeymoon further away than a seaside cottage belonging to a Venn aunt, about five miles from Queensport. And on the next day Ella, summoned by a mysterious note from Bessie, met her in Queensport, at the house of an old servant.

Ella had been alarmed by the note, which said only, 'Meet me at Lizzie's today at Queensport. I'll wait all day for you. You *must* do this. – B.'

She was surprised to find Bessie quite calm and self-possessed.

'What is it, Bessie? Where's James?'

'I don't know and I don't care. I've left him.'

'Left him!' cried Ella. 'What do you mean? Where have you left him?'

'For ever. I've run away from him and I *won't* go back.'

'But what has happened?'

'Nothing, except that I can't bear him, and I'd rather die than go back to him.'

'But, Bessie, what can you do? Where will you stay?'

'If Papa won't have me back I'll stay here. Lizzie would be delighted, she hates James already.'

'Of course Papa will have you back.'

'That's what I want you to do – to ask him.'

Ella hurried home. But James was before her. He had rushed

straight to the Villa. Indeed, the man's distress had taken from him suddenly all the dignity, the starched airs of the Professor. His very clothes were infected with diffidence. He seemed once more uncouth and clumsy, in an unfamiliar world. At every moment he jerked his big feet, his elbows, knees, hands, cleared his throat. He exclaimed: 'I can't understand it, I can't understand it. She seemed so gay, so happy – only a moment before she was laughing. I can't understand it.' And his voice, his glance, his expression showed a kind of horror at this mysterious event, so inexplicable to his intelligence.

It seemed that Bessie, on the first night, had jumped out of bed, run out of the room, and locked herself in the parlour. Afterwards she had dressed and gone from the house, leaving a message that she would not return.

Venn, who had lately been in bed with a return of his former illness, an ulceration of the stomach, was quite revived by this event. 'Bless me!' he cried, standing on the library rug in his dressing-gown, as he had come from his room, and smiling from one to another of the party. 'What a thing to happen. Really – really!'

His little curious smile, his animation, made Rose colour. She kept murmuring, 'Papa, please Papa. I'll speak to her. Poor Bessie, she didn't understand.'

'But that's so surprising, in Bessie,' said Venn.

Rose turned hastily and took Groom by the sleeve. 'I'm so sorry, James, but you will forgive Bessie, won't you? She's only rather hasty and thoughtless. I'll speak to her at once, she's probably very sorry a already.'

'But where is she?' cried Groom, taking two enormous strides and knocking over a footstool. 'I was sure I should find her here. This is fearful.' He threw out his hands. 'It's so unaccountable – she was so gay, so happy. Laughing up to the last moment, I couldn't believe—'

'And you mean that she's gone, gone right away?' cried Venn.

'Oh no,' cried Rose, 'she couldn't. Bessie is too sensible.'

'I haven't an idea where she is,' cried Groom. 'Not an idea.'

'Bless me! – Venn smiled at them with his delighted air of the explorer who discovers new landscapes. 'What an odd business. She must have been quite desperate. And Bessie! I thought she had more *savoir vivre*. Now if it had been little Ella, she might be a bit ticklish on that sort of occasion.'

'Papa, please, please!'

'Yes, yes, I understand. Oh, I leave it to you, Rose. Certainly to you. But really – ' rising on his toes once or twice.

It was at this moment that Ella arrived. She burst into the library to find the conclave, and her expression, her excitement, at once betrayed her news. 'What,' said Venn at once, 'my little Ella knows something. Well, where is the matrimonial delinquent?'

'Oh, Papa, I wanted to see you.' She gazed from James to Rose with a look of apprehension.

'My dear Miss Ella,' said Groom, stepping heavily forward. 'if you have any news for God's sake tell it me. Tell me at least that my poor Bessie is safe.'

'Oh yes,' said Ella. 'That is, please Papa, I was asked to ask you something.'

Ella insisted on giving Bessie's message to her father in private. They withdrew to the little parlour. But Venn, however curious and impartial in the study of human nature, was quite certain of what was due to social law. 'My dear child,' he said with kind but decisive vigour, 'Bessie has my deepest sympathy, and of course this will always be her home. But Groom has certain rights, the thing is not so simple. However, that is Rose's business. Rose will explain . . .'

And Rose was even more decided, though for different reasons. She was frightened, agitated. 'Of course Bessie will go back to you. She has no idea of what she has done. She will be very, very sorry – she will *want* you to take her back – oh, I'm quite sure. But I must go to her.'

'No, let me; let me go first," said Ella. 'I must explain.'

'Darling, I don't think you had better come at all, you always encourage poor Bessie. Do you understand how terribly serious this is, for Bessie herself?'

'I *must* come,' cried Ella, looking fiercely at her sister. 'I won't leave poor Bessie to be bullied.'

'Very well,' Rose sighed. 'But there's no question of bullying. It's a question of Bessie's whole happiness.'

The sisters left at once for Queensport. To Ella's delight, Bessie met Rose with calmness and resolution. 'No,' she said, 'I can't go back to James, and it's no good asking me why.'

'But Bessie darling,' Rose begged her, 'this is not the time to be unreasonable. You must tell us why.'

'Thank you, but it's my own business.'

'No, it's Papa's business and mine and Ella's – it's the business of everyone who loves you – if you ruin your whole life out of a mere whim . . .'

'It's not a whim.'

'What is it then? What has the man done? Has he beaten you or even been rude to you. And suppose he had, what would you think of yourself for running away from him after one day, or even a year. I thought you had more pride.'

'Oh, Rose,' cried Ella, 'don't you see that Bessie is wretched.' She flew to Bessie, who pushed her angrily away. 'Do let me alone, Ella – everybody.'

'Of course she is wretched, and so am I,' cried Rose. 'How can anybody not be wretched in such a wretched silly business. But it's better for us to be wretched now than to let Bessie be wretched for life.'

Rose's vehemence of conviction startled the two young girls, and they looked at her in silence. She suddenly took Bessie's hand. 'Think – how will you feel if you give way now – if you do this silly, childish thing. You may live forty, fifty years. Are you going to throw them all away for a moment of weakness.'

'It's not weakness.' Bessie was trembling as if she would fall. 'I'm not being weak – if you only knew, how disgusting—'

'Disgusting!' cried Rose, gazing at Bessie. 'Good gracious. Ella, would you mind, darling, if you would leave us for a few minutes.'

'No, how can I, Rose?' said Ella, torn once more between the two. 'How can I leave Bessie, when she depends on me.'

'Thank you, Ella,' said Bessie.

'Very well then, it's your own responsibility, Bessie. You say that something happened which was disgusting?'

'Rose,' ejaculated Ella, 'you can't—'

'Be silent, Ella!' Rose cried loudly, and now her face was a deep crimson. 'Do you think I *want* to discuss such horrible things in public.'

'Yes, they are horrible!' Bessie exclaimed, 'and you are horrible.'

'They are *not* horrible,' Rose interrupted, almost distracted in her complex feelings towards this mystery which was at once so gross to her imagination, and for that very reason so sacred to her creed. 'You have no right to think them horrible. They should be wonderful, sacred. What God Himself ordained could never be horrible. Didn't you even listen to the marriage service?'

'But *you* don't listen, you won't understand,' cried Bessie, who began to be desperate and furious at the same time. 'You can't understand, it's not what you think. I shouldn't mind that – no, if I loved a man I should be proud; he could kill me if he liked. I'm not a ninny. I'm not a ninny. I don't mind the *thing* – it's him, its Groom.'

'So it's not the disgustingness at all, it's only the man, whom you know is good and honourable, and who loves you with his whole heart, whom you are hurting so terribly.'

'It is, it is the disgustingness. Because it's Groom, who did the *thing*, or wanted to do it.'

'Oh, what nonsense, Bessie! You say you aren't a ninny, but isn't that being a ninny and wicked, too. Isn't it you who are disgusting in making so much of the thing and taking it all wrong? A thing that if it isn't religious and blessed and holy, is just nothing. Poor James loves you, he worships you. Didn't he promise to worship you with his body. And you say he's disgusting.'

Bessie tried to cry out and fell into hysterical screaming. Ella ran for salts. She was glad to have an excuse to leave the room. For its air seemed to be charged with a pressure of feeling, of violence, which made it hard to breathe. Besides, she did not know what to say or do. Her heart was with Bessie, but her mind and something deeper than her sisterly love and her intelligence, a feeling so deep and mysterious that it frightened her, was with Rose. Its voice seemed to say, 'Rose is right.' She had been strangely moved by the words 'ordained by God, a thing which ought to be holy and wonderful'. They stirred in her body as well as her soul, they made her heart beat with a kind of triumphant confidence. She did not say to herself, 'When I am married I shall not be silly like Bessie. I shall know how to suffer, how to triumph', but she felt within herself that urge, that leaning towards the future, when, of course, she too would be married, with exaltation. So that it was with an absent-minded air that she came into the kitchen.

The nurse, a plump pale woman of fifty, was sitting in the kitchen with a cup of tea. 'Oh, Lizzie, have you any smelling salts, you know, or ammonia?'

''Monia.' She got up. 'Well, now, and how is poor Miss Bessie – I should say, Missus Groom?'

'She's a little better,' said Ella, and she wondered if Bessie had given way yet. For it seemed to her already quite certain that Rose must win. She was so right.

And indeed, within the hour, Bessie submitted. She made no

conditions, and Rose, anxious perhaps that there should be no further breakdown, took her back to Florence Villa.

Groom and Venn were found in the library. The bride walked up to the two men and said coldly and indifferently, 'Here I am, then. What do you want with me?'

Groom, who had got up with looks of alarm and confusion, stared. Venn, who was studying Bessie with his curious and indulgent smile, said, 'You should ask your husband, my dear.'

Bessie turned to Groom: 'Very well, Mr Groom. What next?'

'I beg your pardon, Bessie, dearest? I don't quite gather – '

'I mean, where shall I go? Do we stay here, or go back to those horrid lodgings. Not that I mind. Rose says that the horrider they are – the horrider everything is – the better.'

Groom was still nonplussed by this imperious Bessie who, with a face like paper and furious eyes, snapped out these phrases. It was Venn who stepped forward, took Bessie's hand, put it in his, and said, 'Take her away, man, take her away. And be kind to her. Don't you understand that she's yours.'

Groom took Bessie away and, actually, since he was a man with little sympathetic imagination, returned to the same lodging, the same room, where Bessie, however, being prepared to suffer, was pleased to take humiliation to her breast and press in the thorns.

'Oh, what a day, what a cruelty,' said Ella, 'and to send Bessie, my Bessie, into the arms of that boor. Of course, she had to go back, she had married him and made her promises, but why did Rose force her to marry him in the first place – that stupid, clumsy lump. When she could have had anybody. But Rose never can see that; she never sees anything. She won't admit even that she loved James herself, and wanted him for herself. Yes, that marriage was a crucifixion for her. And I often think that was why it was a kind of pleasure – oh no, I mustn't, I mustn't.'

And entering the room, she said, 'How do you feel now, Rose, darling? Shall I get you a clean glass as well.'

'No, thank you, Ella, I have all I want.' But her voice did not dismiss Ella. The two sisters looked at each other. They knew that the matter between them was not concluded. It was the defect of Ella's sudden flights from Rose that they were always circular. She had to return, if only out of compunction and dependence. And then she found the situation precisely as she had left it.

Ella, unable to fly a second time, lifted her heels a fraction from the ground, her father's trick, and said in a high, cheerful voice, like that of a professional nurse, 'Yes, yes. Yes, I do think you're better.'

'Ella, I have something to tell you. I've asked Robin Sant here for the weekend.'

Robin was their cousin, a smart young man about town of thirty-two. 'But Rose,' Ella breathed, 'he hasn't been here since he was a boy. He will be bored to death. I never expected—'

'I asked him a month ago, but he never got the letter.'

'Oh dear, these post offices.'

There was a short pause. Rose did not look at Ella, but it was obvious to both that she refrained from doing so.

'So I wrote again,' said Rose, 'and Mrs Hendy posted it for me. He's coming tomorrow. Get some claret from Queensport, the best they've got, and put him in the white room. Then he can use the new bathroom.'

Robin Sant was a lawyer in what was called the family firm; that is, a firm which had been started by Ella's uncle, a certain Wilkes Sant, in the eighteen fifties. His son, Dick Sant, was now head of the firm, and Robin was his nephew. He was therefore Amanda's second cousin, and the same age, within three weeks.

Robin had done well at Oxford as a classic, and had become a lawyer because, as he said, 'it's no worse than the civil service and better than highway robbery: so much more certain.' He was lively, popular, always well dressed, and very much the man of the city world.

The aunts were used to pitying Robin, who always looked ill. His thin white face, out of which a large snub nose stuck like a monument in the desert, was lined and worn as by illness; but when he talked, laughing and moving his head, eyes, lips, all together, he seemed like a small boy whose thinness is a mark of his quick growth, of vitality. In fact, Robin's health was extremely good, and he was capable of talking all night and working all day for a week together.

Some years before, to the indignation of his mother, a widow, and his Uncle Dick, who at sixty-five was beginning to look forward to handing over the business, Robin had joined a glider club. Almost at once, he had broken first two gliders, and then, in a further accident, his back and left shoulder. This had left him with that shoulder slightly higher than the other; a defect which he tried to compensate by holding his head to that side.

He was nearly six foot tall, but looked much shorter on account of his big head, covered with very thick black hair, and his narrow crooked figure.

Ella, hearing wheels in the drive, had run down eagerly to greet the young man whom she called nephew; anxiety at Robin's visit caused her to be assiduous in welcome.

Robin, however, did not at once enter the house. He was, like a

smart young man, an enthusiast, and having taken his luggage from
the car and paid it off, he stood admiring the house.

'Why, Aunty, what a picture!' And as Ella descended the steps to
greet him he walked backwards across the gravel in front of the
house, to the grass verge.

'Marvellous, marvellous!'

'And how are you. Robin? How is your poor back?'

'*Very* well, Aunty. How I love the dear old villa. Those windows,
so light. The whole place is in such perfect taste.'

Ella looked with surprise from the house front to her nephew
and back again. She thought, 'Oh dear, what does he mean – what
does this mean? Why is he being so nice?' For she could not believe
Robin was in earnest. She had never before heard the house
admired except for its large rooms and the fine entrance hall.

It was in what is called the Italian style, still very unfashionable.
Ella's grandfather had built it in 1832 and called it Florence Villa,
in memory of his wedding trip. Not that it much resembled
anything to be found in Italy. It was British Italian; in white stucco,
a block two stories high with very large windows framed in plain
flat pilasters. A panelled balustrade running round the top gave
height to the walls and hid a third story of attics in the low roof; a
roof which was wont to leak. The hall, filling the whole centre
from back to front, and going to the roof, was divided by Ionic
pillars into two halves, of which the back contained the main
staircase, in marble, with a delicate iron railing.

A wing, on the east side, was set back in order not to spoil the
balance of the front, which was, however, not quite symmetrical.
The drawing-room on the east end of the front having three
windows, while the breakfast parlour, on the west, had only two.
But this, which had been a cause of complaint to other observers,
was beauty to Robin.

'I always loved the front and the way the door is placed, just the
right touch of informality. So completely *civilized*.'

'It's not very convenient, I'm afraid,' Ella murmured, 'the maids
complain—'

'And the hall,' cried the young man, as they entered the hall, his
face shining with appreciation. 'Space just thrown away, so
extravagant. And the high rooms. It makes you feel somebody just
to be in them.'

'And how is dear Katherine, Robin?'

Katherine was Robin's young wife. They had been married four years, and were said to be on bad terms.

'Katherine – oh, she's quite well. But I say, Aunty, you can't believe how marvellous it is to be back again in the dear old place. I'd forgotten how wonderful it was.' He peered through doors with a smile of delight. 'Even the bobbles on the parlour mantelpiece.'

Robin, while he spoke, always very fast, continually jerked his head, shoulders and legs, so that he reminded one of a sparrow on a dusty road. 'And how's Cousin Amanda? Is she at home? I hope so. I've been longing to see Mandy again. She's *quite* my nicest cousin.'

Ella, who had been smiling in sympathy with the young man's delight, ceased to smile; she started and looked anxiously at him, thinking, 'Just what I thought. That's why he admired the house. He's been sent for to see Amanda. Rose knows they were friends.' She answered in a nervous tone, 'Amanda is out. She has gone over to a farm to help with the lambing.'

'I didn't know Amanda was a farmeress. What a good idea! What a marvellous idea! Amanda must teach me farming. She and I were terrific friends at Oxford.'

'Were you? But of course you hadn't met Katherine then. What a pity you didn't bring her with you.'

'Katherine is not devoted to the country, I'm afraid. She's even more of a townee than I am. But I must see Amanda's farm.'

And after the young man had paid his visit, a long and private visit, to Aunt Rose, he and Ella walked over to Brook.

'But this is better and better.'

Ella, trembling with suspicion, thought to herself, 'Yes, she's told him to interfere, to warn Amanda and work on Harry,' and in her excitement she cried, as if carried away, 'Isn't it?'

'It's very easy to forget the feel of the country, don't you think?'

'Yes, yes,' said Ella, confused between her apprehensions and her natural tendency to like all young men who liked nature. 'That's what I always say – at Brook you are in another world,' and she looked round at the sky, the cottages, the Brook valley, in order to give them proper appreciation. 'It's so private.'

And this was a good description of the valley at that moment, as well as its special attraction for Ella. The woolly white clouds which moved slowly through a sky of pale gold seemed to belong only to the scene, peaceful and remote. The sky indeed had the same delicate but opaque surface as the clouds, as if it had been matched with them. It was a limit, a roof rather than a heavenly window. It was like a local sky belonging only to this valley, in which the sixteen cottagers of the village, the farmers, the rector and Colonel Hicks at Kashmir Cottage, lived apart from the world, in a privateness upon which visitors even from Florence Villa, just over the rise, were intruders.

'It is the nicest farm I know,' said Ella.

'I hear it is in rather a bad way.'

Ella's suspicions returned upon her. She thought, 'So that's the plot they've been making up between them. Oh, how cunning she is, how obstinate.'

'Oh no, no,' she cried. 'Harry Dawbarn is a splendid farmer. Though I believe, of course, there is a debt. Yes, it's very sad – poor Brook. And all it wants is a little money, a little capital. How important that is – money. Money makes all the difference. But really I think people worry too much about money,' and by some hidden course of thought she continued, 'Poor Katherine, how sad it is for her to have no babies. Of course, there is plenty of time.'

'She didn't want one – we both thought it would be better to wait until we had a bigger flat.'

'Oh dear,' said Ella, 'do you think that is wise? I know everybody does it nowadays – it seems so unnatural, but of course it's your own business. You have to think of – your own happiness.'

At this the young man made a kind of pounce, like a dog on a bone.

'So you think there are more unhappy marriages now, Aunt Ella, than there were in your time. Of course there are. There must be.'

'Oh dear – but let's not talk of it – not now,' said Ella, upon whom the influence of the scene was now having it's effect; a religious effect. 'There's the fold,' she cried, as one might have said 'There's the church.' 'Doesn't it look splendid in this light – really it's a privilege to be out on such an evening.' She turned her eyes to delight and her heart to worship.

The lambing fold, though a rough job, was transformed by the sun which had now found entrance underneath the low roof of cloud into a small celestial city of golden or at least, cast, brass walls, against the ebony hedges sprinkled with emerald buds. A great noise of baaing and maaing from the same quarter showed that the breeding ewes were being driven into the fold for the night.

'But we must hurry,' said Ella, striking across the valley from the path. She was eager to be among the maternal flock.

'Of course, Aunty,' said Robin, turning towards her with that air of impulsive candour which had pleased her before, 'you're perfectly right, we should have had a baby at once.'

'Oh yes, Robin – I feel so sorry for you – but you mustn't give up hope.'

'It would have nailed us down, wouldn't it?'

'Nailed you down?' cried Ella, looking alarmed.

'That's it,' said Robin, with enthusiasm. 'Put us right up a gum tree. And that's probably what we wanted, what everyone wants. You've got the right idea there, Aunty.'

Ella's ecstatic expression had a suggestion of one spoken to during service, and determined not to hear. 'Quite beautiful – it's like a Bible picture.'

The half acre of cabbage eaten bare by the sheep was, in fact, to the critical eye, a desert of reddish earth out of which the less edible stumps stuck at all angles, like the relics of some miniature palm forest after a flood. Among these stumps the ewes-in-lamb, enormously wide in their thick wool, were proceeding slowly, in little groups, towards the folds, driven on by the old man Bobby who, at a distance, jerked his gnome-like body and waved his skeleton arms at them in a respectful and exasperated manner due to their condition and touchiness.

'And if you don't like it,' said Robin, 'so much the better.' He pressed down the wire for Ella to climb over the fence. 'The great principle is to acquire a pain in the neck in order to cure the megrims.'

'So much happiness in the world – and simply – given to us. Oh, nice dog – how busy he is.' She stooped to pat the old sheep dog, called Shep, who, tied to a hurdle, was staring at the folds with a disgusted air. He gave a short broken bark, the exclamation of a dog in extreme humiliation, twisted his back and neck into a complex and unnatural position, and turned up his filmy eyes to Ella with an expression which seemed to say, 'Look what they've done to me: put me out, taken my sheep from me.'

'Nice dog,' said Ella. 'What is your name? I'm so bad at names. How serious you look. This is such an exciting time for you, isn't it? Listen.' She laughed with pleasure. 'The mothers calling to their babies – how absurd.'

'Of course, the great advantage of being a sheep is that you don't know you are a sheep,' said Robin, raising his voice and looking round with indignant surprise at the flock. 'I say, what a row they're making.'

In fact the noise had suddenly become deafening. The reason seemed to be that ewes had begun to call to their lambs in the far fold, reserved for lambs of three days upwards, and some of them were not sure yet of their mother's voices. An old south Devon ewe of enormous girth, near Ella, was uttering a deep 'Maw-aw' to which at least three lambs, hidden by the high straw walls of the fold, answered each time 'Mee-mee' and 'May-may'. Whereupon another ewe in the same fold echoed with the peculiar bubbling note of a ewe to her own lamb, 'Mal-law-law'.

'How worried they are,' said Ella, laughing at Robin with the same delight. 'They're all sure that some disaster has happened.'

'Lucky devils!'

'Oh no, Robin.' Ella was suddenly indignant. 'You mustn't—' Aunt and nephew looked at each other with surprise, and Robin said, 'But I wasn't meaning any disrespect to maternal devotion, far from it.'

'Oh, but you mustn't even want to be – like an animal – no, that's so dangerous.'

Robin opened his mouth to shout a reply, but could not be heard. The chorus of driven sheep had been taken up by those in the stalls, probably because they expected their hay. Robin and Ella, both with surprised and perturbed expressions, stood by the pen hurdle to let the flock thrust past them into the folds, already full of sheep and lambs in active movement.

Robin was meanwhile apologizing to Ella, who, catching the word Christian in her ear, understood that he was regretting the fact that he had not, by good luck, been brought up in the faith. But she vigorously shook her head. She was not so much indignant with Robin for holding so cheap his human soul, as mildly put out by his interruption of her devout feelings. The falling sun, however, making her face bright crimson, caused her to resemble an indignant Judy in argument with an up-to-date Punch. At the same time, the ruined cabbage patch had been turned into a mysterious landscape of dark damask and saffron; the straw fences and their thatched roofs into sulphur shaded with rust. The tall, uneaten kale stood behind like a dense hedge of green with halos of lime round each head; and in the fold vast golden sheep with faces of sloe black, lilac white and russet surged among a deep litter of glittering bronze straw. In the outer division a little crowd of lambs was running together in a game of follow my leader, a very young lamb with a grey-blue fleece was sitting in a dry water trough with a sedate expression, and a lamb entirely black was standing by itself in a corner, as if in deep thought.

'Oh, the poor thing,' said Ella, as the noise lulled, and suddenly turning to Robin, she exclaimed with fervour, 'No, no, Robin – I'm not a good Christian – not at all.'

'But, Aunty, who could be more unselfish? See how you have nursed Aunt Rose.'

Ella looked about her, and her feeling was one of beauty, of richness, of an intensity of life impossible to express, except to music. 'No, no,' she said urgently, 'I'm a very bad nurse.'

Remorse overwhelmed her, as though in some holy place. 'The truth is, Robin, that I've nearly killed her more than once. It's my temper – oh, I oughtn't to come near her. But she won't have anyone else. She didn't even want Mrs Hendy – that's the night nurse.'

'But, Aunty, you have the sweetest of tempers, all the family know that – the very sweetest.'

'No, please Robin. I have a very bad temper. Not exactly a bad temper, but a bad disposition. Rose thinks I hide things from her. That upsets her terribly. But she told you about it just now, didn't she?'

'No, Aunty, not a word.'

'It isn't quite true, of course. That is, I do hide some things which might upset her too much. And sometimes other things, too.' Ella looked at the folds now full and, as it were, boiling with sheep and lambs. And to her even the clouds of dust kicked up from the dry earth, the broken straw, the hot smell of greasy fleece and fresh urine, a great stain of blood on the ground close to her feet, seemed part, and not the least significant or unnecessary part, of a sacred mystery. 'For instance,' she said, 'I lost the letter asking you to come, the first letter. But she told you about it?'

'No, Aunty. You lost a letter?'

'Yes, I lost it – that is, I forgot to post it. But of course Rose guessed and wrote another and sent it by Mrs Hendy. So you mustn't admire me as a nurse.' Ella smiled hastily at her nephew, who answered with a murmur between incredulity and politeness. He was unused to Ella's habits, well known in the district, of confessing her faults to anybody at hand, even the baker or the garden boy.

Ella thought, 'It's all very well to confess, that doesn't make it any better. And the real question is how did I come to count on Rose's death – it's astonishing. How could I be so spiteful and stupid. For what would I do without Rose. I should be quite lost.'

But suddenly catching sight of Harry emerging from a pen, close by, she called to him urgently, 'Harry, Harry.' It was as though she flew to Harry for reassurance.

Harry did not hear, or pretended not to hear her. He had not shaved, and his chin glittered in the last rays of the sun as if gold wire had been scattered on a ground of old copper. His long neck with its prominent apple projected from a collarless shirt. A bottle stuck out of each pocket, containing different sheep medicines, and he held sheep shears in his left hand. He touched the brim of his ruinous hat with his short wooden crook, and shouted in a drawling tone, 'Ni-i-ce evening.'

Ella could tell at once by the man's voice and look, and his not wearing collar and tie, that he was dejected. Harry was rarely out of spirits. His habitual mood was a kind of nonchalance, varying only towards the sardonic, on the one hand, and a stoic humour on the other. But he had his depressions when he was taciturn, unshaved, sometimes unwashed, and spoke, when he had to speak, in a native drawl.

The effect of Harry's depression was to terrify Ella. She imagined at once enormous catastrophes. Amanda had been unkind, there had been more trouble with that village girl. She called more urgently.

Harry for answer made a dive into the thick mass of sheep and hooked a ewe by the hind leg. The ewe stood still and Harry sang out in a drawling tone, 'Am-a-anda.'

Amanda came from a pen where she had been feeding a lamb. She was hot and dirty, and wore an air of anxious alarm, quite novel on her face, and also unsuitable to her placid cast of features.

Amanda, like Ella, had found Harry dejected. His father had decided to retire and live with a sister at Pillbay, and the bank had demanded their arrears of interest.

'Knowing I haven't got a happeny for 'em.'

'But how can your father retire if he has no money?'

'He's all right. He's got a bit somewhere where they won't find it. And he bought that house for Aunt ten years ago so as to have something in hand. Well, I don't blame him. But he hasn't got anything to spare for Brook. So out I go.'

'They haven't said so yet?'

'But why shouldn't they? And if they didn't, why should I stay – to work for 'em.'

Harry's gloom, Amanda found, had communicated itself to her own nerves. That is to say, she was not only sorry for Harry, but some mysterious dismay in her flesh seemed to protest against the instability of Harry's affairs, and even blamed him for it. An hour's work in the stifling pens, coaxing stupid lambs to suck, and persuading angry ewes to take orphans. had increased this physical resentment. She exclaimed now with indignation, 'It's a wicked shame to treat you like this, after all your hard work.'

'So it is,' said Harry. 'The whole place is a disgrace, and you mid well say I've made a mess of things.'

'I never said so.' Amanda was startled to find in Harry a mysterious response not to her words but to her irrational feeling.

'You'd have a right to,' said Harry, with tact. 'Ah, I ought to have gone into the engineering, like Fred. If I'd gone into it when he did, I'd have my own garage by now; he has three. But there – I always was a fule.'

'But Harry, it isn't your fault.' Amanda repaid the tact.

'You don't know, Amanda. I've got the damned fulishest bone in me. And don't forget it. Over with her!'

Amanda took the ewe under the fore leg and gave a heave, which the ewe, spreading out her forelegs, resisted with all the patient humble obstinacy of a sheep. But Amanda, in spite of her pale scholar's looks, was a strong girl, with a powerful back. She took a firmer grip of the leg, lifted the ewe off her fore feet, and with a careful heave laid her on her side.

'A real fule's bone, or I shouldn't be here. I hate a starved farm,' said Harry. 'But what could father do – he had to buy in '18 at the Venn sale, and he paid a fine price to your Aunt Rose. War price. Half in mortgage. And he's been borrowing and going downhill ever since the crash in '20.' He stooped down to examine the ewe's belly. 'Ah, I thought so, wool all round the tits. No wonder that lamb couldn't suck.' He clipped the wool round the two small teats and muttered, 'Ought to've been done last week, but nothing gets done properly at Brook. It's a good riddance of the whole place.'

'But Harry, if Aunt Ella can arrange with the bank?'

'And how is she going to do that?' said Harry, standing up and staring at Amanda.

'I suppose she will pay off the debt.'

'Has she the money to pay off two-three thousand pounds?'

'I don't know,' said Amanda.

'What I hear is she hasn't anything to matter, till the old lady dies. But you don't know.'

'No, I'm afraid not.'

'Well, I suppose you don't think much of money, where it goes or where it comes.' Harry spoke this with a peculiar inflection, something between irony and admiration. 'Let her go.'

Amanda released the ewe, who scrambled to her feet and plunged through the straw, careless of the weak grey lamb staggering after her.

'Now I think of it,' said Amanda, 'Aunt Rose pays all the bills, even for Aunt Ella's clothes.'

'Oh!' said Harry. He climbed the hurdle into the outer fold where Bobby was raking hay. This abrupt exit was as good as a long speech on the subject of Amanda's lack of money sense, Ella's airy promises, and his own desperate state.

'Amanda, darling,' Ella called anxiously. Amanda walked to her through the sheep. She felt confused, as if the complications of Harry's problems were revolving in her like broken wheels. She looked with great disgust at a dead still-born lamb, lying among the kale stumps, and picked it up.

'Oh, Amanda, has Harry lost a lamb?'

'Seventeen,' said Amanda. 'Did you know that Mr Dawbarn has retired and the bank may turn Harry out?'

'Oh no, Amanda! Oh, it's impossible.'

'You'd better ask him,' said Amanda with such unusual roughness that Ella was startled; she flushed and looked guilty, as if she had done something wrong.

Amanda walked off with the dead lamb, to throw it into a pit already dug at the corner of the field. As she turned, Robin offered his hand. 'Cousin Amanda.'

'Why, Robin, I didn't see you. It's getting so dark. I'm afraid my hands are rather too bloody.'

'By Jove, have you been acting as midwife? – how wonderful.'

'No, I'm not an expert. I come to help with the odd jobs.'

'Have we met since Oxford?'

'No, I suppose we haven't.' But Amanda was preoccupied; she returned to the fold gate and looked across the pens.

Ella, at her ear, murmured, 'Oh, but my darling, are you sure? How could the bank do such a thing?'

'My dear Aunty, why shouldn't they?'

The sun was falling, and as it fell a blue shadow rose with a slow but perceptible movement, up the posts supporting the roofs of the pens. The sheep below were already in a shadow which with its flatness and cold transparency, resembled water. Above, the sun still illuminated the dust, in a halo like thin fire. As the old man Bobby came out with a lantern and made his way from the outer fold, with a complicated motion due to his stiff legs, and the hop, step and jump progress necessary for one picking his way among lambs, ewes, straw, feeding racks, watering troughs and spare hurdles, the chorus of maa-ing and baa-ing first broke out more loudly, then died away into a continuous but less noisy and agitated movement in which only one or two ewes were uttering at any one time, and the answers of their lambs could be distinguished. Instead of a loud and strident chorus, one heard first a single 'aw-aw' from some old three-crop mother, followed at once by a hearty 'mey' from her stout lamb; then a 'baa' from some first year, and at once a wailing and distressful 'mee' from some new-born youngster not at all sure even of its own voice.

'Come, Aunty,' said Amanda, taking her aunt's arm, 'we must go.'

'Aren't you going to say goodbye to Harry?'

'No, he doesn't want me just now. He's too worried.' She turned towards the road, and suddenly felt Robin's hand on her other arm. 'How nice this is,' he said, 'how tremendously nice to see you again. Do you remember that party in Holywell?'

Amanda did not remember the party. She was still absent-minded and, to Ella's ear, depressed. But as Robin spoke to her about the party his liveliness gradually stirred her interest.

'What a memory you have. I suppose I'd only just discovered D. H. Lawrence.'

'That's what we thought. But of course Lawrence was the craze then. Heavens, how long ago! At least a thousand years.'

'Yes, indeed.'

'And now we're Victorian again, or at least we'd like to be.'

'Is that the latest?' Amanda smiled.

Robin kept looking at her with delight. At last he exclaimed, 'You wear your hair long; how nice that is.'

'Aunt Rose likes it long, but it's rather a nuisance. Why do you say you'd like to be a Victorian?'

'Did I? I don't know. Still, life was rather nice then, so easy and simple.'

'I wonder.'

'So do I. Do periods really have a character? But they must have. For instance, the D. H. Lawrence period?'

And the two cousins became deeply involved in a discussion about the character of periods, whether it was a true character or only that of some group or class which happened to catch the eye.

Ella, walking beside them, full of consternation at the threat to Brook, was greatly irritated against them. 'Oh, how clever that is,' she murmured, as if with warm appreciation and envy. 'Oh, Robin, you were always so clever, and Amanda is enjoying your visit so much. Yes, it is a real treat for her.'

But as soon as she was alone with Amanda, just before dinner, she darted at her with a birdlike peck: 'So you like Robin. I knew you would like him, you always liked clever talk. Yes, you like him better than Harry.'

'Oh no, Aunty, Robin is an old friend, too. Do you know why he came?'

'Aunt Rose sent for him – to talk to you. Yes, she thought you would like him better than Harry.'

'Oh, Aunty.' Amanda was reproachful as of an obsession. 'He came on business – legal business.'

'But Uncle Dick does all our legal business.'

'Dick has sent Robin this time – it's something about Aunt Rose's will.'

'Her will!' cried Ella. 'But she made her will years ago. It can't be about her will.'

'Perhaps she would like to make a new will.'

'Oh no, why, that's absurd. It was a very good will.' Ella gazed at Amanda with an expression of terror, then suddenly flew towards the library.

Ella did not speak to Rose while she walked round the bed, arranging the toilet cover on the bedside table, taking up an empty glass. At last Rose, who had been reading her evening prayers, said to her, 'My dear Ella, what do you want?'

'Nothing, Rose.' Ella turned to escape. 'I was only wondering – would you like to see Robin before dinner?'

'No – unless he likes to waste his time with a very old woman.'

'Very well.' But she waited as if expectant.

'Ella, you know that Robin is here on business.'

'No, Rose.'

'I meant to tell you later, Ella, but you may as well know at once. I am changing my will. You understand, Ella dear, that any changes I make now are meant for your good – yours and Amanda's. As a safeguard for you both.'

'Oh yes, Rose, of course.'

'I meant to wait until Robin has the new draft ready, but you may as well know now.'

'Oh no. Rose, please!' Ella was in retreat towards the door.

'As you like – I shall show you the draft when it arrives.'

'But I shouldn't understand a word – I'd rather not. I'll just go and—' She darted out of the room and hurried upstairs. 'So she's plotting with Robin – but how can she do anything to Harry? I have my own money – I have two hundred pounds – more. It's been accumulating for years.'

She hurried to Amanda's room. But even as she reached the door she heard from within Robin's lively voice raised in discussion.

'In her room,' Ella reflected. 'But of course Amanda would ask him to her room – for clever talk. And what nonsense he talks.' She stood with bent head listening with rage to the voices of the young people, first Robin's tenor, excited and questioning, then Amanda's contralto, slow, thoughtful.

'Discussing – discussing . . .' Ella said to herself. 'Taking things to pieces – but what is the good of it?'

The door opened unexpectedly and she saw Amanda before her. She darted away. 'Aunty, Aunty, don't go away.'

'Yes, I must – change. I must write a letter. No, I haven't a moment.' She turned back and said to Amanda in a low voice, 'I have my own money – I have two hundred pounds – I'll give it to the bank.'

'But, Aunty, the Dawbarns owe thousands.'

'Oh, that's impossible – and what are you talking about in there with Robin? What are you talking about, Robin? But don't tell me, I shouldn't understand. It would be too clever for me.'

'Don't you detest cleverness, Aunty!' Robin cried, looking at her eagerly. 'I think it's the great danger of the time, clever talk. It spoils everything, like fly blows.'

But Ella suspected that he was laughing at her. She turned back and glided quickly into the passage, murmuring, 'Of course, real cleverness – one must admire. Your Aunt Rose is clever. Oh, she was cleverer than most men in her time.' She disappeared. Robin said to Amanda with a note of complaint, 'I like Aunt Ella, but she doesn't like me. She wouldn't even play for me this afternoon – and I was looking forward to some real old romantic piano, with the genuine macassar flavour.'

'Aunt Ella is very shy.'

'And then she wants you to marry the farmer's boy – and she's afraid I'll cut him out.'

'Don't be absurd, Robin.'

'Aunt Rose thinks there's a danger of it – I thought so, too, this afternoon. But why not – he'd suit you very well.'

'Now you must go – I need a bath after those sheep.'

'I'm frightfully sorry, Amanda. Kick me if you like, only don't throw me out.'

'But, Robin, it's twenty past seven.'

'Dash dinner. I want to talk to you. I haven't enjoyed anything so much for months. Have a heart, Mandy.'

Amanda, surprised and amused, said that there would be plenty of time for conversation after dinner. She had supposed that her cousin, with his London graces, was paying her a compliment and making it strong for her provincial taste. But at ten o'clock, after Ella had played, and after she had retired, not to work but to smoke and to brood anxiously upon Harry's troubles, which, it seemed, were now her troubles, Robin walked in. He stayed till one o'clock, and when he had gone Amanda was much surprised to find how late it was.

'I'd forgotten what it was to talk,' she reflected; 'that is, really to discuss. And I'd forgotten, if I ever knew, what a good mind Robin has.'

It had been expected by Rose that Robin would go back to London to draft the new will. But, instead, he went only to Exeter, where the firm had a branch, and returned the same evening. Thus it seemed to Ella that the talk between the cousins, which exasperated her so much, had barely been interrupted.

'Oh dear, these intellectuals!' she said to herself. 'How I hate them, undermining everything. And Robin is the worst kind, he's so charming. I see that Amanda is fascinated. But I can't even warn her. Oh no, it would be quite fatal to say a word against Robin or intellectuals, it would make her furious.'

And meeting Amanda next morning in the passage, she said to her, 'How nice it is that Robin is back so soon. How nice he is. What a pity that he is so—'

'So what, Aunty?'

'Such an intellectual. Yes, I shouldn't mind a bit if I didn't like him so much – but it is so sad – so tragic.'

'But Aunty, Robin is not an intellectual – he's rather anti-intellectual.'

'There, you're furious with me. I knew you would be. I'm so stupid, But I never was an intellectual.'

'Aunty, you're not at all stupid, but I never quite know what you mean by intellectual. Is Professor Moss an intellectual?'

'Oh no, he's so nice and so sincere, so dependable. But then he's not a friend of yours, is he? Not an intimate friend.'

'Who else is there then?'

'I really don't know. If Robin is not one. And he's not a real friend, I suppose. You don't respect poor Robin.'

'I do rather respect Robin,' said Amanda. 'He has such an honest mind, and he has absolutely no shop window.'

'There, I knew it,' said Ella with a tragic look. 'Oh, what a fool I am – what an old stupid.'

She hastened away with a gesture of despair. But five minutes later, when Robin and Amanda were chatting together in the parlour, she was back again, pretending to look for some old music. For Ella was fascinated by this talk, which alarmed her and angered her so much.

'It's a swindle, of course,' Robin was saying, 'but what I can't stick is – it's such a cheap swindle.'

'You mean the politics?'

The young people were discussing a favourite subject, modern civilization.

'That of course; but probably it has to be a ramp. I meant, has there been any improvement since – say 1066?'

'I think women are better off, really better off. And divorce is rather easier under the new Bill.'

'But is divorce a *real* improvement – or only just a botch? Oughtn't we to go on another line altogether – the trial marriage?'

'My dear Robin,' cried Ella, 'but you don't mean it?'

'I do indeed, Aunty. Suppose it had been possible for me to have a trial marriage with Amanda at Oxford, I should probably be her husband now. And that would be very nice.'

'Oh dear, do you think so? I don't think that would have done at all.'

'Two people would have been a good deal happier,' said Robin.

This oblique allusion to his marriage shocked Ella. She looked at the young man with a blank face and round eyes, as if astonished into stupidity. This expression hid her violent indignation. She exclaimed to Amanda, 'Don't forget you have to take Flash to the vet.'

'Did I promise?'

'You know Harry phoned.' And she said to Robin in a very serious tone, 'Flash is a most dangerous dog. I wouldn't go near him. But he would do anything for Amanda.'

'So I'm told would Mr Dawbarn.'

'No, no, that is – of course Mr Dawbarn is an old friend – oh dear, is that your aunt's bell?' Ella darted into the corridor, furious with Robin, furious with herself.

'Poor, poor boy!' she said to herself. 'But I mustn't blame him, he can't help himself. But why does Amanda like him so much – I'm sure she likes him. I suppose it's because he is unhappy, and because he likes her. Oh dear, how foolish girls are, especially clever girls.' Shaking still, she stood at Rose's bedside. But she had forgotten the excuse which had brought her there. She gazed at Rose with wonder and murmured, 'Darling!''

'You've come at last,' said Rose.

'But did you ring?'

'I sent for you after breakfast.'

'Oh yes, I was just coming.'

'I wanted to give you this.' Rose drew out a long blue envelope from under her pillow. 'This is the paper I spoke of, Ella – my new will. Robin brought it last night, and I want you to read it over very carefully. It is not signed yet, and so it is not really a will. I wanted you to see it before it was signed.'

'Please, Rose, I'd rather not read it. I know you wouldn't do anything unjust or unkind.'

'My dear Ella, this is not a matter of sentiment, but business. I'm asking you to read it because you will be responsible for it after I die.'

'Oh, Rose, I couldn't. And you're not going to die.'

'I won't ask you to look after it,' said Rose. 'Not that I don't trust you, but that it would be better in the lawyer's hands. So when you have read it, bring it back to me. I have written you a letter also, it's in the envelope, explaining what I have arranged and why, and the letter, of course, you will keep. It is for you alone.'

'But Rose, you know I shouldn't even understand the legal writing.'

'My dear child, it's very simple. I am leaving you just the same as before. You know what that was.'

'The Villa and the Queensport shops.'

'Yes, but this is the change – they are now to be settled for life – in trust for you. And then they will go to Bessie's children and grandchildren, with the residue. And there is a change for Amanda, too.'

'Oh please, you needn't . . .' Ella made a gesture as if to drive away a threatening enemy.

'Ella, dear, this matter has given me my heaviest anxiety. And it is so important that you should understand everything.'

'But Rose – I don't need to.'

'The change for Amanda is that she is to have a little more, so long as she is single. She will have three hundred and fifty. If she marries, she will only have a hundred, but the hundred will go on to her children. So that she gets a little advantage and the children will have some protection.'

'Of course. Oh, Rose, is it necessary to go on?'

'You fully understand the new position, Ella.' Rose, with her strong honesty, was determined that nothing should be obscure. 'You have the same, but in trust. That means that you will get the income but you won't be able to use the capital; you won't be able to sell the Villa or the property in Queensport.'

'Yes, why should I?' But Ella, in fact, was not even attending to this point. Her feelings were still recoiling from the shock of perceiving that Amanda would lose most of her income if she married; above all, that all these arrangements were aimed at preventing her marriage to Harry Dawbarn.

'And that if Amanda marries, her income will be reduced. That is quite usual in wills – to prevent money going out of the family.'

'Of course it is. Oh, it is – a very good will.'

But Ella felt as if a weight were slowly increasing and crushing her down. The weight was not yet unbearable, but it would soon be so; she felt it upon her breast, her heart. She said in a breathless voice, almost like a gasp, 'It is better because – I am so stupid about money.'

'You are not a good business woman.' There was a short pause. Rose took Ella's hand. 'My darling, I would not be honest if I did not tell you why I changed my will. I mean, my whole reason. I have been afraid that Amanda—'

'No, don't tell me.'

'I should like to see Amanda happily married. I had hoped that she would marry Professor Moss. But I don't wish to see her pressed in any way towards marriage.'

'Oh, but Rose,' Ella, in terror, interrupted. 'There is no pressure, none at all. How could there be? No, you always think that girls are led away by young men. You thought that I was led away by Geoffrey Tew. But you were quite wrong, quite, quite wrong. I led him away.'

'Ella, what nonsense.'

'I – I did. I was just as bad as he – though you blamed him for everything. Yes, you made out that poor Geoffrey was a bad – influence – and you said that he had no principles, because he didn't go to church. But James was an atheist.'

'Ella, please stick to the point.'

But Ella had no intention of returning to the point. She was flying from it, into a ground where she had long planned, in her imagination, the campaign which she had fought with Rose only in her imagination. 'Yes, you stopped my marriage because you said

Geoffrey was an atheist, but James was an atheist, and you made poor Bessie take him.'

'Ella, are you out of your senses? How can you say such things.' There was a short pause. Rose took breath. 'I've explained the whole plan to Amanda and she quite approves. She sees that Bessie's children have a better claim and, of course, as a married woman, she can expect to be supported by her husband.'

'Yes, I—' Ella turned her eyes about her with a look of terror. 'Oh, my knitting.' She rushed at the knitting basket and hastened towards the door.

'But dear, you have forgotten this.' Rose held up the long blue envelope. 'You remember you are going to read it.'

'Yes.' Ella took the envelope in her other hand.

'I shall want it back as soon as possible. You'd better read it at once. And don't leave it lying about – we don't want the maids prying into our affairs – I notice that Mrs Hendy is very curious.'

'No, no, that is, yes – I'll—' Ella hurried out of the room, basket in one hand, envelope in the other To open the door she was obliged to put the envelope into the basket.

She glanced at it as she hurried up the stairs. 'I mustn't take any risks with that.' She stopped to recover it from the basket in order to carry it gripped firmly in her hand. 'It is so important, so fearfully important.' She looked at the blue envelope. 'How extraordinary that it can be so important, a bit of paper. This envelope holds our whole future in it – my life, Amanda's life, Harry's life, a dozen people's lives and happiness.' It seemed to her that that long envelope was like Rose's hand stretching out and gripping their lives. She held it away from her in a kind of horror. 'Oh, what a terrible power. She feels it herself, and well she might. It was what she said to me last week. It was what she said to me when she took me from Geoffrey, when she broke my heart. But I mustn't say that. She thought she was right. No, I mustn't blame Rose. That would be wicked. And what if I have suffered, so has Rose. Yes, Rose's life has been a martyrdom. That's why she is so – but I mustn't think that – where am I – why did I come here?'

She was in the linen room, the basket in one hand, the envelope in the other. 'Oh yes, I wanted to see if those stockings were dry.'

She looked round for somewhere to put down the basket, and balanced the envelope upon the top of the hot tank. She thought, 'It's under my eye there, but gracious! it's not really a good place. Suppose it slipped.'

For down at the back of the hot tank, between tank and wall, there was a narrow deep gulf impossible to see or reach into, and recognized by everyone in the Villa as a standing trap for small articles like handkerchiefs and stockings. 'It's not really a good place,' said Ella. 'I should have put it away first. If it was to slip down it couldn't be got out again without taking out the whole tank, or cutting through the floor. It would be simpler to make a new one – yes, that would be the best plan.' And Ella, reaching up to the row of stockings suspended above the tank, imagined Rose learning of the loss of her will, and then commanding Robin to make another. 'This evening, perhaps. But Robin hasn't got his books with him; he would have to go back to the office. So he would not begin to write out the new will till tomorrow evening – no, the next day, and that's Saturday, when lawyers don't do very much. It would not be till next Monday – five days, and anything might happen in five days. No, I must be careful.' As she spoke she dropped a stocking, grasped at it and caught her sleeve or bangle upon the envelope, which instantly shot down the back of the tank.

Ella stood horrified. Then she shook her head. 'How did that happen? The worst thing that could have happened – the very thing I feared. One would think I did it on purpose. Rose will think so.'

She shut the door of the cupboard, gathered up her basket, and went slowly down the passage. She felt confused, as always after a calamity, especially one in which she had been guilty of some fault, some carelessness. 'But it isn't true. I *am* trustworthy. I have a conscience just as strong as Rose's. Yes, yes, yes. Or if not, it is a reasonably good conscience, and I can't bear one of those looks of Rose's, or those thoughts. I would rather be beaten than have her think so of me. One can't defend oneself against a thought. Oh, I must get the envelope back. I simply can't tell her that I've dropped it. I shall get a piece of wire and bend it round on a hook. I could get it at an ironmongers, in Ferryhill, so that they won't wonder so much what it's for. I'll go tomorrow morning. Rose can't expect it back till tomorrow. I'll say I haven't read it yet. Yes, and it's quite safe where it is. Of course, I *should* tell her.' She was hurrying down the passage as if pursued, 'I ought to tell her at once. I am being a coward. But if I am a coward, it is Rose who has made me so by her thoughts. Oh, Rose's thoughts!' As she flew down the passage she seemed to be flying from some terrible power, unseen, eternal, a power against which it was impossible to fight or even argue; a spiritual force more terrible than racks, whips. 'It was

Rose's thoughts that forced Bessie to marry James Groom. And it was her thoughts that made it impossible for me to marry Geoffrey.' And Ella, feeling a strong temptation to be angry with her sister, as a set off for the accident to the blue envelope, said to herself, 'Oh, it would be easy to hate Rose for hating poor Geoffrey. But it would be wicked. Yes, even if she ruined both our lives and spoilt a great, a wonderful happiness.

And Ella was transported from ethical problems, to her father's table, fifty-six years before, where she sat listening to a young man talking about modern art. Geoffrey Tew, a rising poet, had been captured for the weekend by her father, who now sat smiling at the head of the table, quiet and watchful, elate with calm triumph. For he had achieved the double purpose of entertaining the latest genius and shocking his brother magistrates.

Ella herself, out only that year, hardly knew how to eat. She was afraid to touch her glass in case she spilled her wine. She felt naked in her low frock, shocked, exalted, and she wanted to laugh and cry at the same moment. Her delicate eyebrows rounded in amazement as she gazed at Tew, whose speech seemed to her of a music and meaning unheard before, but quite incomprehensible, like a song in some foreign language, which could give her the most moving sensations without her understanding a single word of it. He was quoting:

> See in the moon, moon-flesh
> Caught in the shadowy mesh
> Of dreaming lilies.
> Oh girl, your beauty's whiter.
> Moon of your breast yet brighter.
> Your swoon more still is
> Than rapture of all lilies.

But it was so long before she discovered that this verse was English, that when, terrified to find herself smiling at such strange and passionate language, she shrank back in her chair and bent her head, the young man was already in the middle of a discussion with Lord Slapton on the meaning of his poem.

'Unintelligible?' the young man was saying, raising his delicate nose in the air as if at a bad smell. 'But why should a poem mean anything. Poetry is the music of the feelings.'

Lord Slapton, who had once been a classical scholar, uttered a loud snort, and asked, 'Whose feelings?'

'The poet's,' said Tew, quite unperturbed. 'Whose else – for how can anyone else know another's feelings?' And he began upon the theme of art for art's sake. Art, he said, could have no object but itself or it ceased to be art. It became utilitarian, commercial, *grossier*. And Tew, who liked to use a French word, tapped his white forehead for a translation. 'Vulgar.'

This kind of argument infuriated all the older gentlemen and therefore delighted Venn, who grew always a little more malicious towards the middle-aged, not so young looking or so active minded as himself. It pleased him to call down the long table, 'I suppose we can say, my dear Mr Tew, that all this has been accepted for the last ten years.'

'It is almost a bore,' said Tew. 'Since the Whistler case I haven't heard the voice of a philistine – not, that is, among decent society.'

The meaning of this argument made no impression on Ella. But she could feel that it horrified and enraged most of the party, and especially she could feel in Rose, as she sat next Tew, a deep indignation and contempt.

Ella herself had laughed with *Punch* when it caricatured the æsthetes. She agreed warmly with Rose in detesting the modern poets from Swinburne to this new young man. And yet she felt such intense sympathy with Tew that she trembled at Rose's brow and could have killed Lord Slapton.

The reason was not because Tew was good-looking, with smooth fair hair and grey eyes, or because his arguments convinced her, but because he was young and alone.

'Your argument then, Mr Tew' – the vicar leant forward to deliver one of those logical knockdowns for which he was famous in those parts – 'is that this modern art of which you tell us has no object whatever?'

'Certainly.'

'May I then define it as useless?'

'Quite, quite useless.'

The Vicar drew himself up, and the country gentlemen also drew themselves up, ready to see the enemy destroyed by their champion.

'Mr Tew, do you expect us to find any value in what you agree to be useless?'

'I saw your charming garden this morning. But flowers are useless. I'm told that they're even poisonous to domestic animals.'

There was a silence. Ella trembled so much that her chair creaked. Lord Slapton stared; he could not believe his ears. The Vicar grew red. Suddenly Rose threw up her head.

'That is a very interesting remark, Mr Tew. It agrees so perfectly with Mr Ruskin's argument in Modern Painters, that beauty is essentially divine, and the contemplation of beauty, true beauty, a moral act.'

'Ah,' said the Vicar. 'Aha,' said Lord Slapton.

'I'm sorry, Miss Venn,' said Tew, 'but I cannot agree that art has anything to do with morals.'

'But Mr Ruskin is himself an artist – a great artist.'

'That's precisely the trouble. Ruskin writes a pretty prose, but he knows nothing about any other art.'

And when Lord Slapton cried, 'Oh!' the young man recalled the Whistler case, and asked, 'Was it a moral act for a rich man like Ruskin to ruin a poor painter by a piece of ignorant criticism?'

'Ignorant?'

'Ruskin praised Turner, an impressionist, and he abused Whistler, another impressionist, for doing exactly what he praised in Turner. Why? Because he didn't like Whistler and he'd made a hero of Turner; that is, for moral reasons.'

No one had an answer to this. And Rose was glad that the time had come to catch Lady Slapton's eye. Ella following into the drawing-room heard Tew abused for a conceited young man, without principles of any kind, whose only object was to advertise himself.

Ella did not speak. Neither did she know how to defend Tew, because she did not understand what he meant. But she was ashamed of herself for keeping silence, and at bedtime, when the guests had gone, and Rose came, according to her custom, to say goodnight to Ella in her room, she ventured to ask, 'Do you really think Mr Tew so conceited?'

'Conceited!' Rose flushed with anger. 'Much more than conceited – a thoroughly bad man.'

'Oh, Rose.'

'A bad – an evil man,' said Rose, flushing. 'He ought to be whipped. If I were a man I should take a whip to him.'

'Oh, Rose, you don't mean it!' Ella gazed at her sister in horror. She was astonished by this revengeful hatred in a woman whom she looked upon as good and wise.

'Yes,' said Rose, 'that's the only way to make a creature like that feel anything.'

Rose was shocked by her own rage, which she scarcely understood. But it was very natural rage, based on the fear and offended moral feeling which is directed against any new gospel. Gladstone was one of Rose's gods, and Ruskin another, for Gladstone had made politics religious and Ruskin had made art and beauty functions of the moral law. He had justified beauty by preaching that to love it was to love God, and to ennoble the character. Ruskin exactly answered the hungry demand of such as Rose, eager, warm-hearted, for beauty which they could permit themselves to love, for an æsthetic which enabled them to delight in form and colour, and feel at the same time that they were not idly wasting time upon frivolity and self-indulgence.

But for the very reason that she was sensitive to romantic beauty, Rose felt the danger of Tew's arguments. They stabbed her to the heart because her breast was open to them. She was terrified for Ruskin, for all the beauty that she had loved. The Tews, these pert young men with their ridiculous lilies and roses, their disgusting sensualities, would destroy her Ruskin, her Tennyson, everything great and noble, and leave her world a desert.

She looked at her younger sister with an intense stare. 'Selfish, light-minded, cheap. The only thing he loves is himself, and his own gratifications. What else does he mean by art for art's sake, that *means* art for gratification – sensuous pleasure and nothing else. Your Geoffrey is the worst kind of bad man, because he doesn't believe in anything at all except self-indulgence. He hasn't enough truth or honesty anywhere to lay hold of. That's why he finds it easy to argue and to make fun of such a really good man as Ruskin. That's why I say he ought to be whipped. He could feel that.'

'How can you be so cruel?' said Ella, astonished.

'How can you be such a ninny, Ella, to be taken in by such cheap rubbish.'

'Me – taken in?'

'Yes, everyone noticed it. No one could have helped noticing it this evening. They only had to see your eyes while you looked at him, or to hear you laugh at his cheap jokes.'

'Oh, Rose,' cried Ella, 'I never laughed!'

'I heard you myself – the whole table heard you, when he insulted poor Lord Slapton in that disgraceful way.'

'Laughed at Lord Slapton?' Ella was astonished. To her Lord Slapton was not only a great man but a dear friend who had always spoilt her. 'But I don't think anything of Mr Tew. No, I know he was talking nonsense.'

'So are you, darling,' said Rose. 'Go to bed, you're much too excited as it is. And forget Mr Tew as soon as you can – even if he has nice yellow hair. He's not at all the sort of young man who would suit you as a friend.'

The sisters, in whose relation there was so much of mother and child, kissed tenderly, and Ella continued to undress. But she was still full of astonishment. 'Did I laugh?' she asked herself. 'Did I look at him? Am I attracted by him? What was happening to me this evening?' And the question started up in her mind, 'Is this love?'

Ella was a dreamy girl but not an introspective one. Her life was too happy, too preoccupied. Her serious thoughts were given to her music and her daily four hours' practice, which did not leave her time or inclination to reflect.

But that secure busy happiness rested upon an assumption so deep that she was scarcely aware of it, that she would presently fall in love, and marry, and have children to whom she would be devoted. Her whole life, indeed, from day to day, was like a waiting time, until her destiny should be accomplished. Not only Rose, but everyone assumed that destiny. The Vicar spoke from the pulpit of the duties and privilege of womanhood. And when he did so Ella felt, 'Yes, I am a woman. I can't escape from it. Please God I shan't be a disgrace to womanhood.'

But the gateway to this fascinating and terrifying life was love. Even Bessie, it appeared, had been in love. For Rose assured her that Bessie had always loved Groom, and she plainly loved him now.

Ella was therefore always prepared to fall in love. And now as she examined, with confusion and curiosity, her feelings as revealed to her by Rose, she asked herself, 'Am I really falling in love with Geoffrey Tew? Did my eyes really show some unusual feeling? What do I feel about him?' and she could not sleep for excitement. For sometimes it seemed to her that she might be a little in love, and sometimes she thought, 'But I haven't even spoken to the man. He probably doesn't even know my name. And besides, it's quite true what Rose says. He has very bad principles. It is very wrong to say that art has no morals. What would happen to the world if art began to encourage wickedness and immorality? That could be fearfully dangerous, because art is so attractive, so beautiful. Oh no, as Rose says, Mr Tew is quite wrong about art, only I'm quite sure he's not immoral himself. He couldn't speak like that, he couldn't recite so beautifully if he were really bad. No, he's not bad, he's only rather too fond of paradoxes and shocking people.' On long reflection, she had decided that she did not love Geoffrey Tew; it was improbable after so short an acquaintance.

But now, as with her agile but rheumatic legs, she climbed the stairs up which, fifty years ago, she had danced, she thought, 'Yes, I did love him, even then – I loved his voice, his eyes, his hair, the way he twirled his glass, even his long nose. Oh, I don't know what or why I loved – I loved him, *him*, the man he was. That is, I was beginning to love him, I had begun to love him, to feel a special feeling about him – and Rose made me feel my feeling, and that was why, the next time I was going to meet him, I changed my frock three times, and even then I could hardly go into the room, especially when I realized that my father and Rose hadn't come down yet. And as soon as I came in, Geoffrey took me by both hands and said, 'How lucky this is – it is just what I hoped for, that you would be the first. I wanted to thank you for backing me up so splendidly last night.'

'How did I back him up?' Ella asked herself in wonder, as she had asked herself a thousand times since. 'I didn't say a word – I didn't dare. I was such a coward. But it seemed that he felt my sympathy. 'Why,' he said, 'I was talking for your benefit half the evening. In fact, I talked a good deal of nonsense. I got rather above myself. But you are an exciting person – so spirituelle.'

'Oh,' thought Ella, entering the box attic and sitting down on an old trunk, 'how can I forget how I felt then. And he saw it, he felt it, too. He turned pale and said in quite a faltering voice, 'I have been longing to see you again.' And when Rose came in just then he screened me: he took off her attention. At least he tried to.'

'How quick he was, how sensitive,' Ella reflected. 'Yes, he seemed so assured and confident, he horrified me by the way he spoke to Rose – just laughing at her. Yes, he was really rather impertinent to Rose. But that was because he was so sensitive – he was that kind of young man, like—' The image of Robin Sant appeared in her imagination, but she at once rejected it. 'No, no, not a bit like Robin. Robin is just flippant and not a bit sensitive. But Geoffrey was very highly strung – he used that abrupt manner as a kind of protection.'

'Excuse me, ma'am, Miss Amanda was asking—'

A maid was in the door. And Ella jumped up. 'Oh, Polly, how you startled me. I was just looking for—' She sidled out of the attic and went towards the back stairs. This led past the far end of the east corridor and Amanda's rooms. Amanda was not in her room, and Ella looked curiously over the desk covered with neat heaps of paper, the open files, each with its bundle of notes under a clip. She glanced at the book open and turned face downwards on the arm of Amanda's chair. It was Pushkin's 'Captain's Daughter'. Aunt Ella made an angry face. 'Oh, these Russians.'

In her mind and in Rose's the Russians were a source of moral degeneracy, especially in girls. All the troubles of the modern world, for the old ladies, had arisen from France and Russia. Ella drifted out of the room, reflecting upon Amanda's perversities, so dangerous to her career as a woman, and suddenly came upon Amanda herself in the passage. The encounter made her blush, for she felt that she had been prying.

'What are you doing, my dear?' she said with a sharpness which made her voice sound like that of Rose. 'Isn't it tea time?'

'Yes, Aunty, I was looking for you. I sent Polly.'

'Is Cousin Robin there still?'

'Yes, of course, he's staying till tomorrow.'

'But he could catch the four-thirty if he were quick – and then he would be back in town tonight.'

'It's a very bad train, Aunty. Besides, he is coming with us to Brook tomorrow morning.'

'Oh, why did you ask him to Brook? He will detest it – it is too dull for him there. Besides, he is so dull himself.'

'Dull, Aunty? Robin?'

'Yes, very dull. But of course you like him – you like him very much, and he's much too fond of you.'

Amanda, preoccupied, did not hear even these words.

'I know why you are so attracted to Robin. It's because he likes to tear everything to pieces. Even his own marriage.'

'Poor Robin!' Amanda murmured.

'Yes, you would like him to live here. You were glad when he said that he would leave his job in London so that he could spend all his weekends here.'

'He doesn't mean it, Aunty. He's worried about Katherine.'

Ella's nervous chatter seemed to both the young cousins like the twittering of a bird in a cage; to people deep in the anxieties of life. Robin had been troubled by letters from his wife, who complained that he did not write. 'But how can I write when I know she only wants a letter to show her power.'

And on the next day when a wire came, 'No letter yet,' he complained, 'You see, she's putting on the screw.'

'But why not write, just a note?' Amanda urged.

'So that she can criticize every word and say, How like Robin. Feed her hatred on it.'

'Not hatred, Robin?'

'Of course it is – what else?' Robin spoke in a cheerful tone which accorded with his smart suit in striped grey flannel, a bright blue shirt, and a glossy new hat.

They were walking through the paddock towards Brook. Ella, who had insisted on joining them, as chaperone, hung a little behind, because she felt that she was not wanted. Her ejaculations of delight at the beauty of the day came to them now and then with an apologetic and beseeching note.

'Robin, how can you talk so? I'm sure Katherine doesn't hate you, she writes every day.'

'I don't say it's a violent hatred, Aunty. But it's very persistent – it's a woman's hatred or, perhaps, just a wife's.'

'You mean a kind of critical feeling?' said Amanda.

'No, I mean hatred. Don't you feel all this hatred – it's about everywhere. People hate everything – their jobs, their wives and husbands, the government, whatever it is – the weather, themselves. It's in the air. Of course you get used to it and don't notice it, like the smell of a dissecting room. But it's not really a nice atmosphere.'

'But you're not spiteful, Robin.'

'No, I like a lot of things. For instance, lobster mayonnaise.'

Amanda laughed. Robin, to her surprise, looked at her with a cold and critical air. Then he said, 'But I don't like humbuggery, so I don't mean to write to Katherine.'

'Oh how glorious it is today," Ella murmured, just behind Amanda's shoulder, and she looked in despair at the two backs before her, the bent heads, Amanda's stoop which always enraged her, and Robin's long white hands clasped on a pair of bright yellow gloves. 'And what does it mean – it can't mean anything. But perhaps it does mean something – it's so hard to tell.' And trying to forget her anxieties, she fixed her eyes on the sky. 'That shower has cleared the air – how *washed* it looks – like Jap silk. I hope it doesn't rain again – but the clouds are too thin and high.'

'Of course it was always a rubber match,' Robin was saying to Amanda. 'From the first night. It didn't seem to matter at first. The really *interesting* thing was how it went bad on us, quietly and steadily, and how we couldn't get away from it. Why, we hated each other even while we were in action – that's marvellous isn't it? It makes you laugh; it made me laugh only last week right out in Kathy's face. She was rather surprised.'

'Last week?' Amanda was mildly startled.

'Yes, last week, but that *was* the last.' Robin looked at Amanda as if to say, 'That surprises you, doesn't it?'

'Oh, a perfect picture,' said Ella in a voice of desperation. They had reached the field path, which led by way of Florence hill behind the Villa, to the Brook valley. The valley was in sight at the end of a narrow deep lane, as if at the end of a telescope. It formed a brilliant miniature landscape in palest greens, blues, silver-white and the heliotrope of wet distant plough, framed in a dark circle of hedge and overhanging trees.

'The very last,' said Robin, and smiled at Amanda.

'Why is it the last?'

'Because I've cut loose, isn't that marvellous? And isn't Kathy surprised?'

'But how do you mean?'

'I answered her wire to say I wasn't coming back, and, what's more, I'm not going back to London either. I've asked for a transfer to the Exeter branch.'

'But Robin!' Amanda turned red with surprise. 'Isn't that rather desperate?'

'That can't be Harry's tractor – it's not his field,' Ella said behind. 'No, it couldn't possibly be Harry.' But neither Robin nor Amanda turned their heads.

'Oh dear,' thought Ella. 'How abominable to talk like that, but I mustn't be shocked. I suppose it's quite allowed nowadays. And what did he mean – about not going back? He can't not go back – he must go back to his wife and his work. If only Amanda wouldn't be so *sorry* for him. She is so sympathetic – how dangerous that is. But I mustn't be angry with Amanda for being kind. No, I know that isn't Harry's tractor.' She turned in at the field gate. 'Oh, how beautiful it is up here.'

In fact, in climbing out of the lane Ella seemed to have ascended into a different world. Below it had been dark, oppressive with the sight of last year's decaying weeds, the smell of rottenness – a narrow gloomy pit. Here above it was brilliant with the morning sun, slanting its rays through an atmosphere so bright and clear that it seemed, like a diamond, to confer sharpness and brilliance upon light itself, which at once gave to all colours a surprising clarity, and took back from them their native and substantial force. So that the farm lying below her seemed like a toy, painted in the most delicate pastel shades. The plough fields at the top of the valley had the colour and texture of foxglove petals; the meadow fields with the new grass coming up among the old bents, all wet with the morning shower, had a shade like the hairy leaves of primrose. The slate roofs of the farm were pale like cuckoo flowers; the stream, still full, with broad pools and a sparkling fall at the dam, reflected a sky of which the blue was so pale that it could scarcely be called a colour: and so clear and sharp to the eye that it seemed the bluest possible sky, the very soul of blue. And this piece of sky reflecting water with its quivering motion which divided the valley into two unequal parts, gave to the delicacy of its colours an unsubstantiality of foundation. It seemed that all this petal beauty upon which the shower, composed of single drops not bigger than a pin's head, lay like bloom, was supported on nothing but sky; it was a phantom, a vision, a work of the fancy.

'You could blow it away.' Ella formed her lips as if to blow. 'What beauty, what a miracle!' she said, adoring and seeking by adoration to make the world admirable. 'Yes, now one can believe in God, and in – but it can't be Harry.' She looked at the tractor roaring up the long field, a field of rough old grass now being torn up. 'No, it's quite impossible.'

Ella took care never to ask much from providence. She feared perhaps to be discouraged. She sought strength and hope in adoration alone.

CHAPTER 10

The cousins, now alone in the lane, found themselves quarrelling. Robin had suddenly proposed to Amanda, but in such ambiguous terms that at first she had not understood him. Then she was dismayed. 'But Robin, you don't mean it? You can't be in love,'

'Why the devil don't you think I can fall in love?'

Amanda was even more startled by her cousin's violence than his proposal. She saw all at once that his liveliness of mind had two edges to it. Its keenness arose from a nervous tension that could be irritable as well as sensitive.

'But you're still married,' she said.

'Kathy and I have split And I'm only suggesting that we give the thing a try out. We could do that now. Absolutely without prejudice on either side. Kathy and I lived together for more than a year before we took the high jump and no one suspected anything, or if they did, they didn't worry us.'

'But Robin, does that even help, does it prove anything?'

'What a cold card you are, Amanda.'

'It's you who are cold. Your whole plan is like an experiment on animals.' Amanda was now all at once very indignant.

'Aren't we animals? Isn't that pretty elementary? Let's be honest at least. I should have thought a lot of animals manage things even better.'

'Oh, I wish this hadn't happened. Life is complicated enough.'

'What the deuce do you think I've been driving at all this week? You really are a fish, Amanda.'

'But how could I tell? I thought you were a friend. I thought you had more sense.'

The tractor, now roaring overhead, suddenly stopped so that the last words sounded very loudly in the silence, causing Amanda to look still more disconcerted. She turned deep red when Harry's voice came from above, in a soft drawl, 'Amanda.'

'Why, Harry, are you up there?'

'Your Aunty says you want to see me about the dog.'

'I'll come up.'

Amanda, grasping some stout beech stems in the hedge, climbed the bank, and reached out for Harry's long arm. He handed her over the new pleached hedge, and they strolled back towards the tractor.

Amanda, like Ella, was also aware of a change of atmosphere, from oppression and dankness in the lane to wide views, clear sparkling air above. She felt it and squared her shoulders as if throwing off that oppression. And reaching out once more for common sense, a dignified sanity, she looked severely round her and reflected, 'All the same, it *is* a starved farm, and those roofs which look so nice are full of dry rot inside and holes outside.'

Harry was examining the shackle which attached his tractor to the double gang plough.

'What are you doing in this field, Harry? Isn't it Okeys?'

'Hire job. Plough and cultivate.'

There was an embarrassed pause. Then Amanda said, 'You saw Aunty, then?'

'She told me you were in the lane and she said I ought to marry you quick before you got too taken up with somebody else – meaning the London chap.'

'She didn't!' said Amanda.

'She didn't put it like that, but that's what she meant. What's the latest about the will?'

'You got my note?'

'I did so. Just in time to stop me paying for the ring. It was a good thought to write so quick. Dom this shackle!' He picked up a large stone and struck the pin.

'I wrote as soon as Aunt Rose told me.'

'It's aimed at us, that new will, to stop your Aunty Ella giving us a start. It's made a big change.'

Harry, having knocked the pin out of the shackle, picked it up and put it in his pocket. Looking then at the distant horizon, he said slowly, 'You see, Amanda, if we lose Brook I mid have to go for a foreman. They'd call it a manager, but it'd be a foreman's job. We can't go blind into a thing like this, we mid find ourselves in a nasty hole.'

'And it really depends on the bank,' said Amanda. She thrust her hands into her coat pockets and glanced round at the broken clouds, the clear pale sky, as if to say, 'It's a workaday world, let's have no nonsense.'

'That's about it,' said Harry.

'But the bank might let you stay in Brook. Haven't you heard from it yet?'

'They want to see me.'

'You mean that whether we get married or not depends on the bank?'

'That's about it.'

'Not a very romantic view of things,' said Amanda in an uncertain voice, as if not sure of her own feelings. And Harry did not trouble to answer the remark.

There was a silence, interrupted by a shout. Amanda started. She had wanted to forget her cousin waiting below. She stepped to the hedge and looked down into the lane, where, in shadow, Robin stood turning upwards a face made white by the cold blue reflection of the sky. This effect was that of one damned soul looking up from a small private hell. It was an effect which at once struck Amanda, and it caused most of her indignation against Robin to disappear. For she thought, 'It's not fair – Robin is not really a futile person. He's only been rather silly, and so was I. And he happens to be looking upwards, which always makes people seem like lost dogs.'

'Here,' said Robin, in a voice between rage and distress, almost a tearful voice, 'I'll go back.'

Amanda answered him in the voice of a nurse or a sister: 'But Robin, Aunt Ella is waiting for us at the farm. Go on down the lane and I'll meet you at the bottom.'

'Oh well.' The young man had failed in his attack on Amanda's conscience; now he was wobbling. 'I suppose it's as broad as it's long.' He turned reluctantly and walked slowly down the lane towards the farm. He looked foolish. And Amanda knew that he knew it, and that he knew that there was no gait, no speech, no action that would not have looked stupid in the same case. Sympathising deeply with her cousin in the injustice of fate, she thought, 'Poor Robin, I treated him very badly. I quite lost my head.'

Harry, to her relief, had remained in his place beside the tractor. He had not seen Robin being foolish. He had not troubled to turn his head to look over the hedge. Amanda felt warmly grateful to him.

'We'd better go on, Amanda, your Aunty will be waiting for us.

I'll take you down on the tractor. I want to oil up, anyhow.'
He unhitched the plough and climbed into the seat. 'Come, my
dearr.'

Amanda mounted the tool box just below the driver's seat and
put her arms round Harry's waist.

'But what do you mean to do if I don't marry you?' she asked.
'A foreman needs a wife even more than a farmer.'

'Yes, he needs a foreman's wife.'

He started the engine, which went off with a roar, and drove the
swaying clattering machine askew across the slope of the hill.

To Ella, who had hastened to Brook, they seemed already like an
engaged couple, and she went out eagerly to greet them. Her smile
was so eloquent of congratulations that both by a common impulse
avoided her. Harry strode off towards the main yard; Amanda,
putting up her hair, shaken down by the rough passage, turned
towards the house as if to find a mirror.

'They must be engaged,' said Ella to herself. 'Amanda was very
much agitated, and they both ran away from me. Young engaged
people always hate their own relations to know anything about
them. Yes, they are engaged. How happy I am. Or perhaps they
have quarrelled. Amanda looked so untidy. Oh dear, one must
thank God for life, and farms, and cows and horses, so patient, so
humble, so simple and true. Why, Robin, did you walk here? But
of course you walked.'

'Amanda left me planted in the mud and went off with the boy
friend. Where is she?' And he passed through the main gate of the
farm towards the main yard. Ella pursued anxiously. 'But you
mustn't call him a boy friend. And I'm sure Amanda did not mean
to desert you.'

'Yes, she did. She thought I was getting too fresh – what a filthy
hole this is.'

In fact, Brook main yard was not in good order. It consisted of a
quadrangle of byres, barns, stables, cart sheds and stores in every
state of disrepair from broken doors to complete ruin, surrounding
an immense midden, in which three large white pigs were rooting,
and from which a carter, at the farthest corner, was loading muck
into a cart.

A raised causeway, paved with stone, ran along in front of the
buildings, but as many of the stones were missing, and their place
was occupied by deep and dirty pools, it was not clean or easy

walking for town shoes. Robin, running from door to door, and pushing his pale face into one dark, smelly interior after another, was soon splashed to the knees.

'But Robin,' Ella protested, 'you won't find Amanda in the pigstye.'

'Why not, she seems to have a fancy for dirt and farm animals – brutes of all kinds. But all these girls are masochists.'

'Really, Robin, I don't think that is very nice to Amanda – though I don't know German.'

'There they are,' looking through the gate where Amanda and Harry could be seen approaching slowly. 'Canoodling.'

In fact, the slope of Amanda's neck as she looked at Harry, and the solemn expression on Harry's long face as he looked at her, were very much those of lovers.

'Amanda,' Robin shouted, starting towards the gate.

'But Robin,' Ella protested urgently, 'I don't think we ought to – to break in upon them – just now.'

'Why not,' and he called out again.

'She wanted to speak to Harry – by herself – about the dog.'

'I want to speak to Amanda. I've got a lot to say to Amanda.'

But suddenly a large greyhound stepped out of the back door of the farmhouse and placed himself in the middle of the gateway.

'Oh, take care of Flash,' said Ella. 'He's dangerous – so suspicious of people.'

Flash stood silently and gazed at the young man. He was a heavy brindled dog, striped in bars of black on dark brown, like a gloomier species of tiger. His eyes, too, like a tiger's, were a bright pinchbeck gold. Set in the big flat head, they had a look of indescribable ferocity, the glare of a serpent rather than a dog.

'Amanda,' called Robin.

The dog uttered a long growl, and Ella cried, 'Do take care, Robin.'

Amanda waved her hand to her cousin as if to say as much. She had only that moment caught up with Harry and was still breathless. Robin's intervention startled her and suddenly she exclaimed, 'But Harry, after all, it's rather a queer idea – to leave everything to the bank. And it's for me to break it off.'

'Yes, but if the bank—'

'Do you think I'm made of wood, Harry?' And now she was mysteriously agitated so that she felt, 'I'm just like Robin.'

'Ah!' Harry was perplexed. 'Why, no—'

'I'm not going to break it off,' said Amanda. 'We've made up our minds – why change them?'

Harry seemed to reflect. But when he spoke it was plain that he did not take this bravado seriously. 'No,' he said, 'it's good of you, Amanda, but it's not a reasonable thing. It's your maiden pride, and the trouble is, that's not a working article.'

'You don't have a very good opinion of me, Harry.'

'Yes, I do,' said Harry, 'but you don't know what you're offering. Poverty is a terrible thing, Amanda, real terrible; it's a creeping thing. It gets you down, it makes you over most completely. And marriage, too, it's such a long slow sort of a job, long enough for the worst of things to work themselves out on you. Lie down, Flash!' he shouted angrily at the dog. 'Ah, my dearr, there's many a black eye come to a woman, yes, and carrying too, because her husband thought so much of her he couldn't bear to see what he'd brought her down to. No, no, I couldn't – I couldn't do it to ee. Flash, Flash!'

Robin had made another attempt to pass the dog, which immediately uttered another long growl. Harry advanced hastily. Amanda touched his elbow and said, 'Wait a minute, Harry.'

'Amanda,' shouted Robin, 'where did you get off to?'

Amanda, now less than five yards away, gave him a wave and smile, then sought once more to restrain Harry. 'If I go on with it, then I shan't be able to complain, shall I, even if you *do* give me black eyes?'

'We'd better see what the bank means to do.'

'I will *not*. How can you be such a fish, Harry?'

Harry gazed at Amanda with a crumpled forehead, as if to say, 'Who could believe it.'

But suddenly Flash's growls became a snarl. Harry rushed forward and pushed the dog aside with his knee. 'Get back, you devil.'

'What happened to you?' said Robin to Amanda in an angry tone. 'I thought we were meeting at the bottom of the field.'

'Oh yes,' said Amanda, whose cheeks were very red, 'I'm afraid—'

'You forgot.'

'No, but—'

'Your conversation with Mr Dawbarn was so interesting.'

Amanda stooped to pat Flash's head. The dog gave a low growl and Ella said nervously, 'Take care, my darling.'

'He's only saying how d'ye do,' said Amanda.

All looked down at the dog, which, feeling eyes upon him, raised his own.

'The nasty brute,' said Robin. 'No one has the right to keep a dog like that.'

In fact, Flash even in this moment had a savage look. His eyes, though turned upwards in that manner which gives to most dogs a look of appealing sympathy, seemed only more wretched, without losing any of their malignity.

'He's not too good with strangers,' said Harry, 'but he looks worse than he is.'

'Oh, I'm not afraid of him – I only say that no one has a right to keep such a dog. But dog fanciers never were remarkable for considering other people.'

He looked at Amanda, who, astonished at his rudeness, murmured, 'I'm sorry, Robin, about the walk.'

But suddenly Flash gave a different furious growl and leapt at Robin. Amanda snatched at the dog's collar. Robin, who had jumped a yard backwards, ejaculated. 'By God. it nearly had me!' He glared at the dog. He was obviously most upset. His voice complained, 'I wasn't even looking at the brute. Why should it pick on me?'

The dog, with his hair standing round his neck, was growling still, as he tried to drag forward. At the same time, he wagged the tip of his tail. This cat-like movement of his tail especially gave him a look of menace.

'I can't hold him. Perhaps you'd better get into the car,' said Amanda to her cousin. And suddenly she added in a sharp nervous voice, 'Don't be *silly*, Robin.'

'I'm not going to run away from the brute,' said Robin, in a rage. 'Why should I?' and he turned his face towards the dog with a furious expression. Thus his big projecting nose was directed straight at the greyhound's sharp profile, revealing an odd similarity of expression. 'You needn't hold him – just let him dare to bite me, the filthy brute!'

'But Robin, he really might bite you.'

'Let him try it on, that's all. I'll kick his guts in.'

'Well,' said Harry mildly, 'I'd sooner you didn't lame him – he's wonderful after the rabbits.'

At this moment Flash, by a powerful jerk, did escape from Amanda, and at once seized Sant by the leg. He, in attempting to kick, fell back into the kitchen passage. It was Harry who, with a thrust of the foot against the dog's shoulder, sent him aside against the wall. 'Down, Flash! Where's my whip? Ah, you'm a wicked one.' Harry spoke dialect to his dogs. He drove Flash out of the passage by hopping on one foot and waving the other, with its heavy boot, in his face.

Ella and Amanda ran to help Robin to his feet and to examine his hurts. Torn trousers showed a very white skin on which blood oozed from a shallow hole.

'It's nothing,' said Robin, trying to make the torn cloth cover this wound. 'You go on to Ferryhill. I'll walk back to the Villa by myself. No, I'm *quite* all right.' His voice, like his face, was quivering with a mixture of feelings, rage and desperation. 'I knew it would happen. Dogs always go for me.'

'But we must worry about you, and you must let yourself be worried about,' said Ella. 'How should we feel if you got lockjaw or hydrophobia. You mustn't be so thoughtless.'

'Oh, I know I'm a nuisance, but I'm used to it. If you'd only let me be a nuisance to myself instead of to everybody else, that's what I can't bear. No, I'm not going to be driven home by Amanda. Amanda doesn't want to drive me, and I want to walk.'

'Bobby will take you,' said Harry, and so it was arranged. Robin consented to be driven by Bobby, because the old man, being half blind, very deaf, and crippled in both legs, seemed to be of the least possible use to others, and the most dangerous possible conductor for himself.

'A funny thing,' Harry murmured, among the group in the gateway, 'Flash never did that before, not to a visitor, that is, and not in *this* yard. This is public, you mid say. Yes, it's bad. I'll have to do something about it: give the old dog a dose of cure-all medicine.'

'Oh, Harry, you wouldn't shoot poor Flash?' cried Ella.

'It's due to him, pretty near,' said Harry, for whom dueness was a conception which looked several ways, not only towards right, but also to justice; and even duty. 'It would be due to me, too,' he said, 'if that young man went mad and bit the furniture.'

'But he's not mad yet.'

'No,' Harry conceded, 'but he's a right to be angry. It was a bad business, very bad.'

'Shall I take Flash?' said Amanda.

'Ah, but I think I'll come with you. I'll see the vet myself.' And after a pause he added, 'And I mid see the bank, too.'

'Oh, the bank doesn't matter,' said Amanda. 'Let it wait.'

'Yes, I'll see the bank,' said Harry, and when Bobby returned with the car in ten minutes, the party set out for Ferryhill. It was a silent party. Amanda drove with a depressed air. Harry, in the back seat with Flash, looked out critically on the fields. Ella reflected anxiously upon the accident at the farm. 'Poor Robin,' she thought. 'He made himself quite ridiculous. But I must be careful not to say so, ridiculous people seem specially attractive to girls like Amanda,' and at last she ventured, 'Poor Robin! But really he behaved in rather a silly way.'

'Robin had very bad luck,' said Amanda in a gloomy tone, 'to be bitten just because he wouldn't run away.'

She changed gear on the hill and Ella was obliged to sit in silence and alarm until the car drew up at last opposite the vet's, who lived in a neat but ugly villa at the very top of Ferryhill's steep and narrow Fore Street.

The party met on the pavement with a little chorus of friendly cries: 'Flash didn't say a word, Harry. Amanda drives so nicely.' 'Ah, she has a real lady's hand for the machines,' and then suddenly, as by a common understanding, it flew apart. Harry went into the vet's with Flash, Amanda invented a necessary visit to the library, and Ella hurried away to her shopping. Moreover, all three faces expressed relief at this separation.

It had been arranged, by a device of Ella's, that Amanda and Harry should return by car while she, whose shopping might keep her in Ferryhill most of the morning, would take the bus. The meeting place for Harry and Amanda was to be the car, at the vet's; the time in half an hour.

In twenty-five minutes Amanda returned and placed herself in the car so that she could command Fore Street below, and the Bank building from which Harry might be expected. She had a Compton Burnett novel from the library and a new copy of the *Economist* from the bookshop. She kept the book for her room, for concentrated pleasure. She opened the paper for immediate relief and detachment. But to her surprise she could take no interest in a carefully reasoned article on German economic policy in the Balkans. She could not even grasp it. She dropped the paper and said mournfully to herself, 'I wonder shall I ever get back to work again?'

Her eyes, glancing now and then down Fore Street, at last perceived Harry descending from the bank. His long legs moved across the street with his usual scissor gait. 'At last,' she reflected. And suddenly she gave a deep agitated sigh. But to her surprise, Ella came suddenly from the shop near the bank and accosted Harry. They stood talking together for some time.

'About me,' Amanda sighed again. 'Really nobody seems quite sane today, except Harry, who is too much so. I was furious with Robin for calling me cold. I ought to have been delighted. Really I behaved like a lunatic.' And then the reflection, still more depressing, occurred to her that the unreason of people and life, of her own nerves, of Robin, of Ella, might be normal. 'Because I *have* been living rather out of things – rather an escapist's existence. Yes, perhaps I have no right not to be insane, and that's what Robin meant, and why I was furious. Nature is trying all the time to put me back in to the stream – by making me insane.'

CHAPTER 11

Aunt Ella had not consciously gone into ambush for Harry. She had been telling herself a story in which she had met Harry just outside the bank, and he had said to her: 'Amanda and I are going to be married at once, Miss Ella. We know all about Miss Rose's new arrangements, but we don't care because we are so uncommonly in love that we can't stop for anything or anybody. Time enough afterwards to think of the cash.'

This story had given Ella a little consolation in her extreme distress of mind, and afterwards she had improved upon it by another chapter in which her sister claimed Harry as a nephew-in-law and changed her mind about the will. 'Though I'm afraid she'd never do that,' Ella mused, wandering into a grocer's, which was next to the bank. 'No,' she reflected, taking her stand at the counter beside two labouring women buying tinned meat. 'That's very unlikely. The marriage would be a great blow to her – yes, it might even kill her. How fearful that would be.'

At this moment the shopman asked Ella what she wanted, and Ella, who did not, in fact, enter this grocer's once a year, could not think why she was there. She stared at the man. At last she made a strong effort and faltered, 'Marmalade, yes.' She smiled with pleasure, 'Of course, that's always useful – with a man in the house.'

While the assistant was getting a two-pound pot of special bitter marmalade, Ella, gazing through the window, saw Harry strolling from the opposite pavement. 'What a lucky chance,' she thought, and thanking providence, she ran out of the shop to intercept him. 'Oh, Harry.' She paused. What could she say that would not seem too intrusive? She dared not ask, 'How is it between you and Amanda?' She feared to provoke an unfavourable reply; even an unfavourable action. She was, like most women in personal relations, a born diplomat, keenly aware of the importance of the right approach, the right word.

Ella dared not speak at once of Amanda. She made a gradual approach, 'Oh, Harry, the bank is not being troublesome?'

'Well, Miss Ella, I suppose that's its job, to go after its money. And I'm sure father can't pay.'

'But what would you do without Brook, Harry?'

'Me? I can always get some kind of work. My brother Fred would give me something at his garage while I looked round.'

'But that's so far away. Oh, you must get a farm, Harry, somewhere near Brook. Oh dear, but I hope this won't unsettle *all* your plans.'

Harry understood her at once. 'Well, Miss Ella, Amanda and I did have a kind of understanding, but there seems such a lot on the other side that I don't know if we ought to go on with it.'

He gazed thoughtfully over Ella's head towards the Longwater below, where a small yacht was trying its new spring suit of sails.

'An understanding!' cried Ella breathlessly. She was pink with excitement. She raised herself on her toes. 'Of course you ought to go on with it – for all our sakes.'

Harry gave his head a short quick shake. 'It wouldn't be right, Miss Ella, it wouldn't be fair to either of us.'

Ella, as white as she had been pink, opened her lips as if to utter some last desperate appeal. But Harry lifted up his cap peak, an inch further than usual, perhaps out of a feeling of sympathy for all concerned, for Aunt Ella, Amanda, himself, and the bank; then went slowly up the street towards the car.

He found Amanda reading her book, and said, 'I'll just go in for the dog.'

'But what did the bank say?'

'It was what I expected. Pay or get out.'

'And what about us?'

'Why, my dearr, that's off, I hope.' He went into the house. On his return in five minutes, with the dog, he found Amanda in a difficult mood. She frowned at him, and said, 'You understand, Harry, that I don't want to break it off.'

'Ah, Amanda, don't be unreasonable,' with some impatience. He started the engine. Amanda said in a defiant voice, 'We mustn't quarrel, Harry. But I am asking you.'

'We've got to be reasonable, Amanda. Being unreasonable in a thing like this, why, you mid as well cut your throat and make a clean end of it before you begin.'

Amanda said no more, but it was felt between them that they

were obstinately indignant with each other. Amanda's last words to Harry, given with red cheeks and a tremulous voice, were 'Goodbye, Harry, and we're *not* quarrelling are we, because we never have quarrelled, have we?'

This confirmed and acknowledged their quarrel.

CHAPTER 12

Ella had continued staring after Harry for a moment as if in half a
mind to follow him, then slowly descended the street towards her
usual shops. She felt light-headed, and could not tell whether this
was due to the steepness of the ground falling away from her feet
or giddiness. 'And he's going away, right away,' she thought. It
seemed to her that this disaster had always been inevitable merely
because she had feared it. 'It was bound to happen. I ought to have
seen that nothing could stop it, even if Rose hadn't changed her
will, even if she had died last year when she so nearly died, only
the doctor happened to be in the house that very moment. Oh,
how lucky that was – wonderful, wonderful luck.' And as she
turned into the chemists to buy various soaps and medicines entered
on her list, it occurred to her that she could not wish even not to
be defeated, 'For suppose he hadn't come. And he didn't come to
see Rose, only to borrow one of Amanda's books. Yes, it was a
providence, God saved my poor sister for me. Oh, I mustn't
complain. And as for the bank, that's just a machine – for counting
up money, even if it ruins the Dawbarns, ruins Harry's and
Amanda's life.' She could hardly breathe with her sense of
wretchedness. 'Nobody can fight against a machine.' And growing
more resigned, she reflected, 'Besides, nothing I do succeeds. Even
if my poor darling hadn't lived, even if she hadn't changed her will,
something else would have gone wrong – Amanda would have
refused Harry, or—'

'Aspirins and the drops,' said the chemist, completing her order.

'Thank you, Mr Colley – and I've just remembered – I want
some of that sleeping draught. You have the prescription. Two
prescriptions, I think.' She sighed and thought, 'No, it's no good
doing anything, Amanda will die an old maid. Poor darling!'

The chemist was looking at the book. He returned to the desk.
'Yes, Miss Venn, there are two sleeping draughts prescribed for
your sister – one London one in 1934, and one by Doctor
McCracken, in 1937.'

'Now which is it?' said Ella. 'How stupid of me. But yes, I think I'll have both.' And gazing at the immense green bottle in the middle of the window pane, she thought, 'I am a stupid person.' And at the same time she was noticing the beauty of the green liquid in the bottle. 'I wonder how much such a bottle would cost. How good it is of chemists to take so much trouble and to go all that expense, simply to give pleasure. It is so rare, distinterested goodness. At least, in public. In private, of course, it is quite common. Look at Rose; think of all those like Rose who sacrifice their whole lives for others. Oh, I mustn't be angry against anybody – not even the bank. Bankers have to obey the rules, poor men, or they would be put out. Thank you, Mr Colley. What a nice day it has been.'

'Lovely day, Miss Venn. We've started well for the spring.'

'We'll hope it goes on.'

'Yes, indeed – while there's life there's hope.' They both laughed, and Ella was feeling, 'That's why I can't bear this – this—' she couldn't describe her frustration. 'Because it's – so – so' – the word 'irresistible' occurred to her, but she did not want to accept it – 'it's so – complicated. One doesn't know even what to feel.'

'Thank you, Mr Blake.' She was accepting the boatman's hand as he helped her into the ferry boat. 'How nice it is today.'

'I'm afraid it won't last, 'm. Not with this breeze.'

'No, I'm afraid it's going to rain before evening.'

'You can bet on it, 'm.'

Ella enjoyed these smiles, these greetings. She felt that she was popular; she knew herself more popular than Rose. But she did not value popularity at a high rate. She would say to herself, 'They like me because I never worry them to do anything, and because it's so easy to cheat me. And they hate Rose because she's not afraid to tell them when they're neglecting their children or charging too much on a bill – because she isn't afraid to do her duty.' And as she hurried up the drive to the Villa she thought, 'Suppose she is dead – suppose she has died while I was away . . .' She stood trembling, listening in the hall. 'How fearful even to think of a world without Rose – with no one even to know me.'

She tiptoed to Rose's bedside with anxious eyes and alarmed features to whisper, as if barely expecting an answer, 'Rose – Rose, darling.'

'Why, what's wrong with you?' Rose was much startled by this cautious approach.

'It seemed so long since I'd seen you,' and she gazed nervously even guiltily, at the old woman's minute wrinkled face. She was thinking, 'She would have been dead four years, and what might have happened in four years? It would seem like an age, a lifetime.'

'Have you read the paper, Ella?'

'No, yes, I did begin . . .' Ella remembered that she had read the address on the envelope. But ashamed of this evasion, she added, 'Not exactly read it.'

'You must do it at once, dear. I've arranged with Robin to explain it all to you, to explain the *legal* effect.'

'Today?' said Ella, trembling as if she would fall.

'No, tomorrow morning. Robin is in bed today.'

'Oh – oh!' Ella was suddenly and visibly relieved. The colour returned to her cheeks. She cried briskly, 'Oh dear, I forgot about Robin. I must go at once.'

'Don't forget to read the paper,' Rose called after her. But Ella took care not to hear. She ran to Robin, whom she found sitting up against the pillows, in pink silk pyjamas, smoking a cigarette and talking to Amanda.

Ella was much startled by the sight of the two young people, so close together and plainly in deep and confidential discussion. She stood and gazed at them, reflecting, 'But how can they be so close, just after Robin's making that dreadful exhibition of himself. How can they be so unembarrassed.'

'Oh, poor Robin, how is the poor leg? How ill you look.'

Robin's very pale face in contrast with the pink silk, looked so livid, so worn and suffering that Ella's last cry was full of sympathy. 'Hasn't the doctor come yet?'

'Yes, Aunty, he's tied me up. I say, Aunty, I am most frightfully sorry for making such an ass of myself.'

'Oh, but Robin, you didn't – it was most unlucky.'

'But I did. Amanda and I have just been going over it, and wondering why—'

'But Robin, oughtn't you to rest?'

'And what we think is, that I simply got a fit of the old trouble.'

'What trouble?' Ella was confused.

'The old love trouble – you see, I'd rather fallen for Amanda, as you've noticed, haven't you? and then suddenly I got most tremendously jealous of Dawbarn. Though it appears it wasn't necessary.'

Ella looked with terror at Amanda, who, however, made no protest. She was gazing at the air with an absent-minded frown.

'And then that brute of a dog – why should I have run away? I object to running away.'

'It isn't running away,' said Amanda slowly, 'to avoid a lunatic.'

'But I don't like to run away from lunatics, either. Why should I?'

'Oh, I understand how you *feel*.'

'Well, do you, I wonder.'

Both pondered with eager curious expressions. Ella gazed and thought, 'Look at them, the same eyes, they might be twins, they might be husband and wife, closer even. Oh, but that's what I might have expected. Robin and Amanda will *never* quarrel. They'll always *talk* themselves together – they've talked themselves already into a kind of – honeymoon. Yes, of – of nuptials. Yes, that's what they love, talk, but it would be madness to say so. And she exclaimed, 'I'm sure you oughtn't to talk too much, Robin.'

'And, after all, everything is lunacy,' said Robin. 'Well, look at me this morning.'

'Or me,' said Amanda softly. 'Yes, lunacy – all day.'

'Love's young dream, it makes you laugh.'

'Oh dear,' said Ella, 'do you think so – but you don't really think so?'

Both gazed at her as if she had uttered her cry in an unknown language; and going up to Amanda, she tapped her on the back and said, 'Do sit up, darling, you're getting into a complete hoop.'

Amanda sat up and said in eager agreement, 'Yes, really extraordinary – and so subtle. I mean the way it makes a complete idiot of you – and spoils everything – everything sensible, the way it makes you take up attitudes which you know all the time are perfectly silly – and yet you have to go on being silly.'

'It's a racket.' Robin's voice was full of amusement. 'And if you try to stay out, you get held up for blackmail; the only really happy people are the born crooks or poor devils who are right on the spot. They're so frightened that they haven't time to ask if life's worth living. A recipe for enjoying life – put yourself on a spot.'

Ella flew down the corridor. She was horrified by the dreamy absentness of Amanda's expression. She thought, 'She didn't even hear – probably they are only playing a kind of game. How does one know when they are being serious. Their worst nonsense may be seriousness, and if they see you think it's nonsense they make it into seriousness. Even Amanda – oh, how stupid I am – I should have agreed with them. I must always agree.'

A few moments later she found herself once more at the door of Robin's room. Robin on his pillow, Amanda from her chair, sat with their bowed heads almost touching, while they smoked into each other's eyes and discussed the wiles of nature, in her ruthless determination to propagate life.

'It's not only the physical nuisance,' Amanda was saying, 'but the mental. You behave like a pernickety child -- everything is brought down to such a petty level.'

'A huge bloody swindle,' said Robin. 'An enormous complicated mass of dirty work at the crossed roads.'

'And of course,' said Amanda, 'about three-quarters of the crime and quarrelling and vice – even nationalism and racial hatred, come from sex in some form or another. Do you want me, Aunty?'

'No, darling, I only came in to see about—'

'How right Tolstoy was,' Robin was saying. 'The old boy's logic was rather weak, but his intuition was dead right. He hit the bull every time.'

Ella, who at the far end of the room was affecting to look in cupboards for some household object, gave a kind of groan, and changed it into a cry of 'Oh dear, how stupid of me. What did I come for?'

Amanda got up and came towards her, but with her face still turned towards Robin, and with the same tone of one in a trance, she murmured, 'Which Tolstoy do you mean – not Anna?'

'Good God, no! I mean the one where he really spills the beans. Don't you know it? It's terrific. Sex – the whole dirty game – is the root of all evil – and that's all about it. Marvellous stuff!'

'Yes, Aunty,' said Amanda. 'Can I help?' But she was still looking at Robin, or rather at a point about a yard below Robin's nose, where, Ella thought, the subject itself might be imagined to hover. 'Yes, of course, you could make a case for that. Rather academic perhaps.'

'Academic,' cried Robin with enthusiasm. 'Not he. You should read it. Especially when he shows up the racket of locking up girls in the nursery till they're fat enough for market, and then bringing them down half-naked, to catch a husband and get put in the family way, so that they can have babies to dote on.'

'But I don't see,' Ella muttered. 'If there were no children what would happen to the world?' With a scared expression, she stood halfway to the door.

'But, Aunty, the point is that perhaps the world ought not to go on, that's what we've been discussing.'

'Oh dear, oh dear!' Ella stopped as if to speak.

'What Tolstoy says is, "If there is a God let him save the world without all this fraud and filth, and if there isn't a God, why go on with it?"' said Robin, laughing in delight at this argument, and suddenly he looked extraordinarily young, like a small boy who enjoys something that moves and jumps, a toy horse or dancing bear. 'You see, Aunty, there's no way out. It's absolutely watertight.'

'All the same, Robin,' murmured Amanda, now back in her old position at the bedside, 'Savages find nothing improper—'

'Oh, but they do. They feel shame, they know there's something wrong somewhere, something nasty. Yes, Aunty?'

Ella had uttered another groan. But she had not answered Robin. She went slowly, if as reluctantly, out of the room. As she closed the door behind her, she heard the creak of Amanda's chair as she leant closer to her cousin, and her voice saying slowly and dreamily, 'Yes, one ought to know more about primitive psychology. I did read Frazer on the Old Testament, but I've rather forgotten the general line.'

'But am I wrong?' Ella, wandering once more in the passages, felt bewildered. 'Am I deceiving myself? Is it really true what Robin says that the only difference is between the silly ones who are cheated and the wise ones who see through all the plots? How did I fall in love with Geoffrey? – why, it was quite extraordinary. I didn't even agree with him. I was horrified that evening – oh, what a terrible evening! – when he argued with Rose and she said that he was trying to make a sensation and he lost his temper and said that Ruskin was an ignorant old eunuch.

'I was quite as angry as Rose, but still, I was in love. I went into the garden just before he left that night so that he might come to look for me to say goodbye, and then of course he proposed – that is, he didn't say anything at all. He simply took me in his arms and kissed me, and afterwards I heard him say, "So we're engaged." And I don't even remember what I said or how he made all those arrangements. Was that a swindle? Was it a physical thing? I had no idea of any physical thing. Oh no, I was in love with all my soul, and if my body was excited it was part of my soul. Yes, that's why I was not ashamed – why, it was so splendid, what incredible happiness. I did not know how to hide it. I tried to hide it, but everyone knew at once – Papa, Rose. Rose challenged me before I'd been in my room for ten minutes. "What has happened between you and that young man?"'

How beautiful, how frightening she was in her anger. Was she right? Did she know that I was being cheated, that love was all nonsense? Of course Rose did know all about the physical part. She must have. Bessie had had her first baby and she told me it was expected. Did Rose only pretend to believe in love? Did she say, 'I'll keep Ella innocent so that she can fall in love, but I'll take care that she falls in love with the right person. Was it all just a – scheme?'

Ella sat down upon her bed and gazed at the wall where hung many photographs of her father, mother and sisters, especially of Rose. Then suddenly she exclaimed, 'Oh, what is true – what can one believe – except this pain – this shame . . .' She pressed and wrung her fingers together, as if to hurt them, and to seize upon the memory of grief. 'That I left him – oh, how could I be so weak?'

CHAPTER 13

Rose had very soon made Ella confess the scene in the garden, that she considered herself engaged to Tew, and that he was to see her father on the next day. She had pointed out at once how little Ella knew of Geoffrey, how foolish it would be to marry a young man of such bad character and prospects.

And on the next day, of course, Venn agreed with Rose. He sent for young Tew and asked politely for some account of his resources.

It appeared that the young man was reading for the Bar, but did not mean to practise. Meanwhile he lived on an allowance from his mother and a guinea now and then for a poem or an article.

'Splendid!' cried Venn. 'How right that is, to put your art first. Yes, we are all in your debt. But perhaps just for the present you would find a wife rather an expensive burden. Shall we wait till your income is more settled?'

And he asked Tew not to write to Ella. 'It will only upset the child to no purpose.'

'What if she writes to me?'

'That would be most unfair to you. I shall explain to her that she must not write.'

But Geoffrey of course had written. He had even sent a poem. And then Ella herself had suggested an accommodation address in Queensport for a regular correspondence. The young couple contrived even to meet, once in London when Ella was staying with Bessie, again in Exeter. After a year, when Tew was rather poorer and less eligible than before, he proposed an elopement, they should run away and get married. Ella did not like this suggestion. She said that it would seem too much as if she were afraid of Rose. She preferred a secret marriage. And she even suggested the arrangements. She would, in six weeks, be going on a visit to Bessie, whose second baby was expected, and at Bessie's she would have much more freedom than at home. She could easily escape for an hour or so, long enough to be married in, and return without exciting any special curiosity.

Unluckily the plan was discovered. Ella, as soon as she reached town, sat down in Bessie's little parlour, to write to Geoffrey. Bessie was out taking exercise. Suddenly she came in, and Ella jumped up to greet her. Bessie, brilliantly dressed, in spite of her pregnancy, began at once to talk about her own affairs, her James, her daughter Alice, her servants. and the parties she was giving or must give.

'I have to entertain so much; it is necessary for James's career.'

Ella gazed with wonder at this sister, so altered by marriage. Bessie had been very ill at the birth of her first child, and had never fully recovered her health. She had lost all her looks and was now a plain woman. But to Rose's anxiety, she had continued to love gaiety and to flirt. Her conversation was a strange mixture of young men, parties, children, servants, and James, for whom she had a devotion at once passionate and critical.

'James didn't want me to dance,' she cried, walking about the room to show off her frock. 'But James is such a stick. He drives me mad with his fuss about what is proper and what isn't. And it's not as though I don't consider his position. I never flirt with his students except in private, and unless they are very nice.'

'But are you well, Bessie? Are you happy?'

'Oh, I'm never well. How can I be – but what does it matter. I'm used to it. Last week I was spitting blood. But never mind, I don't intend to die – life is too nice. Oh, you must be married, Ella, only not to any of those great oafs round Queensport. I shall soon find you someone. I have several in my eye. What you want is a thoroughly sensible sort of man, not too clever and fairly rich, with a taste for music. He will have to be very good tempered, because you will be a bad housekeeper and you are so unpunctual, and he must adore you and kiss your feet. I insist on an adorer, because you will have to make him give parties, you will turn him round your finger – what's this, what have you slipped under the blotter?' She took up the note and read, 'Darling Geoffrey, I have arrived.'

'Well!' said Bessie. 'I just wondered what you were up to.'

Ella jumped up to snatch the note, but Bessie turned her shoulder and continued to read, 'And I could meet you tomorrow in Shoolbred's.'

Ella snatched away the note. 'How dare you read a private note?'

But Bessie was now the matron. 'My dear Ella, perhaps it's just as well I did read it. Who is this man that you make secret appointments with in draper's shops? Geoffrey – is that Tew? Is it the young man Rose wrote about – quite a worthless person, I gather.'

'He's not, he's not! You don't know him.'

'What do you know about men, or about anything?'

'It's not your business to look after me. I'm over twenty-one.'

'Oh, if you take that tone I have nothing to say. You can be as silly as you choose.'

Bessie said no more about Tew. But Rose arrived the next morning. She would not admit that Bessie had wired for her and given her the news. Neither did she contradict it. But it was no use for Ella to cry out, 'It's not fair, Bessie deliberately spied on me.' Bessie had always been indifferent to reproof, and Rose brushed aside this charge as an irrelevance. She went straight to the centre of the matter. 'How could you go behind our backs in a thing like this? How could you lie to us, as if we were your enemies? We, who love you.'

'But I knew you hated Geoffrey.'

'You had only to wait. It was by your own wish you agreed to wait.'

'We knew it was a plot to stop our being married, but you shan't stop it. And I'll see him if I like. I'm old enough to know my own mind.'

'Have you some arrangement with him?'

'I shan't tell you.'

'So you have an arrangement. You are going to him?'

'Why shouldn't I go – if you are so unkind?'

'Good gracious!' cried Rose, 'what a dreadful accusation.' She tossed her head like a girl in the nursery. But her lips trembled. Ella, startled by these childish attitudes in a woman of thirty, looked at her sister in surprise.

'All the same, it's not very nice,' Rose went on. 'I thought we were such friends – however, I don't care.'

Ella, to her amazement, saw tears in Rose's lower lids. She flew to her. 'Rose, *darling*, but I never dreamt of hurting you.'

'Oh, I don't care, but I did think that you were different – not like Papa and Bessie.'

'But Rose – Papa thinks the world of you, and Bessie – '

'Bessie, she triumphs over me. But I'm used to it – I don't care,' and she walked up and down the room with crossed arms and a Napoleonic air.

'Triumphs?' Ella's lips stood open in amazement. Could Rose be jealous of Bessie?

'Why, where are your eyes? In every look, in every word. But she was born possessive and competitive. She was always a flirt. I knew she would carry James away from me, and flaunt his children over me – yes, even her condition. She makes it a triumph, and going to dances like that. To show how she dominates poor James.'

'But, darling Rose, she worships James.'

'Yes, of course she does. She must have that, too; she must be more devoted than any other woman could be. She must have a king for a husband, and then she can be a queen and have the glory of turning a king round her finger.'

'Do you really believe Bessie thinks like that?'

'She never thinks about anything. She *is* that. And she won't even help me with Papa. But I don't care.'

'With Papa?'

'You know he goes to see that woman every day now – Mrs Wilmot.'

'But I thought it was – the other one, you objected to?'

'Oh, there were half a dozen before, but this one is worse.'

'I thought it was Mr Wilmot he went to see. Mr Wilmot is his friend, isn't he?'

'Mr Wilmot is a paralytic, who never leaves his bed. You don't think Papa goes to see *him*. Nobody else thinks so. Mr Wilmot himself doesn't think so. He threatened Papa!'

'But how could he – what does it mean?'

'He threatened to write to the Lord Lieutenant. He wrote to me and I had to tell Papa. It was a terrible thing for a daughter to say to her father. And do you know what Papa did. He smiled and kissed me and said that I was not to worry. Nothing would happen, because Mr Wilmot would write no more letters.'

'What did he mean?'

'I don't know, but I know that the nurse was sent away. And Mrs Wilmot does all the nursing herself, everything. Nobody sees the husband except herself. I suppose he is a kind of prisoner, and Papa goes there still, every day. But what does it matter – the only thing is not to care what happens.'

'Rose, of course you must care. And Papa is devoted to you.'

'A lot of good that is – if this woman ruins him and I can't stop her, and now you're going to ruin yourself, too. But I don't care – not one farthing. I shall soon get used to not having anybody.'

Ella stared. 'But Rose, I'm not turning away from you. I couldn't, never, never.'

'My darling, don't you see,' Rose rounded on her impetuously, 'that you will, you must be changed – with a man like that, he will spoil you, coarsen you.'

'But Geoffrey is not coarse and hard.'

'He wants your body. How could he love your soul? He doesn't even know it. No, he is a fleshly young man. He dresses up his nastiness in pretty words, but he is animal – animal. He has no idea of Christian love, and he will corrupt you, *because* you are good, because you have such power of love, because you are pure in mind and heart. Yes, already he has begun to drag you down, in lies and deceit.'

'But Rose, that wasn't Geoffrey, that was me. I suggested the address in Queensport.'

'Yes, he plotted with you, and you are glad to sacrifice yourself, even your truth, your very soul.'

'Oh Rose, I know I have been selfish and thoughtless.' Ella was confused and excited by a mass of new impressions. She was suddenly presented with a new father, human and fallible, a new Rose, suffering and what was more extraordinary, dependent on Ella herself for something that only Ella could give. She perceived vaguely that for Rose in her thirties, life was growing hard. She felt as if her world, bright as the Villa gardens, had opened suddenly huge cracks, from which dark fumes rolled along the landscape.

'I don't mind for myself,' said Rose, 'but not even telling Papa. After he was so kind, so forbearing. For you know that Tew has absolutely no prospects, no family connections. How could you forget so much, Ella?'

'I didn't think, I didn't think.'

'Could you not at least write to Papa and tell him your plans? I don't ask what they are, but tell him, at least warn him. Remember that Mama left him to our love, our care.'

'Oh yes, I'll write to him now, and of course you must know, too. I'll tell you the whole thing.'

And within an hour after that confession she was undertaking to put off the registry office wedding for long enough to enable her father to come to town and attend it. And so sweet was the sense of being free of guilt, and once more approved by Rose, so delightful it was to sacrifice herself in atonement of her fault, that before the next morning she had proposed, on her own account, to wait until proper banns could be called in Brook Church, and a proper wedding arranged from her own house, as befitted a Venn bride.

Then having given all her feelings, bent all her powers to console the betrayed Rose, she had suddenly to think of Geoffrey, and no sooner had she begun her letter to him, with the words 'My darling', than into the phrase there rushed such a passion of tenderness, of excitement, that she could not write any more. Her hand shook too much. Rose, coming in a few minutes later, found her weeping hysterically. She took her unto her arms, into her lap. Ella clung to her as to a mother. 'I can't, I can't, I must go to him.'

'Darling, but you're not fit to see him today.'

'Oh yes, yes. You needn't be afraid. I shan't change again. Oh, I must go to him! I could never bear to think that I'd behaved meanly and cowardly to him.'

'But you aren't doing anything mean and cowardly. You're doing the brave thing. The proof is that it's so difficult.'

'Yes, it is. Fearfully hard. Yes, it must be the right thing.' Ella pondered. 'Of course it is.' She slipped off Rose's knee.

'You know the address? Is it anywhere where you can go by yourself?'

'He has rooms in Grays Inn. I was just to walk in.'

'To walk in!' Rose was startled. 'But why are you putting on your hat?'

'I must go at once.'

'My dearest, it's within half an hour of luncheon, and you must eat or you will be ill, which wouldn't be very kind to Bessie.'

'No.' Ella fell back, sitting on the bed. 'I've been terribly selfish.'

Rose kissed her with anxious sympathy. 'Oh, my darling child, how I wish I could save you from this wretched business.'

They cried together and were calmed. Ella, exhausted by agitation and misery, lay down on her bed to rest. Half an hour later lunch was brought to her in her room, by Bessie herself. Ella had no appetite, but she was glad not to be obliged to face her brother-in-law and the servants at table. And Bessie's company gave her strength. For Bessie, in spite of the turmoil in which she lived, of her feverish looks and hectic impatience, had a kind of power which Rose did not possess. Where Rose was passionate, earnest, Bessie was careless. She did not coddle Ella. She expressed her sympathy only in the words, 'What a mess it all is. What a nuisance for you.' Bessie was like a man of affairs who is so much preoccupied with matters of State that to smaller troubles he brings a rather aloof, and therefore more impartial and invigorating, judgment.

'But I don't think you need fret if it doesn't come off at all. Your Geoffrey is no great catch. You ought to do much better. You're a very pretty girl, and very attractive, much prettier than I ever was. And you ought to get as good a husband. Of course, I was lucky. James is exceptional, I mean, in being so distinguished. But you can be just as happy with an ordinary nice man even if he isn't famous. An older man, if I were you. Geoffrey is rather young to be a real husband.'

'He's twenty-eight,' said Ella, indignantly.

'That's only five years older than you, and a man of twenty-eight is often quite a child. No, I couldn't have married a man under forty, or say thirty-five at the youngest. No,' shuddering, 'no, I simply can't imagine it.'

'But Bessie, surely—'

'No, no,' Bessie cried, throwing up her chin and showing the thin cheeks, which contrasted so strangely with her stout body. 'You don't understand, dear. You don't understand what marriage is. It would be quite impossible with a boy, quite indecent. Oh, I couldn't be married except to a real man, a man you can respect all through – under *all* circumstances.'

'And yet you didn't—'

'Of course,' Bessie interrupted quickly, 'when I fell in love with my James—'

'Oh, Bessie!'

'Yes, I did,' said Bessie, suddenly becoming again the spoilt little girl who had argued so fiercely in the nursery. 'That's just exactly what I was. I was fearfully in love with him, but I was afraid of such happiness. I ran away from being married to him *because* I was so frightened of being inadequate. And of course I am. But he is so good, so kind – oh, I can't tell you how patient he has been. Heavens, is that Ally? Really, that child!' As Bessie opened the door a child's cry, which had been inaudible to Ella, was heard faintly from the distant nursery. Bessie picked up her skirt and hurried out, with exclamations full of wrath and importance.

And Ella found herself, by some mysterious sympathy, so much encouraged that she at once made her preparations to go out. 'After all, it's not so bad – it's only waiting another few months.

And then Papa will have to agree. And no one will be able to say that we are acting wrongly.'

She went down in hat and coat and sent a maid for a cab. But before the cab arrived, Rose came in. She had been to Grays Inn.

'My dearest,' she said, 'how lucky I caught you in time. I've seen Geoffrey and explained everything – he quite understands.'

Ella was astonished, furious. 'How could you do such a thing! What will he think of me? But it was a trick. You wanted him to think badly of me.'

'I wanted only to save you from a wretched interview, and it was no trick. I suddenly thought of it – I saw that it was a good opportunity while you were resting.'

'And what did he say?'

'He is quite agreeable to put it off. He behaved quite well, considering.'

'But what did he think of me, Rose? I must go to him. I'll go and explain.'

'Ella, my darling, is that a good plan? Would it be kind to him? Besides, he is writing to you. Wait at least till you hear.'

Ella waited. The letter came and broke off the engagement.

'As I could not hold you to a promise which has caused you so much disagreement with your own family and so many moral embarrassments. Our love perhaps accuses us of imprudence, but not less for that fault, so unsympathetic to the bourgeois mind, shall be to me at least a memory so perfect, so sacred, that I could not bear it to be entangled now with recriminations.' A postcript begged her not to answer this note. An answer would only annoy her family and distress them both. And he would not get it as he was going away at once into the country.

'Bad temper and bad English,' said Rose indignantly, 'such as no gentleman should write.' And Bessie agreed with her. 'It shows how right we were about him,' said Rose. 'Too young,' said Bessie. 'Just at the worst age. In another five years he'll probably be rather nice – especially if his hair goes back. He needs more forehead. But you don't want to wait five years for any boy to grow into a man.'

Ella did not argue with her sisters. Her mood was too bitter. She herself only gradually became aware of its depth and extent, that it had left her a changed woman.

She did not defend Geoffrey. She felt his spite as well as his contempt. But it was the contempt that hurt her most. It was a poison which stayed in the wound. And she could not reproach him for his revengeful cruelty. She had betrayed not only their own love, but love itself. She felt like one who has committed a crime against God, and she felt it still after fifty years.

'Oh, I was despicable,' she said. as she sat in her little bedroom, crowded with those relics which made Amanda smile. 'I don't know how I could bear to live after such a base treachery.'

The big hall clock in the depths of the house struck seven, and without knowing that she had heard it, she got up and walked musing towards the stairs. It was time for her to ask Rose what she would like for dinner.

'But how can I blame poor Rose for thinking it was all a childish fancy. I didn't know Geoffrey and he didn't know me. Our letters were a kind of poetry, all about poetry. How could Rose know that I was really in love with him – that I should suffer so much. And why did I suffer? Oh dear, if I didn't know Geoffrey, what did I love so desperately – a dream: a kind of phantom: an idea called love?'

Again her whole mind swayed like an old decayed structure shaken by an earthquake. 'Was it all a fraud – a made-up thing?'

She fled again for help to the past. Bessie adored James. But how? No, she never adored anyone but her children. She made James her great man. Yes, really, she almost – made James up. She created James for herself – yes, and for the world, too. It was Bessie who made Brent Square a kind of palace where people would go up the steps with quite a special expression – I've seen them taking off their hats four steps from the door. They felt they were approaching a kind of holy of holies of science, where the great James Groom reigned in glory with Queen Bessie.

'Yes, Bessie and Rose invented James's greatness. But why did Bessie always pretend that she had loved James from the beginning? She didn't really believe it herself. It was a kind of idea. She was always making things up. Yes, she made her whole life up; she made James up, her James, that is. And her James was quite different from the real James. She turned his brutality into manliness. Yes, I believe she liked him to hurt her and force her to have all those babies and miscarriages; she called his lustfulness, love, and his stupidity, dignity – she made virtues of all his vices and she laughed at the only good thing about him, which was his honesty and simplicity. But why? To deceive herself. Was she deceived? – and wasn't it all a kind of fraud just as Robin and Amanda say? Bessie cheated into a cruel marriage, and then cheating herself into a kind of artificial happiness, from pride and desperation – because there was nothing else to be done. Oh dear, oh dear, I mustn't even think such things.'

'Yes. Ella dear?'

Ella found herself at her sister's bedside. She started at Rose's voice.

'Rose, dearest, I came to see you – about dinner.'

'Have you brought that paper?'

Ella gazed at the old woman on the bed with a face of dismay and astonishment. She had not heard the question; she was wondering how she had come to the bedside without preparing her face and her words.

'That will – draft, Ella, the legal paper. Have you brought it?'

'Oh dear, I forgot it. Rose, is it safe to interfere in people's lives?'

'What are you thinking of?'

'Nothing. But you know you were wrong about Geoffrey.'

'I was right about Geoffrey. I saved you from a drunkard and worse than a drunkard.'

'No – no – never. It's not true.'

'Your Geoffrey died in an asylum, after writing some of the most disgusting poems in the language, and he deserved to die. God punished him for his hideous life with a hideous disease.'

'No, no,' Ella cried. 'He was driven to it – by me – by you.' She was distracted with rage and excitement, but at the same time some part of her mind was saying calmly, 'She always hates me even to speak of Geoffrey, and when she is angry she will forget the paper.'

'What nonsense, Ella. He told you so, I know. And that was like him, too. A cowardly contemptible action. But no man worth anything was ever ruined by being jilted. Your Geoffrey took to drink and vice because he was a weak vain creature who wanted to make himself notorious – famous, if you like – and had neither training nor character to work honestly and sincerely even at his chosen art.'

'His poetry is beautiful, and it is beginning to be appreciated at last. There was a book about him only last year.'

'His poetry is rubbish, and all rubbish comes back into fashion in a rubbishy time. This is a rubbishy time, and so your Geoffrey will be trotted out again. And you know that as well as I do. You know that he was a wretched show-off creature.'

'No, I don't, and you don't. How can we tell, about anybody?

Geoffrey was highly strung and susceptible. But so was Bessie – so were you.'

'Come, fetch that envelope if you haven't made away with it, or lost it.'

'No, I won't. If you want to change your will and tyrannize over us all.'

'Tyranny? Ella, it is you who have planned this crazy scheme from the first, and entangled Amanda. How, I don't know, but you have always been so persistent in getting your way.'

'I never have had my way. How could I? You've seen to it that I have no home, no money, no freedom. You've ruined my whole life as you ruined Geoffrey's, as you killed poor Bessie. Yes, you forced the poor child into that great brute's bed.'

'Oh, Ella, I can't bear – ' Rose put her hand to her heart. Ella, in sudden panic, ran for the drops. But the attack was severe. It continued for twenty minutes, and during the whole evening the old woman could get no relief. Ella went in and out, haggard with anxiety and remorse. 'Why did I quarrel with her? What does it matter about the will – if Amanda is stopped marrying poor Harry? Why did I ever meddle – why shouldn't Amanda be happier as an old maid?' she felt such desolation, such a pressure of urgency, that she could not be still for a moment.

Robin suddenly appeared in the lower parts of the house, in dressing-gown and slippers, propped on Amanda's arm. The young people were deep in their analysis of love's follies.

'It's all nonsense about savages being so reasonable. They only have a different kind of madness.'

'I should call it more a cult. Hullo, Aunty, what about some Schubert – we want to get an atmosphere?'

Ella declared herself too anxious, too busy; but after dinner, because she was angry with Robin for appearing at table in pyjamas, she consented. And the music gave her instant conviction.

'Of course there is love,' she said. 'It's ridiculous to doubt it. Love is as real as I am.'

But when she ceased playing and saw Amanda, with a dreamy look, turning over the pages of the newspaper, while Robin, thoughtful, scratched his chin and gazed at the ceiling, she was seized with a kind of impatience and a secret indignation. She went out of the room. 'No, they have never learnt to feel. Amanda is not at all upset about Harry's going away. She does not know what she is losing. Perhaps she would have been poor, but what would that matter? How wretched Geoffrey made me, but oh! would I have been without a single moment of what he gave me, even the pain? That is what Rose can't understand. No, she speaks of love, of Christian marriage. But in her heart she is jealous of all lovers. Because she lost her own fulfilment, she wants to deny it to others. And there is nothing to be done. No, I can't interfere – it would be madness to speak to Amanda – and wicked to risk the least quarrel with poor darling Rose. Never, never! When she asks again for the will I shall give it to her, and Harry will go away and Amanda will go back to her books and never come out again. In a few years now she will be dry and bent and grey – but it doesn't matter.' And Ella, quite distracted, darted along the upper passage between her room and the stairs. 'She will be quite happy – quite pleased. So why should I mind for her? I don't mind at all. No. And I can't do anything more.' She crushed her fingers together. 'I have not even the right to interfere – no, not even if I knew that Amanda were going to be unhappy.'

At ten o'clock she stood at Rose's bedside. She had so strange, so distraught a look that even Rose noticed it. 'What has happened, Ella?'

'Darling Rose, are you in pain? Will you sleep?'

'You never brought me that paper.'

'Rose, *must* you make a new will?'

'Please, please, no more, not now. Isn't it time for my draught, I must have one tonight.'

Rose often took sleeping draughts when restless or in pain. They were permitted by Doctor McCracken under a general instruction that they were to be used only in need. 'It's a choice of evils,' he had said to Ella. 'Sleeping draughts are bad for the heart, but so is a restless night. Your sister is impatient, she frets at her helplessness, and you must use your discretion.'

Ella, in great agitation and flurry, ran for the box of sleeping draughts made up in cachets, and packed by Mr Colley in two separate green boxes, one for each prescription.

Ella handed a box to Rose, who received it in some surprise. Ella usually made up the dose in water.

'But I can't take it dry, can I? Are these different?' She looked at the box through her spetacles.

'But Ella,' she stammered, as if shocked with surprise, 'these are not—'

Ella turned white. 'Oh, how stupid of me – it's the wrong box. It's the other prescription – the London one.'

'The London one – that was the one that made me so ill. But how did you come to have it – and the box is new?'

Ella tried to take the box from Rose, but her hand was shaking and her fingers did not grip with conviction. Rose easily kept her hold.

'You *ordered* them?' said Rose.

'I can't imagine what I was thinking of – yes, I – I thought I might need them myself.'

'You never take sleeping draughts.'

'But I thought I might need one I've been so worried, so dreadfully worried. And – yes, I knew I should need – the strong one. I'm so strong.'

'I suppose you have always hated me, from the very beginning,' said Rose.

'Never, never.'

'You want me to die.'

'Oh, Rose, how can you even suggest such a thing. It was my stupid head – I seem to get more absent-minded every day.'

'But why did you put the box in my hands? You've never done so before, you always made me up my draught'

'How can I tell, I – just did it – differently.'

'So that you could say to yourself that you gave me every chance to see what I was taking. But you hoped I wouldn't notice.'

'How can you think I ever wished you dead when I need you so much?'

'You never wish anything, you're too weak. You only plot and wriggle—'

'Rose, Rose, my darling! Don't, I didn't know what I was doing. I was dreaming.'

'You were dreaming of my death. Oh, how wretched it is, how horrible, how cruel! That you should hate me so much. Oh, what loneliness – after seventy years together.'

Ella fell on her knees beside the bed and caught Rose's hand. 'Rose, I swear.' She was breathless in terror. 'And you know that it's not true. I couldn't even think of such a thing.'

'Go to bed, Ella. Leave me.'

'Rose, Rose, you must say that you understand. That you don't believe those dreadful things of me.'

'I understand,' said the old woman, in a voice of indeterminate quality.

'What do you mean?' said Ella. 'Do you forgive me?'

'I understand what you feel, what you must feel. Of course you've been adding it all up, things that I have forgotten fifty years ago. It's your nature – and you've nothing else to do.'

'I know I'm selfish and thoughtless, Rose, but at least I have known what you have been to me – how loving and patient.'

'I'm too tired, Ella. Go to bed now.'

'But you forgive me?'

'Yes, yes,' sighed the older woman. 'What is there to forgive? You are you and I am I, we are past changing. I have been lonelier than I thought – but what does it matter. It was better that I didn't know.'

'Rose, you've haven't been alone. Don't say I've been no good to you.'

'I might have expected it,' muttered the old woman, wrapped in the gloom of her own aloofness, and perhaps of her general indignation. 'I might have seen that it's impossible to do one's duty, to think for others and not to be hated by them.'

'Rose, Rose, don't go on saying that I'm angry with you. I couldn't be.'

'Go to bed. We must both rest. Goodnight.'

'But you won't worry about this stupid accident. You will sleep.'

'Yes, I shall sleep – I *must* sleep . . .'

Ella put down her face. 'Kiss me, Rose, and bless me.'

'No, no, go to bed.'

'You haven't forgiven me, then . . .?'

'Yes, but I can't . . .' Rose made an effort and said in a mournful, broken voice, 'But what does it matter. Goodnight, my poor child, and God be with you.'

Ella, in tears, kissed the old woman and went out of the room. She was exhausted by the scene, and she could barely creep upstairs to bed. At six in the morning she was awakened by Amanda with the news that Rose was very ill.

'Ill?' she said, sitting up and looking intently at Amanda's face. '*Very* ill.'

'Oh, Aunt Ella, I'm afraid—'

'Is she dead?'

'We have sent for the doctor, but I'm afraid . . .'

'Oh, God forgive me, God forgive me, I've killed her. I've killed my darling.'

'But Aunt Ella, you couldn't help being asleep.'

'No, no.' Ella was distracted. She was plainly scarcely aware of herself, or of what she was saying. Amanda, with difficulty, persuaded her not to rush down at once in her dressing-gown. But she would not stay in bed, and when Doctor McCracken was examining Rose's body, already cold, she appeared suddenly in the library, crying, 'It was my fault. I gave her the draught.'

'No, no, Miss Ella,' the doctor soothed her. 'I prescribed a draught. You don't remember perhaps. And it was quite proper to give one in the circumstances.'

Amanda and he finally persuaded Ella to go to bed, and mixed her a dose of bromide to calm her hysterical excitement.

CHAPTER 14

Aunt Ella's first words to Robin were, 'Will there be an inquest, Robin? I ask you as a lawyer, and you must tell me the truth.'

'I don't see any need, Aunty. The doctor has been attending Aunt Rose for more than a year.'

'Oh, there must be an inquest: I don't want to hide anything – I want them to ask me questions so that I can explain.'

The inquest, of course, was not needed. The doctor was able to give his certificate, and the funeral was arranged. 'I can't go to the funeral,' Ella said. 'Yes, I must, I must go.'

But at the funeral she alarmed her friends very much by her wild looks and speeches. 'Of course,' she said to a group of tenants standing by the grave, 'we never really made it up, and now I can't explain.'

It seemed to Ella, gazing into the grave, that Rose, pressed down beneath the varnished planks, was complaining. 'It's not fair – I never had a chance,' and she gave a loud cry, 'Rose, Rose darling, I didn't mean – I wasn't—'

When Amanda and Robin took her by the arms to lead her away, she gazed at them in confusion, and said, 'Rose thought I was ungrateful, but I knew how good she was,' and suddenly she exclaimed, 'I killed her, you know, and so cruelly. But of course you don't believe that – nobody believes it.'

They soothed her. Robin especially was gentle. He had, when he gave his mind to it, sympathy and tact. 'But, Aunty dear, you were very patient with Aunt Rose. It's because you nursed her so devotedly that you're run down now – you want a holiday.'

'Oh no, never. I can't go away. I have so much to do. Is that poor Harry in the field, Amanda?'

'No, Aunty. Harry was at the funeral.'

'Yes, of course. Did you speak nicely to him? But you never speak to him now. You have treated him badly, darling. You don't mean it, but you don't understand – how sensitive men are.'

They put her to bed and the doctor prepared an injection to calm her and to make her sleep. But she would not have it. 'No, I'm not ill – I'm only rather confused. There's so much to do. And I am so bad at business. Rose did all that, you know. She was always afraid I would forget something, and she was quite right. I am forgetful. And now I'm responsible for everything.'

Under Rose's old will she was certainly responsible. The Villa and the furniture were hers absolutely, and only the income from the investments was under trustees.

Robin and the family were much perplexed by the disappearance of Rose's new will, as drafted in the Exeter office of the Sant firm. During the third week of April, a clerk from the London office, with some help from Robin and the maids and Ella herself, searched Rose's desk, the cupboards and books in the library. 'It must be somewhere,' Ella would say. 'Yes, I'm sure it's somewhere in the house.'

One day she remarked unexpectedly to Robin, 'I never saw this will – goodness knows what has happened to it.' At once she blushed and went hurriedly away. 'How can I tell such lies?' she asked herself. 'Though it wasn't really a lie. I only saw the envelope. And I have to think for poor Harry and Amanda. I must be careful.'

And two days later, after breakfast, she suddenly announced to Robin, 'Of course I saw the envelope – it might be under the floor.'

Just when the search had been given up as hopeless she declared, 'Even if it wasn't signed, it might be important. If Rose put in a letter asking that her wishes should be respected. Of course, that would have a great deal of influence on us, on me – it must have.'

'I have notes, Aunty, which she dictated to me.'

'But that's different,' said Ella hastily. 'Oh, it wouldn't be any good to show me your notes. Only her own solemn letter, signed – but I never saw such a thing. Perhaps there isn't one.' And she went away as if in flight. She was in fact horrified at her own imprudence. 'Why did I tell him about the letter? It's because I'm not brave enough to hide things. Yes, I used to throw everything on Rose, and now I throw it on – God – or just luck. But that's enough, I shan't say another word.' And meeting Amanda in the upper corridor, she said, 'How sad you look, child. I suppose Robin has upset you again. He always makes you wretched. I wish he would go away. You know, my darling, I wonder if that paper is down the back of the cylinder in the linen cupboard. Things often fall down there. I lost a pair of stockings there only last week.'

'But, Aunty darling, that isn't a very likely place for Aunt Rose to put her will, especially as she never went upstairs.'

'No, of course not. But then so many things are unlikely, if you knew. I mean, they only look likely on the outside. And if I were Robin, I should just take a peep behind the cylinder.'

Robin, however, took not so much interest as his uncles, aunts, and cousins in the search for the will. He had formed a plan to live at the Villa, and thought his Aunt Ella would be a kind landlady.

'I've resigned,' he told Amanda. 'I wrote yesterday – yes, chucked up the job. Wasn't Uncle surprised – and Kathy? The shock of their lives.'

Amanda was also startled. 'But Robin, what are you going to do?'

Robin looked gloomily at her. 'So you're surprised as well. Didn't you think I had it in me? Did you think I was a born louse – a slave of the desk – a little wooden city boy on wheels. Well, I'm not.'

'No, Robin, of course not. But how will you live?'

'I've got a little of my own, you know, enough to keep me while I look for another job. My idea is something in the open air.'

'It takes a lot of experience to farm.'

'Well then,' said Robin, who had perhaps meant to suggest farming, 'I might try as an estate agent. But just now I want to know if Aunty will take me here, as a P.G. of course. That's what I'd really love.'

'I'm sure she would welcome you.'

'But you don't.' Robin's decisive action had left him in a suspicious mood.

'Yes, of course I do. Yes, we must ask her.'

And Ella, approached to accept Robin as a guest, cheerfully agreed. 'Oh how nice – yes, Robin – that is a splendid idea. And Katherine can come and see you at the weekends. You shall have the big double room in the west corridor. Amanda, let us go and see about sheets.'

And going into the linen room she said to Amanda, 'How sad you look, child. I suppose Robin is worrying you. How different he is from Harry – have you seen Harry lately?'

'But you know Harry has left Brook. The bank has put in a manager.'

'Yes, poor Harry. Without a farm. One can hardly imagine it.

Oh dear, money is a great trouble when you haven't got enough of it.'

Ella made these remarks in the most anxious and earnest manner, and every day she grew more preoccupied and busy. She would go down to Brook for long conferences with Hannah, who was acting as caretaker, or visit the agents at Queensport.

'Do you think I could sell the Villa?' she asked them.

'Certainly, Miss Venn – and store the furniture.'

'Couldn't I sell the furniture, too?'

'That's a common arrangement. To sell the furniture first, and then the house.'

'Can I really do this?' said Ella, astonished. She looked at the large quiet office with its three desks and three clerks, its large, old-fashioned bow window looking out upon a builder's yard, some cottage gardens full of early roses, and beyond them, a triangle of the Longwater, as calm and flat as a china plate. 'Just as sleepy as ever,' she thought, 'and yet it has such power – I suppose it is upsetting homes and breaking up families all over the country. And now I have started it going, unless the clerks are only humouring me.' And she asked the old, bald chief clerk, 'I suppose I had better put it in writing?'

'No, Miss Venn, it's not necessary. I can make a note of it now.'

'Not necessary, and you can really sell it all? Just by word of mouth – the furniture, the Villa itself?' She opened her eyes wide, as if to comprehend this amazing scene of the empty villa, no longer inhabited by Venns.

'Certainly, Miss Venn.'

'Then do, please. Yes, I feel sure I want to get rid of it. At least, I want the money. And one must decide, Mr Watkins, mustn't one?'

'When would you like the sale, Miss Venn?'

'Oh, as soon as possible – next week – to get it over.'

It was explained to her that this date would not give time for the necessary prospectuses. 'The furniture must be listed and numbered and arranged.'

'Yes, of course, but do it as soon as you can.'

'We can send a man next week to begin the inventory.'

'That is so kind of you. Thank you very much. Only not in the morning. I don't want my niece to be disturbed. The afternoon is better, between half past two and four. And Thursday would be the best day, when my nephew will be out.'

'Certainly, Miss Venn.'

'It is too good of you – most kind.'

A fortnight later, when Amanda came in from her afternoon walk, she found six men moving furniture. taking down pictures and rolling up carpets. She was told that this was for a sale, and when she sought Ella to find out the truth, she could not discover her; she had taken care to be out for the whole afternoon. When at last just before dinner, Amanda intercepted her in the hall, she said, 'The sale, oh yes. I thought I'd told you, dear,' and immediately rushed upstairs to her room. Ella still had evasive tricks, but she could not long evade Amanda, any more than Rose. It came out that she had given orders for the sale, not only of the furniture, but of the Villa itself.

'And where will you live?' said Amanda.

'Oh, I hadn't thought,' said Ella. 'But there are plenty of places. We could go to some nice farm, where things are happening all the time.'

'But, Aunty, you couldn't run a farm.'

'No, no, I couldn't *run* a farm, but we could *live* on a farm.'

'Isn't this rather a sudden change?'

'Oh dear, yes, it's dreadful! Oh, don't tell me, Amanda. But one must *decide* – one must choose, it's no good shilly-shallying.'

Her voice had so strong a note of Rose that Amanda looked at her again, and thought, 'She even looks like Aunt Rose when she throws up her chin like that.'

Robin, returning after tea from his visit to Exeter, was found standing in the hall uttering cries like a hurt child. 'But what's happened?' And hearing the facts from Amanda, he protested furiously, 'But, Aunty, you can't sell a place like this; it's unique.'

'Oh dear.' Ella looked round as if seeing the Villa for the first time. 'But I thought you all thought it so ugly – Amanda would not have a single chair from it.'

'Amanda is completely out of date – absolutely provincial – you don't really *like* that chromium-plated stuff of hers, Aunty. You can't. It's impossible.'

Ella looked wondering at Amanda, who listened to the attack on her taste with a calm and interested face, and thought, 'Robin can say anything to her and she doesn't mind.'

'Horrible stuff!' said Robin. 'Cocktail-bar vulgarities.'

'But I thought it was – the latest fashion.'

'Yes, exactly – a fashion,' cried the excited young man. 'But don't you see, this place is above fashion. It's like a shrine. I'm not

joking, Aunty. Oh my God, how can I make you understand . . .!'
And Robin actually seized himself by the hair. 'Life is different
here, Aunty. One *feels* different. One realizes that people can live
with *dignity*. Oh, Aunty, don't you see that a house like this is
irreplaceable – it's not something that's made, but something that's
happened – that came to us, like a stroke of luck – yes, like a
religion.'

'Yes, I'm sorry, Robin.' Ella was startled by this vehemence. 'I'd
no idea . . .'

'Why, Aunty, to destroy the Villa – it would be simply a sacrilege.
Of course we understand, perhaps you have not been so happy
here – but now when it's your own and you can do what you like
– don't you see it will be quite different.'

'Yes, I just didn't think – thank you, Robin. Of course, as you
say – it is different. I must be more thoughtful, mustn't I?' and as
she went towards the stairs, where two men were rolling up the
carpet, she said to herself in amazement, 'But do I hate the Villa –
is that why I'm in such a hurry to sell it? Robin thinks I have a
right to hate it, because Rose kept me here. Yes, he thinks I had a
right to hate Rose – and that now I needn't hate the Villa any
more.'

She looked over the banisters at the hall below, which already
seemed like an old furniture shop, and exclaimed, 'But I never
hated it. It was Bessie who hated it.' She stopped a man on the
landing, carrying off a chair. 'No, leave that – leave everything in
the front bedroom; but never mind if you have taken the furniture
already. No, please don't trouble to put it back.'

She went into the front bedroom, the great marriage chamber,
which had been her grandmother's, her mother's, her father's, and
at last, before her illness, Rose's room. The room of the mistress, a
huge and high room, papered in flock, magenta and gold, a royal
paper. There remained in it only the huge bed with its walnut half-
tester, an immense wardrobe, the marble-topped washstand with
its cupboards, and two chairs covered in shabby red plush.

Ella entered this room, as always, with a soft and cautious tread,
as into a sacred place a centre of power, and looked round the
walls from which dozens of framed portraits, photographs and
drawings had been removed. Their disappearance gave Ella a
tremor of fear, and something like triumph. She felt like the outcast
who defies a sanctuary. But at once the bright spaces of the purple,
which marked the sites of pictures, accused her like angry ghosts.

She defended herself: 'But they could not have stayed there for ever – nothing stays anywhere.' She sat down on one of the chairs. 'And Bessie would be glad to see them go. She would say I was right. Yes, I blame myself for quarrelling with Rose – but Bessie had fearful quarrels with her. Often she hated her. And even Rose could not say that Bessie was evil. Or was she – worse than I – more cruel – more unjust.'

And looking at a space over the washstand, where a group had hung, she said: 'That group was taken just after the worst quarrel, and Rose hung it up and kept it. Why did she keep a record of that miserable time, over her washstand, where she saw it several times a day. Why, why – was it for James? Or was it to punish herself? – oh, I must look – how stupid I was to let them touch it. I must – I must find it.

She jumped up and ran out of the room, to hunt for the photograph. Some hours later, after supper, Amanda, who was helping the maids to sort china, came into the library and found her rummaging in a hasty, furtive manner.

'What do you want, Aunty?'

'Oh, how you startled me – you shouldn't tie up your hair, dear – it makes you look – so spinsterish and old.'

Amanda, who had tied a handkerchief over her head to keep out dust, was quite aware that the fashion, by enlarging her features, made her plain; but at the moment, being depressed, she was in the mood to look plain.

She answered, therefore, with some weary impatience. 'Yes, Aunty – but what are you worried about – what have you lost?'

'Nothing, dear – it was only – but it doesn't matter.' She pulled out a frame.

'What is that – a family group?' said Robin's voice.

Robin, who never seemed to be far from his cousin, put his hand over her shoulder and exclaimed, 'There, Aunty, look at that for a masterpiece – a real primitive, and you want to throw it away. Take care – the glass is broken.'

'But this one isn't so old and it's very dull.' Ella made as if to carry off the photograph. She wanted to look at it in private, to explore it for the real Bessie, the real Rose.

But Robin was reaching out his hand. He took the frame from her and carefully disengaged the photograph from the broken glass and dusty backing. 'Dull! It's wonderful!' He held it up. 'Look at the grouping. What an instinct they had for the group.'

It was a group taken in front of the dining-room window. It showed a tall man with a white beard and white hair sitting in the midst of a family party with a straw hat on his knees. A little woman with wide cheek bones, thin cheeks and large black eyes, staring fiercely, stood behind, next Rose, who wore a large garden hat. Four children, of various heights, were ranged by the women; and on the grass in front with crossed legs was a dark young man with a bald head and a long thin nose, looking at the camera in resignation, as if to say, 'I suppose I must go through with this – it's only polite.'

'A classical triumph,' said Robin. 'It's history. But I mustn't take it from you, Aunty.'

'No, I think perhaps – ' Ella was staring at the photograph as if fascinated. She thought. 'Yes, it is full of hatred and fear and despair – look at Bessie's eyes. What was she thinking, what had she done? Had she any right to be so furious against Rose – was Rose hateful? Sometimes. Am I not so wicked—?'

'Look at those trousers,' said Robin, 'even the faces are period. There's a whole ideology in the grouping itself. Uncle James in the chair, paterfamilias – the two women standing. Aunt Bessie, the wife has her hand on his shoulder – Rose, the sister, is only allowed to rest her's on the chair. And Bertie, the eldest son, against his knees – on the steps of the throne.'

'Poor Bertie – how bored he is.'

'But look at Aunt Bessie's expression. She's quite fiercely proud.'

'She was certainly a devoted wife. She had nine children, including the ones that died.'

'And the interesting thing, the really fascinating thing, is that when she lost her last, she adopted you.'

'Yes, they say she nearly died when she lost that baby.'

'But that's not what I meant – the point is—'

'You mean that she was more interested in motherhood than wifehood,' said Amanda, hastily intelligent.

'There *is* a sensuality of the mother, don't you think?'

'I suppose there is – yes, of course – undoubtedly.'

'It's much commoner among primitives than the Freudian stuff, which is after all only egotism. And it fits in better with the central idea. I mean, Nature's idea to carry on the race – the maternity racket.'

'You think the primitive family is simply mother and child.'

'Aunt Bessie obviously liked having babies. I'm not sure that she isn't about six months gone here. Hullo!' Aunt Ella was leaving the room with the photograph. She had skilfully and quickly taken it away while Robin, at the height of his argument, had turned to watch its effect on Amanda's expression.

'Excuse me,' Ella muttered, 'I have to see about the men.' She hurried to the kitchen, which, as she had hoped, was empty at this time of the evening. The remaining maids were in their own hall. 'Oh, horrible, horrible thing!' she muttered, pushing the group into the fire. 'Oh, why did I look for you – I wish I'd forgotten about you.' But the photograph seemed to be damp. It burnt very slowly, and when Ella, fearful of some interruption, thrust the poker at it, the iron went clean through the figures. Suddenly the cardboard, curling slowly upwards, showed Rose with a great torn hole through her breast. Ella fell back from the fire with a twisted face and uttered a cry, 'Rose, Rose, what have I done? Oh Rose, don't, don't – I didn't mean!'

She flew to grasp the tongs, to save the photograph from the fire. But as soon as she touched it it crumbled, blazed up and fell apart among the coals. Ella's tongs gripped only a corner of blackened paper, showing part of a pair of spongebag trousers and rather clumsy boots: the feet of the young man on the grass.

Ella, still trembling and white, looked at those trousers and said to herself, 'Bessie used to choose his clothes, and she wouldn't let him eat sweets in case he spoilt his figure. Oh, but Ernest couldn't have been what Rose thought – he was like a child to Bessie. He complained to me that she treated him like a boy. But what did that mean? When we were at Sandling Bay that time she made him bathe, on a freezing day in April. And only a tiny rag for a bathing dress. Men's bathing dresses were really indecent in those times. And how he hated it. Ernest was always so sensitive to cold. And I was going to protest, too, until Rose protested. Then, of course, I was all for Bessie. And Bessie, of course, had her way. There she sat gazing at him – and, yes, what a strange smile she had. One would have said she was enjoying his misery as well as – oh dear, I hated Rose when she said that Bessie was not a true wife.'

The cook came in, with a haughty expression, carrying her chin high. She had given notice at the first news of the sale, but she still resented intruders upon her kitchen floor. Ella laid down the tongs, picked up the fragment of burnt photograph, and fled from her. 'What did Rose mean about Bessie? Did Bessie simply use me when

she made me so angry with Rose? Oh, my poor Rose! Was all your
life a martyrdom, as well as your death. Was Bessie false and
revengeful against you? What did untrue mean? When I listen to
those children I begin to doubt everything.'

The celebrated crisis in the Venn family, commemorated by the ambiguous photograph, had taken place in 1905, when Bessie was forty-three and Rose fifty-one. Bessie had always flirted, and as she grew older these flirtations had become bolder, more defiant. Bessie was already grey and haggard. She had had eight children, and when she came to the Villa that summer she was far gone with a ninth. Pregnancy terrified this fragile woman, who gave birth with such difficulty and at so much danger to her life. And as her time came near she grew always more reckless in speech and conduct. She even carried herself with something of a gangster's air, who swaggers the more because he has a price on his head.

Bessie used to spend most of her holidays at the Villa, partly for economy, partly to please her father, who would complain that he did not see enough of her. Venn, who had once made a pet of Ella, now preferred Bessie, and they would caress each other in a very affectionate manner. 'How is my darling?'

'Oh, Papa, you get handsomer every year; you are growing quite irresistible.'

And it was true that Venn, at seventy-two, was much improved, both in mind and body. Frightened possibly by his illness, disgusted by the squalor of a disorderly life, he had reformed. He drank only a little claret, and used the diet of an ascetic.

As for his affair with Mrs Wilmot, now a widow, that had been unexpctedly adjusted some years before by his own eldest son. Theo, at the age of forty-two, after eighteen years in Paris studios, when his own family accepted him as a failure, and all Queensport said, 'We knew that spoilt boy would never do anything with his art,' had suddenly had a great success at the Salon. His picture had been bought for the State. His name reached even the local papers. Thus Rose, Bessie, Ella, and especially his father, had become full of pride and the strong affection which grows on the stock of remorse.

Theo, for the first time in twelve years, came home, prematurely aged, silent and preoccupied. He seemed older than his father and much more serious. They walked about like brothers, arm in arm, and Theo's high forehead wrinkled while Venn spoke enthusiastically of art. Even Rose felt in Theo's presence the authority of his character, intensely sincere, a character like her own, but without her passion.

She had spoken to him of their father, whom both loved in their different ways; and, of course, of Mrs Wilmot. Theo had at once opened this subject with his father. And then to Rose's stupefaction, he had gone to see Mrs Wilmot, not once, but several times. It was made plain that he liked her, that he approved the affair.

Indeed, before his departure for Paris, and, it was understood, a career of triumphs and honours, he had said to Rose, 'You are all wrong about Mrs Wilmot. You should ask her here, unless you want Papa to marry her. It is stupid to make it so difficult for him to enjoy her company.'

'But Theo, are you sure you understand?' Rose cried out, and her face, wluch had grown very thin, flushed painfully. 'How could we – in the circumstances.' Her tone expressed utter impossibility.

'Simply ask her as a friend. However, it's not my affair. And I admit I have not gone into it very deeply.'

Theo went and Mrs Wilmot had not been invited. But his approval of the affair had made an effect in Queensport. He had indicated a course. Lord Slapton, now a widower, called on the woman, and a good-natured magistrate's wife, whose husband admired French art and hoped to visit Theo's studio in Paris, asked her to tea. In a surprisingly short time, Venn's liaison had become accepted and reasonable to all but his daughters and a few old fogeys.

Thus Venn, proud of his son, happy in his mistress, and extremely well disciplined in health, was now a fitter man and in a real sense a younger man than he had been ten years before. He deserved those compliments in which he delighted, especially from his darling Bessie. He would pinch her chin and say, 'Is that the way you tamed your big lion in London?'

And though Bessie did not smile, and even frowned a little at this remark, there was suddenly a strange likeness between them, as if both, in their different ways – Bessie more instinctive, Venn more deliberate – had something of the buccaneer in their dealings with life. But Bessie adored her father, and he would make her sit on his knee and lecture her on taking proper care of herself. 'You must look after your hands, my dear. And where did you get those boots? I know that women's boots and feet have been degenerating for thirty years, but those are an atrocity. I shall order you a pair from my own man.'

'Oh, Papa, you are a darling,' throwing her arms round his neck like a little girl. Perhaps both of them liked to pretend that she was a little girl. Two days later, when he discovered that he must go rather earlier than he had expcted to his party in Wales, he suddenly turned to Bessie in the hall, tapped her cheek, and said, again as to a child 'And no flirtations, my dear – not in the country. Not at least till James arrives to take care of his property.'

'But Papa, I never flirt.'

'Is it so serious? All the more need to be circumspect. When in Rome, my dear – that is, Queensport – one must be Roman. That is extremely proper.' And he added, 'After all, one owes it to one's neighbours as well as oneself. It is a question of good manners.'

After this sermon, unusually serious and therefore spoken lightly, with a smile, he kissed Bessie very warmly and, still smiling, but with a more ironical air, stepped down to his carriage.

His engagement was to grouse shooting; or, rather, it was said, to amuse the ladies of the party, while the men climbed the mountain. Venn loved Bessie, but he could not bear children, especially her children, who were noisy and unmannerly.

Rose was pleased by his last warning to Bessie. She said, 'So he heard about last year.' Last year Bessie had flirted with the curate.

'And forgotten Mrs Wilmot,' said Bessie, who, on that same afternoon walked down to the gates and came back with a young man called Ernest Cranage, a demonstrator at the Groom Academy. Bessie, it appeared, had asked him to share her holiday, and had taken rooms for him in the village.

Rose had heard of him already. He had been Bessie's friend for two years past, and there had been already a scandal about him. His wife, from whom he was separated, had come to the Groom's house and made a scene, accusing Bessie of stealing him from her.

He was thirty-three or four, a small dark man, prematurely bald, but good-looking in his effeminate manner.

He worshipped Bessie, and was her slave. But when he came to the Villa he paid court also to Ella, and to Rose. Rose coldly refused his offers to run her errands. But Ella, who at thirty-eight found herself very shy of men, and very conscious of her provincial dullness, her lack of any kind of attraction, was surprised and flattered. She did not know how to refuse these atentions, especially as Bessie, far from showing any jealousy, would hand over Cranage to her service, saying, 'Don't you get up, Ella. Ernest, go and bring Ella's knitting bag. Where is it, Ella?'

'I'm not sure, and I'm afraid Mr Cranage won't be able to find it.'

'Ernest will find it, he's very good at finding things. Run along, Ernest.'

And Cranage would silently disappear into the villa to discover, among its sixteen rooms, Ella's knitting bag. Moreover, he always did discover what he was sent for in a very short time.

But he did not serve Ella only as Bessie's slave. He courted her when they were alone. He asked her about herself, her tastes, he exchanged confidenccs with her. He described the unhappiness of his own life. He was the son of a Crimean officer who had married, as an old man, a pretty housemaid, and died when the boy was eight years old. The widow had maried again in her own class, but had tried to give the boy a good education. Cranage had taken scholarships, but he had ended without a university degree.

'I wasn't so much idle,' he said in his dispassionate voice, 'as dreamy. I hadn't any ambitions because I didn't know that ambitions were necessary. I enjoyed life so much, and it didn't seem to cost anything. One got books from the library, and the fields were free. And really, you know, I was quite happy in my first job – I was clerk in a small chemical firm, and I lived in the country. But then I was moved to the London office, and I found I was too tired to read; the journeys to and from work, the crowding, the noise, they took something out of me – the power of enjoyment. And then, of course, I married and I was finished.'

'Oh dear.' said Ella. 'Was it an unhappy marriage?'

'As unhappy as possible – we separated almost at once. We had nothing in common.'

'Then why – how did it happen?'

'I was very young, very romantic. Boys of twenty-one are children in any woman's hands. I was prepared to love all women, good women, and to think all women good. And then I so desperately needed affection, and – to give it. In a world so completely sordid.'

'Oh, I do understand that,' Ella would cry. 'To love something – that is more necessary than to be loved.'

They played duets together. Cranage was a ready, though a very slapdash, pianist. He admitted his inferiority to Ella. 'I never mastered the piano. I have never mastered anything.'

Ella set herself to encourage him. She made him play and praised his touch. She was full of tender sympathy for this man, so gifted, so modest, so ill-used by fate.

But when she confided these feelings to her sister, Bessie said, 'Do not pity Ernest whatever you do, it's very bad for him.'

'But he has suffered so much.'

'Yes, life was really too hard for him. It is a desperate struggle in that class, you know – the half and half. You can't afford to feel like a gentleman on twenty-five shillings a week with holes in your boots and a bad digestion. I wonder poor Ernest lasted so long. Of course, when James found him in hospital he was completely wrecked. He used to cry when we spoke to him. We had to build him up for weeks before he had the nerve to teach even in an elementary physics class. But if you sympathize with him, he expands too much, and then he collapses suddenly and you have to start all over again.'

'He has great possibilities. I'm sure of it.'

'Goodness knows if he'll ever come to anything, but he certainly wants someone to look after him.'

'He adores you, Bessie.'

'I wonder – he's rather like a dog in that way. He'd adore anyone who pets him and beats him a little.'

But Ella insisted that Cranage adored Bessie only. She wished the sister whom she admired so much to be adored.

Under the influence of this feeling she was hardly for a moment shocked when, going into Bessie's room one hot evening, she found her in a very flimsy dressing wrap, stretched on the bed, while Cranage, sitting beside the pillow, was brushing her hair.

'Oh, I didn't know you weren't alone,' said Ella, blushing.

'Do come in,' said Bessie languidly. 'I've such a head, and the only thing that does it any good is to have Ernest brush me out – Ernest is better than any lady's maid. Don't take him away from me just now.'

'Me, take him away,' cried Ella. 'But how could I?'

'He loves to turn over for you, don't you, Ernest? Ella is much kinder to you than I am – she thinks you're a wasted genius.'

'I do think Mr Cranage should go on with his music,' said Ella.

'There's only one standard of art – the first class,' said Cranage with his air of acceptance, 'and I should never reach it.'

'Hear him,' said Bessie. 'Ernest loves to tell you he's a good for nothing – it saves him so much trouble.'

'But he didn't mean that,' cried Ella. 'He meant that if you can't, you can't. And how true that is. Rose wanted me to give a London concert and take engagements, but I knew I'd never be good enough – not nearly.'

'People do give concerts who aren't half as good as you,' said Bessie.

'I'd be ashamed.'

'Yes, you're just another Ernest. Too proud or not proud enough.' But Ella defended artistic standards, talking with such energy that the situation seemed not odd, but natural, more natural than her usual constraint at the Villa.

She was astonished afterwards to find Rose in a fury against Cranage, Bessie, and even herself. Rose, indeed, after tea, when Cranage proposed to go back to Bessie's room, in order to read to her, intercepted him and demanded what he was doing at the Villa. 'I don't remember asking you here at any time.'

Cranage did not show either surprise or anger at this attack. He did not even apologize. He went away with the impassive resigned air of one who suffers a change of weather, unforeseen but quite natural to the climate.

Rose then rushed into Bessie's room and told her that she would not have Cranage in the house, if neither he nor Bessie knew what was due to themselves or to James.

Rose, in the last six years, had shown a great change in appearance and even in character. Her face had become narrow, her whole framework bony and angular. No dress sat well upon her, and she seemed to have given up the attempt to appear attractive. She was dowdy and often untidy. At the same time, she had a new awkwardness of manner. She who had been the neat and dignified mistress of the house was apt to lose her head, utter strange exclamations, rush in and out of rooms, and bang doors. And with this excitable conduct, which startled even herself, so that she would often stand gazing with a look of wonder, she was more reckless in judgment, more impatient of speech.

'What an extraordinary thing to do,' cried Bessie. 'What are you thinking of – what are you suggesting?'

'I suggest nothing. I can see. If only James could see.'

'James is just as much a friend of Ernest's as I am.'

'I don't believe it, but he can't do anything because a scandal would ruin you all. And you know that quite well and take advantage of it.' Rose was breathless and crimson.

'That's a lie, and you know it's a lie,' Bessie screamed. 'You've always been jealous of me because I make James happy.'

'Call me what you like. I'll write to Papa.'

But this enraged Bessie so much that she could hardly speak. She was frightened only of this, that her father would be sent for.

Since his reformation, Venn had grown dangerous to annoy. He felt perhaps that he deserved some return for that self-discipline. He would punish Rose, for instance, if she bothered him, by forgetting to give her the household allowance. Behind all the affectionate kindness between father and daughter, there were sanctions which both had to respect, tacit threats, polite silent reprisals and manœuvres for position. If Bessie made herself a nuisance to him, without good cause, she knew she would suffer. Her Papa would find, perhaps, next time she wanted help with the children's school bills, that he was himself short of money.

Therefore Bessie was enraged by Rose's threat. 'Go away,' she screamed at Rose, 'go away, how I loathe you. Go and write to Papa. He'll understand, he's not an old mummy.'

And Ella, for once asserting herself, had pulled at Rose's sleeve and said, 'Don't, don't, Rose, she doesn't know what she's saying – and think of what might happen.'

Rose had rushed out of the room. But in spite of Ella's appeal, she had written to her father. 'I don't care what happens,' she had said. 'It's time someone grasped this nettle.'

'But how strange we all were,' Ella reflected. 'Of course, Rose was in her change – she used to fly into fearful rages. But Bessie and I were mad, too. When Bessie said she would leave the Villa and stay in Brook to be near Ernest, I rushed off on my bicycle to find her a room. Yes, I thought Bessie and Ernest were the noblest people in the world and Rose an evil-minded woman. I wasn't even forgiving when Rose gave way, when she came to me and begged me to help her, because she couldn't do anything with Bessie by herself.'

CHAPTER 16

Cranage had come once more to the Villa, every day, and Bessie caressed and used him, even more than before, because of Rose's silent rage. Ella gave her eager support.

'You should write a book,' she urged Cranage, 'you explain everything so clearly. I never understood the atom before. I'm sure lots of people would like to know about the atom.'

'I have no qualifications, Miss Ella.'

'You have your diploma from the Groom Academy.'

Cranage was silent, but afterwards he explained to Ella that the Groom diploma had no value outside the Academy. 'I tell you this in strict confidence,' he murmured. 'Even Mrs Groom must not hear it, she would never forgive me.'

And Ella felt the great privilege of this confidence, which was indeed one of Cranage's attractions for women. He was always putting his life at their discretion.

It was true that the Groom diploma, in spite of the professor's signature, in his heaviest and thickest hand, had no value outside the Academy and Bessie's imagination. It was one of Groom's complaints against the world that his diploma was not accepted by the universities or the Board of Education. The fact was that the Academy was suffering the common fate of pioneers, to be surpassed by its own followers, to become old-fashioned. In the fifties it had discovered and answered a demand for popular scientific teaching. In the eighties and nineties, the polytechnics, with modern buildings, qualified instructors, took up the work and did it better.

The Groom Academy, in three dingy terrace houses off the Euston Road, was not yet a joke. It was supported by the piety of old students who owed to it their start in life, and who admitted only among themselves that the Professor was behind the times. Indeed, to him science was complete. Faraday, Darwin, Tyndal, Lister, had left nothing more to be said or discovered.

Groom was still a distinguished man, even more distinguished perhaps since he had given up his whiskers and grown a beard, and since the penny papers had begun to print scientific articles. For he had always been a good propagandist, fervent and uncritical. His popular reputation was rising at the same time as the Groom Academy was losing its own name and the best of its staff.

'I have really no qualifications of any kind,' Cranage said to Ella, 'and you know in this world you must have a label, or how will people know what you're good for.'

Rose warned Ella against Cranage. 'Don't listen to that man, Ella. He's an adventurer – he lives by playing on women's feelings. He got round Bessie and now he's getting round you.'

Unluckily Bessie detected, by some sixth sense of telepathy or intuition, this move of Rose's, and at once took the offensive. One day at table, before two guests, and the two maids, she exclaimed, 'It's no good glaring at Ella, Rose, because she has been out with Ernest. She's quite old enough to do without a chaperone.'

Rose turned white but made no answer. She was perhaps even intimidated. Rose's weak side, as Bessie knew, was her disgust for brutality, and especially for that coarseness of feeling which does not respect other people's sense of decorum. Bessie, who despised scandal was at the same time a reckless scandalmonger, who would repeat or invent the wildest stories, apparently on impulse.

'James says radium is a fraud,' she declared one day, 'and the Curies simply faked the whole thing.'

'Not a fraud,' Cranage protested, 'and not faked.'

'And they got that prize,' said Ella, who had a great admiration for Madame Curie. 'The Nobel prize, isn't it?'

'Yes, they faked it to get the prize – they must have faked it, because, James says, radium is impossible. And you'll see it will soon be found out. After killing a lot of poor fools who go in for every new fashion in quackery.'

'I beg your pardon.' Cranage had a certain persistence on small points. 'Doctor Groom did not say faked, he said they had drawn mistaken conclusions from—'

'It's the same thing. Run along, Ernest, and get me a handkerchief – they're in my nightgown case.' She looked round the table with her feverish defiant eyes as if to say, 'Go to the devil, all of you.'

The neighbourhood of Queensport was soon full of such stories. It was a long time since it had had such rich gossip. But one morning a wire came from Groom to Rose, 'Is Cranage staying at Villa?' and half an hour later a second wire to say that Groom himself would arrive that afternoon.

'He's had an anonymous letter,' said Bessie. 'People are always writing to him. The Academy ought to be called the Acattery. They wrote to him about Ted, and that idiot Maurice, and now they're writing about poor little Ernest. We had four letters last term, all in different hands. James was awfully upset.'

'I'm not surprised,' said Rose. 'I'm only surprised that you give cause for him to be upset in such a way.'

'I can't help it that people have mean, nasty little minds, especially common people. But here's Ernest. Don't let Ernest hear about the letters. It would upset him fearfully. He's so fond of us both.'

Groom's fly drove through the gate just before five, when all the party were at tea in the garden. They hurried to the gate to meet the great man, who was all the more *their* great man because of his shaken reputation in the world. Rose, Bessie, even Ella, paid him the more deference, insisted the more on his dignity, because of that weakness.

Groom himself was not so confident. He had grown suddenly old in the last ten years. At seventy he had the melancholy look, the slow, heavy gait, the hesitating speech of an old man. And although he would repeat the old rolling phrases about the scientific mission, the power of truth, he spoke them without the old resonance. There was a crack in the bell. He did not, indeed, doubt the truth of his creed, but he was not so sure of its conquering force. It seemed to him that the modern world was indifferent to truth, and maliciously inclined to slight its champions.

Bessie kissed him with impulsive sympathy and said, 'What's wrong, James? You haven't had another letter?' Rose embraced him on both cheeks with a slow pressure, which to the other sisters, if not to him, revealed her desire to stand first with him, at least in trust and friendship. She wanted him to understand that he could depend on her. Ella gave him a light, rapid kiss, which was still an honest kiss and not a peck. For though she hated the necessity, imposed by Rose and Groom himself, of kissing this brother-in-law, she felt that she had no right to refuse so important a person any little gratification that he might ask from one so insignificant. Cranage shook hands with his master and hoped that he had had a good journey.

'Yes, thank you, Mr Cranage. I have a letter for you.' He drew a letter from his pocket and handed it to Ernest. 'From Mrs Cranage.'

The young man's dark skin took on a greenish tinge. 'From my wife?'

'Yes, your wife. She called on me. But perhaps you had better read it and consider it more at leisure. Just now, if you'll excuse me, I should like to speak with Mrs Groom.' He waved his hand as if to say, 'Spare me explanations.'

'I beg your pardon.' Cranage went away into the house. Groom and the ladies turned towards the tea table.

'What is all this?' said Bessie fretfully. 'Why did you send Ernest away? He's dreadfully hurt.'

'I'm sorry, my dear. But I'm afraid all our feelings may be hurt before long. Mrs Cranage threatens to divorce her husband.'

'Oh, but she can't do that.'

'She believes so. She declares that she has evidence.'

Groom took his seat by the table. He seemed very tired, as an old man is tired, suddenly and completely. Rose hastened to get him a cushion.

'But it's perfectly ridiculous.'

Groom was silent.

'Hardly ridiculous,' said Rose. 'She has had much provocation. Mr Cranage ought to have left the Academy long ago.'

'You don't believe this woman, James?' cried Bessie fiercely.

'Of course not, my dear. How can you ask?'

'All the same,' said Rose, 'you don't want to ruin James and the Academy at one stroke.'

'What can I do? I can't send Ernest away. It would kill him. But I see you are longing to speak to James about my iniquities, so I'd better go and comfort the poor boy before he worries himself into a fit.' She toiled into the house.

Rose turned upon her brother-in-law. 'James, are you going to let your life's work go for nothing because of this mad infatuation, because of Bessie's wicked selfishness? Are you going to stand up to Bessie? It's now or never.'

'But we must – consider,' said the old man painfully, as if framing his ideas with difficulty, 'that to send this man away might be an injustice, a great injustice. Bessie would have every right to resent it.'

'Nonsense, if you won't speak to her, I shall.'

'And then she's in a certain condition. We have to consider.'

'I'm tired of hearing about her condition, she trades upon her condition. But if you won't let me deal with Bessie, at least I can speak to Cranage. He is a poor thing, but he seems to have a genuine affection for Bessie. He would not willingly ruin her.'

Groom struggled again with the enormous obstacles of his discouragement, his fear of Bessie, his shame of feeling humiliation.

'Well?' cried Rose fiercely.

'That – certainly – appears to offer a solution. That is a possible way out. I could even use what influence I have to get the young man a post elsewhere. But Rose, Bessie must not know.'

'I'll see to that,' said Rose. 'He must resign.'

She went to Cranage that evening, after Bessie had gone to bed. And on the next day Cranage resigned by letter. It was a good letter, affirming his esteem for both the Grooms and his desire not to bring upon them any kind of misfortune. He begged that he might be spared a parting interview, so painful to all parties.

The letter, brought by a messenger, was in James's hands after breakfast. The great man, quite reanimated by this deliverance, showed it to Rose. They congratulated each other on their sagacity. Suddenly Bessie, pale, nervous, with her waddling gait of a pregnant woman, entered the room.

'What is that, James? Why is Rose so pleased this morning?'

'My dear, prepare yourself. This is a letter from Mr Cranage: he resigns his position.'

'So that's where Rose went last night.'

'He begs us not to see him or discuss so painful a matter. Indeed, he is going away at once – has already gone.'

'What business is that of Rose?'

'But Bessie, you must realize that there has been gossip. Your father himself, when he sent to me—'

'So you wrote to Papa,' cried Bessie, glaring at Rose. She snatched the letter from Groom. 'Pray God Ernest hasn't killed himself already.' She tore up the letter and threw it on the floor. 'Ella, order the trap – I must go to Ernest.'

'My dear,' Groom interposed, 'but he has gone.'

'He can't go – he couldn't – more likely he has cut his throat. That will really make a nice scandal for you, Rose. And ruin us, and bring James into the Villa at last, into your clutches. Oh, how I hate this horrible house, it's soaked in your hatefulness.'

Ten minutes later, Bessie drove to the village. She found Cranage sitting in the window and smoking a cigarette. He had not even packed or given notice. He had not been able, he said, to find courage for the project of leaving his only friends.

Bessie, in triumph, brought him back to the Villa, and kept him, after dinner, so long in her room, reading to her in bed, that James was visibly divided between his weariness and the fear of interrupting this happy reunion. He was very glad, next day, to allow Ernest to withdraw his resignation.

CHAPTER 17

'And Bessie never made up that quarrel with Rose. She hated her too much. It was the first quarrel between any of us sisters which was never made up. Not that it made any difference – ' Ella, finding herself in the library to which she had wandered, watched two men taking down her grandparents' portraits in the library, from the places where they had hung for seventy years. 'Quarrels are impossible to keep up in a family – a real family like ours. Yes, even when we hated each other we knew we should have to go on being sisters. Oh, that doesn't prove that Bessie didn't hate Rose. She did, she did hate Rose – even when James had that photograph taken to show that we were all friends together, and that the scandal was nonsense, and that he had no reason to be jealous of Ernest. It was a bitter hatred. Even in that picture you can see how Rose and Bessie were raging against each other. But they were both like mad women at that time – Rose so fearfully unhappy in herself, and Bessie, my poor Bessie, so terrified of what was coming.'

And Ella remembered a day that winter, in Brent Square, where she had gone to be useful in the last weeks before Bessie's lying-in. She had been playing the piano for Ernest, who sat beside her to turn over the pages, when Bessie came limping in with a basket on her arm, and demanded, 'What are you two doing? Wallowing in Schubert. I thought you were going to write out that list for me, Ernest, and address the envelopes for the reception.'

'Yes, of course. I was just turning over for Miss Ella.'

'Are you falling in love with Ella?'

'Where are the addresses?' Ernest jumped off the piano stool.

'I finished them myself – see, Ella, what you've done to my knight.'

'Mrs Groom, I—' Cranage, in distress, stood before Bessie like a small boy about to be whipped.

'Yes, I know, you're all mine. I saved your life and so nothing is too much.' Bessie planted her basket, full of children's mending, on a chair and cried, 'Would you jump out of the window for me, Ernest?'

'Mrs Groom,' the man spoke in a low voice, 'I do owe you more than I can ever—'

'I believe he would,' cried Bessie to Ella, as if discussing, between women, some freakish animal. 'If I really meant it. Wouldn't you, Ernest? I could make you. But that's because you're a fool about women. You think we're soft and gentle because we have soft breasts, but we're really as hard as iron. We have to be or we would be ground to pieces among you fools and lumps of men with your great knees and elbows. But you're not a man, you're a woman, and that's why I tolerate you. No, you're a child, and that's why I'm a fool about you – women are soft only to children, and even then only to their own children. So mind you're my own child and no one else's.'

'Yes, Bessie could be frightening. She was angry with life in those years.'

Ella gazed at the portrait of her grandmother now standing on the floor. A young woman with a black formidable glance. 'How like Bessie she is – and they say she used to ride her horses to death. Is it true the baby who died, Ruth, was Ernest's baby? Oh no, I can't – I won't – I won't believe it.' Ella flew to her room and shut the door behind her as if to escape from some terrifying and revengeful pursuer. 'But if it was true – how can I blame her – with my own crookednesses – and secret angers.'

And it seemed to Ella that the whole world of human relations hung over her like a thunder sky in which the clouds, charged with fury, might at any moment reach an unbearable tension and break into lightning to blast and kill. She fell into her armchair, small and narrow, which had been hers from the nursery. 'No, no,' she protested as if against an intolerable oppression. 'It's too dark – too wretched – I can't breathe. O, I wish someone could tell me – what ought to be done. Oh, darling Rose, how I miss you.'

She sat silent, a little confused by this last conception. Then she reflected, 'But at least I can know – had bad I am – yes, I shall find out soon now.'

As usual, resignation brought her peace, and in the peace, her energy stirred. 'Lot 117' she read off the ticket affixed to her chair. 'I never noticed they were going to sell this. No, I don't want them to sell it. I must have somewhere to put things that are not to be sold. Of course, Amanda's room is to be kept out of the sale, but I mustn't put anything there. It would interfere with her work. No, there is really nowhere. And what does it matter, if they hang me. Though I hope the police won't come till after the sale and after I've paid off the debt on Brook. They ought to come now.' She said calmly and cheerfully as she got up, 'I've no right to be at liberty.' She walked along the corridor. 'And certainly I mustn't make any more plans for other people – when I'm so confused in myself. No, it would be very wrong. I might do fearful harm – I must stand aside.'

'Amanda, darling.' She knocked at Amanda's door and thought, 'I hope she's alone.' Fortunately Amanda was alone. Robin was writing necessary business letters in the library. Ella, entering the room with a cautious glance, and a discreet rather dignified step, suddenly changed both for that mixture of shyness and impulse which she commonly showed to Amanda. 'Oh my dear, I wanted to ask you if you'd mind my leaving one or two special things in your room – Rose's reading lamp and my little armchair. I don't want them to get mixed up with the things for the sale.'

'Of course, Aunt Ella, I have plenty of space in my book closet.'

'I don't want to make your pretty study uninhabitable,' said Ella, looking round at the quiet room, with its sad colours of grey, brown and beige. Although Ella was supposed to have free access to that room, she had never entered it without hesitation, without a sense of its enmity to herself and her world, and what was more important, to her ideas for Amanda. It was her rival.

'The book closet will hold almost everything you want to keep.'

'Yes, but – ' Ella murmured, 'suppose there wasn't room in the closet. No, it's not a good plan – it was only a sudden idea. I hadn't considered your work.'

'I'm not doing much work just now,' said Amanda, with a patient weariness.

'No, of course. All this is such an interruption to you. Poor dear, you look so tired! How is Robin today? I thought he looked so ill at breakfast.'

'Very well I think. He's very tough.'

'I always wonder that Kathy lets him go away alone when he is so ill, and they say she is such a nice sensible girl. Have you written to poor Harry lately?'

'I hadn't thought of it, Aunty. I don't know his address.'

'He's at his brother Fred's. It would be so nice for him to hear from you. I see they're shearing at Brook, but I suppose you don't want to go – I couldn't bear it.'

'I'm afraid it's impossible today. I promised Mrs Jones to go through the pantries.'

'No, the book closet is too small. I mustn't interfere with your work – that's so important.'

Amanda reassured her, and she went away in much perplexity. However, the lamp, an ancient sealskin coat and a dress stand known as Maria Jane appeared in the book closet during the afternoon. They were joined the same evening by a brass fender, a mahogany step ladder, and a pair of plush curtains trimmed with gold, which overflowed into the study and prevented Amanda from reading the scientific magazines stored in the closet.

But when Robin sympathized with her on the invasion of her study she answered only with a shrug. Both the cousins were depressed, Amanda by the dust, the confusion of the house; Robin by Ella's failure to prevent the sale.

For though the auctioneers, having fixed the date of the first sale, of the furniture, in mid-June, made their preparations at leisure and by fits and starts, it had become plain that Ella did not mean to change her scheme. This surprised Robin very much, and after several days' discussion he proposed the hypothesis that she could not help herself. 'She's like a force of nature – they say mushrooms will lift a cathedral if they're put to it.'

'I suppose they have to if they're going to live.'

'The force of life might almost be measured in foot pounds.'

'What I can't understand is Aunty's idea of being a boarder in some farmhouse.'

'Wasn't the idea more that she should be aunt-in-law at Brook and enjoy the vicarious satisfaction of your marriage bed and babies?'

'I've thought of that. But why now? Brook is done for.'

'A regular spinster's complex, if you'll excuse the jargon,' said Robin.

'I suppose so.'

'She's overlooked one factor – that Harry Dawbarn wasn't a force of nature – he looked before he leapt.'

Amanda was silent. She did not like to explore her secret indignation against Harry. She was only glad that Harry had removed himself from Brook. She felt at the moment a disgust with all sentiment and congratulated herself often that Robin had not again tried to make love to her.

'Yes,' said Robin, brooding over his defeat and the loss of his sanctuary at the Villa, 'Aunty is just a terrific old maid. She has an appalling force of will, as if all her vitality had got dammed up except for one little crack where it shoots out like a water cannon, to knock you where she wants you.'

'I suppose you're right,' Amanda sighed, too languid even to discuss. 'But oughtn't we to move if we're meeting Aunty at three?'

They strolled together in meditative silence towards the road gate of the Villa, where Ella was to join them for their usual afternoon walk. The June day was warm and gloomy, with a thick sky of cloud, which, though bright to look at, darkened the ground and gave all colours a sombre intensity. The poppies in the green wheat seemed like pieces of mediæval glass, a foxglove in the hedge was like a fragment of thunder sky, the white of bindweed flowers hanging from a fence post seemed phosphorescent, the tarred road was the burning blue of hot clinker.

'How stuffy it is,' said Amanda. 'If it's going to pour, I wish it would get it over.'

'And then what,' said Robin, in an impatient voice.

Ella came swiftly from the lane, in her black dress and large black hat. She smiled at them – or, rather, she passed a smile across them – and said, 'You didn't bring your umbrella, Amanda.'

'No, Aunty, but you haven't one either – shall I go back?'

'No, dear, there's not time. We're late.'

The young people fell in one at each side as she hurried forward.

'Have you an appointment, Aunty?'

'No, but – we might look in at the shop for some oatmeal. Did you see that the men had taken down your Aunt Rose's dressing-table? I never meant them to touch that.'

'You could make them put it back.'

'I'm afraid it's too late,' Ella sighed. 'And they work so hard, these men. Is that Mr Veale, Amanda, on the bicycle? Isn't that a helmet?'

A policeman rode out of the Queensport road with a man in a brown suit.

'Oh dear,' said Ella. 'I was afraid we might meet them – you were so late, but really it's a very good time. Good afternoon, Mr Veale.'

The policeman and the man in brown got off their bicycles and saluted Ella, who said to the policeman, 'You got my letter?'

'Yes, ma'm. We were just coming to the house. But perhaps we could see you here.'

'Oh do, please.'

The two men looked at Robin and Amanda, and Ella said, 'You'd better walk on a little, my dears. I have business with Mr Veale and his friend.'

'This is Detective-Inspector Parry, Miss Venn.'

'How do you do, Mr Parry. I hope I'm not giving you too much trouble. I could come to the station.'

'But what is this, Aunty?' said Robin. 'What do they want?'

'I wrote to the police about something, about your Aunt Rose's death, and they've come down to see me.'

'But, Aunty, you mustn't make these statements without proper advice – you should have consulted a lawyer.'

'Should I? Yes, I suppose I should. I've probably done everything wrong – but these gentlemen will excuse me.' She turned to the policemen: 'They will understand. You will make it legal for me, won't you?'

'It's a small matter, ma'm,' said the detective, 'about certain information' – he glanced at Amanda – 'but perhaps you'd rather we stepped up the road.'

'Not on your life,' said Robin indignantly. 'What you have to say to Miss Venn is to be said in my presence, as Miss Venn's legal representative.'

'Very well,' said Ella, 'if that's the proper arrangement, and I suppose everything ought to come out.'

'Following your letter, ma'm, we found Mrs Bates.'

'Yes, old Batey.' Ella turned to the young people, 'That was an old nurse of Bessie's, you never knew her.'

'And she confirms what you said, ma'm, about the young lady.'

'But what did Miss Venn say?' said Robin. 'What is this statement?'

'I'm sorry, Robin, but I only wanted to help. I only want them to know exactly what happened. If it wasn't for me, my poor sister would still be alive – I think that's quite certain. I was the cause of her death.'

'What nonsense, Aunty! That's absurd!'

'And of course these gentlemen want to know particulars.'

'Excuse me, ma'm, we were not making any enquiries at the time you wrote.'

'No, but people in the village were talking. They were bound to talk. So I thought I should tell you myself about Miss Groom – that she's my daughter.'

The inspector drew out a notebook and read out, 'Born, April, 1906; registered father unknown.'

'Yes, but I've never seen the certificate. My sister did that for me. And I didn't know my husband had not been registered.'

'Your husband, miss?'

'I call him my husband, of course. We meant to be married, and he would have married me, poor man, if he could have done so. At least I think so. It's so hard to know what people might have done, if things had been different.'

'And you say that you and the late Miss Venn had a difference of opinion about your daughter?'

'Oh yes, it was very difficult, even when we didn't speak of it. What I mean is – that if you were looking for a motive – in murder cases that is important, isn't it, the motive?'

'But, Aunty, what are you talking about? No one has suggested that you committed any murder. It's absolutely ridiculous.'

'There's no charge whatever,' said the detective. 'This is a voluntary statement by Miss Venn.'

'Yes, of course. Oh, I do want to get things straight.'

'You understand,' said Robin to the policeman, 'that Miss Venn's death was quite natural and expected.'

The policeman said nothing. Ella exclaimed, 'Yes, of course. Doctor McCracken gave the certificate. And Rose took the cachets of her own free will.'

'Exactly,' said Robin. 'The doctor's prescription.'

'But, then, why did she take three cachets?' said Ella. 'That worries me so dreadfully – and even one was too strong.'

'Three, Miss Venn?' said the detective

'Yes, the doctor didn't notice, but I did. There were twelve cachets in the box and only nine left, so my poor sister must have taken three. She didn't mean to wake up again. Unless of course she was only leaving it to God.'

'Thank you, Miss Venn. I won't ask you anything more. I hope I haven't given you any distress over the young lady.' He touched his cap to Amanda, who, however, did not notice the gesture. She was looking at the cottages opposite, with a preoccupied expression.

The constable and the inspector mounted their bicycles and rode off. Aunt Ella said to the two young people, in her lively voice which sounded now a little feverish, a little too lively, 'But I suppose that is what the Bible means, 'Thou shall not tempt the Lord thy God. Yes.' She walked on towards Brook and they fell in beside her, as if acknowledging, for the first time, her right to set the pace. 'And if poor Rose took three cachets just to challenge God, then it wasn't suicide, was it? But I don't think Rose would do that. It's more like me. I'm always tempting God. And I quite see why it's a sin. It's weak and cowardly. But I didn't tell the officer about the three cachets to make him think Rose committed suicide. I told him because it occurred to me just then. I don't want to deceive him in any way.'

'So Amanda is your daughter, Aunt Ella?' said Robin, causing Amanda to take a step slightly in advance.

'Yes I'm surprised you don't know. Your father must know. Your Uncle Dick knows. I'm sure everyone in the village knows. Oh, I have a dreadful name in the village, considering how nice they are to me, it's surprising. But it never seems to make any difference in the country. People who believe the worst things about you are often the nicest to you.'

'And the man was married?'

'Oh, I didn't know that he couldn't marry me, not when I went away with him. Or if I did, I didn't admit it even to myself. I thought we were getting married at once. At least I think I thought so. And I knew all his plans. We were going to America together – it was a very good plan. And he told me everything. He confessed to me at once. He was the soul of honour, Amanda's father.' Ella spoke loudly as if to make sure that Amanda, still a pace in front, should hear. 'He was the best and truest of men, who never wished harm to anyone, least of all to me or to her.'

'Although he deceived you about his wife.'

'Oh dear, Robin, he didn't deceive me. I think not. I think I only pretended to be deceived. I behaved very badly. Yes, I think that's quite clear. Why, I should have stayed with him always if it hadn't been—'

'For what, Aunty?'

But suddenly Ella's mind changed. She looked at the young people and saw their melancholy, thoughtful faces, absorbed in some private reflections into which she could not penetrate. She felt their mysterious distance from her, and especially that Amanda was suddenly removed so far from her that she could not reach her, even in imagination. She thought, 'Goodness knows what they're thinking about – perhaps it is all ideology to them – words.' She answered Robin in a depressed voice: 'Something that happened – which really doesn't matter now. My dearest Bessie agreed to adopt Amanda and I went abroad for some years. I went to Italy with a friend – oh, look, they haven't finished shearing at Brook. Shall we go now? How lovely the sheep look when they are sheared, so clean and neat. And they seem so relieved to get rid of all that weight. But no, Brook is not Brook any more – we'll go back.'

She turned towards the Villa and hurried so fast that even Robin had to stretch his long legs.

'How sad Amanda looks,' Ella was thinking. 'But it is dreadful news for her – a fearful shock. I can hardly believe it myself – that I ran away with a married man. How did I – how could I do such a thing? Of course, Rose thought I was a silly old maid who was desperate to get married – and that Ernest was a swindler who took advantage of me.'

'What's happening now?' said Robin in a fretful tone. 'Are you moving today, Aunty? You never tell us things.'

They had reached the drive and found it blocked by a pantechnicon, standing at the front door.

'I don't think so,' said Ella, gazing with suspicion at the van. 'But of course, they don't tell me either.'

The pantechnicon proved not to be taking away furniture from the Villa, but bringing more. The men were in the act of carrying a large mahogany table across the steps; another, already unloaded, stood in the hall, beside a cheap yellow chest of drawers and a strange wardrobe.

'What *are* these things?' Robin asked. 'Where on earth do they come from?'

'I don't know, dear,' said Ella. 'But please don't say anything to the men, they mightn't like it. And they've been so good.'

Robin was indignant. He pointed out that the Villa sale was bound to attract a large number of buyers because the house was full of good furniture. 'And these people are going to pass off a lot of shoddy stuff as yours. It's simply a fraud.'

'That may be it,' said Ella, 'or perhaps there is another reason which we wouldn't understand.' She looked timidly at Amanda, as if to say something, and Amanda turned round and made as if to speak. Then both changed their minds, and Amanda went into the house, followed by Robin, who, passing slowly through the door impeded the men with the second table. It was the protest of a moralist.

Ella sat down upon a sofa, in crude Turkey plush, which had been placed on the grass beside a worn Wilton carpet covered with immense pink and white roses. Several old chairs and one moth-eaten bear holding a brass dish were scattered at various angles round the sofa and a footstool in cross stitch, badly stained with some pink dye possibly cherry juice, stood before it. Ella placed her feet on the stool and folded her hands in her lap.

'Perhaps Rose was right – perhaps I was getting queer – perhaps Ernest was a rascal. Oh no, no – not a rascal. And I loved him. Oh, what can I tell Amanda? It must be the truth.' Ella spoke severely to herself. 'It's not safe not to tell the truth – certainly to Amanda. So I must be very clear in my own mind. If only people were not so mixed up.'

'Excuse me, Miss, shall I put it here?' A young workman with a red face was clasping a bust of Phryne. 'It doesn't want to get broke, does it?'

'Oh, please,' said Ella. The young man put down Phryne on a large gilt armchair and rubbed his hands. 'Nice stuff!' he said, looking round.

Ella thought anxiously, 'He wants a tip and my bag is in the house – but I don't think I'd better.'

She didn't want to go into the house in case of meeting Amanda.

She felt guilty towards Amanda. 'Of course, she has not got accustomed to having a father – I mean, a real father – she must feel very strange – like a different person. Ernest's daughter. And suppose she asks me questions?'

'I don't think I've ever moved such a nice bit of stuff,' said the man, and Ella, having no tip, suddenly smiled at him and said, 'But you're – I know you quite well, don't I? Is your mother – '

'Yes, Miss Ella, thankye. Mother's pretty well.'

'I'm so glad, and I'm so glad to see you so well, too. You'll remember me to her, won't you?'

'Yes, thankye, Miss Ella.' The young man walked away and Ella thought, 'He's not disappointed.'

And pleased with this escape, even smiling a little, she sat gazing at Phryne, who with her blank plaster eyeballs, and a smirk on her chalky lips, returned the look with an intensity which gradually penetrated Ella's imagination. Her eyes grew large, her lips parted; she gave a little cry and half started up. 'Why – where is this?' She looked round at the unfamiliar objects which had so silently gathered about her, as at the substance of a dream, in which her past life was as fantastic as the extraordinary carpet, the strange chairs and tables, the enigmatic Phryne.

She sank back on the sofa. 'Oh, but – it did happen. I did run away – I must have plotted – I must have known. How could I not have known after what Bessie said.'

She saw herself and Cranage after Bessie's dry remark, 'Ernest is falling in love with you.'

Bessie had gone out of the room, probably to show her indifference to these intrigues, and Ernest had turned to Ella.

'I felt that he was going to say something – about being fond of me – so I didn't look at him. I began to avoid him – but no, did I avoid him? Or did I only pretend?'

CHAPTER 18

It seemed to Ella that, at one and the same time, she had kept aloof from Cranage and thrown herself in his way. She was always meeting him, going into the same room with him, and then, once in his presence, she had placed herself at a distance, and this distance itself created a tie, a tension between them, like stretched elastic.

'Was I really encouraging him – or only excited?'

Ernest came every day to Brent Square, where he was indispensable. He wrote letters, typed, went shopping, paid bills, kept the accounts. He attended for Bessie's instructions like a butler. But as soon as Bessie was brought to bed he was suddenly excluded from her room or close intimacy. The child was sickly from the first, hard to keep alive, and the whole of the mother's time and thought were given to it. Bessie herself was ill. She had had as usual a hard and long delivery, and was slow to recover from it. Illness and anxiety made her impatient rather than bad tempered; she went about with a calm, very white face, and ejaculated cynical comments upon all persons and things.

'Look at Ernest,' she would say, 'terrified that I'm going to be rude. I wonder why he comes here at all, except to see Ella. Play something to him, Ella, so that he can say nice things – that's what he does really well.' On the other hand, if Ernest did not come, she would send for him. 'Where were you yesterday, Ernest – I was expecting you all the afternoon, to add up my books. You knew it was my account day. But I suppose you are annoyed with me about something: if so, I apologize. I know I'm very bad tempered just now, it's this weather, and that fool of a nurse – and that idiot of a doctor, and that brute Beal. Oh, I wish someone would kill Beal – if you really were my friend, you would kill him for me.'

Beal was a well-known young scientist of fifty, who had written to a newspaper contradicting one of Groom's popular articles. His letter was clever and rather spiteful, in that style which has always marked the quarrels of dogmatists. Groom had answered it in a high moral tone, and laid himself open to a damaging reply. 'Long-established prejudice is not yet, we hope, a substitute for the habit of enquiry and a respect for truth. Professor Groom is, of course, entitled to his professorship because it is that of the Groom Academy, founded by himself. It is not his fault that its degrees have never been accepted by the educational authorities. But it is, we suggest, within the power of any gentlemen who sets up to teach the young, to acquaint himself with the rudiments of his subject.'

Groom had threatened a writ for libel, but meanwhile it was noticed that there had been a further fall in the number of admissions to the Academy; and one of the two papers which published his articles on popular science had asked him to send no more 'for the present'.

This conflict had enraged Bessie, who saw in it a conspiracy to ruin her great man, out of jealousy and spite. 'Nasty little creatures like Beal always hate men like James, really great and noble minds, because they can't understand them.'

She commanded Ernest to write an answer to Beal, which perplexed him very much. For, as he explained to Ella, Beal was right. 'It's his own subject, and he knows more about it than anyone in the Academy.'

'But is James really a kind of impostor?'

'No, I think he is, or was, rather a remarkable man – it took great vision and energy for a young student without money or friends to start the Academy. But of course he is not a born scientist – he has no idea of detachment, of impartiality – he ought to have been in the Church.'

'In the Church?' cried Ella.

'I mean, he has a religious mind. He wants to teach, to convert. He doesn't really care about facts at all as facts, but only about morals which he thinks he can find in the facts. That's why Beal hates him. Beal is a real scientist. I mean, he really loves what he calls facts. And he really hates religious-minded people.'

Ella and Cranage were thrown together by Bessie's preoccupation. They went shopping together on Bessie's errands. And Ella was glad to find topics of conversation interesting to her companion.

'But how awful to be like Beal,' she would say. 'To hate good people.'

'But are they good who teach what isn't true? It's very dangerous.'

'You don't mean that the Academy ought to be stopped?'

'I wish I could leave it – the question is, if I am fit for anything better.'

'Of course you are,' cried Ella, forgetting all discretion. 'You know you are. You are a wonderful teacher. Your students worship you.'

'Poor things, they have no standards.'

'Oh, Mr Cranage! But why, why will you depreciate yourself in this wicked way?'

Cranage was silent and reflective. He said at last, 'I am not qualified to be a good teacher because I don't know enough, but I know what good teaching is.'

'Then you should have a school of your own.'

'That's been suggested, but to start a school needs capital.'

'I have money,' said Ella instantly. 'How much would it need to start a school?'

Cranage smiled and said that he could not take Ella's money. Also it appeared, on enquiry, that Ella's money consisted only of a hundred and seventy odd pounds, in Consols, left her by her aunt.

But now the friendship of the couple became far closer. They were entangled in a scheme of action, of hope. They had a future to discuss, even if it were only a future of dreams. And when the time of Ella's departure came close, Ernest admitted that he could not bear to lose her.

'You have given me courage, a new life.'

'I wish I could – I shouldn't feel quite so useless.'

'Useless, you are the very soul of usefulness. Without people like you, nothing is any use.' And suddenly he proposed to her. Ella was startled.

'But Ernest, I thought you had a wife.'

'She's dead. I mustn't say, thank God! But I feel it.'

'Dead?'

'Last week – in hospital. She had been in for a long time.' He gave particulars. And now it turned out that he had been meditating this proposal for some days There was an opening in South America, at a school for British children, where it would be possible, after a few years, to buy a partnership. 'We could save enough for that as we go – we only need enough money for our passages and necessary kit.'

Ella was startled at such an adventure. Why, she asked, leave England?

'Because there is no opportunity here – in South America I can soon have a school of my own. I could make a fortune.'

Ella, after very little hesitation, agreed.

'I knew you would do it,' said Cranage, in his calm, rather melancholy tones. 'I knew you had courage for anything. But, dear Ella, there's one other difficulty – we shall have to keep our intentions secret.'

'Why, Ernest, do you mean a secret engagement?'

'We must even keep our marriage to ourselves. We must arrange to meet somewhere and be married quietly, immediately before we leave the country.'

'But why? I don't see—'

'Otherwise we mayn't be married at all; we shall be prevented. I have a confession to make, dearest.' He took her arm. 'I owe certain debts – if anything of our plan came out I should be arrested.'

'They can't arrest you for debt.'

'Yes, they can arrest me and send me to prison for what is called contempt of court. That is, not paying a debt under an order of the court. And I have such an order against me.'

'But can't I pay the debt?'

'A debt of over a hundred pounds. We shall need every penny for our journey. Afterwards, of course, I shall pay, but just now we have to count our resources, or we shall never get out of this slough of despond.'

'Oh yes, yes,' said Ella. 'we must be careful. We must think only of that, to escape, to take you away.'

And she became even more determined than Cranage upon the secret elopement. She was eager to run away, and running away was now easy. At over forty, she enjoyed more liberty than she had had as a girl. Bessie allowed her to go and come as she chose. Even Rose had relaxed her government, which had never been the paltry tyranny of a small mind, but a spiritual power. Rose had never pried into Ella's affairs, and she had acquiesced without comment in that new freedom brought to women merely by the mechanical progress of the age: corridor trains which gave them the power to change their compartment, if invaded by drunks or exhibitionists, and restaurants where it was possible for them to rest or eat without taking the risks of being turned out or accosted, which might have been their fate if they had dared, alone, to enter an hotel or public-house.

Ella's arrangement with Cranage, therefore, was simple. On leaving Brent Square, at the end of her visit, she met Cranage at Paddington and went by the night train, not to Queensport, but to Liverpool, where a room had been engaged by wire at the best hotel. They were to be married that morning and sail on the next day for the Argentine.

But on arrival, in the early morning, Cranage appeared so dejected that Ella herself was made uneasy. 'Has anything gone wrong, Ernest? You look quite ill.'

'Because I am a wretched creature, I've deceived you. I've brought you away on false pretences.'

And he confessed that his wife was not dead. She had been very ill, and he had thought that she might die, but she had recovered. In fact, most of the debt of which he had spoken was due to her as arrears of her separation allowance.

'I've known this for weeks, but I couldn't bear to give you up. You were my only chance. And of course she is a bad life, she may die any day. This South American offer seemed such a good opening. I thought that we could still go as man and wife. Nobody would have known either of us and we couldn't be traced. I arranged for the maintenance order to be paid regularly through a bank, and even the bank wouldn't know where the money came from. I didn't mean to tell you all this,' he said in his level tones, 'I meant to pretend something had gone wrong with the arrangements here and that we could be married in the Argentine. I thought that when I'd got you to South America, you couldn't make difficulties about living as my wife. A thoroughly mean calculation. My only excuse is that I wanted you so badly. But you see, I'm not even good at carrying out a dirty trick. I've lost my nerve already. Luckily no harm has been done, you can go back to your home, you can say you missed a connection, and Rose – Bessie – no one – need know anything at all.'

Ella reflected only for a moment. Then she said, 'If you need me, I'm coming with you.'

'Ella, my darling, do you mean—'

'We can be married in South America. You say your wife can't live very long.'

'The point is that I shall have to tell the steamer people whether we need two cabins or one.'

Ella was startled. She turned red and said at last, 'But must we—'

'You must choose, of course – it's always easier to get a double cabin.'

'How terrified I was,' Ella reflected. 'But I felt so guilty, too, at adding to Ernest's difficulties. Yes, I felt wicked. It seemed that I was being mean. But I didn't really make up my mind to give way. I simply ran to him, quite unexpectedly, and put my arms round him and said that I would be his wife – whenever he liked.

'And then I felt quite proud, and very, very happy. But of course I knew quite well – that I couldn't be his real wife. I was taking him from his real wife. And even now, yes, I feel glad. I am ready to thank God for a sin – for poor, darling Ernest's weakness.'

A slight sound made her look up. She stared with a horrified, astonished face.

Before her, on the gaudy, threadbare carpet, which undulated upon the rough untrimmed grass like the magic rug in the picture books, a girl had appeared who, in her white mackintosh and green knitted cap, reminded her of Amanda. 'I beg your pardon,' Amanda's voice said to her, 'it seems I've got to meet Kathy at the station.'

'Oh – it's you, Amanda – I thought—' Ella did not finish the sentence, for it seemed to her that Amanda was indeed someone else; a stranger not only in feeling, but in form. She thought, 'But this girl is so plain and stooped, and old – and her expression is so – distant – no, I don't know even what she's feeling.'

'She phoned just now and said that she was stuck at the station, but my car is still at the garage for the new plugs.'

'Oh yes,' said Ella. 'Has Kathy come – where shall we put her?'

'She says you wrote to her'

'So she did – I'd forgotten. That is, very nearly forgotten. I'm so glad you reminded me.'

'She'll have to wait until I can catch the bus – but I told her to get herself some tea. Why did you send for Kathy, Aunty – I mean—' The strange girl, before Ella's eyes, turned red, and Ella said, 'Oh no, darling, I think perhaps—'

'You wouldn't like me to call you—'

'No, no,' said Ella hastily, as if there might be explosive in the very name mother, so strange to her. 'I should feel – and then people would wonder – even if they knew – it would be so awkward for them.'

She looked at Amanda with high-raised brows and a deeply-wrinkled forehead, as if she had never seen anything like her before.

'I'm terribly sorry,' said Amanda awkwardly. 'Of course I understand how it happened. You mustn't feel—'

'You think – I shouldn't have given you up?'

'But then you were deserted by that creature.'

'Oh, you mustn't – he was your father.'

Amanda said nothing to this, and Ella thought, 'She is a very strange kind of girl – or perhaps I am strange.'

'Yes, I mustn't.'

'You see, you wouldn't be here – I mean – there wouldn't be any you if it hadn't been—' Amanda looked round her and then, as if surprised to find herself on the extraordinary carpet, stepped carefully off it and disappeared behind the sofa. Her voice murmured behind Ella's back, 'And he never took you to America after all. Was that a fraud, too?'

'No. He meant to take me – at least I – think so. But he had such bad luck. And Ernest, your father, always underestimated difficulties so much. He couldn't get a cabin in that ship – there was some mistake about his letter. And then we had to go on staying at the hotel – such an expensive hotel – and spent all our money. So Ernest had to take a cheap lodging in Liverpool and look for work – of course, under an assumed name. And work was so hard to get, any work. Your father often had to go as a labourer and conditions in those days were fearful. The dirt and the drunkenness and the fighting, they affected him very much. He was so sensitive, so gentle.'

'But *you*. Did he ever think of you?'

'Oh yes, he was terribly anxious about me, especially after I – when we knew that I was going to have a baby. That was the worst part of his trial, to see me scrubbing and cooking, and going among those dreadful people. He thought it was bad for me, that he was killing me. But, of course, it was nothing to me, I was really – yes, I was really enjoying it. I didn't think so then, when the women so terrified me with their fighting and drinking. But really, I was so happy that I used to lie awake worrying—'

'Excuse me, miss, just a minute.' Two men had seized the sofa by the ends; Ella got up hastily and they carried it away. Ella finding herself face to face with Amanda again, was panic stricken. She exclaimed, 'But you will miss your bus.'

'I'll see it coming over Brook hill. You don't mean to say you liked being worried to death.'

'It does seem strange. But perhaps I needed something to worry about. Something really important. Yes, I'm sure that often, even when I cried out of worry, it was really a happiness – to be so dreadfully worried. It was so real – we were so poor – and I suppose real life is always rather worrying.'

'Here you are, miss.' The men had come back with an enormous club sofa covered in faded leather of a dirty mud colour. It smelt even in the open air of stale tobacco. They placed it in front of the ladies, and gazed from it to them with the air of those who have done a considerate and knightly act. But Ella and Amanda, apparently on a simultaneous impulse, after one glance at this enormous dissipated sofa, turned their backs on it and walked slowly away, about a yard apart, towards the front door of the house.

'You can't really mean happiness,' said Amanda.

'Oh yes, yes, because if it had never happened I shouldn't want to have lived. But, of course, that's really silly, too. How can I tell what I should be, if it hadn't happened.'

Amanda gave a deep sigh and remarked, 'All the same, happiness has a definite meaning, and I can't see—'

Robin approached with nervous step, and Amanda said to him, 'Kathy's coming.'

'Kathy! Why Kathy?'

Ella looked round anxiously, but Amanda had disappeared as if into space. She said, 'Oh, Amanda's gone – but of course—'

'What's this about Kathy, Aunty? Is she coming here!'

'I don't know – I thought it would be so nice for you to see your dear little wife.'

'You know, of course, that I've asked Kathy for a divorce – she's agreed to it – so that I can marry Amanda.'

'Oh, Robin. How can you?'

'I really think I'd suit her better than Dawbarn even if he were available. Honestly, Aunty, can he appreciate Amanda? I mean, her really unusual *quality* of mind, her pluck, her guts, her *straightness*.'

'Oh please, Robin – and really Amanda – I noticed just now her stoop is worse than ever. I know of course you didn't mean her back, but really it's so important – for a girl to have a straight back. I wish you would speak to her. She won't listen to me. She's very angry with me.' Ella took a step towards the stairs. 'But I must go and see about Kathy's room.'

'So she really is coming,' said Robin, quite astonished by the reality of this event. 'Not that it matters.'

'Oh, Robin, you know you can easily make it up.'

'Not on your life, Aunty. It's too easy.'

CHAPTER 19

Kathy, whom neither Ella nor Amanda had seen before, proved to be a small, rather plump girl of twenty-four or five, with reddish hair and a very white skin. She was smartly dressed in a coat and skirt, severely cut. The whole effect was that of a discreet young person, very sure of herself as well as her clothes. She greeted Ella with a handshake, and said 'How good of you to ask me.' She spoke with a smile which was full of good nature.

'I'm so sorry, my dear, that I couldn't put you in with Robin – the men cleared too many of the rooms.'

'But I like to be by myself,' with the same smile, which was now seen to be a habitual gesture, 'and you are all in the throes.' She looked round the hall, full of cheap wardrobes and washstands, already dusty and squalid. 'Poor Aunty, a sale is quite the worst.'

'I had no idea how bad it would be, and such a long time before.'

'That reminds me, I have a note for you, from Dorothy.'

Dorothy was Bessie's youngest daughter, wife of a general. At her name Ella said nervously, 'Is she very upset?'

'They're all very upset. They've called a family meeting and they're applying to the courts – for something called a caveat, to stop the sale and everything. But here's Dorothy's note; she may be coming herself.' Kathy, still smiling, hunted in a white leather bag, overflowing with small bright articles.

'Oh, but she's not coming,' said Ella. 'No, I can't see her – must I see her?'

All were surprised by her agitation. When Kathy put the note into her hands she hastily dropped it into a wash-basin standing among other bedroom crockery near the door. 'No, you must tell her – there's no room. Yes, Amanda, please wire at once.'

'You're not afraid of Dorothy,' said Amanda coldly, and Ella looked at her daughter in panic. 'No, no, of course not – it's only that – she's always been so nice – so kind. Your Aunt Rose liked her so much. And, of course, your Aunt Rose didn't want a sale. Robin thinks it wrong, too.'

'Robin adores family relics and everything else that's stuffy. But he doesn't have to dust them,' said Kathy. She turned to Robin, and husband and wife looked at each other curiously. Then Robin said in a friendly tone, 'Did you have a good journey?'

'Moderately. I had lunch and tea. I didn't know you were staying here permanently.'

'Yes,' said Ella, fluttering round the couple like a nervous hen. 'He came to stay – it's so nice for us – and it's so nice you've come. I am so delighted – only I'm afraid I haven't got a double room. But there is a door between your rooms.'

'Has it a key?' said Kathy.

'Oh no, but you don't want – and really it is quite appropriate. Your Aunt Bessie and Uncle James came back to those rooms from their honeymoon.'

'But then we aren't on our honeymoon, Aunty. Quite the other way,' said Robin.

'No, I forgot. Still, it is really a honeymoon. You are so young, and – having no children yet. But of course there's plenty of time.'

'Can I show you your room, Katherine?' Amanda led Kathy away and Ella reflected. 'I shouldn't have said that. But, oh dear, they are all furious, and Dorothy is coming. I know she'll come. And she has always been so sweet to me. Perhaps she doesn't mean it, but she has such a kind, affectionate smile – and holds her neck so prettily. No, even if Amanda is furious I must be nice to her. I must be firm and do what is right. I must be firm with Robin, too. I must tell him he has no right to divorce such a dear little wife. She loves him so much. Yes, I'm sure she loves him. She wouldn't put on that nice dress for travelling, and have to wear a coat over it, unless she wanted to please him.'

'I've phoned a wire to stop Dorothy,' said Amanda, returning.

'Oh dear, I hope she won't be hurt.' But Ella's spirits revived and at supper she exclaimed to Robin and Kathy, '*You* don't want visitors, do you?

She insisted on treating Kathy as a bride, and proposed her health. So that as she herself went up to bed her conscience was troubled again, and she said, 'Why didn't I think of Mama's room? It was really hers, before Papa handed it over to Rose as the mistress. But yes, I've been afraid of that room and that bed. So I never think of it, and I'm going to spoil those children's marriage because I'm afraid of – really, what am I afraid of? But I won't, I won't. I shall speak to Robin.'

She was too agitated to sleep. It seemed to her that mysterious enemies were plotting against her, enormous forces were joining to attack her. She mwmured once, 'I'm quite safe from Dorothy – she would never come here – she has not been here for five or six years. She thought us a couple of old bores, and she knew we would always give her her cheque at birthdays and Christmas, whether she came or not. She is really a very selfish person. If only she wasn't so sweet.' She gave a long sigh and relaxed in her chair. 'But perhaps the police will come first and take me away' – a reflection that calmed her.

She dozed in a chair and was waked suddenly by voices which seemed to come from the dining-room below her window. She thought, 'The windows have been left open and somebody has got in – but perhaps it is Robin. Yes, I know Robin's voice – he is talking to Amanda. Oh dear, suppose Kathy hears them. But I must pretend I can't hear. I'll shut the window.'

Robin's voice came clearly through the window and Ella went downstairs to the dining-room. She opened the door with precaution, and saw, on the sofa opposite the centre window and well lit by the moon, a kind of agitated bundle. The bundle instantly broke up into two forms, and she perceived that it had consisted of Kathy and Robin. Gently Ella drew the door back and turned to fly, but already Kathy was calling 'Aunty.' She came from the door. 'Do come in, Aunty, we couldn't sleep either.'

'But, Kathy dear, I wouldn't break in upon you.'

The girl, who was in a brilliant wrapper of blue satin trimmed with swansdown, was smiling broadly, with a candid enjoyment. The smile, broadening her cheeks, made her seem like a little charming cat. 'But Aunty, do come and play to us – we were so bored.' She drew her back through the door.

'But there's no piano in the dining-room.' Ella, in her embarrassment, was flustered.

'Oh yes, look, quite a lot of pianos.'

Ella looked with amazement at four cottage pianos ranged against the wall. She murmured, 'But where – where did they come from?'

The big room, without its curtains, was full of the moonlight thrown across from high windows in bars like the limes of a theatre and falling on piled furniture, tables covered with dinner sets, tea sets, huge old tureens, the enormous family meat dishes of the past, bedroom crockery, and bundles of steel knives, worn into waists, tied up in old lingerie ribbons and stay laces.

Kathy opened the nearest piano and struck a chord. 'It seems to be in tune – I've heard so much about your playing.'

'But does Robin?' Ella looked apprehensively at Robin, who, in his pyjamas, was standing alone by the window. 'You know you don't want me – you and Robin are so happy by yourselves. I am so glad, Kathy, to see you so happy.' And seeing Kathy's affectionate smile, the swansdown next her delicate skin, her whole air of the youthful bride, she said, 'And then when you have your baby, how nice that will be.'

'Kathy is not so keen,' said Robin from behind. 'She thinks babies are an overrated pleasure.'

'Oh no, Robin, Kathy knows very well' – and Ella tried by a spcial effort to provoke this knowledge in Kathy – 'how wonderful it is. Every woman does.'

'I think my family were rather *too* keen,' said Kathy. 'You see, I'm an only child, and they always gave me dolls for Christmas till I could have screamed.'

'Oh, but it's always there,' said Ella, 'the feeling – in quite young girls, in their feelings of being girls. Isn't it, Kathy? Yes, even though of course they don't know – it will hurt them. They know they want a baby. Even a little *because* they must suffer. But Kathy understands.'

Kathy was in the act of lighting a new cigarette from the old one, but even in the act she raised her pretty eyes and looked sympathetic and intelligent.

'It's so hard to explain,' said Ella, 'but Kathy knows – that secret feeling – of being a woman. And you know, when you're having a baby – that's much stronger – it's quite strange – how different it is. No, even when Ernest – Robin has told you about Ernest, Kathy?'

Kathy's smile appeared to reflect both knowledge and a tactful benevolence.

'Even when Ernest asked me how I felt, I used to say, 'Very well, darling,' or something like that, because, of course, I couldn't tell my true, real feeling. There weren't any words.'

'What are you doing?' Amanda's voice sounded from the door. 'You've been keeping me awake for hours.'

'Yes, it *must* be a funny feeling,' said Kathy.

'Oh, but quite ordinary, too,' said Ella, anxious that Kathy should not be alarmed. 'Of course it is – they say that some girl is married every second, and some wife is having her first baby every single second—'

'A perfectly horrible idea,' Amanda murmured.

'Oh – quite ordinary,' said Ella, 'but of course rather alarming, too. I used to feel – who am I in all these millions of women? Who cares if my baby is never born. Yes, that was a fearful thought – that no one cared about one's baby – that it wasn't even worth talking about – except of course to some other woman – with the same kind of feeling. But, oh dear, I'm talking nonsense, and you think I'm a very old-fashioned person.'

'Give me your old-fashioned period any day,' said Robin.

'But I love it, too,' said Kathy. 'The novels. The people are so marvellous. The way they *talk*. I love your novels, Aunty.'

'Three sets of lovers,' said Amanda from the background, 'and appropriate clothes and upholstery, but how hot it must have been under all those petticoats.'

'I don't know,' said Ella, turning frightened eyes towards Amanda, 'I wasn't allowed to read novels.'

'Now that's a point,' said Robin, becoming more animated, 'that's interesting, that the novels were rather a by-product than an inspiration.'

'But how extraordinary,' said Kathy, who was now extremely serious, as if realizing for the first time what tyranny could be. 'Fancy anyone daring to stop people reading novels.'

'Your Aunt Rose was quite right,' said Ella. 'Novels are bad for people – a waste of time.'

'And what else did they stop you from doing, Aunty?'

'Our mother died when I was eight and I don't remember her very well. She was so much abroad – it was your Aunt Rose who brought me up. I always said my prayers to her. She taught me everything.'

'Housekeeping?'

'No, I never learnt to cook – or house-keep. There were always – servants, and I had my music.'

'But what did Aunt Rose teach you?' asked Amanda.

Ella looked with surprise at the group and answered at last, 'I suppose – yes, my prayers.'

'Was that all?'

'Yes, she taught me to have faith. Yes, to trust in God – in goodness. She gave me all my happiness and courage. Perhaps I should never have had the courage to run away – if it had not been for Rose. Yes, it was because of Rose – I trusted love.'

Ella paused, and said in a peculiar voice, amused and rueful, 'How strange – that I should elope – with a married man – because of Rose's teaching.'

'Fascinating,' said Robin, looking round for Amanda, who was once more prowling in the darkness. 'Yes, it's extraordinary how things work.'

'Yes, when I think of it,' said Ella. 'Really, I owe *everything* to Rose. And her reward was – to be murdered.'

Suddenly to Ella's surprise the young people were standing round her. Kathy was smiling in a kind manner, Amanda was frowning, Robin had an expression which terrified her, so that she got up from the piano stool, and stepped back crying 'Children.'

'You're not to say that, Aunty, not to think of it.'

'It's too absurd,' said Amanda.

'It's a complex,' said Kathy. 'We ought to get her psychoed.'

'Aunty, listen to me. You had nothing to do with Aunt Rose's death.' Robin glared at his aunt.

'But Robin, I did. I did kill Rose. I was so angry with her. I wanted her dead. And you mustn't hypnotize me. I don't like it. No,' Ella spoke firmly, 'I won't be hypnotized.'

'Aunty dear,' said Robin, touching her arm and speaking in so affectionate a tone that she was astonished and touched, 'she hurt you, too. And you know that Aunt Rose rather tyrannized over you – we all thought so.'

'She gave you a guilty complex,' said Kathy, bringing out the term with satisfaction. 'My psycho man says that's the worst kind, it's so unreasonable.'

'You see, Aunty,' said Robin, 'Aunt Rose taught you to be devoted to her and to feel guilty if you fell short in any way in that devotion.'

'She was always *grieved* when anyone fell short,' said Amanda. 'She did it to me, too.'

'Of course, how could she help being grieved?'

'But Aunty dear,' said Robin, 'it's a system, a scheme for pushing people around when you're not allowed to push. The rule of love – and guilt. You teach people to love you and to feel very wicked if they don't do what you think right. It's the only way you can have a rule of love.'

'The love produces the guilt,' said Amanda.

'It's so unnecessary,' said Kathy, 'a guilt complex – and so unnatural. Animals don't have it.'

'But Robin, your Aunt Rose never demanded any kind of sacrifice – she hated to put anybody out,' said Ella.

The young people all looked at her with that strange expression which made her feel like a complicated piece of antique machinery in a glass case, and she stopped with the reflection, 'But of course that's just what they mean.' For the first time she gave her mind to the argument.

'But do you think, then,' she looked round at the group with raised astonished brows, 'do you think we couldn't help ourselves?'

'You couldn't help feeling guilty, Aunty. And you can't now – and that's very dangerous. You see, Aunty dear, people who don't know you might misunderstand. For instance, you shouldn't have written to the police. Of course, they know the facts; but still, they are often rather simple-minded men, they might get a wrong idea.'

'You think I only feel guilty?'

'You were conditioned,' said Kathy, who plainly supposed that she possessed complete freedom of judgment.

'Conditioned,' Ella murmured. 'Yes, I suppose I was – I must be careful, mustn't I?'

'You see, Aunty, it's a complex.'

'Oh God!' Robin seized himself by the hair. 'Don't throw that bloody word about. Let's leave the hokum out of it.'

'Sorry.' Kathy smiled joyfully as if pleased by this unexpected effect of her words. 'But Amanda said—'

'I see, I see,' said Ella hastily. 'Yes, Robin dear, you mean I mustn't talk to the police – in case they find out too much, in case they arrest me.'

'But they *can't*, Aunty, they *can't*. Don't you understand . . .?'

'It is so strange,' said Ella, 'when they arrest so many people for quite small things. But, Robin dear,' she hastily interposed, seeing her nephew once more contorted as with agony, 'I *do* understand – and besides, dear Rose would hate so much to have any scandal fall on the family. I hadn't thought of that. She would be horrified. Yes, I must be careful what I tell the police.'

'Come, dearest,' said Amanda, taking Ella's arm, 'it's quite time you were in bed.'

'Yes, but I do understand,' said Ella. 'Thank you very much, darlings, it's so kind of you. I do really see exactly – what Kathy means about the complex – and being conditioned. Of course, I can't help – being rather old-fashioned – and stupid. I never went to school, and Miss Simpson – she was our governess, didn't even believe in Darwin. She *said* she did, but when Papa used to talk about evolution and mammals, she used to leave the table.'

'Come, dearest.'

'You're too kind to me,' said Ella, with tears in her eyes. 'Yes, too forgiving, when I've ruined everything for you. Poor Robin, when I think how you loved the Villa . . .'

Robin embraced her and, with Amanda, discreetly drew her out of the door. But she still murmured apologies all down the passage.

'I'm not worth it – all this love, this kindness – if you only knew,' and, looking at Amanda, she exclaimed, 'I've spoilt your life, my darling. Rose warned me that I should – she warned me not to tell you about your father.'

'But I'm very glad you told me.'

'No, I've spoilt your life, just to please myself. Because I wanted to feel – that you were really my daughter.'

'How on earth can telling me the truth do me any harm?'

'But it has. I can see it already. It's just what Rose said. That there was all the difference in the world between not knowing where you came from and knowing that you had been born from a – wrong connection.'

'I suppose I was born from the usual thing.'

'There, you see, already you are bitter and – and coarsened. Oh, Rose warned me—'

'But I'm not blaming you for anything – I think it was wicked the way they treated you. You were brought up for marriage and then expected to do without even a lover.'

'But, oh dear, you mustn't think of it like that, that's so wrong.'

'Like what?'

'It wasn't that I needed – a lover. I loved your father as a husband. I thought of him as a husband.'

'But I shouldn't mind if you'd just gone on to the street. Why shouldn't you, it would have served them right.'

They had reached her room, which was now heaped with furniture, old chairs, carpets, hangings.

'Oh no, no – oh, why did I tell you – but you must go to bed – your eyes are quite sore – you must wash them every morning in cold water. Bright eyes make such a difference.'

'Now Harry isn't here it doesn't matter so much.'

'You think I worry too much about a girl's being attractive.'

'I suppose Aunt Rose made you wear low frocks when young men were about, and they were very low in the eighties.'

'Yes, dreadfully low, and I was dreadfully ashamed the first time – Rose had to come and persuade me – she was very amused. She herself had a most beautiful neck, she was very proud of her figure. But, oh dear, how can I make you see – it was the right thing to wear low dresses – it was only polite.'

'Almost religious.'

'Yes, yes. No, you're laughing. But Rose would have thought it very rude and – ungenerous of any woman not to make herself as attractive as possible. But you don't believe me. How could you. Good night. Oh, I shouldn't have told you.'

The two women kissed nervously, remotely, and Ella left the room as if in flight from that remoteness. Amanda sighed, 'If only she would understand how little it matters.'

Amanda knew that she would not sleep. She was both tired and excited. She looked about her with disgust, exclaiming, 'I believe she's brought in some more stuff today. Really, there's no room to move – and everything so fusty.'

In fact, the furniture and relics, piled against the walls, now took up most of the floor. A dark monumental wardrobe blocked the inner closet; three bedside cupboards, in the shape of corinthian columns, hid the fireplace; Maria Jane, a grey presence, was next the window; and in the corner, an alp of quilts, cushions, and bed curtains rose to the ceiling.

'*She* never liked the room,' Amanda said, 'and now she's nearly beaten me out of it.'

She sighed and lay down on the bed with a book. But she found it impossible to read, and when at last, letting the book fall, and thrusting the sheet below her chest, she dozed, her dreams were terrifying, full of vague and horrible images, blood-stained, grinning monsters which seemed to threaten and to coquet in the same action. From which she waked suddenly and sat up with a cry of terror, throwing back her bed-clothes as if she would spring out of bed.

And suddenly she saw again the corners of her room, now in the direct rays of the moon, not as a store of relics, the relics of an age, but as the living witnesses of that age. Margaret Venn, mother of seven, had worn that coat; Aunt Bessie, mother of nine, had looked at herself, many thousands of times, in that cheval glass; with what feelings of self-pity and of contempt for that self-pity, as she saw herself growing old and grey in her twenties, as she tried to hide a new pregnancy in those dresses of the eighties whose tight-fronted skirts served only to exaggerate it.

And Amanda felt suddenly not that genial allowance for Victorian objects; that sentimental tolerance for the age, which had been her mood with Ella, with Rose, but horror and loathing. The red-plush padded chair with its sloping shoulders on which a tattered antimacassar hung like a fichu, seemed to hold out its fat stumpy arms, not with comical welcome, but with an animal sensuality, gross, sheeplike; the bedside cupboards seemed like grotesque priapic monuments; the grey headless Mary Jane in the corner with its absurd tortured waist, its forced-out chest and stomach, became the characteristic form of that for which it stood as representative Victorian woman, a sensual victim and machine, a fleshly device for the production and nourishment of other little lumps of flesh, a creature as little free or noble as the segment of a tape worm; and beyond, in the corner among the confused heap, one saw a huge sideboard carved with grapes, a washstand holding apart its thick crooked legs, a hat-stand flourishing horns against the dim portrait of which nothing could be seen but a white neck rising from a low-cut frock; and draped behind, the great plush curtains drooping with crimson folds like the walls of some immense womb.

Amanda was stifled, nauseated. She felt that she would be sick if she could not escape into the open air. She threw back the clothes to jump out of bed. But the sight of her own white and plump leg thrust into the moonlight startled her into a new horror – of herself. She felt her own flesh, and it, too, was part of this hideous world of the flesh. She, too, was woman; meat for lust; a walking womb; a cow to yield milk; a slave to nature, which had given her a heart only that she might be a servant to her reproductive organs. An animal constructed from top to toe only to continue the species, so that life should not perish from the world.

She turned out her light with a violent movement which shocked her and further excited her. Her bed and the room were now in darkness. But she could not relax. Then quickly pulling on her dressing-gown she ran out from the room and down the back stairs into the garden.

The moon was now passing down behind the tops of the trees, and the shadows of the leaves, on the short grass of the lawn, made a pattern like Brussels lace against oyster-coloured velvet, on which the beds of roses seeming in the pallid light like artificial copies of the real, stood motionless like embroideries.

Amanda, looking at the white walls of the Villa rising from the gravel of the drive, remembered Rose, 'proud of her neck,' and thought 'The very house is like a woman in a low frock, sitting here waiting to be admired, half undressed to excite some man. But this is absurd. This is the way girls go mad.' She let her dressing-gown fall back so that the cold wind blew between her breasts, and looked round her not at visions, but at trees, grass and sky. 'A lot of space and some indifferent vegetables,' she said to herself.

Suddenly as she passed along the high windows of the dining-room for the fifth or sixth time, she saw at her elbow behind the central pane a white motionless figure like some ghost peering out. She stopped in surprise. Robin was standing within, close to the glass. They looked at each other for a long moment, without speaking. Then Robin moved his mouth, as if to say, without uttering the words, 'Come in.'

Amanda shook her head.

Robin drew up the sash and leant across the sill. 'You needn't worry about Kathy – she's gone to bed, and she wouldn't worry.'

'Why aren't you in bed?'

'You don't want to talk to me?'

Amanda was silent but without offence. She seemed to reflect. 'Are you annoyed with me for entertaining Kathy?' said Robin.

'Did you?'

'She came to me and we had our usual quiet clash with the usual trimmings, really out of exasperation, I suppose. A gesture of disgust, a sort of go-to-hell. The whole thing had absolutely no importance. It never does.'

'Isn't that a pity?'

'Why?' said Robin. As usual, when alarmed, he spoke sharply and looked old and pinched. 'That's just absurd. What do you mean – you *know* it doesn't matter. Kathy has agreed to a divorce, that's the important thing.'

There was a longer silence. Robin's expression changed from wrath to anxiety. He gazed at Amanda with raised eyebrows. At last he yawned in an embarrassed manner and said, 'Don't be annoyed with me, or offended, or forgiving – it would spoil something that does matter.'

'You mustn't think too well of me, Robin. I always seem nicer than I am.'

'Don't we all?'

'Goodnight, Robin,' said Amanda, who had been drifting carefully away.

'No, you don't want me?'

Amanda pretended not to hear. Seeming to be absorbed in her thoughts, she went slowly along the path. She did not want any company. It seemed to her that she had too much already, she was pressed upon by company, a vast company of feelings which were at once as thin as phantoms and as fleshly and gross as bodies, bodies without minds, stupid, sensual. At the same time, because they were phantoms, creatures of the imagination, they could not be pushed away.

CHAPTER 20

At ten o'clock in the morning Amanda, Kathy and Robin, sitting at breakfast, laid on one corner of the parlour table, heard a sweet and rather lisping voice calling from the hall, 'Aunty – Aunty Ella.' All three jumped up, and Amanda exclaimed, 'Lady Grab.'

This was the family nickname of Lady Pedley, who now suddenly appeared in the doorway, and advanced upon them with a ravishing smile, uttering little cries of delight. 'Robin! Kathy! Amanda! but how delightful. What a pity I can't stay. Lady Malley was going to Plymouth and kindly came this way so that I could look in. My dear Amanda, what a mess!' She turned and looked round at the piled magazines, guns, game-bags, fishing rods, tennis rackets which were stored in the parlour. 'I'd no idea the old woman would have the nerve – but why didn't you stop her?'

'It's hardly our business.'

'I should have thought it was. However, she can't sell the house. We're going into court, as I told her. Even if she does sell anything we'll make her pay it back. Where *is* Aunt Ella? But I suppose she's hiding from me somewhere.'

She walked into the hall and called again, 'Aunty – Aunt Ella.'

Robin and Amanda looked at each other. Kathy said in an amused tone, 'Isn't she just—'

Dorothy Pedley was the youngest living of Bessie's daughters, but she had long assumed the place of the head of the family, of which she regarded herself as the most important, not because of her social importance, or brains, or wealth, but because of a quality which she called *savoir faire*.

She meant by this, the ability to get out of life certain satisfactions which, though she depreciated them, she seemed to consider worth having. She was a woman who complained of the trouble of her possessions, but was always adding to them, who groaned at committees, parties, charity balls, but was always sitting on committees and contriving charity balls. Her life was spent in a round of small vanities, small appetites, small envies, fashionable fancies and conceits, but she herself was fully aware of the fact and would say, 'What nonsense it all is. Really, I don't know anything more absurd than to be an imitation duchess and open a village institute. *So* middle class.'

She had produced one daughter, with a great deal of self-praise, but refused to have more children on the grounds that it wasn't fair to ask her to waste time and health having babies when she was so busy and far from strong. Yet, while she got all the glory possible out of being a mother, she would laugh and say, 'We mothers of one, what bores we are.' She had, however, no sense of humour. She laughed at herself because it was fashionable and popular to take nothing very seriously.

'I don't know why I'm worrying about the old things,' she said as Robin and Amanda reluctantly followed her into the hall. 'Goodness knows I don't want any more knick-knacks, but I can't bear to see dear old Aunt Rose's treasures just thrown on the dust-heap – look at this desk. I remember it so well. Oh, I must find room for it somewhere. And the dessert service, what's happening to those nice old blue plates?'

'You mean the Crown Derby?' said Amanda. 'They're valued rather high in the inventory.'

'We know those valuations,' said Dorothy. 'And dessert services fetch nothing in the country. Aunt Rose said that I should have that service. Ella can't really go against all Rose's wishes. But where is she? Robin dear, do you know where the dessert service was put? I don't see why I shouldn't take it now.'

'I see several reasons,' said Amanda. She went to find Ella, whom she discovered at last in a shady corner of the paddock, near the pleached alley, a tunnel of interlaced lime and beech, which guarded the paddock on two sides. But Ella refused to come.

'Oh no,' she murmured, 'I couldn't say she mustn't buy things when they're all for sale.'

'But she won't pay anything like the value of what she takes.'

'Oh, you've every right to be cross with me.'

'But I'm not cross – I only want you to protect yourself.'

Ella moved a little further back into the shade of the valley, which, in the morning sunlight, from one side, displayed before them on its green wall a series of arched shadows in a darker green. The effect was that of a garden cloister, all of gardener's stuff, a gardener's place of meditation.

'How nice it is here – how beautiful,' Ella murmured. 'Why not bring out a chair?'

'But – ' Amanda frowned, 'Dorothy's waiting.'

Ella looked with terror at this new Amanda, who could frown, and said, 'Why – why did I tell you?'

'It hasn't made any difference.'

'Yes, of course it has. I can see it every day.'

'Please, we must decide. If you won't come, may I say no to her?'

'Oh, please – we mustn't offend her. I'll come in a minute, as soon as I've seen – they say the gate is broken.'

'The gate's been broken for years.'

'Yes, I thought it seemed rather – urgent. Now you're furious with me.'

'It's no good running away. Dorothy knows you're about the place.'

'Oh no. never. I'm not running away – I'll come at once – almost,' and as Amanda turned back to guard the house against Dorothy Pedley, she hastened all the faster towards the lower gate into the field, saying to herself, 'Oh, why did I tell her – it's just what Rose said? I'm not fit to look after my own daughter. Oh, Rose, how I have raged against you for hunting me down – for setting the detectives on us. But Amanda owed everything to you. More even than I have thought. At the very beginning you said that we had to consider the baby. Yes, if it hadn't been for Rose, Amanda would have been quite different – a slum child, among other slum children. Among the poorest. For we should have had more children, as Rose saw. A lot more. Because I adored Ernest and he was so – his nature was so affectionate. Besides, I was so much older. I wanted to give him everything. I was always afraid that he might grow tired of me. He was so good looking, so young in himself – we should have gone down and down. And to bring up children under such conditions, so that they would never know anything better, with a slattern for a mother. How could Rose help being shocked, at the very sight of me then.'

Ella saw a grey-haired charwoman, far gone with child, in a sacking apron and clogs, who was pushing a worn broom across a pavement foul with grey mud. Behind was a narrow street of dirty brick houses, in which some ragged children were kicking about the garbage from the flowing gutters. Other women with brooms, buckets, jugs, were passing to and fro, or gossiping in the door-ways; young and old, clean and dirty, they had the same grey or bloated faces of the very poor. Overhead, a bright spring sky threw down a light in which pavements, gutters, garbage, rags, dirt, every rotting brick in the house fronts, and each wrinkle of care and want in the faces, was revealed with a severe candour. It was as though some cruel judge said, 'Look at this squalid hole – you will see that every inch of it is polluted with dirt, ugliness and despair, where even goodwill and devoted courage is made futile by all conquering poverty.'

'Oh, it was hideous,' said Ella, trembling. 'How could I have expected Rose to understand my feelings.'

Rose had not at first recognized Ella, pointed out to her by an officious neighbour, under her false name of Finn. She had stared at this drudge, whose pale face, shining with perspiration, was exactly like the other faces in that slum; where wood, coal, hot water were expensive luxuries.

It was Ella who had dropped her broom and cried in panic, 'Rose.'

Rose, as she kissed Ella, broke into tears. She could not believe her eyes that this worn-out, grotesque old woman was Ella.

To Rose, the sacking, the clogs, the thick-darned stockings, the whole appearance of poverty and its makeshifts, were marks of degradation as well as misery. Her cry of 'Ella, is it really you?' still sounded in Ella's ears with all those overtones of horror, of disgust, of that critical thought instantly perceptible to the younger sister. 'But of course I might have expected something quite as bad.'

And she remembered Rose's little sniff as she had entered Ella's kitchen-parlour, with its smell compounded of rotten floors and walls, decaying wallpapers, bugs, and the garbage outside, a smell which no amount of scrubbing could remove. That room, the cheap furniture, the dirty cracked ceiling, had been like a contamination to Rose. She belonged to a generation that loathed dirt with their soul, because they lived in a society but lately emancipated, in all classes, from a great deal of dirt, whose mission, perhaps, was to hate dirt and muddle. There was a Nightingale in Rose when she said indignantly, 'Ella, how could you live like this?'

'There's such a shortage of lodgings everywhere,' Ella said. 'They can't build them fast enough – and then we couldn't afford more than six shillings a week.'

'We – we!' Rose ejaculated. 'Do you mean your husband? Is he your husband?'

Ella was fustered. She had often imagined the encounter with her family when she would explain, calmly but firmly, that though she could not be married to Ernest, yet, in the eyes of God, she was his wife, and could never be separated from him. She liked especially the phrase, 'in the eyes of God', for in her situation it seemed to her profound and true; to express, like no other form, the feeling of the nature, at once sacred and private, of her tie. But taken by surprise, with dirty hands, and bedraggled skirts, in a sacking apron, she could only stammer to Rose's question, 'Not exactly – I mean – we couldn't get married because—'

'So it was all true what we heard,' said Rose, 'and you really have been living with another woman's husband.'

'She left him – at least – she was impossible. And he did try for a divorce. But, of course, it would have taken so long.'

'And you couldn't wait.' This meant, you were so mad for a husband that you could not think of anything else. Ella understood her sister. 'Perhaps I was wrong,' she said. 'But not Ernest – he tried to stop me.'

'I see you're wearing a ring – I suppose you call yourself Mrs something.'

'Oh Rose, I had to – how could I go about like this, without a ring?'

'I couldn't live with a lie on my finger. But I suppose one lie leads to another. Oh Ella,' Rose burst out again, 'I won't reproach you now in your dreadful position, but how could you go away with such a man and call him husband. And never tell us a word all this time.'

Rose pulled down Ella on her lap, where Ella, breaking down in tears, could only mutter, 'But I loved him, I loved him.'

'He picked well, he knew where to find a soft heart,' Rose said, stroking Ella's grey hair. 'Yes, he knew how to make a fool of you.'

'You don't know him, Rose. He is the kindest, the best of men.'

'And brought you to this,' looking round at the miserable room. 'and made you work like a charwoman – you, in your condition. When is the baby coming?'

'I don't know. I think I must be over my time.'

'Have you seen a doctor?'

'No, but there's a woman down the street who knows about these things.'

'I know those women down the street. And this man was prepared to let some wretched gamp look after you.'

'But it's not Ernest's fault, Rose, that we're poor. He's worked dreadfully hard. He's out at work now in a warehouse, but that kind of work, labourer's work, is so badly paid. And he can't get any other.'

'Of course he can't. No one will give employment to a man of his character.'

'There's *nothing* against his character.'

'My darling Ella, he's a common swindler. He was turned out of two offices for stealing – stealing *money*.' Rose emphasized this word. It seemed to make the sin worse. 'Oh, we know all about him. He took money everywhere he went, from two different offices. Even at the Academy he cheated in the accounts. Bessie knew and used to make it up.'

'He never stole, Rose, never. He used to get into debt and perhaps he borrowed a little sometimes.'

'My dear Ella, don't you see he's a common swindler. Thank God at least I've found you! I can take you to a proper lodging.'

'But, Rose, what do you mean? I can't come away with you.'

'How can you go on like this? What will happen to you? Can you believe that Cranage ever meant to marry you, an old woman ten years older than himself?'

'I don't care,' cried Ella, desolated by this stroke. 'I don't care what he's done or may do. But I love him and I won't leave him while he wants me, while he needs me. And he does need me now.'

'As his charwoman.'

'No, as his *wife*, as the only person he's got who doesn't misjudge and despise him. I may be older than he, and I may be a silly old woman, but at least he *trusts* me.'

'He knows he can twist you round his finger.'

'Say what you like – I belong to him now and I'll never, never leave him.'

'I can see that, but he might leave you.'

Ella was struck with terror by this suggestion.

'You couldn't do that, Rose.'

'I didn't propose to do anything. I was suggesting only a possibility – a very likely one in a case like this.'

'No, no, you can't think of such a thing. You don't know what you're suggesting . . .'

'But, Ella, you must face the facts. Why did this man elope with you? He's never done anything except for money. He's had all yours and isn't it at least possible that his whole idea was to get money out of the family?'

'Then give him some, but don't drive him away.'

'Give him some. Ella! Think, how could one give such a man money without some conditions, some thought for your position?'

'He isn't such a man, he's a good and gentle soul. Only a little discouraged. Oh, how can I make you understand anything.' Ella became hysterical and began to cry out.

'If you spoil my happiness, Rose, I'll never, never forgive you. Go away – go away!' She clutched at her sides and screamed. Rose made her lie down, called in a woman from next door, sent an urchin for a cab. In half an hour Ella was in a nursing home. The hospitals refused her, but Rose was not a woman to be thwarted. She found the home and though it had not a bed to spare, imposed herself so thoroughly upon the matron that a nurse was sent to an hotel for the night in order to accommodate Ella. Her daughter was born nineteen hours later.

Ella cried out incessantly for her husband, and Ernest, in a new suit, duly appeared at her bedside. He explained his more prosperous appearance by saying that he had obtained a better job. And after Ella was up he took her to the Welsh seaside for a month; to lodgings which were perhaps not fashionable, but certainly not of the cheapest. He explained that he had had an advance of pay. He had never been more charming, more attentive; he delighted in the baby. But one afternoon, at the end of this month's holiday, he did not return. Instead, Rose appeared. As tactfully, as gently as she could, she explained that Ella would not see Ernest again. That night he would be on his way to South America. Rose was moved, and the effect of her news made her anxious. At first Ella could not or would not believe her. Then she cried out, 'But he wouldn't go without telling me. He wasn't a coward – you told him some lie, but still he would have let me know, explained – where is his letter, I know he wouldn't go like this without any explanation?'

Rose was in a difficulty. For part of her bargain with Ernest was that he should not communicate again, in any way, with Ella. 'He did wish to write, but we thought it best to make a complete break. We thought it might upset you less. I must say, Ella, he behaved very well at the last – he was considerate and reasonable.'

'He's been told lies,' Ella exclaimed. 'I must go to him at once.'

When she heard that this was impossible, that Cranage would have sailed before she could reach the port, she became hysterical. And this violent, uncontrolled grief, which frightened Rose for Ella's reason, and perhaps her life, made her also impatient and severe. 'What is the good of giving way like this, Ella. You know the man is worthless. He jumped at my offer.'

'You don't understand, Rose,' Ella whispered. She lay exhausted but she still protested. 'You could never understand a man like Ernest. Bessie did, but you are – too different, and so you made him – seem bad. Because he knew he couldn't make you understand. Because he's too discouraged – and proud – to fight against the stupid meanness, the cruelty. Of course he was glad to go. You've taken him away from me. I knew you would. I knew, if you found us, you'd take him away, you'd play on his weakness, on his lack of self-confidence. Oh, I know he's weak, like me. Perhaps that's why I understand him. He's been made weak by injustice and badness. But he's so good, so gentle, so loving. And now he will despise himself more than ever – he will go down and down.'

'My darling Ella, you must rest. For the sake of your baby. Perhaps I don't understand Ernest, and at least he has seen his mistake. I shan't say another word against him.'

'I shall go to him,' Ella said, 'afterwards. I shall find him. You will help me, Rose. I'll need money.'

'Get well, dear, first. Get strong.' Even in this crisis Rose would not promise what she did not intend.

And in fact Ella never did follow Ernest. She had no means of doing so; no money of her own, no way of earning money. But she heard from him. A month later, when, growing at last stronger, she came in from the beach with the baby in her arms, Rose handed her a thick and heavily sealed letter, with the remark, 'This looks like your Ernest – it's a South American stamp. He promised not to write, but of course he hasn't kept his promise.'

'I'm glad, I'm glad, he's quite right,' said Ella. 'He never promised – it was you made him promise.'

CHAPTER 21

The hedge of the field below the paddock, at the Villa, ran straight across to the back avenue where there was a cart gate. Ella had now reached the gate, and at once, after a cautious glance towards the house, she hurried by the avenue to the back door, and thence by the back stairs to her room. There, agitated more by fear of Dorothy Pedley than by her climb, she stood for a moment to catch her breath. Then she stooped slowly and unlocked a bottom drawer in her desk, from which she took a tin cash box. This box she unlocked, and from under the tray drew out a letter in very large blue sheets. She sat down in her chair and read:

Buenos Aires
8.4.06

My Dearest,

I promised not to write and perhaps I am wrong to do so, but I can't bear any longer that you should think badly of me. You must think me a coward and worse, to leave you like that. But I had brought you nothing but wretchedness, and I did not see any way of escape. As your sister pointed out, our whole enterprise had gone to pieces. How did it happen? How did I fail? Your money would have taken us to South America, and I might, I should have, got a job there. You've been told, no doubt, that the school I spoke of never heard from me, because I was afraid to write; and that I had never even tried to get a berth on the steamer. So that, of course, when you agreed to travel as my wife and I went to get a berth, there were none available for more than a month. A story to damn better and honester men than I have ever been.

Darling, I should not dare to hope for understanding from any but you, and even from you I don't know how I dare ask for it. Can you believe that all this miserable contemptible failure came first from one thing, my fear of losing you. I told you lies because I wanted you so badly, needed you so badly. You were my only hope, not just of happiness, but of self-respect, of life itself. I had to persuade you to come away with me. You will say, but why did you allow all our money to be wasted? That was what really ruined us. I remember you used to ask me if we weren't spending too much at the hotel. Why did I squander our money, or rather, let it sink away from us, in bills we never saw, and that I never asked to see, and put out of my mind? I myself still wonder at that six weeks of calm madness, while I stayed passive and let our money and our chance waste away. Did I expect some other miracle to save me, or did I simply feel that my happiness could not last, that it was a kind of dream, to be enjoyed only as a dream.

Your sister Bessie once compared me with a puss moth caterpillar on which the ichneumon lays its eggs, so that its grubs may feed on living flesh. But first the fly drives its proboscis into the brain of the caterpillar grub and poisons its central nervous system, so that it cannot move to crush the ichneumon eggs or to shake off the grubs while they slowly eat it and torture it to death. It is kept alive and fresh, to be a living meal for the little ichneumons, beasts of prey.

Was it my faith that was paralysed, my very soul of action that was poisoned?

Do you, can you believe such a fantastic explanation for an act that destroyed us both? Darling heart, even if it is incredible to you, believe that I loved you and that with you at least I was honest and sincere. Try not to think meanly of me. You used to hate injustice, and that would be unjust.

I do not blame Rose. I am the last man to attack her standards, her ideals. My own mother sacrificed herself to give me what education I had. And with you for a few months I lived in that heaven for which I must thank not only your true soul, but the sister who brought you up. No, I am no revolutionary or anarchist. I know that I am a poor thing beside Rose, and even if she misjudged me, perhaps that was necessary, too.

Perhaps it is even necessary that her ideals of life should bring into the world cruelty as well as happiness, purity and chastity for some women, prostitution and disease for others.

We know that the world is a tissue of injustice: children in the womb are already condemned to be cripples, blind, stupid, weak, unstable – in a word, to be slaves. And others, no less undeserving, are marked down for genius, for power beyond all wealth, and delight beyond all happiness. But for the born slave, the soft-skinned caterpillar, the world is a cruel place. Did I ever have a chance? I can't tell, but I think it was a small one. And it was because you didn't condescend to me, my darling, that I first loved you. Bessie was good to me, God bless her. She did not judge meanly or cruelly. Because she is gay by nature and no moralist, I know that she is blamed. Perhaps, as some would say, she too is a spendthrift of the capital guarded by such as Rose. But she gave me back my life, even if it was life without hope. For it was you alone who gave me hope, who did not merely pity me but entered into my life and lent it your energy. You alone, simply by the power of imagination, comprehended what I had suffered – the grind of poverty and squalor, on body and soul, in sleep or waking. Squalor of the mean street, the dirty office where everything was shabby, inky, dusty, the fearful squalor of the city, the tangled mass of filthy barracks without a single trace of beauty and dignity; above all, the squalor of mind and interest. I'm not saying that the poor devils who worked with me were worse than any of the rest – they were simply victims, like me, of fate. They were ignorant and narrow because they had been born into ignorant and poor circumstances. They were mean because they had to be mean – they were fighting for their lives. They pursued poor cheap girls and ruined them, if they could, under false names, because they had natural appetites and could not afford to marry, because they wanted some adventure and the risk seemed to give it dignity. So that if they were caught, like me, if instead of being the beast who preyed, they were the prey of beasts still more worthless and cunning, the half-prostitutes who blackmailed them into marriage, they were looked upon as unlucky, or as fools who had not been clever enough to hide their traces. I was looked upon as the poorest kind of fool, because I was caught by a few tears. And so I was. I was a fool because I should have known that my only chance, in that world, was to have a heart of iron, and see that girl in the river before I married her, that she, even at sixteen, was a cunning animal fighting for herself only, as I should have fought for myself. It was her cunning, her tricks, against my brutality, my fists, and I wasn't a brute. And so I was finished for life, I couldn't divorce her even when she was openly unfaithful: I couldn't afford a divorce. And I had to pay her drink bills when she had deserted me for trying to stop her drinking. According to your sister Rose, the law was quite right. Marriage must be protected. Hard cases make bad law. A dictum which wraps up the legal mind in five terrible words, which says, Justice is impossible, but law is necessary, to save some rags of honour, some fragments of peace, truth, and nobility in a world of damnation. Perhaps Rose and the lawyers are right. Who am I to doubt them, a cripple of the will, perhaps a cripple from birth.

*Indeed, my whole experience cries out, the world is a world of beasts,
and only the strictest law saves it from vileness and misery beyond
imagination. And so I asked myself, when Rose came to me, not only,
Can I make Rose understand, but can we fight the world that Rose
represents; and one much stupider and without any of Rose's good
qualities, without even honesty and truth? Can we face a world which
is saved from utter barbarism only by law, and a law as savage as a
watch-dog kept on a chain to make him murderous against every
wandering humble beggar who might steal a little peace or comfort?
Ought I to have asked you to bear the spite, the incredible small-
minded cruelty of people who would delight in punishing your children
for what they would call your vice? Cruelty against which you would
have no defence, for it would make you see your helpless children
suffer for your acts. Darling, believe me, that I left you not solely
because I was weak, but because I did really think it was the best
course for you. And that I went with seeming abruptness and
callousness because it was the kindest way, indeed, the only possible
way. For you would have wished to prevent me. Goodbye now, my
darling wife, at least I may call you that in a letter which is only for
your own eyes. You gave me the only justice, the only true love, the
only happiness I ever had. Through your sweet and true soul I knew
for once a faith, I dare not say faith in God, but faith in goodness.
And it changed my life, for that one year which now seems all the life
I ever had. May God bless you and keep you and bring you some of
the happiness you deserve. I hope at least that the child may make up
to you something of what you have suffered by me. My darling, here
at least I can sign myself your loving husband.*

Ella laid the last sheet carefully in its place. She was moved, but
not passionately, not violently, by words read so often and known
by heart, and she made for the thousandth time the same comments
in the same order: 'He should not have gone. But what would have
happened to us if he had stayed? What would have happened to
Amanda?' And then, with the letter before the eyes of her memory,
stretched out like a landscape of the human agony, she grasped, for
a moment the full meaning of that trite phrase, 'Life's a battle'. She
had a glimpse of enormous masses of helpless creatures marching
and counter marching, trampling each other down among cries like
the yelping of jackals, the screaming of cats; shouts of argument,
triumph, and patriotic hysteria. She felt rather than saw the eternal
conflict of ideas, of wills and faiths, inspiring those cries, driving

those masses, and sudden frightened, she put the letter back in its box and locked it in its drawer. 'My poor Ernest, it wasn't fair – but how strong Rose was. What courage she had – what fearful courage, to decide lives. She wasn't even afraid to be unjust. Oh, one must be strong.'

She had walked to the stairhead, attracted unconsciously, in the manner of a housewife, by the sound of voices in the hall. But suddenly, recognizing that one of them belonged to Dorothy Pedley, and that it was growing louder as its owner ascended the stairs, she went quickly to the remotest attic, where, opening a trunk to explain her purpose there, she said to herself, 'Yes, one must be firm – and I shall not see Dorothy. No, whatever happens.'

At lunch-time, when Amanda went to seek her, she was found apparently sorting old dresses.

'Dearest, what are you doing?'

'I was just looking for – is Dorothy staying to lunch? I do hope she is staying.'

'She went two hours ago, thank goodness. Her friend couldn't wait.'

'I'm so sorry – I should have liked to see her.'

'She says she'll stop the sale of the house. That will mean a bigger muddle than ever.'

'You're angry with me.'

'No, please don't say that – it only makes things difficult – and why should they be difficult. It's all so ordinary – too much so.'

'Yes, of course. Forgive me. I can't help wanting you to be happy – I want that so much.' But seeing again the girl's white, worn cheeks and dark-ringed eyes, terrified by her look of weariness and exasperation, she suddenly lifted up her face, like a child asking for forgiveness, and said, 'Don't hate me, don't—'

'How could I?' Amanda kissed her and tried to make the kiss frank and convincing. 'You've been an angel to me.'

Both were embarrassed. They walked silently down the corridor and descended the stairs, a step apart.

But at the bottom step Ella suddenly asked in a timid voice, 'Could you call up a number for me, dear.'

Ella was still nervous of the telephone. She had been used to depute the calling of numbers to a maid. Now that all the maids except the between-maid Polly had left, she was obliged to ask members of the family.

'Yes, of course,' Amanda said, with a cheerful obedience which only overlaid the embarrassment, so that she began slowly to blush. 'What number, dearest?'

Ella gave a number in Ancombe village, and Amanda looked it up in the book, saying, 'But who is it?'

'It's a lodging. Harry is staying there.'

'So he's come back?'

'Yes, I think he wants some work. And I thought he might like our hay. They always had it before, when at Brook.'

'What can Harry do with our wretched hay? It's never more than one little cock, and they can't get a mower through the gate.'

'Oh dear, I'd forgotten, but I must ask after his poor father. Yes, perhaps I'd better have the number.'

Ella's message to Ancombe, it appeared, had after all referred to hay. Just before eight o'clock, while the June sun was still high, Harry and old Bob arrived at the Villa, in an ancient Ford, with scythes, and at once began to cut the broken and tangled paddock. Ella asked old Bob to take supper in the kitchen, and Harry to dine, but Harry returned answer that they were too dirty and too much pressed for time. Beer and meat were therefore sent out, and at half-past ten, when Amanda. on the excuse of sleepiness, said goodnight, Ella asked her to go first down the paddock and see that the harvesters had all they wanted.

'It's so good of Harry to do this work for us. I've sent out some supper, but ask him if he would like some more beer.'

'Must I see him?'

'No, of course not, but it would be kinder, I think.'

'To him or to me?' said the girl, in a bemused voice. She leant against the garden door to gaze at the mowers, who, having cut about a third of the little meadow, were now at work in the shadow of the house, and approaching the slope which fell suddenly away to the north. They appeared as two blue-grey shapes against the pinkish-violet of the opposite hillside, still illuminated by the sunset.

They were scything in echelon, the old man leading, by right of seniority rather than strength, for the work was plainly hard for him. Almost hunch-backed, he thrust out his lizard neck, and pivoted on his stiff leg in a swing contrived of his defects, in broken arcs. Yet it had the rhythm of efficiency.

Harry's long back and long thin arms, swinging a wider circle, showed more graceful motion, but not more precision. The two, harmonized in time, stepping together, seemed to be performing a complex symphonic dance, to the accompaniment of their own four foot Devon blades, and the smell of the new-cut grass, now wet with dew, threw up so rich and intense a mixture of scents that it seemed to change the nature of the air itself into a sort of ætherial mead, or honey brew, cooled in the breeze off the water.

Amanda drew a long breath and said, 'They're like machines,' and suddenly she scratched herself angrily, thrusting her hand into the open front of her blouse.

'Amanda, dear – really you're getting so rough.'

'But I feel so filthy. There's not the slightest chance, you know, that Harry will marry me.'

'Why, he's been in love with you for years.'

'But my financial future is rather uncertain. Suppose the other will did turn up. The country people are all ready for the worst.'

'Harry would never marry for money.'

'But he'll go where money is, and he's quite right. He knows what he wants, at least.'

Ella was already bringing the beer, and Amanda, as if set in motion by the cool touch of the jug in her hands, moved away.

The mowers had finished their downward cut and were now returning. Their bodies rose above the top of the slope into the pink light, and were gradually swallowed into the blue shadow of the house. A chimney-pot obscured old Bob before his partner, but Harry's hat still had a touch of pink on its crown when Amanda called out, 'Good evening, Harry; good evening, Uncle Bob. How kind of you to come.'

Old Bob touched his bald forehead; Harry crossed the wet grass.

'I've brought you some beer.'

'Thank you, Miss Amanda – that's very welcome. It's warmer than you might think. Here's to us all and luck where it goes.' He took a pull.

Amanda peered at Harry through the dusk. She had feared to find him changed by misfortune: dejected or bitter. But he seemed merely thinner and a little more flamboyant. He wore his hat at a more careless angle, as if with defiance.

'And how are you, Harry?'

'Going along. Well, I hear they're going to stop your sale.'

'Who are?'

'The family – some ladyship that went to the auctioneer.'

'Very likely. I'm not a good proposition, Harry.'

'Nor me. Less than ever I was. Look at me leaving Fred's and coming back here. An't I a fule?'

'It's your own home place, and you like farming better than a garage. So should I.'

'Getting in Okey's hay.'

'And your friends are here. I hear Nelly's had her baby.'

'Why should that bring me back?'

'I'm not meaning anything, Harry.'

'No, I didn't come back for Nelly. I came back because I was a fule. I told you I had a fulish bone, Miss Amanda, and so I have, as thick as a bull's head.'

'Why Miss, Harry? But never mind, is it going to thunder?'

Harry made no answer to this. He drank and said, 'I've been offered a horseman's job up to Okeys.'

'You won't accept a job like that?'

'Who knows,' said Harry. 'If my fulish bone took a jump that way.'

There was a silence. Amanda leaned languidly against a beech stem, looked across at the fields, and said, 'Is Nelly going to swear her baby to you?'

Harry lowered his jug to his chest and looked doubtfully at Amanda across the rim.

'She mid try, but what would be the good. I couldn't pay anything, and Nelly wouldn't want to send me to gaol.'

'Poor Nellie, poor baby. Or perhaps lucky Nellie.'

'Ah!'

'Does she like her baby, Harry?'

'I've not seen it as I don't own to it. But she'd be bound to keep it nice. The Rafts have got their pride – too much.'

'Can you have too much?'

'It seems so, Miss Amanda, if I couldn't come down to a car-washer; and too little, too, if I go for a horseman. Did Nelly see you?'

'No.'

'I wondered why you were aiming at me.'

'But I don't feel like that at all. I couldn't blame you, or Nelly, or anyone, for – for such a natural thing. No, I rather admire you.'

'Well now, that's kind, but I don't admire myself so much, and I don't think little Nelly would feel so.'

'I meant because the baby was born.'

'Ah!' Harry took another long discreet stare at Amanda. Then he said, 'Been pretty well?'

'Yes, thank you, Harry. Don't I seem well?'

'You didn't sound too good.'

'We've all been rather busy.'

'This thunder weather is very bearing down. All the girls have headaches this week.'

'Did you come back for the girls or the place, Harry?'

'I hear you've got a friend yourself, Miss Amanda.'

'Is that why you call me Miss?'

'He's a smart chap, just the thing for you.'

'Are we quarrelling, Harry? I should hate that.'

'Never, not I.'

'Nor I. I wasn't being prim about Nelly or the girls. I wish you all the girls in the world, the nicest possible.'

'Ah!' It was plain that Harry was not convinced by this generosity. But he suddenly decided that if they were indeed quarrelling, nothing could be done about it. 'Look at the sun – I must get on. I'll just keep the jug awhile, if you don't mind. To give old Bob his share.' He strolled away towards the drooping grotesque figure of old Bob, which had stood, during this interview, motionless as a willow stump, split and ruined by age and probably nearly as vacant of reflection.

Amanda returned slowly towards the house. She reflected, 'Were we quarrelling? I don't think so. But why did he call me Miss? To make me feel superior? He knows I don't feel like that, far from it.' She turned to glance back at the mowers now drinking their beer. 'How they love their beer. It quite brings old Bob to the surface. All the same, I could have hit Harry when he said that all the girls had headaches this week. As if we were part of the weather – elementary.'

'How did Harry seem, darling?' Ella, meeting her at the back door, spoke as if enquiring after an invalid.

'I don't know, he didn't say.' Amanda leant against the door-post and gave a long sigh.

'Darling, aren't you too tired?'

'I've got a bit of a head, but it doesn't matter. I think it must be the weather.'

'You must to to to bed at once.'

'I don't feel like bed.' The girl yawned and said, 'I wish there were a party somewhere, a dance. I should like to get drunk.'

'Amanda!'

'I know it's quite stupid. but everything's stupid tonight,' and she exclaimed in a cross voice, as if under a legitimate grievance, 'You never showed me a picture of my father. But I suppose you didn't keep one.'

'I think so, darling. Yes, I have one. But it's very bad, it's not nearly handsome enough.' She handed Amanda some small object.

'Your brooch. But does it open? How neat.'

She stepped into the empty pantry and opened the cameo brooch, which held a miniature of Cranage. The high, bald forehead and cupid's mouth had been rendered with obvious will to draw a character, at once contemplative and sensuous.

Amanda said in a slow voice which seemed to admit an argument under protest, 'He's very distinguished looking, all the same.'

'Yes, yes, that is just what he was – in mind, too.'

'But how could he treat you like that?' Amanda gazed at the miniature with raised eyebrows.

'Wait,' said Ella, trembling with eagerness, 'I'll show you a letter, his last – yes, you will see. He was good – he was noble – you need never be ashamed of your father. No, stay here – Harry might want some more beer.'

'Don't bother,' said Amanda, handing back the brooch. But she did not move, and Ella, as if eager to seize a moment which might never recur, implored her, 'But – it's no trouble – I want to.' She hurried away. At once Amanda, as if she, too, had an important preoccupation on her mind, went to the window and, pressing her nose to the dirty glass, turned her eyes on the mowers. They were on their outward journey, and as Amanda watched them they passed gradually out of the shadow of the house back into the sunset, now a darker pink, so that for several minutes their backs and arms, of a brilliant brick colour, oscillated mysteriously in the air, as if jumped on invisible wires, while their legs and scythes were hidden in the shadow.

Amanda was so intent on this spectacle of unreflective motion that she was still twisting her neck, to see the last of it, as it disappeared over the slope, when Ella, breathless, came flying from the passage. And she gazed with a kind of bewilderment, as if awaked from a dream, at the letter placed in her hand.

'But it's quite long,' she said, protesting.

'Yes, it's the only one he ever wrote to me. He wrote it from abroad.' And when ten minutes later Amanda, not without two or three glances from the window, had finished reading, she exclaimed triumphantly, 'You see – you see. Oh, he was good as well as clever.'

Amanda was silent.

'Don't you feel that?' Ella enquired anxiously.

Amanda glanced out of the window. 'I think you were too good for him.'

'Oh no, no. I was weak.'

'I might have written that letter myself – dodging out of everything, even myself. Yes, I'm his own daughter.'

'Oh, how can you say so?' Ella was in despair. 'It was I who was weak. You're not a bit like Ernest.'

'Did you run away with him, dearest, or he with you?'

'Oh, he did everything – no, of course I didn't mean – but that's a wrong question.' Ella spoke with unusual indignation. 'You wouldn't ask such a question if you knew – how things happen. How they really happen.'

The girl was startled. She looked out of the window and said, after a minute, 'No, but I can imagine. I can feel how they happen.'

'It's so strange – to be in love – everything is changed.'

'But even then, inside things, some people drift and some act.'

'But you have never been a drifter.'

'I've never been anything, anything risky.'

'Oh dear, Rose told me – she warned me.' Ella was almost in tears. Clasping the letter she hurried away towards the stairs.

Amanda went to the door and looked out to see if Harry had returned the jug. It was not there. But the mowers had just finished a swathe and shouldered their scythes. The dark red sun, as they began to climb the slope, illuminated only their heads, and the long bladed scythes which shone as if wet with thin blood, as if the fresh-cut grass had bled upon them. They had the air of weapons, and the gesture of the mowers as they halted close to the yard gate and stood their blades against a tree, was that of disciplined soldiers, who lay down arms after a campaign.

They then wiped their faces, held a short conference, sat down upon an upturned wheelbarrow and a bucket, and in the double light of the sunset and the rising moon, began to take their supper of meat, bread and beer.

Harry's voice came clearly on the barely perceptible night breeze. 'You can't call it hay. 'Twouldn't make feed for wireworms.'

And after a long pause the old man's quavering lips answered in his incomprehensible language something which plainly agreed with this judgment on the Villa's grass.

The idea came into Amanda's head, to go down to the men and say to Harry, 'Where shall I meet you tomorrow?' She thought,

'Harry will know at once what I mean – he can hear a girl's moods when she hardly knows them herself.'

And she had raised her shoulder from the post, to take a step, when a hand touched her arm and Robin's voice said, 'Here you are – sorry, did I make you jump?'

'I thought you were a ghost.'

'Are you going up?'

'Why?'

'Mandy, you said you'd marry me if I got a divorce.'

'Did I? But – I thought you'd made it up with Kathy.'

'You know that was just a silly incident.'

'Very silly.'

Robin pressed Amanda's arm and stared at her in the deep shade of the high pantry light. He appeared doubtful of her mood, as Harry had been. Amanda said in an exhausted voice, 'No, it doesn't matter, does it?'

'Except that it made me see – I'd got to do something drastic.'

'Marry me, in fact.'

'You're my only chance. After all, I chucked my job.'

'Not for me, Robin – but never mind.' She disengaged her arm. 'Yes, I'll marry you, if you're sure you need me.'

'But do you want me?'

'You mustn't ask – you must take – take.'

Amanda ran upstairs and began furiously to undress, throwing her clothes on the floor. She was so tired that she wanted to cry. Yet when she was at last ready for bed she could not lie down. She was too feverish. She drew back the curtains which still hung at the windows and looked out.

The mowers were again hard at work in the deep blue dusk of the evening.

'Swish, swish!' she murmured to herself. 'How they keep it up. They must be made of steel springs – even Bob.'

'Are you ready?' Robin glided across the floor in his pyjamas. Amanda stared at him. 'Be careful, Kathy might hear.'

'I don't care. She'll know tomorrow, anyhow.'

'You mean you want to stay tonight?'

'Why wait? Let's make a jump at it. It's the best way.'

There was a long pause and then Amanda said, 'Wouldn't we feel mean to Kathy? She seems so nice.'

'Of course she's nice – that's her racket, being nice to people. But why think of Kathy on a night like this?'

'It's hard to think of anything, on any of these nights.'

Then for a long time they continued to lean out of the window. In front, the moon having withdrawn among cloud, the mowers appeared as silver shapes on a grey field; steel men moving through an unsubstantial underworld. Only their blades sometimes flashed like blue fire, or a red spark flew up when the point hit a stone.

'How wonderful to work like that,' said Amanda. 'But of course they know all the time that the job has to be finished.'

'Aren't you sleepy, Mandy?'

'I couldn't sleep.'

'You don't want me to go?'

'No, I don't think so. I'm sure I don't. No, you're quite right. We ought to get involved.'

'You needn't mind about Kathy – our lives are not worth living together, they are simply mean, dirty existences.' Robin spoke with emphasis. 'A nasty kind of struggle. All the nastier when we're polite.'

'I can't understand that, but why should I?'

'Really, we spend our whole time trying to do each other down, to make the other admit to something or other.'

'What does Kathy want to make you admit?'

'Kathy? I don't know – that everything is Kathy, perhaps. She wants to swallow me and digest me, turn me into Kathy meat. And I suppose she would say that I want to turn her into me.'

'Perhaps she needs some interest, apart from you, to forget herself.' Amanda moved her head to the mowers swing and counted, 'One and two and one and two. How lovely to be able to swing a scythe.'

'But good God, Kathy has her job and adores it! Hasn't she got her dear boss, who kisses her on the forehead and tells her he couldn't do without her.'

'Yes, I don't know – how should I? I haven't been – involved.'

'Shall we go to bed, darling Mandy?'

But Amanda moved a little away, and after a moment she said in a conversational tone, like one who wants to keep a party alive, 'It's not as if you'd had children.'

'You take the Victorian view.'

'Not at all. I think it was a cruel and stupid age for women.'

'I daresay.' The man moved restlessly. 'Perhaps it was. What then?'

'Obsessed by sex.'

'I should say rather by marriages and engagements and nappies and pap – they put the tiger in a mill and made him grind their corn.'

'Your tame tiger trod down millions of women, like the aunts. There was blood on its feet.'

'Well, he got a sore neck too. They kept the chain on him. But so can we.'

'Yes.' Amanda spoke in a weak voice as if confused. 'What were we talking about?'

'What's wrong with you, Mandy? I'm not saying it wasn't a put-up job, a racket if you like. And every racket has its victims.'

'Yes, but I feel they didn't face the consequences of their racket.'

'All right, I'm not arguing. I give it to you. All of it. And that's twelve o'clock striking at Brook Church.'

'Ancombe. It has a much sweeter bell, and it's always five minutes fast.' Amanda remained leaning out of the window.

'Tell me if you're nervous, Mandy.'

'Yes, I mean, I'm not.'

'It's quite ridiculous you know. A piffling thing.'

'I suppose,' she answered dreamily, 'if you make it piffling, it is piffling.'

'Come, Mandy.' He tried to draw her from the window.

'But Robin—'

'Oh God!'

'I'm not – it's not what you think – I'm not afraid of the – piffling thing, but—'

'Darling, forgive me if I seem a little impatient, but do you know I'm very fond of you? I mean, attracted. It's a genuine emotion.' Suddenly he took her in his arms and kissed her with violence.

'But Robin – oh dear, don't look so furious. There's only one thing – we are going to have a baby, aren't we?'

'What!' Robin let her fall back to the full length of his arms. 'Well, I suppose so, sometime.'

'I mean – now, if it comes. We're not going to try to escape – from any consequences.'

'But damn it all, how long do you suppose a divorce takes?'

'I don't care. I don't care.'

Robin stared at the girl with frowning astonishment. 'But Amanda, this *is* a bit mad. I should have thought we're going to have enough fuss without an appalling scandal on top of it.'

'I'm not a bit afraid of what people may say or think.'

'What on earth are you thinking of then?'

'Nothing – nothing.'

Down below, the paddock had disappeared in a deep blue-green darkness. Nothing could be seen of the mowers. But the noise of their scythes had an extraordinary loudness and regularity.

'Listen to them,' said Amanda. 'It's like music. It's almost as good as fiddles.'

Robin looked at her with indignation.

'I suppose it is music to them – they simply forget what they're doing – in doing it. In doing the job.'

'If you want to change the subject.'

'How do they see – it's uncanny. But perhaps they don't, they do it by instinct. Yes, in a kind of dream.'

'You know, Mandy, it's all very well, but aren't you rather running away?'

'I don't think so – am I?'

'My scheme is quite reasonable. To take the ordinary precautions. And it would make everything safe all round. Why are you afraid of it?'

Amanda made no answer.

'You're not superstitious?' Robin made a face at this word as if it tasted nasty.

'I don't think I've any morals at all. No. I'm sure I haven't. Why should I have?'

'I can see your worry,' said Robin, in a judicious and impartial tone. 'You're afraid that if we started to live together we should begin to hate each other. Like Kathy and me. But I've told you our little trouble is nothing to do with sex. In fact, that's the one region where we can meet.'

'With precautions.'

'My dear old girl—'

'Yes, but—' she spoke in an apologetic tone. 'After all, what *is* this thing. You call it sex, but – isn't that rather a silly little word for rather a big – and rather queer – but now you think I'm only making talk.'

'No, I understand. Only I don't—'

'You must admit,' she interrupted, 'that women are rather specially constructed – for a purpose. And they may be very terribly punished for not fulfilling it – they may even be driven mad.'

'Not you. Come, be sensible. Really, you know.'

'But, Robin, you must see that this power has got its grasp on them – its claws if you like – more than on men.'

The mowers had stopped and a sharpening stone rang suddenly against a blade with a noise which made Amanda jump. Robin put his arm round her and said, 'You're all nerves, and it's my fault.'

'No, I'm running away. Yes, you're quite right, I'm frightened. No, not of you – of – I don't know what.' The girl gave a sharp cry, and Robin exclaimed. Two broad beams had flashed across the field. Harry had turned on the headlights of the Ford which gave to the bushes and the alley, the hollows of the ground, the aspect of a moon-photograph, in black and white, and made the house-wall spring out of the dark, like some ash precipice of the same landscape.

Harry and the old man, now with his braces hanging looped to his knees, appeared in the beams, wearily trudging towards the standing grass. They slowly took position, as if for drill, and without a word swung out their right arms for the first cut of a swath.

'Am I being frightfully silly?' said Amanda, and Robin, to his alarm and astonishment, perceived that the big solid girl beside him was nearly weeping. He hastily gave her a pat on the shoulder and said, 'Good heavens, you're not going to cry?'

'No – o.'

'Don't, for God's sake, let the thing get on your nerves – it isn't worth it. After all, you're just as likely to be right as I am, it's an—'

'Oh, don't say it's an open question; but yes, of course it is. But why, why must everything be open, so awfully open, like wounds.'

The mowers had passed into the lamplight, and two enormous scythemen, three stories high, were swinging and jerking slowly across the back wall of the house.

'Here,' said Robin, 'shall I go away?'

'No, no, please. Forgive me, Robin. I know I'm behaving badly, but it appears that I'm not really a rational being – and you mustn't expect me to be one.'

Robin, having watched the shadow play on the house wall for some moments, remarked in the light tone used for discreet reproach, 'Father Time and Brother Death.'

'Yes, I know how you feel,' said Amanda. 'But I'm not really so – fatal. It isn't quite stupid to – be afraid that—' the girl shivered. 'Don't you think perhaps we might spoil something important. And then of course we shouldn't even know that we'd spoilt it.'

Robin pressed her waist. She could feel that he was being kind and tactful to the unaccountable female. 'Well, dear, aren't you getting cold? I am.'

'Yes, frightfully. Robin, do what you like. Please.'

'It's decided. We'll wait.'

'But then – Kathy?'

'Kathy needn't know that we haven't really given her the evidence. She wouldn't believe us if we did tell her.'

Amanda, cold and stiff, got into bed and stretched herself out, making herself narrow. In a minute Robin's cold body slipped down beside her. He took her hand and, after a moment, he said in a tender, even pleading voice, 'I think perhaps you are right, darling. We'll make a proper old-fashioned marriage of it. Yes, I'm sure you're right.'

'I hope so,' Amanda said in a doubtful tone. 'There's so little to go on, so little real evidence. And this is not very natural either, I suppose. Oh, Robin, I do hope that we'll be happy, that I shall make you happier when the time does come.'

'We'll be all right, my dear, so long as we don't grab, and you couldn't be a grabber if you tried.'

'I hope not,' said Amanda, as if she could not be sure even of her abstention from grabbing.

There was a long silence. The scythes stopped their monotonous tune; Harry's voice was heard, and old Bobby suddenly uttered a strange crow of laughter, a rusty crow like an old cock pheasant's.

Amanda exclaimed, jumped out of bed, and ran to the window. Harry was seen stooping in the lights, about to crank the car. She called 'Goodnight, Harry, and thank you. Goodnight, Uncle Bob.'

'The old man slightly moved the scythe whuch stood beside him like a kind of banner, and raised his skull-like face with its great hollow eye-sockets. Harry turned slowly and gazed upwards. 'Miss A-man-da,' his voice tired to exhaustion, drawled with the deliberate movement of a scythe swing, 'aren't you asleep? It's too late for you, you'll be spoiling your maiden colour.'

'Goodnight, and thank you, both of us.'

'Goodnight, Miss A-man-da, go to sleep.' The car roared and pounded away.

'Miss – Miss – how I hate it.' Amanda thought as she got back into bed. 'I know I was spiteful to him – but a man oughtn't to be so touchy.'

Amanda, waking by long habit, at half past seven, found Robin asleep, flat on his back, with one hand under his neck. He was sleeping so deeply and quietly that he seemed dead. His features had the smoothness of the dead, so that he looked younger than his age, like a young and guileless boy.

Amanda was still examining him with a kind of wonder at her own calmness in this new relation with the world, when she heard the passage creak and hastened to the door, to interrupt Polly with the morning tea. It was only half past seven and the tea was early. Amanda reflected, 'How lucky I waked early.'

She opened the door quickly to find not Polly, but Kathy in the passage. Kathy, with a brilliant smile, glided past her into the room and stood looking at Robin, who was now, with closed eyes, stretching his arms and arching his back, with enormous yawns.

Amanda silently joined Kathy by the bed. She hoped that Kathy's indignation would be turned rather upon her, and she was prepared to attract it. But Kathy continued to smile. She said in a soft, cheerful voice, 'Hullo, Robin.'

'It's you, Kathy.' Robin gazed at his wife with a frown of enquiry 'You heard us, did you?'

'I couldn't help it, both our windows were open.'

'It's just as well, perhaps – you agreed that we should have a divorce.'

'Do you really want a divorce?' said Kathy, apparently surprised. 'This is intended?'

'Very much so.'

Kathy sat down on the bed, with a turn of her body which gave to her pretty dressing-gown a graceful line, looked up at Amanda, and said, 'I hope you will be happy. Really and truly.'

'I'm frightfully sorry,' said Amanda. 'I feel so guilty.'

'It's not your fault, dear, or Robin's, or even mine. Though Robin doesn't think so.'

'Call it incompatibility,' said Robin. 'We clashed.'

'Don't you think everyone is rather incompatible?'

'I don't agree.'

'Some more than others, of course.'

'Meaning that *I'm* impossible.'

'I never expect anything from anybody, and so I'm never disappointed.'

'Meaning that *I* expect too much.'

Kathy was silent. Robin got up and went out of the room, but through the door, in exasperated tones, he exclaimed, 'Goodbye, I leave you in peace.'

Kathy looked at Amanda and said, 'Poor Robin, but he really is rather difficult. He's so suspicious.'

'He's been rather worried lately – I don't think he expected to have to resign.'

'Oh, he always resigns. He's done it twice already, and each time they gave him a rise to get him back. He's rather good at his job.'

'But he hates it so much.'

'He hates every job after the first week.' She paused and looked thoughtfully at Amanda. 'And then, of course, he tends to fall back on the domestic hearth. You'll find him rather dependent – though of course it's the last thing he'll admit. It took me quite a time to realize how dependent he was – on home comforts.' Kathy threw a slight emphasis on the phrase and smiled at Amanda in a manner which the latter found confusing. She said vaguely, 'Oh yes.'

'And, of course, being so suspicious, he needs managing even then.'

'Oh, is he particular about food?'

'Oh yes, he loves his food, but I was meaning more – the amenities.'

Kathy smiled at Amanda, gently, sadly; but Amanda was suddenly disgusted. She murmured an excuse and went out. She thought, 'No. I needn't have a conscience about taking Robin from Kathy.'

She was forced, however, to admit that Kathy was the more civilized house-mate. Her tact, her temper, were a support; her balance, a pleasure. While Robin was surly and silent. Amanda was ashamed of him. She was relieved when on the next day he declared that he must go back at once to Exeter; his mother was expecting him for at least a week's visit.

'It's my fault,' Kathy lamented. 'I shouldn't have stayed.'

'But you've been charming,' said Amanda, moved by a sense of injustice.

'That doesn't matter with Robin. He always thinks I'm trying to do something to him. Robin is a regular lawyer, you know. He can't help getting up a case.'

'I haven't noticed that.'

'No, you wouldn't. He doesn't notice it himself. It's really a kind of complex.'

And despite herself, Amanda had to listen to Kathy's analysis of Robin, which seemed to her like the dissection of a brain with blunt scissors.

'You think I'm imagining things, that I'm being rather too subtle,' Kathy said once.

'Oh, not at all.' Amanda coloured as she spoke. She was afraid that Kathy would perceive the irony. But Kathy answered mildly, 'One has to be, you know, in marriage. Men are so unexpected.'

Amanda could not help replying 'Unexpected?' and was at once put down by the married woman's superiority: 'I can't quite explain, but you'll soon find out. They're awfully dissatisfied, for one thing, I mean, by nature. So restless.'

Kathy's superiorities, no less than her faults, made Amanda glad when, returning from the village one morning, she found her suit cases in the hall and heard from Polly that she was leaving that day. A friend had called for her.

'What name, Polly?'

'Her ladyship, miss. Lady Pedley.'

Ella came quickly from the parlour. She carried a picture in her hand and her guilty look at once alarmed Amanda.

'But, dearest, what are you doing?' She looked into the parlour and saw, assembled round the door, half a dozen of the best pieces in the house – a walnut bureau. a tallboy, a Chippendale mirror, two seventeenth century spice cabinets. She exclaimed, 'But you're not letting her take anything?'

Ella turned very red. 'A few mementos.'

'Grandpapa's bureau was valued at more than a hundred pounds. How can you be so weak?'

Amanda's unusual tenderness was changed to unusual anger, and Ella was greatly alarmed. 'But dear, you see, she is so attached to the family things.'

'Dorothy doesn't care a penny for the family or family things. She has neither the imagination nor the affection.'

'Good morning, Amanda.' Lady Pedley suddenly came out from the parlour at Amanda's elbow. She kissed her foster sister. 'How are you, dear? I just called in for some odds and ends, family things.'

'But has the family given you leave to take them?'

'Yes, yes,' said Ella. 'Dorothy, is this the picture?'

Amanda took the picture and looked at it. 'I thought so, the Turner water-colour, the only really valuable one left.'

'I've just heard,' said Dorothy, 'that Aunty hasn't stopped the sale of the house. Apparently she didn't even read my note.'

'The house is hers to sell,' said Amanda.

'She has no moral right to sell a thing.' Dorothy Pedley was in a rage, which for her was a chilling emotion. Her pretty skin showed red patches, but her voice was calm. 'Aunt Ella, you know Aunt Rose's real wishes. We all do.'

'Oh yes, yes.' Ella visibly trembled before this fierce and authoritative niece. 'I – know it's not right—'

'There,' said Dorothy in triumph. 'After that—'

'But oh dear, I shall have to sell the house – I'm afraid so.'

'But, Aunty, it's simply robbery.'

'I can't help *what* it is.' Ella was extremely agitated. 'No, I can't help it. I must have – the money for the house.'

Dorothy Pedley, who was quite blank with astonishment that Ella should oppose her, now smiled in a significant manner and said 'You know, Aunty, the whole thing seems a little queer. You say you didn't approve of Aunt Rose's new will, and then she dies very suddenly before she has time to sign it, and you go against all her wishes and now you declare that you aren't responsible. But, Aunty, there must be such a thing as right and wrong, or there wouldn't be any police or law or anything.'

'Oh yes, indeed,' said Ella in despair. 'I killed her. But I told the police.'

'You told the police!' Lady Pedley was much startled. 'But what does she mean?' She turned to Amanda.

Amanda placed the water colour in a safe corner and took Ella's arm. 'You haven't been writing again?'

'No, not again. That is, not since – Friday – I wrote on Friday.'

'Wrote to the police?' cried Lady Pedley. 'But, Aunty, you don't want a scandal in the papers?'

'No, no, but what can I do. And there is always plenty – that poor woman in Queensport last week who drowned her little baby, and so much pain and distress in Brook village.'

'Oh, in that class!' cried the other. 'One knows what goes on there. But it doesn't matter to them if they get into the papers, and it does matter most definitely to us. Think of Mark's feelings if the Press got hold of the story.'

'Oh dear, yes,' cried Ella. 'But if I've done wrong—'

'Do consider, Aunty, you don't want to punish the family.'

'No, no, that would be very unfair – but perhaps I could explain to the papers.'

'No, Aunty! Please, Amanda, you won't let her, will you? A letter to the papers would be the last straw. Goodbye, Aunty. and thank you very much.' Lady Pedley, in her confusion, kissed Ella warmly. She then returned to a large car, which was waiting outside, loaded with her booty. Kathy was waiting beside the car. Tactfully she had avoided the conflict in the hall. She embraced both Ella and Amanda with affectionate but gentle warmth, and smiling still, was driven away. The smile remained in Amanda's memory with the flavour of a macaroon. She could not decide whether it was more sweet or more bitter. It was only when she had returned to the hall that she noticed the disappearance of the Turner. She cried out furiously, 'Dorothy took it after all. But when and how? My God, how I loathe that woman – she's such a profiteer.' Then, seeing Ella's startled anxious look, she took her arm. 'Why do you give way to people?'

'I don't, darling – that is, she's not people, is she? She's Bessie's favourite daughter – except you. Oh, I know I oughtn't to sell the house, but I want the money so badly. You see, suppose you and Robin did decide to—'

'But has Robin told you anything?'

'He said something about a divorce. And you know, if he were divorced he mightn't get another post. It's so dangerous to go against the law, unless you're rich or have a position in the Government, like poor Papa.' Ella's notions of government were wide. 'Oh, I must really sell the house for a good price.'

And on that same day she wrote to the agents, commanding the sale of the house as soon as the furniture should be disposed of. She wrote also to the family to come and choose what they wanted. But it turned out that the family was in no hurry. And this was not surprising, for it had been pointed out to them by Dorothy Pedley, who was wont to extract praise for herself even from her failures, that Ella, having undertaken to let them choose furniture, would not sell the house until after their visits. And that this means of delaying the sale was far better than legal threats from Sant & Sant, which were not really legal.

Certainly Ella did not perceive the trick and waited eagerly from day to day for family visits.

'I can't understand why I don't hear,' she would say to Amanda, 'at least from your Uncle Richard, he was so strong against letting the furniture go. But of course he is a busy man, and then he's getting old. And when you're getting old you have so little time except for the really important things – it is so hard to think of business and money.'

'Aren't they important?' Amanda would ask.

'Oh yes, yes, but not perhaps so very important as knowing what ought to be done. They are – outside – like weather. Of course, weather is important. One might be struck by lightning. But it couldn't be one's own fault unless one was very imprudent and carried a steel umbrella or stood under a wet tree – is Robin coming here this weekend?'

'He says he's too busy at home.'

'Oh dear, I'm afraid he's very conscientious,' and, going away from Amanda, she said thoughtfully, 'perhaps I ought to ask him?' a suggestion to which Amanda gave no answer.

'What is happening?' Ella asked herself. 'Why doesn't he come back – does Amanda really love him? And is it right for me to wish that she should – to want them to be together?'

A few days later, about three weeks after Robin's departure, Amanda, making a hopeless attempt to dust the drawing-room which was still used as a sitting-room, heard Ella's voice at her shoulder. 'I do hope nothing is wrong with Robin – or poor Kathy. But perhaps they weren't really suited to each other – Kathy is not really very intellectual. She only pretends. You really ought to have some new hats, dear – nice smart hats.'

'What should I do with hats in Brook?'

'No, of course not – only it's so disappointing for you here.'

'I wish we could get this sale over.'

'Yes, I must write to Robin.'

Amanda continued to dust. Ella looked sadly at her and then went to compose her letter to Robin Sant. 'I hope you will come this weekend,' she wrote. 'We have been dull without you. I have ordered some cigars, Havana cigars, and we found some of my father's claret in the cellar. It is more than forty years old, so I feel sure that it will be good.' After long reflection she added in a postscript the three words, 'Amanda misses you.'

When Ella had posted this letter she was seized with guilt, not only against Kathy and Christian ethics, but against Robin and Amanda.

The two women, during the last weeks alone in the deserted house, had been drawn together by a kind of physical sympathy. An embarrassment remained, which sometimes made conversation difficult, but still they sought each other as if by some magnetic law. And Ella in Amanda's company could not hide long a guilty feeling.

'I really think,' she said, within an hour of posting her letter, 'that I ought to write to Robin.'

'No, please, I'd rather you didn't.'

'Oh dear, do you think it would upset him? Yes, it might be risky,' and quite horrified, she slipped away. 'Perhaps I've spoilt everything – it was a very dangerous thing to do. But still, somebody had to do something. And Amanda is so good – and so tactful.' And she said to Amanda the next morning, apropos of nothing, 'Your Aunt Rose would have written – yes, I feel sure.'

'Would she approve of pursuing a married man?'

'I mean, if Robin hadn't been married, she wouldn't have been afraid of sending for him – she wasn't afraid of anything, anything.'

'She didn't interfere very successfully with you.'

Ella looked at her daughter with anxiety. The two women were sitting in the parlour, a cool room in the morning, mending house linen, work formerly carried out by the sewing-maid. Both sewed badly, and did the work more as a pastime than a duty. But while they worked they talked with less embarrassment.

'But how hard it was for her,' Ella said at last. 'Think what a danger she faced – I was in such a state. I had suffered so much already.'

Ella drew in her breath sharply like one who remembers acute pain. 'You see, it was not as if I was just an ordinary mother who falls in love with her first baby – I was over forty and I'd never expected to have a baby at all. And I'd lost Ernest in such a cruel way. I was really – quite queer about it. I wouldn't let you out of my sight. I wouldn't have a nurse. And when Rose tried to make me have a nurse, the doctor warned her to let me alone, or I might lose my mind. And, really, I wonder I didn't die.'

'So Aunt Rose might have killed you.'

This remark had a startling effect on Ella. She sat, needle in air, and stared at her daughter. Then she turned red and exclaimed, 'Oh, but you mustn't – it's not the same. She didn't want me dead – she wasn't guilty – of a wickedness.'

'She was guilty of a great wickedness, of being cruel to you when you were helpless and unhappy.'

'Oh no, no.' Ella let her sewing fall. 'Yes, it's true – yes, she was guilty. But what is guilt? Can one do anything without guilt?' And for the whole day she walked about with a look of agitation, until Amanda, kissing her, said, 'But you mustn't worry about Aunt Rose any more.'

'How can I help it – when I – but I mustn't say that, must I? Oh, you speak of Rose being cruel, but you are cruel to poor Rose. And she felt it so much, that very cruelty – to be hated for doing – things that some one had to do. Oh, how unfair, how wicked that is – to hate people for daring to do things that one wouldn't dare by oneself.'

In fact, Rose had not dared, for many weeks, to take any further steps in rescuing Ella from what seemed to her a very dangerous position. She saw without the doctor's telling that Ella was in a strange mood. She appeared different and unfamiliar even in character. The Ella who, at the Villa, had been unpunctual, dreamy, impatient of set times and places, now at Roundrock Bay lived by a routine so stiff and narrow that it fretted Rose. She would grow red and furious at three minutes delay of breakfast or luncheon. She left the house for the beach always at the same time, and went to the same part of the beach, even the same rock. She was in terror that someone might get to the rock before her.

This rock stood at some distance along the sands, in a place little frequented. It was indeed very difficult to push the perambulator so far through the sand; for Ella, light and thin, it was an enormous feat. But she performed it often four times a day in order to reach this quiet place which had caught her fancy.

Once established there for an afternoon, it seemed to her, because of her fancy, that she was secure in a special fashion, in her own place. She would sit there a whole afternoon, knitting and looking now and then at the sea; at the absurd little pier, or sometimes at the cliff behind her; a cliff, which like everything else at Roundrock Bay, was moderate and restrained; and at the neat narrow houses, with their coloured stucco fronts, which formed its northern horizon against the pale blue sky.

The perambulator stood beside her. But she never permitted the baby to lie in what seemed to her a narrow and dark compartment. She always lifted Amanda out and laid her on the rug that she might kick and roll. Amanda was a very small and thin, but active baby, with that look of lively intelligence which belongs to thin babies. Her long upper lip, the shape of her mouth, a thin bow, her small sharp chin, gave a look of extreme acuteness to her expression, as she gazed first at the sky, then at some passing figure, at a dog or at Ella's quickly-moving hands.

Ella returned these glances with a grave pondering look, as if she were preoccupied with important questions of the child's health and education. But in fact she was not thinking at all; she was only feeling intensely; and the whole context of her soul might have been expressed in the words of the comic song, 'That's my baby.' But this feeling to her was very far from comic. It was acute, anxious; it was like the feeling of one who has been given the task of conveying some fragile treasure of art through foreign lands, in the midst of revolutions.

Ella could not see or even conceive the dangers that surrounded her, but she felt their pressure. One of the chief, of course, was croup; of which two of her own sisters had died as infants. She had no idea of what croup was like, but she dreaded it. Another was diphtheria. Another was mad dogs. Every dog with its mouth open, in that hot summer, made her tremble. Further off were such ambushes as measles, scarlet fever, and chicken pox, but they were still too far to affect her anxieties except as distant mountains affect a traveller crossing a rope bridge over flooded rivers. She felt their presence only in the general sense that there was no end to the dangers that awaited her.

Rose would bring beach chairs which she set up beside the rock, saying in a voice so gentle that it was almost timid, 'Won't you have a chair, darling, that stone doesn't look very comfortable.'

Ella did not answer her and pretended not to see the chairs. She had not yet brought herself to forgive Rose, and since she had not forgiven her she could not speak to her. She was literally unable to speak to Rose. A silent rage paralysed her tongue.

One afternoon Rose drew up her chair between Ella and Amanda. This was an act which enraged Ella so that she could not knit except by a careful and deliberate effort. But though her hands shook she did not protest, or move. She pretended, so to speak, that Rose did not exist, and could not, therefore, obscure her view of Amanda.

Rose had endured this treatment, the more painful to her feelings because it was instinctive and nervous, without complaint, but this afternoon she was forced to speak.

'Dear Ella,' she said, 'you know I don't want to worry you in any way – but we have been here now more than two months and the doctor seems quite satisfied with you and baby's health. I wonder have you thought at all of the future?'

Ella looked away towards the sea, a gesture which eloquently expressed her wish to be rid of Rose.

'Darling,' said Rose, 'I don't want to worry you, but you know we shall have to come to some decision, and I'm afraid we ought to think of it soon. It is so very important for you and for baby, to make no mistakes. They might be irretrievable, they might spoil your life and poor little baby's life, too.'

Ella now finding it impossible to knit, and afraid that the trembling of her hands might be seen, laid her knitting down and crossed her hands on her knee.

'We have to be very careful,' said Rose, and suddenly she gave a deep sigh, the sigh of one who foresees that a hard and thankless duty is to be no less thankless than his worst fears. 'We are running great risks every day in case we might be recognized here.'

She paused. Ella sat like a stone, and Rose said in a reproachful voice, 'Perhaps you don't mind that, or think you don't mind, but you do realize, I'm sure, that there are things – there must be things – which are wrong from every point of view.'

Ella did not move, but Rose, as if strengthened by the sense rather than the reflection, that she was on firm moral ground, in seeking to save Ella and her baby from Ella's own folly, continued in a more resolute voice. 'Now darling, I have given much anxious thought to your trouble, which of course is mine, too, and Papa is also very anxious. He meant to come and see you, but of course it was the time for his visit to Theo, which means so much to them both. But he agrees with me that we ought to consult Bessie. As a married woman, of course, she is really the proper person to be consulted. And so I wrote to her and she wired this morning that she would arrive by the five o'clock train.' Rose turned as if for comment, then seeing that Ella did not mean to speak, frowned. Rose herself had been ill in the last months, with sleeplessness and indigestion. Her eyes and nose were always reddened, and she complained everywhere of the food. At the same time, she had become more religious and attended early service every day. She ran to religion, as it were, for nourishment.

'You should not be bitter against me, Ella,' she said. 'You don't think I like to see you unhappy, you don't think I enjoy having to plot and meddle.'

Ella rose and walked round Rose in order to put into Amanda's hand the coral and bells, a present from Ernest, which she had dropped on the rug. Then she returned to her seat. Amanda's short arms, jerking in the air, rang the bells with sudden jangles of metal, and each time she did so Ella looked at her – that is, towards her – as if through Rose's back. But she did not smile.

'I'm sorry to have to ask you for anything,' said Rose in a voice that trembled with anger and weariness, 'but I think that we ought to meet Bessie's train. It is due to her, after coming all this way at a time when she has so many troubles of her own – Ruth so ill, William getting such bad reports, and James so depressed.'

James was depressed, as all the family knew, because he had not received a knighthood in the birthday honours; and perhaps Rose felt in Ella's silence, which was for her expressive in varying degrees, a criticism of her hero. For she continued, 'Perhaps you think Bessie has not such great troubles, but then you have always taken a different view of matters of principle. We know that James is above wanting honours for himself. What is shocking to him and to us all, is that they should be given to men like Beal and Wilkins, who are a disgrace to the name of scientist.'

There was a crash of bells as Amanda hit herself on the forehead and Ella's lips moved. She was whispering encouragement and approval in her imagination. 'Bessie has a heavy and important task,' said Rose 'and I hope you will be nice to her. She has come a little sooner than I expected, but it's not for us to choose Bessie's times – we have nothing to do, and she is very occupied with a thousand anxieties. And after all, Ella, we have to make a decision sooner or later, we have to take the bull by the horns.'

There was a pause. Rose frowned and then smoothed away her frown. 'And I wonder, darling Ella, if, for your own sake, we ought not to have something ready in our minds before Bessie's arrival. Bessie is sometimes a little hasty and reckless. She doesn't always consider feelings as she ought.'

Ella leant back on her rock to see Amanda behind Rose. It was conceding Rose's existence, but in a manner which suggested that it was not in a desired place.

'Of course,' said Rose, 'the usual plan in a case like this is to arrange for the baby to be adopted, and I'm told there are various societies which arrange for such adoptions.'

Ella got up from her stone, hastily picked up Amanda and put her in her pram. Then just as she turned away she found words strong enough to break through the wall between Rose and herself. 'You took away my husband by your lies, but you shan't take away Amanda. And I hate you.' Then she wheeled the pram towards the steep path which led towards the road. She pushed desperately to escape from Rose, but Rose did not follow.

Ella's idea was to appeal to Bessie. They had always been close friends, and Bessie was a mother. Ella relied on Bessie to understand the impossibility of separating a mother from her baby, three months old. And Bessie had great prestige in the family. Not only with her father, who still adored her as his pet, but with Rose herself. As a married woman, the wife of a man who, if forgotten by the world, was still to Rose great and influential, the mother of nine children, Bessie naturally assumed the place of chief among the Venn women, and Rose always accorded it to her.

'Bessie will tell her that it's perfectly wicked of her even to think of such a thing,' said Ella to herself, toiling up the street towards her lodgings, and as soon as she had put Amanda in the landlady's hands, she hurried to the station. She hoped, by being on the platform, to catch Bessie before she could see Rose.

The train was not due for an hour, and Ella walked about the streets, sometimes calm in the assurance of Bessie's support, sometimes in terror. 'But of course,' she said to herself, trembling with defiance, 'I don't care what anyone says. I shall simply – go my own way. Yes I shall take Amanda and I shall say to them, 'You aren't my family any more. You are simply nothing and nobody to me.'

Suddenly, to her astonishment, she saw travellers streaming from the station with bags, children, spades and buckets. The train had arrived. She rushed into the crowd and struggled towards the platform. She was in tears of despair. 'How could I not see it was time, and now Rose will be there.'

But Ella, when, at last, breathless, she reached the platform, found Bessie still alone. She was standing among the luggage pointing out to a porter her different bags and boxes. Bessie, like

Rose, never left home even for one night without several pieces of luggage.

Bessie at forty-four looked older than Rose, who was nearly eight years her senior. Rose's hair was still dark, and Ella's was pied with grey, but Bessie's had long been grey, and was now beginning to turn white. This had made her little yellow wrinkled face, full of impatience, seem younger at a distance; but the woman herself appeared like a grandmother. Bessie was very thin. She had ruined what was left of her health nursing the child Ruth, who, at more than a year old could not speak and could hardly feed; who was probably diseased in brain as well as body. But Bessie was determined to rear her. One would have thought that this one sickly baby, kept alive almost at the cost of its mother's life, counted for more to that mother than all the rest of her children.

Ella flew to embrace her, and Bessie, whose first kisses had been merely routine, reminded by Ella's warmth that she needed comfort, pressed her in her arms and said, 'Poor Ella, what a time you must have had!'

'Bessie, has Rose told you?'

'Yes, the green bag,' said Bessie to the porter, tapping her foot. 'How stupid the railway is, it loses everything.'

'Bessie, darling, you know what Rose did – she drove Ernest away.'

'I told you to look in the van,' said Bessie to the porter. 'And now perhaps you will get me a cab, if they haven't all been taken.'

Bessie was imperious with all porters, servants, and yet she was always well served. She gathered up her parasol, book and cushion, and turned to take Ella's arm. She had been lame since her last confinement, and was obliged to wear an iron on her hip.

'Cranage,' she said, turning on Ella her prominent eyes, which seemed always brilliant with pain and contempt for pain, 'you were well rid of that fellow.'

'Oh, Bessie, and after the way you encouraged him. People said you were in love with him.'

'People!' Bessie ejaculated, with a contempt which even Rose could not have touched, a violent scorn. 'They say, let them say. I was sorry for your Ernest. He certainly needed a woman to take him in charge. But he was a good-for-nothing. I simply hadn't the time to pump some backbone into him; it wasn't fair to the children. Is that the only cab you can get me – what a wretched object. I suppose it's full of fleas, and that horse is obviously lame all round. But this Government does nothing for anybody, except creatures like Beal. Help me up, dear.'

Ella placed Bessie in the cab with solicitous affection. Nothing that Bessie could do or say ever changed the love of her sisters, a love of which the sources were mysterious even to themselves. She was still the adored pet of the family, and her careless tongue, her temper growing always more impatient, were never resented. Rose would sometimes reprove her, but only from a sense of duty. Ella would fight with her, but never, as with Rose, retire into sullen anger. Now even while she was furious and revengeful, her touch, her thoughts were full of affection. 'Are you comfortable, darling; it's not far, thank goodness.'

'Thank goodness, with this horse, it's a perfect Ernest of a horse, ready to fall down any moment out of sheer discouragement,' and placing her parasol across her knees like a weapon, she gave Ella a look of indignant defiance.

As the cab jerked and creaked forward, Ella gathered her forces. 'I see what it is,' she said at last. 'You've turned against Ernest because he went away with me.'

'Don't be a goose, Ella. Though it *was* a little surprising – he was kissing me only the day before.'

'That I do not believe, or, if it's true, then it's simply disgusting. That you should allow it.'

'What did it matter if it gave the poor wretch any comfort to kiss an ugly old hag like me. And he was so terrified; but I daresay that was half the attraction.'

'What would James think of you?'

'I told James *everything* about Ernest from the beginning.'

'Oh, Bessie, you mean to say he allowed it?'

'I put it in such a way that he had to be sensible; there's a certain advantage in men's having such a tremendous respect for their own dignity.'

'I see you are just as disloyal to James as to Ernest.'

'You really are too much of a goose, Ella, and don't put James and Ernest in the same basket. James is worth hundreds and thousands of Ernests – James is a man, a great man. I know that people rather laugh at him and, of course, he hasn't been a popular success like Beal and Wilkins. They are rich and knights, somebodies, while poor James at sixty-seven is still quite poor, and nobody in the public eye. But who cares for the public. If it can't understand the difference between a man of real character and cheap pushing mountebanks, it can take the consequences, and be beaten by Germany. James says the German ships are better already because our admirals are uneducated men who despise science, and the Germans are really scientific-minded men.'

'But Ernest is a man of true character, too.'

'He isn't a man at all. What did he ever *do*? Why, even Wilkinses even Government pets and birthday knights are better than Ernests. They do do *something* – they aren't just ninnies and poor rags. You were well rid of your Ernest, Ella. You ought to thank God on your knees. The *real* question is the baby.'

Bessie gave Ella another defiant glance and repeated, 'The baby, and if you want me to do anything about it you'll have to decide at once, because I can't stay away from home a single hour beyond Thursday morning. Even now I'm on hooks.'

'But there's nothing to be done about baby,' said Ella. 'She's putting on weight and the doctor is quite satisfied, except that I mayn't be able to go on nursing her for the full time.'

'You don't propose to keep her,' said Bessie.

'Of course I shall keep her, my own child – who else has any right to her?'

'Well, you *do* surprise me,' said Bessie. 'You mean that you're going to flaunt yourself before everybody as the woman who was seduced by Ernest Cranage and had an illegitimate baby. That may be possible to kitchen-maids, but it's certainly not possible to you in your rank of life. You'd be a by-word.'

'I don't care if I am,' said Ella furiously. 'You say yourself that people are simply despicable.'

'All the worse if they can do you harm – real harm. Muddy boots are even nastier on your face than clean ones.'

The cab had reached the lodgings. Ella hastened to assist Bessie to her room. She was surprised that Rose had not yet appeared, but glad of whatever accident had prevented her.

'Now you must have some tea,' she said, ringing. 'Poor Bessie, you look worn out. You need a real holiday.'

'Quite impossible,' said Bessie. 'James can't be left in his present state of mind. But Ella, seriously, you must have some plan.'

'I shall go abroad,' said Ella. 'I shall go to America to Ernest – I don't know why no one answers the bell.' She went out to avoid argument with Bessie. She felt strengthened merely by her firmness with her.

When she returned with the tray she found Bessie hobbling along the upper passage, and cried out, 'But where have you been?'

'With Rose. She's packing. She says she's going away. Ella, you've really behaved rather badly to Rose. She's very wretched.'

'I won't apologize, never, never. She drove Ernest away and now she wants to take away Amanda.'

'She has done wonders for you, Ella, and for me. And you know half her illness and her tempers are because she hasn't married – because she took our mother's place and refused offers. Think what her life has been and what she has to look forward to. We owe Rose every consideration.'

'Then she must let me alone,' said Ella. 'I won't worry her or you or Papa, I'll go to America.'

'You silly girl, do you think that will stop gossip? And how will you live in America? Where will you get the money even for a passage?'

'Very well, I'll stay here and scrub floors if necessary; I scrub floors very well. I'll be a housekeeper. Now I must go and put Amanda to bed.'

Ella marched to the room which she called already the nursery. She now felt completely sure of herself. In one day, she had broken Rose and confronted Bessie's treachery with firmness. Yet within twenty-four hours she was defeated.

Bessie wired to their father, who, even to her surprise, answered at once that he would be with them in forty-eight hours. Rose was still excited against Ella, but she consented to remain in order to receive her father.

CHAPTER 24

As Ella saw him again, in her mind's eye, on the platform of the little station, sandy with children's feet and bright with the cool sunlight which appeared like a quality of the sea breeze, she felt again an involuntary pleasure and tenderness. He was dressed in a very light grey flannel suit of London cut, a round hat of a fine straw, as specially made for him each year, and light brown boots. Venn had never adopted the modern fashion of shoes.

From a little distance he seemed, at seventy-three, with his delicate complexion, his bright eyes, his active upright carriage, like a young man, slightly dandified and old-fashioned, but all the more distinguished. At a near approach he appeared like a well-preserved man of sixty. And Bessie uttered her own delight as well as a compliment when, kissing him eagerly, she cried, 'Oh, Papa, you're younger than all of us.' Ella, too, had delighted in that youth, that exquisite smartness, neatness of her father, while she sought by the quality of her kiss to express her feelings, her love for him, her desire for his forgiveness and sympathy.

'Theo sends his love, his special love,' he said, smiling at the three women.

'Dear Theo! How is he? How is the picture?' cried Ella.

Theo, for three years past, had been painting the masterpiece which was to confirm his reputation.

'It seems to me very good, yes, a fine thing. I only hope it won't be above people's heads.'

'Theo mustn't mind that,' said Bessie. 'What do the people know about anything?'

'We can't always ignore people's prejudices,' said Rose, causing a moment of embarrassment. She apologized for bringing her father away from his annual holiday in Paris. 'We did not mean you to come, Papa, but only to tell us what ought to be done.'

'My dear Rose, a letter would not have been enough – this is altogether too serious.' And now they could see that the old man was much agitated. For a moment he seemed tremulous, he looked almost his age. Indeed, as Venn grew older, he had become more fearful of public opinion, more conservative. He no longer encouraged young men to come to the Villa and make epigrams; and he disapproved very much of the new Liberal Government, so far removed from Gladstone's economy. His scepticism had penetrated so far that he did not believe the world could be much better or worse. He was accustomed to say of any situation, 'It seems bad to you, perhaps – but think how much worse it might have been.' Any threat to his comfort at the Villa, even a change of servants, would cause him alarm and anxiety.

'Dearest Papa, you're too tired,' said Rose anxiously. 'It has been too much for you.' She was nervously effusive after her quarrel with Ella.

'No, my dear,' taking her arm, 'I don't blame you in the least – you have done very well, very well indeed,' and suddenly recollecting Ella's part in the family crisis, which had upset him so much, he turned quickly to her and gave her a supplementary kiss. 'My poor Ella, you have been very unlucky. But never mind, the great thing is not to blame yowself, and you will find we shall contrive something.'

Ella had been so moved by this kindness that she had burst into tears, an act so embarrassing to her father that he had quickly withdrawn and left her to be consoled by Rose. And since he would not travel four in a cab, she did not see him again until, about an hour later, after he had had a rest and a brandy and soda, Rose brought her to his room.

Venn had tried to avoid this interview so painful to him, but Bessie and Rose had assured him that it was necessary. And he faced it like a hero. For it was probably a greater trouble to him after his thirty years of self-indulgence than a major operation.

He had made Ella sit down with him, not on his trouser-knee, but on the arm of his chair, and spoken to her in a voice of which the slight smell of brandy and cigar mingled, discreetly masculine, with the more delicate scents of his soaps, hair wash, and handkerchief, a compound which for Ella conveyed the sense not only of her dear Papa, but of a world beyond her imagination, the world of the elders, those masters of life and wisdom who made and enforced, or broke laws, according to their own mysterious wills.

'My dear little Ella,' said Venn. 'My poor child, don't think I'm going to reproach you. I know how much you have suffered. All of us feel for you, my dear, but we can't help you so well as we should like unless you agree to be reasonable.'

'Oh, Papa!' Ella began to shake.

'One moment, my darling. The word reasonable sounds very alarming to you, but have you thought of your new responsibility?'

And he spoke of her duty to her baby's future. He pointed out the great disadvantage to the baby of being a known illegitimate child. 'Whereas, if wc could place her in a good home – a recommended home, where she could be adopted, she would start life without a definite stigma. We might even be able to assist her later on, by a little settlement, or an outfit for service.'

'For service, Papa?'

'If it were found suitable to train her for service – good service, of course.'

'Oh, Papa, what are you thinking of?'

'My darling!' Venn spoke with firmness of tone, he was quickly tired by obstinacy. 'We can't pick and choose in this world. And especially not in your position. I do not accuse you or reproach you. I know your crime is purely against convention, but we have to remember that it is often more dangerous to break a convention than a law. The punishment is so much more cruel. I should not be doing my duty if I let you expose yourself and your baby to its action. It would destroy you both.'

'Oh, Papa, how can people be so cruel?'

'They are perhaps not so much cruel as stupid and rather selfish. But stupidity and selfishness are terrible enemies, indeed, the most terrible. They destroy every good thing and you can't even reason with them, especially when they take it upon themselves to act in the name of our best and noblest feelings. Even of a mother's love. My darling, I can understand how you feel towards your baby, your poor, helpless little baby, who starts life under such a grave handicap. You are naturally affectionate, and you love your baby with all your soul. But have you thought what a temptation that may be? My darling, you are not going to be stupid and selfish, you are not going to ruin your dear little baby's life.'

Ella was already in a passion of tears. She sank on her knees, her head fell on her father's lap. 'My darling child,' he stroked her grey head, 'you are too wise, too loving.'

'Dear, darling Papa,' said Ella, as she remembered that homily, once more with tears in her eyes. 'And he had come straight from Mrs Wilmot in Paris. He always arranged for her to meet him there, and they even lived together in the same hotel. Yes, the same suite. Because Theo didn't mind and said it didn't matter in Paris. Poor Papa, it was a dreadful nuisance for him to break off his holiday – how he must have hated it. I remember how tired he was that night, and how relieved he looked next day when at last he was in the train and everything was settled and he was going back to Paris. Darling Papa.' She breathed the name with a tender smile. 'How he hated any fuss.'

And two or three days later, finding a good portrait of her father, she took it to Amanda. 'You should have this, darling, you are so like him. I always think – you have his eyes. And you're so good-natured.'

'I should like to be like him,' said Amanda. 'He seems to have managed his life rather well.'

'Oh yes, he was so restful.' Ella looked anxiously at her daughter. 'Dearest, you shouldn't frown – you are getting such deep wrinkles, and they'll make you look old before your time.'

Amanda was in her room lying stretched at full length on the counterpane. It was ten o'clock in the morning and she was fully dressed in rather a dirty pink frock and the down-at-heel slippers which she wore for comfort while she did household work. For Polly was willing but not very capable.

'But how are you darling? How is your headache?'

'I haven't one.' Amanda sat up and put her feet to the floor. 'Can I do anything – is there anything to do?'

'Dear me, your stockings.'

'Yes, they're scandalous – I haven't had time to get any new ones. That is, I've all the time in the world, but somehow I don't bother.'

'Have you heard from Robin lately?' Ella asked the question with a careless air to hide its connection with her course of reasoning. But Amanda did not mind being analysed by Ella's very simple methods. She answered promptly, 'No, we agreed not to write.'

'Oh dear, have you quarrelled?' Ella raised her eyes from Amanda's laddered stockings to her face.

'No, but Kathy is going to have a baby, so he thinks he can't leave her.'

'Oh dear.' Ella was overwhelmed. 'Oh, my poor child – what bad luck. But of course we ought to be very glad – yes, poor little

Kathy – how nice.' Suddenly she kissed Amanda, who touched her cheek and said, 'It was rather a surprise.'

But that new community between the two women which gave them often so close a feeling of each other's minds, though it made Ella more tactful, seemed often to irritate Amanda. She looked at Ella for a moment with her tired eyes, which, with their fatigue, seemed to have a new boldness, and said at last, 'Kathy offered not to have the baby, but we weren't going to take the responsibility.' And Ella, meeting Amanda's look which defied her to be shocked, as always coloured and looked frightened. 'Offered not to have – oh, dear, what do you mean?'

'You know what I mean, Aunty.'

And Ella reflected, 'Yes, Dorothy and Iris used to speak like that to Bessie. It made Bessie angry with them, and I was angry, too.'

'And we couldn't trust her either,' said Amanda angrily, combing back her hair with her fingers.

'Robin has treated you very badly,' said Ella, feeling Amanda's discomfiture.

'It's not poor Robin's fault, it's just a silly accident. It's really rather funny.' Amanda spoke in a tone of exasperation. 'It makes you laugh.'

'Oh no, it's not at all funny when you'd – got settled to Robin.'

'Kathy is the right woman for Robin,' said Amanda. 'She knows how to manage him; probably he doesn't really want a wife at all, only a mistress. Mistresses are much less trouble.'

'Yes, I think perhaps – he wouldn't have suited you.'

'I don't expect it's very difficult to learn the tricks,' said Amanda, going out of the room. And Ella, scarlet, said to herself, 'How she has changed. But she is lost – so bewildered. I shall have to be very tactful. I mustn't say a word about Harry's being her real true friend – not for a week or two at the shortest. No, that wouldn't do at all.'

But the same day she spoke to Polly about Brook. Polly was laying lunch on the kitchen table. The three women had abandoned as by common consent both class distinctions at meals, and even distinction of food. They all lived upon tea, bread and jam, seed cake, eggs, and an occasional rasher, taken either from some bare table corner, or at best, from kitchen plates on a spread napkin.

'Yes'm,' said Polly, 'it's about time for 'em to be dipping,' and Polly, who quite understood the significance of Ella's enquiry, brought news next day that the Brook sheep were to be dipped on Thursday 'up to Mr Okey's new dip on Brook hill.'

'Thank you, Polly,' said Ella. 'But I couldn't trespass on Mr Okey's ground.'

'You've often been on Okey's fields,' said Amanda. 'Why shouldn't you go to the dip?'

'I hardly think there'll be time on Thursday,' said Ella. 'But it would be nice to see the Brook sheep again.'

On Thursday morning, Ella took Amanda to shop in Brook village, but the girl was not surprised to find their course deviating into the lane which passed Okey's dip.

'You want to see the dip?' she said.

'Does this lead to the dip? Why, so it does. There it is – and I do believe – yes, Harry is there. What a surprise.'

'Didn't you know he would be at the dip?' said Amanda.

'Yes, I believe I did. I believe old Bobby said something about it yesterday when he brought the eggs.' She opened the field gate. 'But it is always nice to see Harry. Oh dear, there is someone else there.'

'It's Mr Sangster from the bank. Do you want me to marry Harry and be a labourer's wife after all?'

'Oh, what nonsense!' said Ella. 'Harry will never be a labourer, he is far too clever and hard-working.'

'But then he is rather unambitious,' said Amanda, 'and rather too fond of the girls. He must be rather feckless to get into such trouble about girls.'

'Harry has never had a chance,' said Ella, indignantly.

'But don't people who succeed in life make their own chances?'

'How can they unless they have some money first? How can they do anything without a start?' Ella perhaps looked upon money as a quality like health, given or withheld by fate. She had no idea of accumulation.

Mr Okey had designed his dip at the top of the Brook vale, two years before, in the latest style, to let to his neighbours, and to lend to his friends. It was built of concrete, like a narrow deep plunge bath with a gentle declivity at one end, and possessed its own water supply from the clear stream which ran from the moors above the vale. A rough shed with a roof of corrugated iron, some wire fences, and pens for sheep made of hurdles, broken gates, and an old bedstead contrasted with the formal neatness of the concrete. Mr Okey was a good farmer, but he did not trouble about looks.

At this moment, in the bright haze of mid-July, when every particle of the air was a mirror, and every patch of rust on the shed roof, and tangle in the wire, was displayed as clearly as if lighted for microscopic examination, the scene had less beauty in the common sense of the word, than animation and interest. The sheep to be dipped were still being driven into a large pen on the right, from which a narrow swing gate led to the dipping bath. Harry and old Bob, armed with implements resembling toothless rakes, were pushing the sheep one by one into the dip, from which they scrambled up a ramp and passed into a second pen at the roadside, where they stood dripping among pools on the trodden earth and sickly grass, poisoned by arsenic.

The barking of the old dog Shep, cantering to and fro on his stiff legs, which seemed to be made of wood, as his coat was like that of a woolly toy, much moth-eaten, the bewildered maaing and baaing of the sheep, the shouts of a couple of village boys, composed an action at once calm and tense. Dogs, boys, and men, patient of necessary toil, but ready to be extremely impatient with unreasoning hitches, had the looks which, in women, go with a troublesome wash-day. Even the gentleman in rather loud reddish tweeds, whom Amanda called the bank man, was grimly busy. With his spudded stick in one hand and his cap in the other, he was assisting old Shep to drive the last of the flock into the waiting pens. His bald head and bandy legs seemed to exclaim, 'We're all farmers, working farmers, here – men of the land. Don't ask silly questions just now.'

The shape of the action was like an hour-glass; the pens at each end were the bowls, the sheep pouring through the dip, the sand, and the dip itself, the waist. Its narrowness enabled the two ladies to come close to the dippers, unstopped by any fence. Harry, who faced their way allowed them to come within five yards without notice; then finally planted his staff between his legs, took his pipe from his mouth and lifted his hat backwards off his head.

Ella, excited by the scene, smiled with encouragement and cried, 'How lovely your sheep look – I mean, oh dear, Mr Okey's sheep.'

'Yes, Miss Ella, they're not too bad.'

Amanda stood a little behind. Although she had foreseen this meeting she was annoyed with Ella for contriving it. She had not seen Harry since their encounter at the Villa hay-cutting, and was the more conscious of having avoided him.

'They're so clean,' said Ella, as if no other sheep but Brook sheep could be so clean.

'Yes, Miss Ella, they've been sheared.'

'And now you've washed them.'

'Why, no, Miss Ella, we're dipping 'em. We used to wash 'em, but washing sheep has been going out this ten years.'

Amanda felt a touch in her hand as of ice. Startled, she did not move the hand but looked down, and saw that Flash had just placed his muzzle in her palm. His eyes were raised to hers with so wretched an expression that she stooped and patted his head. The dog gave a growl, but also moved his tail from the root, showing at once his distrust of sentiment and his tolerance of Amanda.

'Going out,' said Ella. 'Now isn't that strange that you should have fashions in farming, too. What can we do to help, Harry? We want to be really useful.'

'Why, Miss Ella, you mustn't get dip on your dresses – perhaps if you could stand over there by Mr Sangster to stop the sheep from breaking out that way. Good morning, Miss Amanda,' with another backwards flick of the hat.

The Miss annoyed Amanda. She looked at Harry with a frown, meant to be noticed. But just at that moment he uttered one of his peculiar yells at the boy who was supposed to be in charge of the further pen. These yells, which had a ferocious sound, were actually performed by a routine action of the muscles. Harry's face would spring into a form of rage, and then at once, like a rubber mask when the pressure is relaxed, return to its normal expression of experienced or rather sardonic patience, an expression common among farmers' sons, working for other people.

'Is that really all we can do?' Ella cried, disappointed that she could not sacrifice at least a frock in the cause of farming. But Amanda, willing to avoid Harry, was already guiding her towards the nearest slack wire. 'We mustn't be a nuisance,' she said urgently. 'Harry's annoyed.'

Mr Sangster greeted them with warm handshakes. Heaven knows what he thought of the Venns and their affairs, but his manner was one of delight. 'I hear you've taken over Brook Farm,' said Amanda.

'Not exactly, Miss Venn. We've asked Mr Okey to manage it for the meanwhile. But we're looking for a tenant.'

'Why doesn't Mr Okey take it himself?'

'He thinks perhaps he has enough.'

'And Brook has gone down.'

Mr Sangster was silent, but with such blandness that even his silence did not give away his opinion.

'And is Harry Dawbarn back at Brook?'

'Not exactly – I think he's only taking on odd jobs – like the dipping today.'

'Harry's very capable – he's wonderful with stock.'

'Yes, certainly. Oh yes,' cried Mr Sangster, managing to convey by the hearty good nature of his agreement that it was only good nature, and that, in fact, Harry's skill as a farmer was not by any means established. 'So I've heard. Oh, certainly. Hi-hi-hi-ee,' and he sprang with the agility of a middle-aged man, a prompt but self-conscious liveliness, to wave back a ewe as she turned back from the gate.

The last of the flock were now entering the dip, and Harry uttered another of his ferocious cries. 'Flash, Flash, Learner. Where's Learner?' Learner was a young rough-haired terrier who was learning to catch rats at Brook. He had been tied to a stake behind the shed, where he had been barking, biting himself, and tying himself up in the string for the last half hour. Now Ella, gladly seeing a means of being useful, went to untie him. Harry was still calling 'Flash, Flash! Dom that dog.'

Dom was Harry's polite curse, used in the presence of ladies. And at once, modifying his furious look he called, 'Ah, Miss Amanda, but I'm forgetting, you're a visitor today.'

Amanda's aloofness at once disappeared. She was highly susceptible to the contact of real persons, as distinct from ideas about them, and, like Ella, she could not bear to be at variance with anybody. 'But Harry, of course I'll dip Flash. I'd love to.' The eagerness of her own voice startled her and made her turn red. She felt Harry's penetrating glance while he affected only to be busy. 'Shep – Shep – dom you! Shep!'

'Oh, look at him,' said Amanda, fascinated by the old dog's extraordinary gait.

Shep, having done his duty by the sheep, was now moving towards the edge of the bath – but with an action quite undoglike, sidelong, stiff-legged. He seemed like a wooden dog pushed along by some invisible hand, to which, nevertheless, he accorded a sad obedience.

'How he hates it,' said Amanda. 'And yet he knows he must.'

'Get on, you.' said Harry. 'Hi, Flash.'

Amanda turned quickly to catch up Flash, who uttered a growl which was really a groan. For he turned up his eyes at the same time and followed the growl by a whine. Amanda gripped him round his barrel chest, under his long arms, and carried him to the dip. She wished to lower him gently into the filthy liquid, now dark red as blood, so that it should not splash his eyes. But as usual the stupid dog gave a violent twist in her arms and fell in over his head.

'Oh, Flash, you are a donkey!'

'He's a pet, that's his trouble,' said Harry. 'We spoilt him at Brook – in the good days.'

The speech invited Amanda to remember the good days. She perceived it and said nothing. Harry pushed Flash under for a second time.

The silence all at once became unendurable to Amanda, and she said, 'Is it really true that Brook is gone for good?'

'That's right.'

'But—' again she hesitated; then fell to the pressure of what good feeling required: 'What is happening to you, Harry?'

'I'm going to New Zealand,' said Harry, 'soon as I can get. Dom you, Shep, jump in, you old fool.'

'Isn't that rather far?'

'I was entitled to go before,' said Harry, 'before Fred went into his garage. Father said I might.'

'But won't you miss Brook and Ancombe?'

'I don't know yet, but it's only getting used to somewhere else. I should think I'd do that soon enough. Get on in, you dom fool, Shep, you know you've got to do it, so why can't you have sense,' and taking Shep by the wool, like a sheep, he pushed him sideways towards the dip. The old dog neither assisted nor resisted, he became simply an inanimate lump of dog.

'Stand you back, Miss Amanda, you don't want to be splashed.' He pushed Shep over the edge and then thrust him under with the staff.

'Why Miss, Harry?' Amanda asked, and added hastily, 'But it doesn't matter.'

Harry made no comment on this, and Amanda felt that he was already separating himself from all Brook, including herself.

'Doesn't Mr Okey need a manager?'

'Mr Okey is his own manager. He isn't a man to keep a dog and do his own barking. Go on, Shep, you needn't be so proud. If you had no ticks you wouldn't need dipping.' He splashed the dip

behind the old dog, who was walking up the ramp without any of
the frisks by which the sheep had expressed their relief, and
stopping while still knee deep in the water, he gave his thick matted
coat a shake which sprinkled the dippers from head to foot.

'Look at the old brute,' said Harry. 'He did that on purpose. He
was so glad to see me again that he nearly choked himself, and
now he's just as stubborn an old fule as ever – won't do a thing as
I want it.'

'He'll miss you if you go to New Zealand. You won't come back
from there.'

'And will you miss me, Miss Amanda?'

'Oh, look at Flash!'

Flash, having bobbed up from the bottom was stretching his long
arms across the concrete sides of the bath. Too stupid to follow
Shep up the slope, he had yet contrived, by sheer strength and will,
to climb so far up the side, and hung there now staring in front of
him with an air of grim humiliation. His long face might have been
that of some grandee, after the contemptuous ill-treatment of the
mob.

Amanda, having put the dip between herself and Harry, dived
forward and with a heave of her strong shoulders, lifted the dog to
firm ground. He walked off then with his slinking gait, turning in
his hind toes, but suddenly stopped, raising his head and eyes
towards the girl, and looked at her as if to say, 'Shall I bite her or
thank her?' Then slightly waved his tail and stalked down the hill.

'What did you do that for?' Harry was saying. 'Look at you,
Amanda, dip from toe to breast.'

'Never mind, Harry, it's an old frock. Don't bother.'

'Ah, stand still, my dearr, and let me wash you properly.'

The dear made Amanda blush. But now she submitted to Harry,
deliberately and patiently, as to a necessary fate. She said sadly, 'I
can't believe you're really going'

'I'd better,' he said, picking up her skirt with his hand and
splashing water over it. 'And I should have thought you would
wish me to go, Amanda. You used to say I had not enough
ambition.' Amanda did not answer. She was enjoying a moment of
prudence and reserve.

'Pinmouth Fair is next week,' said Harry, taking another handful
of water and dashing it on the thin cotton frock.

Amanda was silent. Harry gave her an enquiring look, and then
turned to pull up the plug which emptied the dirty water of the dip

into a sump. He said then in a gloomy voice, 'I'd have a right to blame myself if I didn't go now I'm disgusted. Twenty-nine next month; it makes me sick to think how I've wasted the best part of my life. And now, just on my middle age, to take a turn downwards and not even to work my own land – no, I'd be entitled to shoot myself if I didn't go.'

'Yes, of course you ought to go, Harry.'

'Well, that decides me, then. Yes, that's all I wanted. I'll get the ticket today. I'll write to Plymouth by the afternoon post. Bless you, my dearr, that's the kindest and friendliest thing you could have done to me.'

Amanda, startled by this responsibility, answered, 'But Harry, you don't need me to tell you what to do.'

'No, no, I wouldn't do that. I wouldn't put it upon you, Amanda, it wouldn't be fair to a girl. It's not that you've pushed me into it, but you haven't pulled me back and made me a bigger fule than I am.'

Harry hauled up the sluice to fill the bath with fresh water. 'Yes, it's a kind thing of you – not to pull me back.'

'How could I?'

'But seeing you're letting me go so far, you mid come with me to my last Fair.'

'But Harry, you mustn't put things on me.' Amanda was indignant. She reacted, like a bird that has walked into nets, with a sudden flutter. 'And you know I couldn't leave Aunty alone in the house.'

'But if I asked your Aunty to let you go?' Harry scrubbed the ramp vigorously with his broom.

'You mustn't, Harry – it wouldn't be fair.'

'But it was your Aunty said I should ask you.'

Amanda was at once furious. She frowned and opened her mouth to exclaim that nothing should take her near the Fair. But suddenly her wrath made a sharp turn, and she said, 'Oh, in that case, I'll – think it over – yes, I'll – see if I can't fit it in. When is it?'

It was as though she had turned upon Ella, like a badgered child, and said, 'Very well, if you *will* go on prodding me, you can take the consequences – whatever they are.'

'Well, that's grand,' said Harry, looking at her with surprise and satisfaction. 'Ah, my last Fair will be a good one, I can see that.'

Ella, having caught Learner, under the belief that it was part of her duty, and refixed his lead, was hovering near the couple all aquiver with hope. But she dared not approach and ask Harry, under cover of Learner's barking, 'Have you and Amanda made it up?' For she feared the answer 'No,' she feared to provoke a no. Like most women, she had a strong sense of the fluidity of human relations, of the promising friendships cut off by a shower of rain, a broken suspender needing attention; of the lives directed, in one instant, for their whole course, by a misunderstood glance, a careless word. She occupied herself therefore by crying to Learner, 'Oh, good boy, good boy!' while the dog, quite hysterical after his dip, and obviously uncertain whether he had been complimented or insulted, flew round her legs and tied her up in the lead.

'We'll get drunk and dance under the trees.' said Amanda, with an air of defiance.

'Ah,' said Harry, looking at her with keen enquiry, 'that's new for you to want to be cider happy.'

'Isn't that the right thing?'

'Certainly,' said Harry. 'It's the properest way at the Fair. I was just telling Amanda, Miss Ella, that I should be glad and proud to take her to the Fair.'

'Yes, yes, Harry, that is a very good suggestion of yours, very kind. And I suppose you don't really need me – you don't want me to go with you, Amanda?'

'I gather you told Harry I was to go alone.'

'Yes, yes, I believe I did say that it would be too much for me. I'm too old to dance. Poor boy, poor dog! He's been so good, Harry.'

Learner was tied to a bedstead to get over his enthusiasm, and Harry walked off with Bobby to restore Mr Okey's mops and buckets to the shed in good order. Okey was a particular man.

'How nice that is,' said Ella, as the two women turned down the hill together.

Amanda took her mother's arm, according to her new daughterly habit, and exclaimed with daughterly frankness, 'Nice! That depends on why you did it.'

'What, darling?

'Sent me to the Fair with Harry. One would think you wanted me to fall.'

'To fall, darling!'

'Like Nelly Raft.'

'Oh, Amanda!' Ella started forwards as if to escape from such an idea. 'How can you – and, besides, poor Harry has never admitted

– I'm sure he could never go with such a stupid common girl as Nelly Raft.'

'Nelly must have fallen at the Fair. It seems to be a good place for falling.'

'Oh, but you mustn't suggest – it confuses me so much.' Ella came closer to Amanda, and Amanda shortened her step so that they might move together. Both seemed to brood on the same thought. 'Oh no,' said Ella. 'Oh no, no. And Harry couldn't have had to do with Nelly at the Fair, because it's nearly a year since the last Fair, and the baby has only just been born.'

'I expect she fell at the Fair, and then went on falling – Harry would go after her.'

'Oh no, no,' said Ella, musing. 'I only wanted you – to enjoy yourself. You've seen so little of Harry lately and he's so fond of you. He would be such a good husband, I'm sure, so domesticated and attached.'

'Needing a regular woman,' said Amanda, 'and regular meals.'

'Darling, I wish you wouldn't speak so. It's not like you. If you know how coarse it sounds, and coarseness is not really pleasing. Men don't really like girls who swear and speak coarsely. I know, of course, poor Robin encourages you to talk like that.'

'I'm terribly sorry. Perhaps I did try to shock you, but I am a little worried about the Fair. I didn't really want to go.'

'Then you mustn't go, my dear. No, certainly, you mustn't go. At least,' she reflected for a moment, 'you must come away early, before it's dark. Before it's *quite* dark. I suppose it would be too unkind to Harry not to go at all, but I'll tell Harry that you must not stay after it's dark.' Ella gave a short involuntary sigh. And suddenly she remarked, 'No, it can't be Harry who went with Nelly or Mrs Raft would have brought an action against him. That's the way Mrs Doe married her Gladys to Tom Ould. It's quite the usual thing round here. And the Oulds have been such a happy couple. That nice little boy at the gate was one of the Oulds. Gladys has five or six now. And such a self-respecting, hard-working woman, she keeps her family in wonderful order. You never see Tom going about in a ragged shirt, or unshaved on Sunday.'

Ella now recollected other such stories, and during the next few days she dwelt much on the old local custom of allowing a young couple every freedom until the girl became pregnant, and then expecting or obliging the man to marry her.

'Is that what the Fair's for?' said Amanda. It was in late July, a few days before the Fair. 'To catch husbands?'

'Oh no, no – though indeed it's very hard to bring some of these country boys to the point. And, of course, if they mean to get married, and are hanging back, it doesn't seem quite so – and marriages about here turn out very well, I think. The village girls get such a good training in making a home, and the men are accustomed to look forward to a home.'

The two women were standing near an ancient rustic summer-house by the road hedge. The corner was a wilderness of elder bushes and long grass, with a strong fetid smell of mildew from the summer-house, of which the rotting floor-boards were covered with a greenish fungus. Bindweed had passed through the gothic windows, latticed with basket work, and again out through black holes in the rotten thatch. Its bright green top leaves caught the sun above, and made the only bright and healthy seeming object within view.

'You don't think it matters very much which female catches them?'

'Don't say female, dear – or you may think female – that is so dangerous for a woman.'

There was a silence. Amanda picked a leaf from Ella's breast and smoothed down her dress with a caressing hand. But she was frowning. 'And this summer-house is where Grandpapa used to bring what I mustn't call his females.'

'Oh, please! Robin thinks like that, but you are a lady. And even a village girl is not a female. No, you can laugh at me, but even a girl like Gladys Ould is not a female – she may seem a very humble person to you, but she has a very good sense of her womanhood, and what is due to it. I remember very well that when they were first married Tommy got a little tipsy one night and tried to go to bed without taking his boots off, but she wouldn't suffer him. She said she would leave him if he did such a thing to his wife. Oh, of course, it is amusing – Robin would be amused by it. But it wasn't at all funny to poor Gladys – it was very serious for her. Tom was still a little sulky with her for making him marry her – suppose he had taken her at her word – and she had had to go back to her mother. A nice welcome she would have got at home – there were three other girls in the kitchen eating their heads off. Oh no, it was a dreadful problem for poor Gladys – whether or not she should just put up with Tom's boots, as many poor wives have done, goodness knows! I honour her for making a stand – I think all women ought to feel grateful to her – but you think I'm a silly old Grundy.'

'I'm not laughing at you, dear, I feel more like crying.'

'Crying?'

'I feel Gladys would have an advantage over me. She knew what she wanted and went for it. She caught her Tom, and caged him.'

'No, Gladys is a good girl. She didn't deliberately—'

'You think she was drunk – that would, make it quite respectable, wouldn't it?'

'Darling, you frighten me.'

'Perhaps she got drunk on purpose so as to have a misfortune without losing her self-respect.'

Ella became more agitated. 'Oh, you mustn't – it's so confusing. I know I'm not strict enough – not like Rose. But it's so difficult in these things – life is so difficult, real life. Is that the officer again?'

Ella for some weeks past had been excited by the notion that the village constable was keeping her under observation. There was no obvious reason for this belief. The man passed through Brook every day by bicycle on his usual round. At the moment, he was apparently standing at the corner between the village lane and the main road. Only his helmet was visible, over the hedge, and it was stationary.

'They oughtn't to watch me,' said Ella. 'I tried to tell them everything, but they didn't seem to understand, I suppose men can't understand family matters.'

'Female family matters,' said Amanda. 'No, indeed.'

'I'm not against the Government,' said Ella, 'but I think they ought to leave private people alone.' Ella was gazing angrily at the helmet about ten yards away. 'How can they judge people's minds – and difficulties – things that one does without even thinking at all – one can't understand them oneself – come, dear, he's listening to me.'

'He couldn't hear from this distance.'

'No, perhaps not.' And then suddenly Ella approached the hedge and called out, 'Mr Veale – Mr Veale.'

The constable's helmet gave a slight start and turned slowly towards the voice.

'Mr Veale,' called Ella, 'it's Miss Venn – Miss Ella Venn. I believe you have been making enquiries about me.'

'No, Ma'm.' Mr Veale's voice showed neither surprise nor curiosity. 'I was just passing through.'

'Oh, I'm not blaming you, Mr Veale,' said Ella. 'You have your duty to do. We all have our duty, haven't we? But I'd much rather you asked me what you wanted to know instead of going about the village and asking at shops. Because they don't really know.'

Amanda plucked her sleeve. 'I don't think Mr Veale—'

'Please, Amanda, let me speak.' Ella appeared calm, but this unusual calmness was by itself a mark of her excitement, and turning again to the policeman, she said, 'I wrote to the station and told them everything I could think of.'

'Ma'm.'

'Can you hear me, Mr Veale?'

'Yes, Ma'm.' Mr Veale's helmet disappeared, but immediately afterwards the man himself passed through a gap in the hedge and stood before them.

'You wrote, Ma'm?'

'Certainly – I wrote and told them about my sister's will – that I did not want her to make a new will – and how I lost the draft – but really I think I must have lost it on purpose – and then I gave my poor sister a sleeping cachet, and she died that night. So of course the new will was never signed.'

'Well, Ma'm, if they know at the station—'

'But they don't know that I had a dreadful quarrel with my sister that very night. Yes,' cried Ella, 'and she said to me, I know you want me to die.'

'Perhaps, if you don't mind, Ma'm, I'll ask the inspector to see you.'

'No, please. Couldn't you make a note of it yourself, Mr Veale? I was just going to say—' Mr Veale drew out a notebook and made an entry.

'Thank you, Ma'm, that will be all right.'

'Thank you, Mr Veale. I hope it won't be out of your way.'

'Oh no, Ma'm, I'll just pass it on.'

'Please do, but tell them that really I don't want to be asked any more questions. I am too busy with more important things,' and as she turned away with Amanda she explained mildly, 'I've told them all I know and they can do what they like. Of course, I've probably done it all wrong. I never had anything to do with Government people – not even the gas. Your Aunt Rose did all that. She didn't like them coming into the house, but she would always go and see them. To the very end, when she could hardly walk, she watched over everything.'

Ella pondered and then remarked, 'I thought of telling Mr Veale how fond I was of Rose, and Rose of me. But then I thought he would think I was trying to avoid suspicion. I'm sure the officer would never understand how Rose and I felt for each other. No man can really understand feelings like ours, between two sisters, between women. He thinks Rose and I hated each other, but we were really devoted – yes, devoted. And it was because we were so devoted that things were so difficult, so fearfully difficult. Oh dear, it is so tragic, that when people are devoted they suffer so much. They must suffer. When Rose took you away from me – Rose and Bessie – I thought I should die. Oh, that first night, alone, when my breasts were so full, so aching, I beat my head on the floor. Yes, it is funny to think of – it makes you laugh.'

'Oh no, darling.'

'Yes, it was funny. I lay on the floor and got so cold. I wanted to die – I hoped I should freeze to death. Oh, what misery that was. I wonder how anyone can go hour after hour in such fearful, wretched suffering and not die of it. But it seems that you can't die of misery – you can go on getting more and more wretched and still not die. I suppose God knew what was in store for people and made them so that they couldn't die of pure misery, especially women. I used to think hearts could really break – split open and bleed – so that a woman could bleed to death. And I said to myself that night, My heart is broken and I am dying, thank God! I thought I could even feel the blood going out of it, but of course I wasn't any the worse – I didn't even catch cold. And next morning I had to get up and wash my face and do my hair, and Bessie made me eat something. And all the time I was getting more wretched, more despairing. You think how silly it was – what a fuss about nothing. Why didn't I make a firm stand and keep you, or be sensible and reasonable. But it was not only Rose, it was Bessie who advised me. Yes, I think after Papa, it was Bessie who had most effect.'

'That's what I can't understand.'

Amanda seemed to be protesting against a personal injury.

'Even Rose gave way to Bessie.'

'So you say – but why?' And Amanda, in her suspended existence, became obsessed with Bessie, so that she spent hours brooding upon that mysterious power. The sale had again been postponed until the autumn season. Even furniture movers no longer came to the house. The two women were alone in a place which was neither home nor store; in which everything was growing dirtier and more senseless, more squalid, every day; in which history itself seemed to be bleeding slowly to death.

'And Bessie's children aren't so successful,' said Amanda one night. 'Alice is a fuss-pot, Iris quarrels with everyone, Bertie is really nothing at all – just a nice man – and Dorothy is a greedy snob.'

'Oh, but perhaps they might be worse – so much worse. When you think what people can be.'

'I wonder was she a good mother after all?'

'She had very strong influence.'

'But why? She wasn't clever, she wasn't very wise.'

Amanda was walking about her room in her pyjama trousers. She had just had her bath and was going to bed. Ella, fully dressed, had come to wish her good night. A month, even a week before, Ella would have protested against the girl's half-nakedness and made her put on her coat, but now neither even noticed it.

'Bessie suffered a great deal, so much pain.' said Ella.

'But why did you all give way to her – why did you let her take me away and change your whole life and mine?'

'I remember very well what anxiety she was in,' said Ella. 'Yes, it was specially hard just then, with poor little Ruth so ill, nearly dying, and she was terribly worried about James, and about the boys, Bertie so clever and so lazy. All those clever boys are so apt to be lazy and waste themselves. Bertie, yes, Bertie had just been sent down from Oxford after his first term; and William, who was even cleverer and so good, so anxious to do right – he did so brilliantly at school – and then he had some religious trouble. Of course, his father upset him – James was quite shocked at anyone believing the creed, and William wanted to be confirmed and then afterwards he began to be dreadfully unhappy about the lie in his soul and the sin against the Holy Ghost.'

'I thought William was rather wild, too.'

'No, never, dear. Oh no. Some girl got hold of him in the war, but you know what girls are in wartime, and William was far too sweet-natured to stand up for himself. Bessie suffered dreadfully for William – oh, a thousand times more than for any of the others, except perhaps Ruth. And, of course, when Ruth died, she had you. Oh, I knew as soon as she saw you that she'd take you. She fell in love with you at once.'

'And everyone gave way to her. But why?' said Amanda indignantly. 'I can see *how* it happened, how she took me from you, but why should she be so strong, why should everyone respect her so much because she had a lot of troublesome children? I suppose she pleased herself by having them. We know she did.'

Amanda threw her hair back with an impatient gesture. Her pale cheeks were damp with sweat which made the shadows under her eyes glisten like grey metal. She crossed her arms and gazed at Ella.

'Sit down, darling, and let me do your plaits,' said Ella, and taking Amanda's fine but rather thin hair, she began to plait it into two short tails

'She *liked* having babies,' Amanda repeated in a resentful tone. She sat with bent head, gazing at the floor, while Ella plaited slowly, enjoying the task.

'It was just a physical thing,' Amanda complained. She was calling up before her eyes the Bessie she had known.

Amanda had been twelve when the woman she had called mother, her Aunt Bessie, had died. She could remember her only by glimpses, pictures fixed in her mind by some special circumstance, a scolding or a present. She saw a thin, ravaged face, white as paper, with immense black, furious eyes, under a tall cushion of white hair, and a wide mouth whose thick lips seemed to her, in recollection, very dark, so that they stood out sharply against the white skin; it was a face all mouth and eyes.

She had been terrified of this little fierce old woman, who would silence her own older children, tall men and married women, with a glance, who would ejaculate, in the middle of a party, reproof full of rage and contempt.

'But I must have loved her,' she thought. 'If children love anybody, if they can love, in their souls.' And suddenly she said: 'Of course, everything is so physical – in the nursery. Nature again. But perhaps nature has a soul, a kind of animal female spirit.'

'Where are your tapes, darling? I wish you had ribbons. Tape is so—'

'And Aunt Bessie wasn't even old when she died.'

'Fifty-eight; but she was quite worn out.'

'What a life – but I suppose she never had time to pity herself.'

'Oh yes, poor Bessie – she hated pain so much. From a child. And she had so much. At least you might have clean tapes.'

Amanda got up from her chair and sat down on the bed. She reached out her hand for a cigarette.

'The power of suffering,' she said, dreamily puffing. 'But really it's so stupid, so dangerous. There's no sense in it, that people should have power just because they have suffered.'

'Bessie could be quite frightening when she was in pain. Dearest, you ought to wash your brushes.' Ella was tidying Amanda's dressing-table.

'I suppose Christian martyrs didn't *like* being burnt, but they all wanted martyrdom. They say some of the women used to beg to be martyred.'

Ella had gone from the room with the brushes. But at this moment she reappeared with a large photograph in her hand which she placed among the pile of relics which now almost filled Amanda's room.

'Perhaps it's a female notion to suffer,' said Amanda, and then seeing the picture, she cried plaintively, 'Must we keep any more rubbish. Who is it?'

'I don't know – one of Grandmama's sisters.'

'What a pity you saw her.'

'Yes, but then – I didn't like to think that she would be thrown on the fire – and quite forgotten.'

Both gazed at the picture of the woman, a dark, handsome, pale face with smooth hair dressed in the style of the eighteen-fifties.

'She looks as if she had suffered, too,' said Amanda.

'She must be forty, but she wasn't married. No, I think she lived all her life here, at home.'

'And what a tartar. No, I expect she was very good tempered – in a Christian way. And proud. Quite a triumphant sadness,' said Amanda. No you mustn't burn it, I'd like to keep it. I must find out about her. Would Uncle Dick know? But perhaps she *is* forgotten already.'

'Bessie did her duty, she was so simple – really, like a child.'

This remark was quite intelligible to Amanda. Both women had become used to a talk in which half the words were missing. She said, 'Yes, that's what I mean, and if she *did* have a bad time, why should she seem so tremendous?'

'She wasn't very dignified, no, it distressed Rose to see her waving her hands and walking too fast. But yes, she had dignity – it was rather frightening.'

'Oh, of course, even a child with toothache, especially if it doesn't cry – one wants to walk on tip-toe. One curses God.'

'Such dignity,' Ella murmured. She drifted to the door, then returned and kissed Amanda's forehead. 'Good night, my darling, God bless you.' But she was with Bessie, on the evening when she had issued her sentence, 'You ought to think yourself lucky that the child can be left and that she's so strong and healthy, and that you know what to do. Because it's your plain *duty* to leave her, and if you were as old as I am,' said the woman of forty-four, 'you'd thank God your duty was so plain and simple. It isn't always so plain. I only wish it were. I wish I could always know what my duty was, between James's work and Alice needing sea air and William so unhappy at school and writing for me to come and see him, and now I've left them all to come here, and it seems I'm going to saddle James with Ernest's baby and my poor children with another sister. Yes, I wish to God, my duty was as plain.'

'And she was right,' said Ella, going into her room and sitting down in the faint light of starlight through the window, still uncurtained. 'Duty, duty, duty is the salvation. It's a hard bed but it is a bed: one can be at peace there, one can escape from that misery of not knowing what is right and what is wrong. Oh yes, yes, teach me, O God, make things plainer!'

Just after midnight, Amanda lying, still half-naked, on the outside of her bed in a restless doze, found Ella standing at her bedside. She started up. 'Yes. What is it?'

'Nothing, darling. Did I wake you? I forgot to bring back your brushes.' And going out, she said over her shoulder, 'Dear me, isn't tomorrow the Fair – I'd forgotten. But you have the blue, I had it washed on purpose.'

CHAPTER 25

On Fair day Harry called for Amanda in a borrowed Ford just before six. Amanda had put on her best cotton frock and a flower in her breast; she had expected Harry to be in his best clothes, and in high spirits. She relied on those spirits to revive her own. But Harry came in market dress, breeches and gaiters, an old tweed coat, a very old check cap with a large horsy peak. He was silent, even gloomy. He smoked his pipe as he drove and said only now and then, 'Dom these buses, they've no right to be so wide'; or 'Dom these fancy drivers, they take all the road.'

'How are things?' Amanda asked him.

'The same.'

'And when do you sail?'

'Next boat but one.'

'What date?'

But he made no answer, and Amanda, seeing that he did not want conversation, was silent. She felt now that she had given too much thought to the Fair, and dressed far too gaily. But upon arrival, when the car had been parked and they had taken their first stroll along the little esplanade by Pin river, and back through the grounds, she saw in the other couples a likeness to Harry and herself which was at once abasing and consoling. All the girls, like herself, were dressed in their best summer frocks, newly washed and ironed, so that even the roughest from some lonely cleve had about her the air of freshness and innocence which belongs to flowers. The frocks, representing to Amanda's eye, so much careful laundering, so much anxiety on crowded journeys by bus or car or waggon, had by themselves a touching look of hopefulness and trust. Like children, they seemed to say, 'We have come to be made happy. Don't hurt us.' But the men, like Harry, had market day expressions, reserved and watchful. As they moved slowly along, with the girls on their arms, they kept well away from the booths, as if in fear that those traps for sixpences might be able to bite the money out of their pockets. To the enthusiasm of the girls they answered nothing, or only those retorts meant to cut down too reckless ambition. Thus one red-faced young man to whose arm hung a little breathless girl in a frock like a peony, answered her cry, 'Oh, Clem, the Noah's Ark. We mun go on the Noah's Ark,' with the abrupt question, thrown down over his shoulder, 'Another shilling one – anything more you'd like?'

The booth flares, the festoons of coloured bulbs or candles in glass or paper, hung across the walks and among the trees of the esplanade, were now being lighted, but they served rather to increase the melancholy of the evening than the illumination of the paths.

The sun had sunk behind the hills which rise steeply all round Pinmouth, but the sky was still bright, a thousand times more brilliant in green and gold than the brightest Chinese dragon lamps, so that the effect was rather that of dawn after an all-night party, when no one has troubled to extinguish dying lamps, than twilight, prematurely dressed out with foggy shades and rusted knots of wire. In competition with the brilliance of the whole sky, lanterns, and even the strong acetylene lamps of the fair theatre, could bring out only the pink stripes upon a few square feet of dirty canvas, or throw deeper shadows into the hollow worn face of some gypsy preparing for another night's battle with the crowd. And all these faces seen by glimpses, from sky or lamp, had a grotesque or even terrible look; the foolish terror of sheep; the staring wonder of lunatics, the brutality of the stupid or bewildered; the resignation of cripples. 'And they're all decent, quiet people from villages like Brook and Ancombe,' Amanda thought. 'These tragic looks are only the effect of the lights. Or is it because it is only by these lights and at the beginning of a fair when there is nothing else to do, that one really looks at faces and sees their true shapes.'

'Who are those?' she asked Harry. 'They've passed us three times.' She was gazing at one of the family parties, a big fat woman in black with no neck and enormous shoulders, bobbing slowly along on two lame feet, with an expression of resigned agony; and a little bandy-legged man beside her in a bright blue suit, his huge head covered by a bowler. His handsome, shrewd West Country face, which in a ducal family would have stood for the mark of many noble descents, wore a look of patient amazement. He seemed to marvel at himself for bearing so much and so long. Five children surrounded the couple; a girl of about fourteen, in a bright pink frock, but the black stockings and boots of a schoolgirl; a boy in a new tweed cap and an electric blue bow tie hooked to his collar; and three smaller children, who were revolving round the father and mother like prisoners in an invisible cage. All these children were talking at once, at the tops of their voices, the big girl complaining of something, the boy shouting to his father, the three others pouring out questions, demands, so fast that there was no time for an answer.

'Poor woman,' said Amanda. 'She has a handful. Who is she, Harry?'

'Wickens. From Ancombe,' said Harry.

'What do they do?'

'Horseman up to Fines Barton.'

'She looks worn out already – she's quite lame.'

'Ah,' said Harry, who was staring with cynical and defiant gloom at the boxing tent, where a barker, a sharp-faced young man with a long nose which had certainly never felt a glove, was shouting out the evening's contests.

'Five pounds for the winner,' said Harry. 'I don't think – lucky if he sees five bob.'

'How much does a horseman make?' said Amanda, trying to imagine the life of Mrs Wickens.

'That depends,' said Harry. 'There's the flea circus again. I'm glad the fleas have come. Wonderful patience those chaps have to teach fleas.'

'She can't be more than forty,' said Amanda.

'The first thing is to train 'em not to hop,' said Harry. 'You put 'em in a glass tube. They soon find out that if they hop they bump their heads. Ah,' he stopped again, staring at a tent on which a large picture displayed a woman's head cut off from the neck, from which pipes full of blood branched into a complicated apparatus. 'The Scientific Phenomenon. I know that one. Victim of a railway accident; only the head left and kept alive by special pumps. She is alive, too. She blinks her eyes and answers questions – you going to take my arm, Amanda. I think you'd better or we'll get separated. And it doesn't mean anything at the Fair, everyone does it. But I don't mind if you don't like.'

Amanda obediently put her hand through Harry's arm and they fell into step, close together, a movement of bodily concord which at once produced a current of spiritual sympathy.

'Yes, we must see the fleas,' Amanda murmured.

'Ah, you'll like the fleas. Why, they fight a duel with swords –

it's only twopence, and you can look as long as you like. No crowding allowed.'

They had come full circle, and once more Amanda saw the Wickens family. Mrs Wicken toiling forward; Wicken a yard behind, his eyes on the sky, his eyebrows arched, his forehead wrinkled; the children rushing round their vast mother like little sharks about a wounded whale. Amanda heard her cry in a little piping voice, exasperated and weary, 'Doant ee, Arthurr, doant ee go on. Doant ee, Margy.'

'I'm sorry, Harry.' She pressed Harry's arm.

'I didn't say anything'

'I suppose you didn't know Mrs Wicken before she was married.'

'Phyllis, yes. We're just of an age.'

'Twenty-nine,' said Amanda, astonished. 'But I can see she was a pretty girl.'

'See that chap, quick, on your left.' Harry spoke in a low, urgent voice. 'No, don't stare, look sideways. That's the Miller.'

Amanda had a glimpse of a huge flat clay-coloured face, and two little eyes buried in pits, eyes at once defiant and forlorn.

'Welter weight champion he used to be, but he's gone to fat. We'll go and see him fight if you like. He's slow on his feet, but he's still crafty – wonderful how he draws 'em in to the kill.'

'How many children has Mrs Wicken?'

'Phyllis? Seven or eight. Some died. And there's the horses going up, that chap is always late. But I like the horses, they've got a steam organ. None of this dommed wireless.'

Half an hour later they were completing their sixth round of the Fair. Overhead it was still light, but with greener, darker reflections; while below the thickening crowd had filled the air with a grey dust which lay upon hats, shoulders, even on cheeks and noses, like a clown's powder. The effect, blue-white, orange, red, was theatrical. The squalor of dust, heat, shabby canvas and cheap music, in becoming more dusty, hot and noisy, had also become exciting and picturesque. But the crowds still ambled, the big booths were still empty; no one was trying his strength at the hammer, or shooting at the ping-pong balls which danced so lightly on their fountains.

'But Harry,' Amanda murmured, leaning on the man's arm, 'when does the Fair start?'

'Start? It has started.'

'But nothing's going yet. Nobody's doing anything.'

'No, but they're entitled to see what they're going to do,' he added in his grim market-day tone. 'It's easy to waste money at a Fair – dommed easy.'

The band struck up in the little gardens between the fair and the esplanade, under small cut trees which looked as if they had been designed for a film set representing some German watering-place of the sixties. It was like a pantomime wood in which the demons were waiters in caps, and the nymphs were plump dairy-girls in print frocks, pursued by the nailed boots of labourers, who hunted, however, at a slow walk, saying in dispassionate voices, 'Is that yew, Maggie? I see yew, but I'm not chasing after yew – it's too hot.'

'It's darker,' said Harry at last, stopping to examine the sky. 'In half an hour it will be dark enough.'

'Dark enough for what?' said Amanda, whose feet were burning and who felt already exhausted.

'Dark enough,' said Harry, as if this was a complete explanation. 'We'd better go for supper, not to miss anything. Yes,' he took another expert observation, 'there's just time for supper, but not too much time,' and he hurried Amanda back to the car park as if, all at once, there wasn't a moment to be lost.

In the dark back seat of the car they ate cold chicken, and an apple pie with thick cream, washed down with draughts of thin sharp cider. Amanda knew by experience the strength of this cider, and took care to drink only one glass, a precaution, even in the dusk, at once noticed by Harry.

'Have some more cider, Amanda, it will do you good.'

'No, thank you, Harry. Farm cider goes to my head.'

'Where else should it go?' said Harry. 'Isn't it meant to do so?'

'If I drink too much I shan't be able to walk.'

'Why should you walk? We've done our walking, Amanda, now we're going to be sitting. We're going to the horses, and the wibblywobb, and between times there'll be dancing.'

'Do you want to make me drunk, Harry?'

'No, not drunk, but it's better for you to be lively at the Fair'

'You said it was the music more than the drink that got the girls into trouble at the Fairs.'

'The girls know what they want,' said Harry.

'Do you think so? A lot of the girls look very simple.'

'Most of 'em have got their eyes on a chap – if they haven't been walking out with him.'

'You think that the girls want to catch the men?'

'I wouldn't say that, Amanda. But both sides are willing enough – especially after a few pints of cider and some quick steps.' And after a pause he added, 'It's got to come to 'em some day.'

'Marriage?'

'Whatever's due to come – it's got to come.'

'Poor Mrs Wicken – did she fall at the Fair?'

'No. Phyllis is a Methody, a touchy maid, not but what her first came at the six months.'

'She must have had a terrible hard life to look like that at twenty-nine.'

Harry took a large mouthful of pie and washed it down with a full glass of cider. He then remarked, 'She's come out well, Phyllis. Yes, she's made a good job of it. They think a lot of her in Ancombe. Come on, Amanda, we're late, my dearr.'

The last words were spoken in a new tone, and marked a new phase both in Harry and the Fair. When Amanda returned to the ground she found that not only its appearance had changed under the dark sky, which gave brilliance to the lights, but the people were different. The crowd was more restless and no longer circulated at an even pace. It formed dense knots in front of each of the larger booths, and when it moved, moved in spurts and at all angles. Boys had begun to run about chasing each other. And on the roundabouts girls were crying out.

'Come on, Amanda,' said Harry, 'we'll have a shake-up.'

Amanda was still reflecting on his phrase, 'It's got to come to 'em some day.' And while she permitted Harry to push her through a turnstile and place her in a little tub chair attached to a long metal arm, she was saying to herself, with a kind of resigned wonder, 'I suppose that is the real philosophy of all these people, to take what nature sends and make the best of it. Even to invite what nature has to send.'

Harry and another couple had climbed into the tub, which began to move. Amanda felt her head swim and then suddenly the speed was increased, her back was pressed against the tub, the other girl slowly fell upon her, an elbow was forced into her breast, and the strange young man's knee ground into her stomach. For an instant she was being suffocated, wounded, outraged, while her brain was just about to faint. Then abruptly the speed relaxed, and Harry said in her ear, in a calm detached voice, 'Scream if you like.' The girl breathlessly began an apology for crushing her dress. 'Oh, I am so sorry. Oh dear—' And then her red lips remained apart, her young pink face became redder, and again, as the tub was jerked round the corner, she fell shrieking upon Amanda, and Amanda set her teeth to bear that agony of the brain pressure, the dislocating jerk, and the squeezing, ravaging hands, feet and knees on her body.

Her hair was coming down, her hat was flying off, but her arms were gripped in the tub. Harry, who was perched on the edge of the tub, defying gravity, took off her hat and said coolly, 'That's better.'

Amanda wanted to scream, 'Stop, stop!' but again they were whirling, and again she set her teeth. She was determined not to scream. And this time the speed was greater, the jerk more violent; the girl's nose was in her neck; hands gripped her thigh, she saw darkness in front of her eyes and heard Harry's voice, betraying at least a certain satisfaction, 'That was a better one.' Countless more jerks, whirls, succeeded until she heard Harry say, 'All right, girlie,' and felt him catch her arm and haul her out of the tub. Her skirt was above her waist, her hair over her eyes. Broken, limp, she staggered into the path on Harry's arm. The girl, shrieking with laughter, kept bumping against her and saying, 'Ooh, wasn't it awful – ooh, I'm all to pieces.'

'Harry, please,' Amanda implored him, 'I must—'

Harry propped her against a tree and expertly turned down her skirt, smoothed up one stocking, adjusted her collar, and then, taking her hair in both hands, curled it over her head with his fingers. Finally, he planted her hat upon the hair and said, 'Now I think we could try the horses – that's a quiet one.'

'Please, Harry, not just yet.' She heard to her surprise a note of humble appeal in her voice. Already it seemed that Harry was in the position of dictator.

'But that's a quiet one,' Harry said, 'And we've not too much time if we're going to do the Fair, to do it proper. Come, Amanda, ah, you should have had more cider.'

He hoisted her upon a horse's back, and almost at once she was rising and falling in great sweeps as the machine swung her round far over the heads of the crowd. She was giddy and held on tightly to the spiral brass column in front of her. Harry perched sideways on his horse and, riding it like an acrobat, rested a hand carelessly on her neck.

'Harry, I'm slipping.'

'No, you won't, I've got you safe. This is nothing – wait till we get to Noah's Ark.'

And five minutes later she was clinging to a hard wooden camel which was tearing her asunder while she whirled through a confusion of light and dark at a speed which seemed always to be at the last degree of the unbearable. But always it got faster, driving hard wood more cruelly into her flesh, wrenching her arms from their sockets, and trying to fling her outwards into the crowd. Until sheer agony of bruised bone and blindness of terror forced out of her lips a little breathless shriek. And the shriek seemed more disintegrating than all the knees, elbows, thighs and fists.

For afterwards as, panting, she hung upon Harry's coat, she found herself laughing and thought, 'I must be getting hysterical.' Harry was dressing her; his hand was smoothing, touching, patting over her body which felt naked to that familiar touch and indifferent to its nakedness.

'Oh, Harry – but not that one again – it's too—'

'That's better,' said Harry. 'And now I think you could do with a drop.' He spoke like a doctor administering a treatment. And in fact, Amanda was grateful for the cider as it poured down her hot throat. She thought critically, 'And this, I suppose, is the next step – to get drunk.' Her whole body acquiesced with the suggestion. All her limbs, her feverish, bruised shaken flesh seemed to say joyfully, 'Yes, let us get drunk.'

'We're going on nicely,' said Harry, as he pushed their way towards the Dragon cars. And Amanda, who seemed to herself to be floating after that arm and hand, as boneless as a scarf, felt herself answering 'Yes, we're getting on nicely,' and then crushed with seven or eight others in the front seat of the dragon car, while it whirled her to the roof; clutching at the air, snatching at some stranger's arm to keep from being tossed overboard; thrown suddenly on the floor among a heap of struggling bodies; pushing out with both hands to save herself from being disembowelled. She reflected, 'But how strange, how strange, the whole process.'

For a moment, as she came to the surface, lying on her back across some stranger's legs, with some strange girl clinging to her waist, she saw Harry balanced high on the side of the car, with one arm round the dragon's neck, and his legs derisively swinging out over the heads of the crowd. He was smoking, or pretending to smoke, his pipe, and his expression was careless, almost bored. Harry, as Amanda had perceived, was one of the Kings of the Fair, a recognized king, for he was permitted to do what was forbidden to ordinary persons; to risk his life, to ride the horses sideways on the croup, the switchback, standing. And seeing him on his proud throne at the dragon's neck, she felt towards him a mixture of homage and pity. She thought, 'Poor Harry! So this is his glory,' and at the same time her whole body seemed to rejoice in that expertness and courage, even in that arrogance.

An hour later, perhaps two hours later, for she had lost all feeling of time, she was dancing under the trees. Harry was clasping her so tightly that she seemed to be melting into his body. But she was glad of that support. She was tired not only in body, but will. She welcomed the feeling of a joint existence with Harry, a perfect clockwork harmony, in which her body and Harry's body and the hammering, throbbing music were all part of one long, slow, complicated intoxication. 'I don't mind what happens,' she thought, as her legs, as if of themselves, joggled slowly through the dusty shadows. 'I suppose that's the whole idea, I haven't got a moral left. And yet I'm not drunk, not very drunk. I'm only soaked with tiredness and noise and flesh and indifference.'

'Yes,' she thought, as they sat under the trees, with glasses in their hands. 'Harry is an expert. How strange that I can see that and not mind.' She was sitting on Harry's knee with her arm round his neck, so that the edge of his cap tickled her nose.

'Oh, Harry,' she murmured, 'my feet are worn out.'

'Take some more cider, my dearr, that will cure your feet.'

She noticed that his hand was inside her blouse, and for a moment she felt panic. She took his wrist and pushed it away. Harry's hand at once yielded, so easily and promptly that Amanda was a little ashamed. 'It's so hot,' she murmured.

'Take some more cider, dearr, that will cool you.'

'Oh, Harry,' and she began to laugh, weakly, with closed eyes. She thought in confusion, 'But what exactly – did I come here for? What *is* happening? What *is* it all about?' And it seemed to her that the whole world about her was swimming like a vast roundabout under an acetylene moon, and strings of electric stars to the music of a steam organ.

Harry's hand was once more about her breast, and now she let it stay. She had no more will for defensive action. She lay passive against the rough tweed of his coat and felt him caress her gently, heard him murmur, 'My dearr, my sweetheart, my darling.'

'It's all – so extraordinary,' she reflected. or rather her mind reflected for her, like a little piece of the old Amanda which still, in the midst of a crazy world, kept its brain, its impartial curiosity. 'I'm like two girls, and one of them is putty, and yet this putty girl is not at all amorous. Anything but; she wants to go to sleep, to sleep.'

They were on the esplanade, seeking the cool air before a dance. Amanda, hanging on Harry's arm, opened her eyes on a scene of peace, stability, on motionless ships, reflected in water which, for all its smooth, slow wrinkling, seemed to belong to a world extraordinary for its solid worth and substantial dignity; upon ship-shape railings, useful and undecorated, and the quiet hillside beyond, of which the outline against the starlight had the weight of some eternal horizon.

Three sailors or yachtsmen were beside her, two perched on the rails, so calm, so removed from her fair-day existence, that she glanced at them as if they might appear as strange as they were remote. One was saying in a thoughtful voice, 'Give me a yawl for handiness.'

There was a pause and then another said, 'But now everyone has an auxiliary.'

Again there was a pause. The third spoke.

'Yes, picking up your moorings is not what it used to be.'

'All the same,' said the first, 'you don't *need* to use your engine.'

'It's done away with a lot of seamanship.'

'All the same—'

'But all the same—'

There was a long pause. Then the third remarked, 'There it is tho', and if you don't use it, it's like—'

'Artificial,' said one of them quite briskly, causing Amanda to start and half turn her head. But Harry was drawing her out of earshot, and suddenly she noticed on the quiet seats, within two yards of the yachtsmen, on each side, couples locked together as she had been, a moment before, with Harry. She wanted to laugh. 'Oh, but how funny. Oh dear, how tired I am – how weak. The wonder is not that girls fall, but that any of them don't fall. And of course Harry is cleverer than most, he's really very clever. So cool and professional. Yes, I'm in the best possible hands, or the worst. Oh dear, I can't think and I shan't try. I only hope Ella will be pleased.'

'And shall I be like Mrs Wicken?' she thought, as once more they were dancing, a slow foxtrot to music which wept, which moaned, which suddenly uttered cries of rage. 'Shall I some day find myself struggling with children and house cleaning and poverty, worn out at fifty, and glad at last to fall into my grave.'

It seemed to her when Harry, putting his arm round her waist, guided her again towards the road, that this was bound to be her fate, and that she was strangely resigned to it. 'After all, Aunt Bessie went through it, it was her life, and it was a real life. I mustn't expect happiness, that's the great mistake. No, I mustn't ask, am I going to be happy, or am I being happy? I must simply do what has to be done.'

She was surprised to find herself in front of the car, the door was open and Harry, gently but strongly, was pushing her in. And she was resisting, not by will, but by inertia. She said in a weak and wavering voice, which was yet amused at its own weakness, 'But Harry – we haven't – seen the fleas.'

Harry made no answer. His urgent pressure increased and half thrust her, half lifted her into the car. He drove off, but not along the Queensport road. They were mounting the hill towards the moor. 'Where are we going, Harry?' she murmured. She scarcely expected an answer, but not receiving one, she thought with surprise, 'Harry is not so cool, he's quite excited. Perhaps he's really madder than I am. Actively insane.'

The car was stopped. Harry got out, opened the door beside her and took her by the wrist. She lay inert. 'But Harry – why—'

'I know a place,' he muttered.

'A place,' said Amanda, suffering herself to be drawn limply from the car.

'A quiet place, up the lane.' He gave her waist a hasty squeeze and Amanda reflected, 'Well, really, is this the way one comes to the crisis of one's life. How simple. But, oh dear, I wish I wasn't quite so tired. I'm really too tired – even to – take notice, to get *any* profit. But I suppose that's all part of the system, too. The Fair, the Noah's Ark, the dragons, the cider, the lights, the dancing, the music, what a complicated way to make wives and mothers and husbands and children, and good wives, tender mothers. At least, I hope so.'

'Here we are,' said Harry, stepping down suddenly into a broad, soft ditch full of bracken and long grass. He reached up his hand. 'Nobody'll see us here, my dearr, we can stay as long as we like.' Amanda slipped down and found herself in his arms. She said, 'Oh Harry, you won't hurt me?'

'No, no, it's nothing to mind.'

'No, of course not,' reassuring Harry or herself, she did not know which, but she thought dreamily, 'No, it's nothing to mind, not this part of it. What is serious is what comes after.' Bessie's face seemed to float before her, followed by a vision of the Wicken family. 'A woman's life, a real woman with husband and children – that is really serious, terribly, terribly serious. You can't get over it, never.'

She saw Harry's cap against the sky, he had not troubled to take it off. She reflected, 'Isn't he even going to kiss me first – but no, he isn't very religious. Or, perhaps, it's because – he is so religious, yes, mediæval – they used to dance and juggle in church. Oh God, I am so tired, I could scream, scream.'

When Amanda reached home at three in the morning she was so exhausted, battered in mind and body, that she sat down on a kitchen chair in the hall, heedless of dust, to gather her last forces for the climb. And at once she fell asleep. Suddenly Ella stood before her, like a ghost in a dream, with a dead white face and great hollow pits for eyes. Her look of horror and despair startled Amanda even in her drowsiness, but in the same moment she perceived that the effect was due largely to the position of the hall light, straight overhead.

'Aunty, did I wake you?'

'What's wrong, what have you been doing?' Ella cried in a sharp, shrill voice, very unlike her usual nervous tone.

'Nothing, dear, I was rather tired.'

'But your dress, your hair.'

'You know what the Fair is like, and Harry insisted on all the worst side shows. Oh,' Amanda yawned and slowly raised her stiff body, 'how I long for a bath.'

'Are you sure,' Ella stared at her, 'that nothing's happened?'

'Happened?' For a moment the two women looked into each other's eyes; their minds seemed to rush together, and then as suddenly recoiled. Ella turned red and exclaimed, 'Did Harry – was he nice to you?'

Amanda yawned and said in a lazy voice, 'Harry was an angel.'

'He didn't worry you – to do too much.'

'Really he behaved rather beautifully – and he's going to New Zealand next month.'

'Next month?' cried Ella, terrified. 'To New Zealand?'

Amanda stretched her arms. Her expression was the false absent-mindedness of the child who avoids enquiry into her private affairs. 'Oh dear, oh dear, I feel absolutely filthy, I simply must have a bath.'

'But – aren't you sorry about Harry?'

'Yes,' she seemed to reflect, 'I think I am.'

Ella stared at her with high eyebrows and a wooden face. She was indignant with her daughter.

'I think so,' said Amanda, yawning. 'He's really – so – dependable.'

'He is devoted to you.'

Amanda was silent. She looked sleepily at the floor.

'And if he goes to New Zealand, you'll never see him again.'

Amanda remembered some words exchanged in the car as Harry drove her home. They jumped now into her mind, like the recollections of a dream, set off by some trigger of association. 'And you sail next month?'

'That's right,' Harry had said.

'But what if—'

And Harry had answered in a voice so flat and weary that it could hardly be recognized, 'You could come, too – you'd have to come.'

'Do you really want me, Harry?'

'Ah,' assenting with enthusiasm but without irony to the statement of a fact. And he added with a bitter note, 'A bit too much, it seems. But there, I've always wanted you. You got me.'

'I'm sorry I led you astray.'

''Twas both of us. Dom those night lorries, always on the wrong side,' avoiding a waggon at a corner.

'I have a little money saved, about a hundred pounds. But, of course, that's nothing.'

'Nothing, you call it,' in a tone of reproof. 'I call it a hundred pounds better than that. It mid make all the difference, give us a start.'

Then they had driven in silence for at least ten miles, but in a silence more relaxed, more hopeful. And Harry, wishing her good night, had embraced her carelessly but warmly, and said, 'No, I won't say I'm sorry if you do take fire. No, dom it, and that hundred. It would be a godsend.'

'A godsend,' Amanda reflected. 'But what has He sent, and did He send it?'

She stretched out her legs and groaned, rubbing a bruise on her thigh. 'Oh, I feel as if I had been beaten with clubs. I'm one wound.'

'New Zealand,' Ella exclaimed in tones of despair. 'It's further than Australia.'

'But I might go, too,' Amanda said in an unwilling tone. 'Why not – we might both go, I suppose.'

'Harry suggested that you might go with him?'

'We might – under certain circumstances.'

'Dear Harry,' said Ella, suddenly full of cheerfulness and alacrity. 'But I knew that he would – he's always been so – oh dear, I hope the boiler's not out.' She rushed away. Fortunately the water was hot enough for a bath.

But now Ella could not bear to leave Amanda. She hovered round her with affectionate cries, and even half an hour later, when the girl, bathed and brushed, was lying between the sheets, she could not leave her.

'And so you and Harry – are just as you used to be. Oh, how lucky you thought of the Fair. I am so glad – to see you so happy again.'

'Am I happy?'

'Oh yes, yes – I can see – you're quite changed. But those bruises. Good gracious, you must take care.'

'They are nothing,' And Amanda, in her lazy voice that was meant to shock, said, 'Really, dearest, one would think I was going to have a baby.'

'Oh,' cried Ella, 'you mustn't say such things! It's too serious. Goodnight.' She kissed her warmly and went out, but turned back at the door to say, 'Of course – I should like you – I hope you will have a baby someday – I hope so indeed.'

And walking along the passage she thought, 'What has happened? They must be engaged. But of course she would never tell me, and these young people nowadays, one never knows what they are thinking of. They're so secret – and they get in such muddles. But New Zealand – they must have an understanding. Yes, but why New Zealand?'

And next day she took her walk past Ancombe, lingering in the baker's shop and opposite the little bay, until Mr Sangster came out into the front garden of his new villa, to tie up his climbers. Ella crossed the road and seemed to be passing. Mr Sangster said 'Good morning, Miss Venn.'

'Oh, Mr Sangster, how lucky to see you. How lovely your roses are. You are wonderful with roses. Can you tell me – but perhaps I oughtn't to worry you about business now that you are on holiday.'

'If I can do anything for you, Miss Venn?'

'I was wondering – the Villa, that's my house, our family house, has not been sold yet, but of course it is quite a valuable house.'

'On lease, I believe.'

'Yes, but it is in such good order. My sister spent four hundred pounds on it only five years ago, putting in electric light and a bathroom, and a radiator in the hall. It's a splendid radiator.'

'How long has the lease to run, Miss Venn?'

'I'm not quite sure. I know my sister used to say she would be ninety-eight when it ran out.'

'Who is the ground landlord?'

'I'm not quite sure, but I think it was some estate. My agents could tell you. But what I want to know is, if it would be possible for me to get some of the money for the house now, before the sale. Of course, I shouldn't want it all. I should only want about a thousand pounds, or perhaps two thousand. Yes, I think two thousand would be better.'

'I doubt if you would get as much as that, if the lease is so short. And a material point would be what the money was wanted for – did you mean it for investment?'

'If you promise not to tell anyone, Mr Sangster.'

'I shall treat the matter as one of strictest confidence.'

'I noticed last week that there was a farm for sale, in working order, at a valuation. And it seemed so nice, the house is right down near the water with a view over the estuary.'

'Is that Quarry Farm at Ancombe?'

'Yes, Quarry Farm. And I'm so afraid it will be snapped up.'

'The bank might consider an investment in Quarry Farm. It's been in good hands. When were you thinking of taking over the farm, Miss Venn?'

'Today, if possible.'

'My dear Miss Venn, you can't buy a farm in a day. There are many preliminaries, the architect's report on buildings stock valu-ation, crop valuation. Remember, there are standing crops. '

'Oh, but the money doesn't matter. I don't mind how much they cheat me as long as I get the farm.'

'Today,' said Mr Sangster, carefully not smiling.

'Yes, today.'

'Would you liko me to speak to the manager on the telephone and arrange an appointment?'

'If you would be so kind, Mr Sangster. I'm so stupid on the

telephone. Tell him I must have the farm at once, for family reasons. Quite at once.'

The manager was as politely amused as Mr Sangster by the old lady's urgency. And it was found that the Villa's lease had barely fifteen years to run. But the bank considered Quarry Farm a good investment, and the transaction was arranged within little more than six weeks. Ella paid one thousand four hundred pounds odd for the farmhouse, and the stock, of which four hundred was allowed to stay on mortgage. The bank advanced a thousand on security of the Villa property and certain small investments.

Ella's tenant, Harry Dawbarn, proved acceptable both to the landlord and the bank. He had a name for handling stock, and Mr Hicks of the Quarry had carried a large head on his ninety acres. 'I never saw such beautiful cows,' said Ella, who visited her farm and its tenant almost every day in the first months. 'They are just like our dining-room table, really like polished mahogany. What are they called, Harry?'

'Devons, Miss Ella.'

'Of course they are Devon cows.' Ella breathed the name as if it were delightful to the taste. 'And do they give splendid milk?'

'Ah, I'd like to see their records,' said Harry, who since his sudden change of fortune from prospective emigrant to tenant farmer, had become even a little more critical of stock, crops, weather, of everything in a farmer's way, than before. That is to say, he had become a farmer, rather than a farmer's son, with first hand responsibilities instead of second-hand troubles. 'But Mr Hicks didn't believe in milk records. We'll have to start from the beginning.'

'Mr Hicks said his sheep were a speciality.'

'Longwools,' said Harry with resignation. 'They mid have been a special lot about forty years ago, but they're getting a bit out of date.'

'Why, Harry, I thought you were so pleased with the Quarry.'

'So I am, Miss Ella. I have a right to be pleased. It's a very nice little place. I shouldn't like to say it doesn't need a bit of doing to, house and garden. But all that will come, we can't afford everything at once.'

'I'm sure you will get the best out of it, Harry. I must send you some roses from the Villa, and you could take the trellis, too. It would look so nice up the end wall, especially if you put out a bay window. Amanda, darling, don't you think Harry ought to make a bay window to the upstairs room. It is the best bedroom, but it is really too small for a double room.'

'Perhaps Harry doesn't need a double room,' said Amanda.

'Oh nonsense. Of course Harry will want to get married, some day. Every farm needs a wife, doesn't it, Harry?'

'Since Harry signed the lease he's not so interested in getting married,' said Amanda.

Harry looked at her with a concentrated expression which meant that he was irritated, and Ella turned pink. She was so delighted by the new and close relations of the young people that she was instantly aware of any unkindness between them. She said in a nervous voice, 'Of course, he's so busy – but where was I – oh yes – I wanted to see – the new boiler.' She went into the house.

Harry said to Amanda in a severe tone, 'Now what do you mean, Amanda?'

'Only that you don't seem very ready to get married.'

'No, you mean I got the farm from your Aunty on false pretences.'

'No, Harry, truly.' Amanda was now ashamed of herself. 'I know you wouldn't do such a thing.'

'You know I want to marry you, Amanda, as soon as ever I can, but when could I have found time in the last month?'

'No, you're terribly busy.'

Amanda, looking thoughtfully at Harry, reflected, 'And you're not terribly keen on getting married. Why should you be? You have all the advantages without any of the troubles.'

'It's not only that,' said Harry. 'But a farm of this order is something on a chap's mind, ninety acres of land, all the stock, machinery, buildings, things that need watching all the time or they just run away from you. It's a big job. I've got to make £170 of rent for your Aunty next year, and keep up the land, too, and bring in a lot of changes – a tricky kind of thing on an old farm.'

'Yes, indeed,' said Amanda, in a sympathetic voice. She was reflecting, 'And I suppose that's just what marriage is for, to tie the man down before he gets what he wants. He's in the trap before he reaches the bait. Like a mouse. But it makes one feel rather mean.'

'Any farm is a responsibility,' said Harry with his new air of anxiety and importance. 'But an old-fashioned place like this is a big responsibility. Because it's been doing well enough before. If anything goes wrong people will say, "Why didn't he go on in the old style?"'

'People are so—' said Amanda in a tone of sympathy but some vagueness. She was saying to herself, 'All the same, it is really rather unfair that women have to be so Machiavellian.'

'But you can't go on in the old way,' said Harry. 'You'd be broke in no time. Look at the way wages have gone up. Only to pay the wages you have to have a bigger turnover.'

'You'll make a success of it, Harry. You're so keen – you hardly think of anything else.'

'I'm not afraid of not making a success of it, if I get a good start. It's the first ten years are going to be the tricky ones.'

'Ten years.'

'Well, say fifteen. It's a nice kind of boiler, Miss Ella,' he said, as they entered the kitchen. 'The idea is, you can cook pig feed in it as well as water or clothes or stew.'

'I'm so glad,' said Ella, gazing at the new copper boiler, behind which the form of old Hannah could be seen jerking to and fro like an agitated gibbon monkey in a small cage. 'How does Hannah like it – how do you like it, Hannah?'

'Waw? Woo,' said Hannah, grinning broadly. She lifted up the copper lid and let it fall with a loud crash. 'Woo.'

'Good,' said Harry, interpreting. 'The old girl swears by a good copper.'

'Ooo-ow – wee-wee,' said Hannah, laughing. 'Ay-woo – wow-aw.'

'She says you can boil in it,' said Harry. 'It's a quick boiler.'

'Really, it's quite delightful,' said Ella, 'and so light and airy upstairs. Have you seen the upstairs, Amanda?'

'Yes, Aunty, several times.'

'But not properly, I think. I'm sure you haven't seen those cupboards since Harry painted them, or the attic with its new floor. An attic is so important to a family house. I'm sure Harry would like to show you the cupboards, darling. Wouldn't you like to show Amanda the new paint, Harry?'

'I could do so, Miss Ella, if she would like.'

'Do show me the house, Harry,' said Amanda, 'and the family attic. Won't you come with us, dearest?'

'Oh no.' Ella was taken aback by such a suggestion in which she detected malice. 'You know very well, Amanda, I couldn't come just now. I have to, yes – see about the garden. I'll look where the roses are to go before I get back.'

Amanda and Harry went through the door leading to the front

passage. Ella started out of the back porch exclaiming aloud, 'Yes the roses,' as if to assure some listening angel spy that it was really necessary for her to lay out a rose garden. But at once, changing both her expression and her voice, as if the angel had been already deceived and out-distanced, cried to herself, 'But what are their relations – one would take them for a village couple – who only get the engagement ring just before they're married. Yes, it must be that – it's really rather nicer like that. More natural,' she consoled herself.

CHAPTER 27

The little house had been furnished with pieces from the Villa, and Harry admired them to Amanda even when she had seen them before. 'It's a good overmantel, that – solid mahogany. I should say it's worth thirty shillings anywhere.'

'Do you like overmantels, Harry? They're rather going out.'

'If they weren't going out that one would be worth three pounds. Of course, it needs patching up, but I'll have that done as soon as I can get round to it.' He polished a cupboard door with his sleeve. 'Beautiful bit of grain, that. Yellow pine. You can't get any more yellow pine like that in these days. Give it a touch of varnish and it would be an ornament anywhere.' This was the chorus of Harry's song at the Quarry, everything was good, a bargain, a little better than anyone else's; but everything needed improvement. He spent all his time when he was not at work poking out the drains in the banks, shaking fences, climbing about the roofs of his new barns and byres, full of an owner's delight, and of the critical suspicion natural to a new owner,

Amanda in at least a dozen visits to Quarry Farm had grown a little tired of the rounds. She was preoccupied not so much with thoughts as with vague feelings of lassitude and futility. In the front room upstairs, while Harry measured the wall to see if he could put into it Ella's wardrobe, Amanda looked out of the window at the Longwater and felt a tedium already domestic. It seemed to mingle naturally with the familiar stretch of water, bright but not sparkling, enclosed by small hills on which harvest was proceeding by stages which were no doubt rapid on the spot, but, at the distance of half a mile, varied the pattern of tawny gold, lemon, lime-green and laurel-green, by changes so gradual that it was impossible to remember where corn had given place to stooks or stooks to stacks.

The buzz of a couple of flies under the low ceiling, Harry's whistle while he stretched the tape, the smell of soap from the new-washed curtains all conveyed to Amanda an enchantment which was sleepy but not delightful. She thought, 'It's a kind of interval – one's hardly alive.' She felt Harry's arm round her waist and he touched her breast.

'Oh, Harry,' she murmured, protesting. 'Do you really want to—?'

Harry turned her gently but firmly to the bed and she patiently lay down.

'You might take your hat off,' she said.

Harry stopped in surprise. A hat or cap, to Harry, was almost part of his anatomy. 'My hat,' he said. 'Well, if you think it makes a difference.'

'No, please don't bother. Really, it doesn't matter at all – in fact, I like it.'

And as, five minutes later, they lay side by side on the quilt, she said, 'How nice to be a man.'

'Ah,' said Harry, at once on the defensive.

'You needn't marry me at all, need you?'

'H'm!'

'You didn't marry poor Nelly.'

'That was different.'

'Is it so different, we're both women. And if I'm six weeks gone already people will soon begin to notice. It's a wonder Aunty hasn't noticed how green I look in the mornings, after I've been sick.'

'But Amanda,' Harry protested, 'you know I want to marry you, just as soon as I can.'

'What did you tell Nelly?' said Amanda, who was surprised at her own words. She thought, 'But I'm not a bit jealous, it's just a kind of silly game to pass away the time.'

'Ah !'

'And did you make her lie down whenever you took the fancy?'

'Now, Amanda, you know how it will be.'

'Oh, I'm not going to make a scene. It's only that it doesn't seem fair.'

'There you go, telling me all about the men having such a nice time, as if the girls never get after 'em and get 'em into trouble, too.'

'I'm sorry, Harry. I know Nelly rather threw herself at you.'

'And promised me there'd be no trouble. Didn't she say it'd be more than her life was worth, with her mother so respectable, and she was up to everything. And so she was, too.'

'So Nelly thought she would nail you with a baby. Isn't that the word.'

'Ah, and everyone knows it. They'd laugh at me if I'd let myself be cot by that old trick.'

'And now I've nailed you.'

'Ah!' said Harry, giving to this expressive syllable a force of disappointed wrath which was more telling than words.

'Poor Harry! Who would be a man?'

'Ah!' said Harry. 'Well, goodbye,' and he tossed up his long legs to roll off the bed. Amanda at once caught hold of him. 'No, no, Harry, I didn't mean it. Don't be cross with me.'

'Dommed if I know what you mean.'

'Oh dear, I don't know myself.' Amanda gave a deep, almost tearful sigh. 'But I suppose I'm not quite myself. With this thing going on inside. And I do hate feeling so – stupid.'

'There now,' said Harry, at once relenting, 'there now!' He patted her with consoling, expert hands. 'I know how it is. It's a dom shame you should be made so sickish. You have a right to be a bit flighty.'

Amanda lay still with Harry's arm behind her neck. She thought, 'Perhaps I've put myself in the wrong not only with convention but with nature, too. After all, the natural unit is not mother and child, but the family. Papa, a settled regular papa, is a necessary part of the arrangement, even among monkeys and birds. And perhaps he is necessary even to the mother's feelings.'

'Was Nelly flighty?' she asked in a dreamy voice.

'Ah!'

'I'm sorry, but really I wasn't thinking. I didn't mean to say a word about Nelly, and I know you'll marry me quite soon.'

'That's more like it,' said Harry, embracing her. 'That's more like you, it's reasonable.'

'I won't worry you again, dear, though I hope it will be fairly soon. Before I get – noticeable. I'm so afraid of upsetting Aunty.'

'Yes, soon's the word. Soon as ever I can. Though now you mention it, Amanda—'

'You'd like to put it off altogether. No, Harry, I was only joking.'

'I was going to tell you myself, it mid be a bit ticklish to get married just this minute.'

'Oh, of course it would – it's always ticklish, isn't it?'

'I mean, with the Rafts. They'd make such a terrible to do.'

'Yes, we couldn't be engaged because of the Rafts, and now we can't get married. It's a great saving in rings, anyhow.'

'Now, Amanda, didn't we agree to keep it quiet?'

'But Nelly Raft's baby is three months old. If she were going to make trouble I should have thought she would have made it before this.'

'She didn't make trouble before because I hadn't anything to get. But now you see, I've got the Quarry. Nelly's not so stupid, nor so thoughtless. It wouldn't be Nelly either, it's old Mother Raft I'm afraid of. She's behind it all.'

'But you'll tell your story, that Nelly was quite ready – a little too ready.'

''Twouldn't be any good. I might swear anything. They'd never listen to me. The bench is always against the farmer, especially when it's one of his own girls. No, they'd give her ten bob a week, it mid be fifteen shillings. And you know, Amanda, Quarry will need every penny if it has its rights.'

'But what are you doing about Nelly?'

'Well, I've got a plan for young Marten to marry her. I'd give 'em a nice present. What's more, I believe I could give 'em a cottage. And that would clinch it. Yes, a cottage would settle it. If the cowman leaves, and he's ready to go to Okey if Okey will give him a rise.'

'And what does Nelly say to that?'

'She'll take it well enough when she sees there's no better offer. Nelly is a nice sensible girl, and always was.'

'More so than me, and a better figure, too – yes, Harry.' Amanda, seeing Harry's brow darken, hastily reverted to the subject: 'Oh yes. Of course she will.'

'And what I hope is, the whole thing will be straight before apple harvest.'

'But Harry, that's three months. I'll be enormous.'

'That's the longest; it mid be only a month.'

'And my reputation doesn't count, does it?'

'Nobody will say a word to your face, and what does it matter what they say behind your back? Haven't they said this ten years that your Aunty Rose was a miser, and your Aunty Ella – was mad, and that you were a sly piece that mid be up to all sorts. Let them talk.'

'It doesn't matter to you?'

'Ah!'

'So long as your Nelly's feelings don't suffer – but that does you credit.'

'Ah well.' Harry once more began to roll off the bed and Amanda hastily prevented him. 'No, please, Harry, forgive me. Stay with me. I don't mind what happens to my waist, or my reputation, or anything. I've got no pride any more, no brains, nothing. You're all I have, so stay with me, use me, beat me if you like.'

'Now Amanda, dearr,' in a warning voice.

'Yes, I'm good now. I'm not going to make any more scenes. Never again.' Amanda remembered with horror how, about a week before, after a mysterious quarrel with Harry, she had found herself in tears. 'Never again' she said firmly.

'You see, my dear,' said Harry, in his most cajoling volce, 'your reputation won't come to much harm, so long as you get your lines before you're too round. And even if we had to wait a couple of months now, and your belt was getting a bit longer, no one will tell it. Why, young Nelly was five months gone before anyone knew anything. Not even Mother Raft herself had any idea of it. Of course, Nelly pulled herself in a little and went stooping a bit and holding her shoulders forward to keep her chest down. But you could do that better than Nelly, because you stoop by nature, and you're bigger by nature, too.'

'Nelly is such a clever girl. I suppose she's clever in a lot of ways, and such a good cook and a good milker.'

'So she was – it was a charm the way she made the stubborn ones give down.'

'And you'd be prepared to throw away this charmer on a cowman. Is that wise, Harry?'

'Ah!'

Amanda turned her head and looked at him. She reflected, 'How handsome he looks and how distinguished, too, carrying off all the honours as well as the maidenheads. And the extraordinary thing is that I feel guilty before him – quite mean and small, even in asking him to marry me.'

'But of course you can afford to pick and choose,' said Amanda.

'Ah!'

'But what I wonder is, wouldn't it suit you better to keep us both, Nelly for the cows and me for – I'm rather good at accounts. And, of course, we'd both be available for – for passing the time.' Amanda gave a laugh.

Harry turned his head, looked at Amanda, and raised himself slowly on his elbow. 'Now, Amanda, you're not crying?'

'No,' said Amanda, weeping freely. 'No – laughing.' And she laughed.

'Don't ee,' said Harry, much perplexed. 'Don't ee, you'll be having the highstrikes.' And he looked round as if for assistance. 'Amanda! Don't ee laugh like that.'

'I'm not laughing,' said Amanda, laughing and crying at once. 'I'm s-sorry, Harry. Yes, I suppose it is highstrikes. But I won't let it get too high.'

'Don't ee,' said Harry, sitting up and taking her by the shoulders. 'Stop it, my dearr! Your Aunty will hear you.'

'Oh dear,' said Amanda, putting her handkerchief to her mouth and uttering another laugh, while the tears jumped off her cheeks. 'How pupperfectly s-silly. I suppose it's because I'm p-pregnant. Of course, that's what it mumumeans, how fuffunny.'

'You stop it,' said Harry, shaking her with energy. 'It wouldn't be funny if your Aunty should come . . .'

'Yes, that's what it means in the Guggreek, wombical – I'm wombical, Harry. Just a womb, in ppossession of a perfectly s-silly girl, such an idiot of a g-girl.'

'If you don't stop I shall have to fetch a can of water and dowse you proper. I'm sorry, dearr, but it's the only way for highstrikes, to save you from a fit.'

'I'm better now,' said Amanda, uttering a kind of hiccough followed by a cry like a puppy in a door. 'I'm better.' Harry muttered an exclamation, seized the jug from the washstand, and ran out of the room.

Amanda jumped off the bed, resolved to control herself, but almost at once was taken with such a fit of sobbing and laughing that she had to sit down on a chair. Harry's voice was heard shouting a protest. 'Dom it, Amanda, stop that!' He appeared with the jug and at once dashed half a gallon of cold water over her head and neck.

'Harry!' Amanda started up. She was furious. As the water poured down her back she shook with anger and disgust. But in the same instant, seeing Harry's solemn critical eye fixed upon her, she lost her anger and said calmly, 'Yes, you're quite right – I'm cured.'

'It's the only thing for highstrikes,' said Harry, putting the jug back into the wash-basin. Amanda could have sworn that he paused a moment to admire the china.

'Thank you, Harry. There's no one like you in a crisis.' She smiled at him, blinking her wet eyelashes.

'Now, now,' said Harry, 'don't give way to it.'

'You needn't be afraid. I'm soaked to the skin.' Amanda shivered. 'What will Aunty think?'

'Never mind your Aunty. I'll tell her you spilt a jug off a shelf. But you must have a change while we dry your duds on the kitchen boiler.'

Perhaps I could put on your pyjamas.'

'No, no. I'll get some things from Hannah – or wait – I'll be back in a tick.'

He carried off Amanda's wet clothes to the kitchen and returned in less than ten minutes with a set of undergarments, not very fine, but well-laundered and smelling of garden lavender. Amanda, having remarked that they were better than her own, put them on, and sat down in the casement to dry her hair in the sun. She said to Harry, patiently guarding the door, 'Old Hannah is rather particular about her underwear – I must thank her.'

'No, you'd better not,' said Harry slowly.

'But why—'

'Well, it wasn't old Hannah. Hers wouldn't be fit.'

'Then whose?' And suddenly putting together Harry's expression, the fact that the Rafts' cottage was not a hundred yards away, and an inspiration that seemed to float on the air, she exclaimed, 'Not Nelly's? No, you couldn't.'

'I never said they were Nelly's.'

'You haven't denied it. Really, Harry, you're—' She began to laugh. Harry started up. In fact, Amanda was very nearly in hysterics. But seeing Harry's jaw lengthen, she made a determined effort and became calm. 'All right, why not Nelly's. It's even rather appropriate.'

'I only thought of Nelly on account of you,' said Harry, following Amanda's mind with that subtlety which always surprised her in a man so little given to reflection, 'because she is so clean and particular in her ways, and so sweet in her skin. I was thinking of you, sweetheart, and what was due to a nice particular lady like you – it would be Nelly who has a right to take me up wrong. But I wasn't minding that.'

'Yes, Nelly might well be offended. Did you tell her the clothes were for me?'

'No, I didn't,' said Harry drily, as if this were a foolish question. 'I said they were for your Aunty.'

'And what if she finds out?'

'That won't matter since it will be all past. Nelly is no fule to make a fuss about what's past and done. She's enough to think of in the present, and so have we all, I should think,' he spoke with some impatience.

'You are a wonderful man, Harry, for bringing things down to the ground.'

'I still think that's where we have to live. And that reminds me, Amanda. I was promising myself to go round by Queensport before five o'clock for a load of cake.'

'If my things are dry we can go at once.'

'Why wait till they're dry, we'll take them with us. Nelly won't want her things back till tomorrow.'

'They won't be ready to—morrow. I must have them washed before I send them back.'

'No need for that, you won't have dirtied 'em in a couple of hours.'

'You don't understand these things, Harry. Nelly's clothes must go back to her as fresh as they came to me.'

'Just what you think proper,' said Harry. 'That's your own woman's business. I'd be a fule to put my nose in it, and get myself scratched with all those hooks and pins.'

CHAPTER 28

The agents, long pressed by Ella, now suddenly advertised the sale saying only that they could take no responsibility for its success, in such a bad month. But every day parties came to poke the chairs, to say in loud voices that everything was very shabby and that the house was inconvenient. Young couples arrived who plainly had no intention to buy, farm labourers with dairymaids on their arms, come to explore this strange world, to admire the pantries and to giggle at the huge marriage bed with its mahogany half-tester in the chief bedroom.

'I shan't let anyone buy that bed,' said Ella to Amanda, 'or anything here.' She had indeed gathered all her own treasures in the room. 'I shall send everything to the Quarry House. Even the bed will fit quite well when Harry throws out the bay.'

'Isn't it a little bit overpowering?' said Amanda, looking at the bed with disfavour.

'Oh, my dear, but we couldn't let Granny's bed go. Why, it was great-granny's – your grandfather was born in it, and all of us.'

'And I suppose they died in it, too.' Amanda was sitting on the couch beside Ella, who was perched on a cushion. This enabled Amanda to lean her head against the smaller woman's shoulder, which pleased them both. Amanda was now feeling very well. As Ella said, she had never looked so well, her cheeks were firm and her eyes were bright. But she was languid and bored to distraction.

'Your great-granny died in it,' said Ella, 'and my mother and two of her babies.'

'And grandpapa, I suppose.'

'I'd nearly forgotten Theo.'

'Uncle Theo. How did he come to die in Rose's bed?'

'Because he brought his wife here and Rose thought they ought to have the state-room. And then, of course, he caught that terrible influenza in 1918.'

'Poor Uncle Theo,' said Amanda, looking at the bed with a slight frown, as if enquiring into this uncle's last moments. But Ella raised her eyebrows in a puzzled expression.

Theo's career had always perplexed the Venns, even Rose. For suddenly, after his initial success, and after toiling eight years upon a picture that was to be a masterpiece, he had abandoned painting for art criticism, saying that he would never be first class as an artist. Afterwards he had married a poor, ugly, and intelligent French woman and set to work on a history of art. But his only child, a daughter, had died young, and soon afterwards Theo had given up his great work, saying that it was good for nothing. He had mistaken his powers.

Amanda remembered him, just before his death in 1919, as a tall, white-haired man with a very long thin face, a face which seemed to defy the world, and which, in spite of its quite different form, had a look of Bessie. He was a silent person, but he had remarked one day to his young niece, for whom his grand and melancholy air had an attraction: 'Paris is the only civilized spot in the world – or was, until it was ruined by barbarians and foreigners. Now there is no civilization anywhere.'

Venn and his only son had always been good friends, though Theo would say of his father, 'A dilettante,' and Venn would say of his son, 'Poor Theo, he's so afraid of being second-rate – and that is so second-rate.'

But once, in a moment of intuition, he had remarked, 'It's my fault, perhaps – I brought him up to value only the best.'

'I was rather in love with Uncle Theo,' Amanda murmured. 'He looked so unhappy – no, not unhappy, but sad.'

'He was a great disappointment to poor Papa.'

'I suppose everyone disappoints his parents. Yes, everyone fails, more or less, generally more. A lot more.'

'Oh, no, Amanda, not you – with your scholarships. Even Rose was proud—'

'Except, perhaps, people like grandpapa who are artful with life-born diplomats. But where did grandpapa die?' Amanda was not to be put off.

'I – I don't quite know. We think – we hope it was here.'

'You hope.' Amanda, having moved her head to a more comfortable position on Ella's stays, said lazily, 'You know?'

'I shouldn't tell you, but you ought to know. Did you ever hear that Papa had a great friend – a lady?'

'A very *intimate* friend, so I've been told.'

'Yes, I'm afraid – things were said. But we mustn't blame him – he was very young when my mother died, and he could have married again. But he told Rose that he would never do so because it would not be fair to her or to me.'

'It was less trouble to keep a mistress.'

'Oh no, darling, please. You shouldn't speak so – Papa was so thoughtful of people's feelings – so truly considerate. And then he was religious, too. I don't mean that he was very – orthodox – but he always supported the Church.'

'It was a good racket,' Amanda murmured.

'Please – that's so like poor Robin.'

'I'm sorry, dearest. I said good – I mean, it worked.'

'And Mrs Wilmot was a very *nice* woman,' said Ella, in a tone of reproach, 'and a widow. She had been married to the Brewery manager. Papa and she were friends for nearly forty years.'

'It was almost respectable.'

In the last weeks the relations of mother and daughter had again changed. They were less embarrassed, more casual; and Amanda had ceased to be quarrelsome. But she had begun to make small jokes at Ella's expense. It was almost as if she felt an equality.

'Oh no, no,' said Ella. 'I didn't mean that. No, I'm afraid it couldn't be respectable. It was always a great grief and anxiety to us all. And that was why, of course, your Aunty Rose was so upset when it seemed that Papa might die in Mrs Wilmot's arms.'

'That *would* have been a scandal.'

'Yes, indeed, quite dreadful. You see, Papa was very well known: Chairman of the Bench, and he'd been High Sheriff, it would have got into the papers. The papers are so malicious.'

'And have a good idea of what the public will enjoy.'

Ella paused a moment as if she thought this remark also savoured too much of Robin. But she never liked to speak of Robin, and after a moment she continued: 'So when poor Papa was taken so ill at Mrs Wilmot's, your Aunty went in the landau – we had it closed – and fetched him away. Of course,' said Ella, enlivened by this ethical conflict, 'people said she did very wrong – that it was a cruel thing. Mrs Wilmot went down on her knees and begged her – she said that Rose would kill him. Oh, she adored Papa, and I'm not surprised. He was such an attractive man.' Ella spoke this in the enthusiastic tone of a young lady speaking of a matinee hero. 'Quite fascinating to women.'

'I can well understand it,' said Amanda. 'He sounds so thoroughly wicked, and civilized.'

'Darling, it wasn't a joke, it was a dreadful thing – and I thought Mrs Wilmot would do herself an injury.'

'You thought – were you there, too? I thought you were abroad all that time.'

'Yes, I was still abroad at Papa's first illness, that year – it was a kind of fit. But though he seemed quite well again, Rose sent for me at once. Papa was a little cross about it. And indeed it was nearly four months before he had this other attack at Mrs Wilmot's. So Rose was quite right to send for me. And she took me in the landau to help in case we had to carry him. I was so strong – much stronger than Rose.'

'She took you to kidnap him away from Mrs Wilmot.'

There was a pause. Then Ella said, 'Have you heard from Robin lately, my dear?'

'Robin? On Monday. He writes every second Sunday. I think Kathy must remind him. But he has no influence over my mind. I haven't got one any more.'

'Don't be so absurd, darling! Of course you have a mind.'

'It's come unjellied. But do tell me about Mrs Wilmot – what did she look like? How old was she? Did she have any babies by Grandpapa?'

'Darling, please – and *by* Grandpapa. As if he were – a horse.'

'She must have been over forty. She didn't really go down on her knees?'

'Papa was in his seventy-ninth year when he died – Mrs Wilmot must have been sixty.'

'And she went down on her knees. How dramatic.'

'I saw her myself, it was quite dreadful. I don't know how I stood it, but of course Rose told me what to do. Mrs Wilmot was such a dignified woman, she always wore black silk and she had lovely hair – quite white, of course. And you know, she was a big, strong woman and Rose was so little and thin. I couldn't help being afraid that she would just push us both out of the room. How awful that would have been if there had been a struggle. But she didn't resist at all – as soon as she saw Rose at the door she seemed quite paralysed with fear. And that was awful, too – yes, it was fearful to see that big, strong woman go down on the floor – she crouched right down and tried to take Rose by the knees.'

'But I suppose that was just what people did then – on the stage.'

'Amanda, she was dreadfully in earnest.'

'Yes, but people are influenced by plays and books in the way they express themselves. And I suppose the way they express themselves influences the people who write books and plays. It's all rather complicated.' Amanda ended on a note of placid tolerance.

'Mrs Wilmot was chapel. I'm sure she never went to a play. We weren't allowed to go to plays either, except Shakespeare.'

'Art forms life and life forms art,' Amanda murmured. 'Especially chapel, I suppose.'

'What does Robin write to you about?'

'Nothing, only talk – and Mrs Wilmot really knelt down in black satin?'

'Oh dear,' said Ella, 'I'll never forget her face. She hardly dared even to touch Rose's skirts. But she felt so guilty. And guilt is such a dreadful—'

'Yes, dearest,' said Amanda quickly. 'Poor Mrs Wilmot, she had been brought up so strictly, she couldn't help herself. So you and Aunty Rose went and took poor Grandpapa away – when he was ill. And he died respectably at home.'

Ella, successfully diverted from her diversion on guilt, gave a sigh and said mildly, 'Yes, I hope so – oh, I hope so. Of course, he was breathing when we carried him downstairs. But I could not be sure that he was quite breathing when we took him out of the carriage. He seemed so cold, and, oh dear, his mouth had come open. But we took him to bed and put hot battles round him and the doctor wrote it down in his certificate that he died at the Villa. So Rose had her way. He didn't die at Mrs Wilmot's.'

'What a horrible story,' said Amanda sleepily. She shivered, drawing her shoulders up and stooping her breasts forward. But she did not feel any horror and her shiver was due to something in herself. 'As if someone had poured cold water on my grave,' she thought.

'Oh no, no, awful if you like. It was a dreadful thing for us – especially for poor Rose. But not horrible, dear – it wasn't like that at the time. The house was very light and clean, and Mrs Wilmot kept her dignity.'

'With her head on the floor?'

'Perhaps not what we usually mean by dignity, but she didn't scream and she looked very neat, as she always was – not a hair out of place. Even when she tried to catch Rose she did not do it in an unladylike way. Mrs Wilmot was not quite a lady, of course, but she was always very ladylike. Rose always called her 'that housekeeper woman,' and really she was very like a housekeeper of the best kind. A very good kind of self-respecting person.'

'And she was still a housekeeper on her knees?'

'Amanda, dear, I don't think it's very kind. I didn't quite like Mrs Wilmot, but I was very sorry for her. She suffered dreadfully; indeed, I think she died of it. They called it influenza, but she died that same year. She could not live without my father. Yes, I suppose she'd really given up a great deal for him. I don't think she'd many other friends, there had been so much gossip.'

'I suppose it is difficult to carry on an affair like that in the country.' Amanda began to yawn, but turned away her head and tried, not very successfully, to adjust her features.

'I don't know, my dear, but country people are very secretive about their affairs – one really knows surprisingly little about anybody, even about near neighbours.'

Ella was gazing, with high-raised brows, at the window which showed an evening landscape in the last week of August: harvest fields, some full of ripe corn, almost roan in colour, some already patterned with stooks, others striped with the different greens of new leygrass, kale and swede. All was in deep and strong colour, like a picture that has grown dark and rich with age, but lost, by the same process, its freshness and brilliance. Even the sky, of an intense blue, seemed impure as if mixed with the gold tints of old varnish. In fact, it was probably full of harvest dust.

'Dear Harry,' Ella murmured, conjoining the ideas of harvest, secrecy and a general sense of the neighbourhood in both its aspects, of rich private character and warm, deep soil. 'I'm sure his harvest will be good.'

'Never mind Harry,' said Amanda, who saw the turn in Ella's mind. 'What about Mrs Wilmot – people did find out about her? But I suppose Grandpapa wasn't very careful.'

'Oh yes, he was most circumspect. But of course it went on so long – and he paid her rent. Indeed, I believe he left her something in his will, because I know Dick Sant was angry about it. Poor Papa had lost so much money in the last years – he had to sell all the pictures – and china.'

'I've heard he spent a lot. How much did he leave his mistress?'

'I never knew. Dick and Rose kept it quiet. Certainly it wasn't read to me. I only heard about my own legacy.'

'You had a legacy from Grandpapa Venn?'

'Yes, of course. Papa left us five thousand pounds apiece.'

'But I thought you said that you had never had an income of your own – never had any independence.'

'Oh yes,' said Ella, 'I had five thousand pounds. It came to over a hundred pounds a year. Yes, I suppose it was what you call—'

She stopped and again gazed out of the window with an air of surprised enquiry. As if, having discovered a new view of herself, she wished to check the consistence of other familiar objects.

'Tell me,' said Amanda, kissing the air near her cheek, 'what happened to your independence? I suppose someone took it from you when you weren't looking.'

'Oh no, no.' Ella was quite astonished.

Polly knocked at the door, opened it a foot, and inserted her round red face sideways through the opening.

'Oh,' said Amanda, 'don't say more people!'

'In a car, miss. To see over the house.'

'Do they look as if they would buy a house?'

'Oh yes, miss. It's a gentleman in plus fours.'

Amanda unfolded herself from the sofa. 'It's really extraordinary all the people that want to buy a house or change houses. I suppose they're so bored they can't think of anything else.' She went out, with a meditative air, stooping languidly and half expecting a reproof to compensate her for her annoyance.

She was provoking a reproof, but Ella disappointed her. She had not even noticed the stoop. She was still gazing at the view and thinking, 'Independence – was that what people mean by an independence? But really . . .' She recalled again her feelings on the day when she had received, at the age of forty-nine, her first cheque-book, and understood that she had money of her own.

'But, really, it's just what Amanda says.' She was delighted to find an answer to a certain perturbation in her conscience stirred up by the recollection of Mrs Wilmot's despair. 'I wasn't able to be independent.'

Some weeks after the will reading, when the legacies had been paid, Ella had gone to Rose and said, 'I think I should like to spend a few days in London.'

'My dear Ella, we can't leave the house before spring cleaning.'

And Ella, red, astonished at herself, but under the spell of her new wealth, had answered, 'I thought – perhaps – I could go by myself.'

This was a startling suggestion. Ella had spent years abroad, but always with an approved friend.

'By yourself?' said Rose. 'Where? Bessie hasn't room for you.'

It now appeared that Ella had wired to an hotel close to Brent Square, and already received an answer.

'And what is your object in going to town when you know I can't be there. To see Amanda, I suppose.' Rose spoke in a sardonic manner. Rose, in her late firties, had, as her family said, calmed down. She was no longer so excitable nor so pious as she had been ten years before. Her dress and carriage were rather stiff and formal, and she gave the impression of one who thought little of the world, and took part in its affairs as a duty, without either much enthusiasm or hope.

'I thought we agreed that when Bessie took the child that you should keep away from her. I took it that was the idea in your going abroad.'

'You said for a few years.'

'I said it would be disastrous for you to see too much of her.'

'But I must see her sometimes.'

'You think it would help the child to settle down if you were to tell her of your relation to her.' Rose in her new sardonic resignation was fond of irony.

'Oh Rose,' cried Ella, 'I shouldn't dream – I couldn't –'

'No, I'm sure you wouldn't mean any harm. You don't think you'd better wait till I can come with you?'

'I've made my arrangements,' said Ella, suddenly obstinate. 'After all, I can do what I like. I have my own money.'

'Very well. You needn't defy me like that. I'm not your gaoler.'

'Oh Rose, I don't want to hurt you.'

'Hurt me. I'm not hurt. If you must make a fool of yourself and ruin Amanda's life, that's your own business.'

She had even driven Ella to the station, in the trap, and given her a farewell kiss, which moved Ella much more than her anger.

But Ella said to herself, 'I can't help it – I can't help it. I must see Amanda. I have a right.'

Ella on her last visit to London, six years before, had noted the address of the hotel. She had even then been preparing, subconsciously, for this crisis. She was not at all disconcerted to find, when she reached town, that the hotel had gone downhill since that date. She was only delighted that it still existed, within two hundred yards of Bessie's house, and Amanda. Its very existence was like an act of grace to her. It seemed to say, 'I, too, have been prepared. Though you did not know it, did not see me, I, too, like your fortune, like the bank, like the railway which brought you here, was waiting for the day of accomplishment.'

Bessie's house was even shabbier than the hotel. There were holes in the stair carpet, darned in wool; the varnished wallpaper was cracked; the plush curtains showed grey patches of thread. But this shabbiness was an accustomed thing to Ella. She knew that Bessie had great expenses. She had sent the older children to good schools, and still had to educate the two youngest girls, Muriel and Dorothy. The two boys and Iris had all been at Oxford, and both the boys had needed a great deal of money.

Bertie, the eldest, scholar of his college, and Ella's favourite, a charming and clever boy, had run up great debts, and had been sent down at last for good. William, the second boy, had had a brilliant university career, but then, feeling unable to enter the Church, had taken an unpaid post at an East End Mission. He was therefore still a charge on the family, and as Bessie wrote, unhappier than ever.

Ella knew that the Academy was doing badly, and that the Grooms, for a long time, had been borrowing money from her father, from everyone who would lend, without hope of return. And yet this poverty had made so little impression on her ideas that the moment she entered the dingy hall of Brent Square and begun to climb the dark, steep stairs, she was exhilarated by the sense of Bessie's life, by the feeling which belonged to Bessie's home, of a rich and glorious activity, a world in itself, full of

history and promise, a centre of European culture – that Brent
Square, in fact, which Bessie had created by the force of her
character and imagination.

She rushed eagerly into the drawing-room, smiling already with
tender excitement; to be shocked, as always, by her first glimpse of
Bessie. It was true that she had not seen her for six years, but she
could not have believed that this old woman was her sister, so near
her in age.

Bessie had not only grown white, but very much thinner. The
whiteness of her hair had caused the colouring of her cheeks to lose
its delicacy and to seem yellow; but had added to her eyes an
extraordinary brilliancy. They seemed to start out of her head. At
the same time, her thinness had filled her forehead and cheeks with
wrinkles, and brought out unexpected bones; a sharp, narrow
bridge to her snub nose, a projecting jaw.

This highly expressive face wore so fierce an aspect as it was
turned towards Ella, that she stopped and exclaimed 'Bessie!'

In the same instant. Bessie's ferocious stare changed into affectionate delight. 'Ella, darling, have you come?' She ran to embrace
her sister.

'Darling Bessie, I've been longing to see you. How are you? How
is everything?'

This was not a rhetorical question. Bessie said, 'As bad as could
be.'

'Oh, Bessie, has Bertie been gambling again?'

'No, but there are bailiffs in the Academy.'

'Bailiffs?' Ella had no exact idea what bailiffs were.

'It's bankrupt – didn't I write and tell you last year?'

'Oh yes, I did hear.'

'But it's been getting worse and worse for years. James's enemies
were never satisfied until they'd ruined him. Because they knew he
knew they were frauds. That's what hypocrites can't forgive. But
there, I'm not going to worry you with our troubles.' She plumped
down on the sofa beside Ella and put her arm round her waist.

'But, Bessie, is the Academy closed?'

'No, but we get almost nothing from it. The creditors take all
the income – they only give James a pittance, just enough to keep
us alive. And they might close it, they're always threatening.'

'Oh Bessie, I'd no idea—'

'*Next* time they threaten I *might* have a surprise for them.'

Bessie looked at Ella with an air which Ella remembered from her nursery days, when Bessie would say, 'I know something that you don't know.' And Ella, as in those days, answered with a look of dramatic interest, 'You've thought of something?'

'I've thought of something – dear papa's money came at the luckiest time.'

'You can pay off the debts?'

'No, no.' Bessie looked triumphant. Even as a little girl she had not liked people to guess her plans at a first trial. 'Guess again.'

'I simply couldn't.'

'I'm going to buy the Academy. To *buy* it, Ella, and paint it and put in all the latest improvements – new sinks and white tiles and a proper ladies' cloakroom.'

'But how can you buy it, from James?'

'Oh Ella, how dense you are. It doesn't belong to James, it never did. At least, not since 1898, when there was the reconstruction. It was on lease, and the lease belonged to the trustees – two doddering old gentlemen who haven't been near the place for fifteen years. But if I take it over from them, I can get a new lease. The only difficulty is, I haven't *quite* enough money.'

'But Bessie, won't these men, James's enemies, go on attacking the Academy?'

'Of course they will, but we shall say to people, 'Come and look at our beautiful Academy.' And it will be beautiful, Ella – I've got plans, from an architect. It will be the best Academy in London. And Sir Beastly Beal and Sir Weathercock Wilkins can keep their knighthoods.'

'Sir Beastly Beal?'

'Oh, I believe it's Sir Walford, but they've all got knighthoods,' said Bessie. 'Those kind of people always do. Thank God James will never have a knighthood – I shouldn't allow it – scientific knighthoods nowadays are cheaper than peerages.'

'Rose seemed to think that James might retire soon.'

'Rose.' Bessie thrust out her jaw. 'Rose is always wanting James to retire. James himself hates the very idea. And he would never agree to live at the Villa, anyhow.'

'His health?'

'He's in splendid health, and his mind is better than ever it was. Naturally, he knows more – he has a wider grasp. He says so himself. He has never done such brilliant work as in the last year. That's why we must save the Academy – you and me.'

'Me?' said Ella.

'You,' Bessie again looked very mysterious. 'That is, if you like.'

'But, of course, I forgot – I have my legacy, too. Yes, I could lend you some money.'

'No, darling, I couldn't allow that, it wouldn't be fair. But I could offer you a share in the new Academy – you can pay for some of the work, and then, of course, you will get some of the profits.'

'I wonder would Rose—'

'Rose! Why should you worry about old Rose – why should you even tell Rose? You know that she'll simply say no. She says no to everything.'

The notion of carrying out any financial operation without telling Rose alarmed Ella very much. Her eyes and thoughts seemed to wander from the subject. She asked after the children. Were they at home?

'Easter holidays haven't started, but Amanda comes home to tea, of course.'

There was a pause. Bessie, like Rose, thought that the less Ella saw of Amanda the better. With Rose this opinion was founded on prudence and morality. With Bessie it arose probably from jealousy. But Bessie had the reckless nonchalance of an old captain who does not trouble to avoid dangerous seas. 'You want to see her – I don't see why you shouldn't. She'll be in soon now. I think Ella, you're missing a good chance in this new Academy plan.'

'Oh, but I should love to help. I'd *give* you the money if only Rose could be stopped from knowing'

'But that's easy. I can manage that, in a minute.'

'Then do – do,' cried Ella. 'Take what you like. Is Amanda like anybody?'

'They say she's like me,' said Bessie, 'but you'll see for yourself.' And when a few moments later Amanda came in, she called to her and said, 'You remember your Aunt Ella?' Her air of fulfilling a bargain was perceptible to both sisters, and ignored by both, as something insignificant, a mere shade in the greater family diplomacy.

Amanda was a thin child of seven, tall for her age, but still round-faced; with fair, crinkled hair in a wave which seemed too heavy for her thin neck. She was very shy and kissed Ella's cheek with a touch so light that it could scarcely be felt. Ella, forgetting herself, suddenly hugged her thin waist and kissed her lips, murmuring, 'Darling, you don't remember me, do you?'

Amanda submitted with the passive gentleness of a shy child, and then gazed at Ella with curiosity, as if counting the freckles and wrinkles on her face. Bessie said sharply, 'Amanda, darling, run and get my work-case. Do you know where it is?'

'Yes, Mummy.' She ran out of the room.

And Ella discovered that though she was allowed to see Amanda, she was hardly able to make her acquaintance.

Bessie's jealousy was not less watchful and much more enterprising than Rose's foresight. She could discover, as by a special intuition, the presence of Ella in the house, and at once send Amanda off on some errand, to carry a message to the Academy, or to buy something in a shop. Amanda was accustomed already to run messages in the neighbourhood – she was a precocious child.

Bessie kept Amanda from Ella, but at the same time she had never been so affectionate, so intimate.

CHAPTER 30

Bertie, coming to see his Aunt Ella, asked her, 'Has Mama been getting you to invest in the comic Academy?'

'I think the Academy is a very good thing, and I'm sure your Mama and Papa deserve all our sympathy and help.'

'I thought so,' said the young man. 'She's been so very sweet.'

Bertie, at twenty-six, was a good-looking young man, who took after his grandfather Venn, with curly fair hair, a fine white skin, blue eyes. His only defect was the white lashes which gave his eyes a look of coldness and insolence. He was employed as physics master in a London school, and languidly detested his work. He affected langour even in his pleasures. When Ella, anxious to change the subject from her investment, asked him to play to her, he answered, 'I'd rather listen – it's less trouble.'

'Bertie, you haven't given up your music?'

'Pretty well. Come, Aunty, you will play to me.'

'Only if you play, too.' Ella had no shyness with Bertie. Aunt and nephew, both musical, had always met as friends, and Bertie admired and respected Ella as a pianist.

'J. S. B.,' said Bertie. 'Not Yohan.'

'Yes, Yohan. Have you got the Forty-eight?'

'I suppose so.' The young man indolently moved his graceful self about the room, discovered the Fugues, and put them on the piano.

'You play the bass and I'll play the treble.'

'It's not kind of you, Aunty, making me work on my holiday. What's the time? One and two and three-four.'

They played the whole afternoon, and the young man, forgetting his languor, made Ella promise to play with him every afternoon when he could escape from what he called his cram-shop.

But Ella had quite a different relation with Bessie's second son, William. She respected this reserved young man as she did not respect Bertie, but she was also afraid of him. She was greatly alarmed when, one afternoon, while she and Bertie were playing, William came in, embraced her cheek in a grave manner, and said,

'Excuse me, Aunt Ella, but Bertie tells me you were thinking of putting money into the Academy.'

William was very tall, very thin, and very pale. Easter was past but he looked like a young and enthusiastic parson who has fasted himself into a fever. He was, however, still a strong critic of the Church, and swore that he preferred the East End hooligan to any parson.

William had the rough tweeds, the foul pipe, the breezy manner of a mission worker; but, at the same time, he was used to fix any interlocutor with a steady would-be penetrating glance which always disconcerted Ella.

'Perhaps I oughtn't to ask?' said William.

'No,' said Bertie. 'It's waste of time. Come on, Aunty.' He opened a music book and placed it upon the piano desk. 'What about our oratorio?'

'You see, Aunty, Mother is not a very good woman of business,' said William. 'Her objects are good, but her ideas are rather wild. We've all tried to persuade her against this scheme, without success. But it seems rather a shame that you should be drawn in.'

'Oh, but Willy, I'm not being drawn in.'

'You'll lose every penny you give to it.'

Bertie struck a chord softly and sang in a high baritone, 'Mighty Lord and Ki-hi-king all glorious.'

'Every penny,' said William. 'It's a hopeless plan. We've told Mother, but she won't listen.'

'Yes, Willy,' Ella murmured, her eyes full of terror, terror that she would be prevented from giving her money to Bessie. Not that she believed in Bessie's scheme. She had a firm disbelief in all women's schemes except those of Rose. But she thought, 'If I draw back now, Bessie will be furious with me and I shall not be able to call and see Amanda.' She said in a weak, uncertain voice, 'I've thought it all over.'

'Saviour True, for Ma-ha-han victorious,' Bertie softly intoned, drawing in his chin like a heavy bass, as if he could thus give himself a bass voice.

'So you *have* invested in the scheme,' said William. 'Aunty, you must get out at once, it's not fair. If you like, I'll speak to Mother myself.'

'Oh no, no,' cried Ella, in a panic, and then, by a stroke of inspiration, she exclaimed, 'And you know, I couldn't invest in anything unless the bank gave me the money.'

'Earthly state thou dost dis-dain, thou do-hust dis-dain,' said Bertie, rounding his mouth like an O, to make his O's round and deep.

'I see,' said William, after a pause during which he had looked very hard indeed at Ella. 'It's in trust, is it? You can only use the income?'

Ella, who did not exactly know what this meant, but knew instantly, by William's look and voice, that she had hit on the right argument, exclaimed eagerly, 'Oh yes, that's just what it is. The bank keeps it, I have a cheque book, of course, but the bank keeps the money.'

William uncrossed his long legs and rose from his chair. 'I'm glad about that,' he cried. 'Of course that would be it. But I was worried.'

'Thank God, Willy is at peace,' said Bertie. 'Go away, Willy, and mind somebody else's business.'

'It's so kind of you, Willy,' said Ella, 'to take so much trouble.'

'Who all things, who all things do-ut-uth sustain.' And Bertie turned round impatiently, 'Do come, Aunty, I'd forgotten what glorious stuff it is. It would make a perfect pirate's chorus.'

'I'm sorry if I worried you, Aunty, but I *had* to say something,' William apologized, and kissing his aunt with an absent-minded air, he hastened away. William was always hastening from place to place on urgent and usually secret business.

'How good he is,' said Ella. joyfully taking her seat at the piano beside her beloved Bertie. 'Where are you? I can't really sing it, you know, but I could squeak.'

'Let's do the whole thing,' said Bertie greedily. 'Come on, Aunt; Christians be joyful and praise your salvation.'

'Oh, but we haven't got there yet, the introduction is so lovely. Will you take the treble?'

'Good God, no, I couldn't. I'd ruin it.'

'Very well. Ready.'

'You know, Aunt,' said Bertie, suddenly turning his face towards her.

'Yes, Bertie.' She smiled at him with that exuberant and as it were conspiratorial affection which subsisted between her and Bertie.

'You *will* lose your money if you give it to Mother.'

'Oh, please, Bertie,' she implored, 'don't spoil everything! I thought we were going to play.'

'Don't you *really* mind?'

'Begin, begin – one-two-three-rour,' said Ella. 'One-two—'

They submitted themselves to be carried away by the music.

A week later Bessie brought her scheme to Ella, whose share was over four thousand pounds.

'Four thousand five hundred pounds,' said Ella. 'But will the bank—'

'If the bank dares to say a word,' said Bessie, '*I'll* talk to them, and if they tell Rose I'll bring an action against them. It's against the law for banks to tell *anything* that their client wants to keep private.'

'Oh, thank you, Bessie, I knew you would manage everything.' Ella was full of gratitude to this capable sister, who, as she understood, was about to lose her money. Perhaps she understood also that she could not prevent her from doing so. Her gratitude to be saved the trouble of ruining herself was really gratitude for peace of mind and conscience.

She noticed, too, that Bessie, after she had received her money, in one cheque, the second and last from the book, allowed her to see more of Amanda, not much more by time, but a great deal by Ella's feeling. And she reflected, with deep affection to Bessie, 'It is really *very* good of her, *true* goodness. Because now she has my money she really needn't trouble about me at all.'

Ella, indeed, having paid over her money, heard nothing more about it. She noticed scaffolding against the blackened walls of the Academy. She reflected with alarm, 'I'm paying for part of that – suppose someone fell off and was killed, should I be responsible?' But she took care not to worry Bessie with questions. Though she was much distressed when, at the end of six months, she found herself unable to pay her hotel bill. The bank, it appeared, had no more money to give her. Unluckily, in this week, Bessie was in great distress about Alice, the eldest daughter, whose husband, Dick Sant, a man twenty years her senior, and son, Arthur, were both gravely ill at once. Bessie went over every night to nurse them, and when she came to Brent Square for some necessary duty, she was more than usually tired and restless.

But when the landlord waylaid Ella on the stairs and threatened to turn her out and keep her luggage, she was forced to speak. As it happened, Bessie did not come home that day. But she had on the morrow her usual Thursday reception, when she would be bound to appear, and Ella was not sorry to be forced upon an occasion when she could ejaculate her bad news in a few casual words and escape before their import had caused its full disturbance.

The reception was a crowded one. Bessie, with dark rings of sleeplessness round her eyes, and hollow grey cheeks, was dressed in a frock of magenta and blue, in the worst and most gaudy taste. This frock, to Ella, was by itself a sign of crisis, for Bessie, when driven to extremity, was accustomed to put on her most gorgeous frock, the more provocative the better. It was a defiance to the enemy, as well as an encouragement to herself.

'Oh dear,' Ella thought, seeing that frock, and Bessie's worn looks and restless movements. 'Poor little Arthur must be worse. Perhaps I'd better not say anything,' and she did not greet her sister.

But Bessie, in her rapid flights from one corner of the room to the other, from Professor Strumff of Leipsic to young Mr Paterson of the Home Office, an admirer of hers whom she was trying to pass on to the second girl, Muriel, suddenly came face to face with her.

'Bessie, darling, how is Arthur? I do hope—'

'Ella!' with a quick kiss. 'Oh, Arthur, he's a little better. But the cook has gone, poor Alice will break down.'

'Bessie, I'm so sorry, but—' Ella stopped with open mouth.

'Yes.' Bessie was on one foot, in the act of flight.

'It's only – about the bank.'

'What bank?'

'They say – I'm sure there's some mistake – that I haven't any money in my account.'

'Oh, those banks!' said Bessie. 'Isn't that just like them?'

'So they *are* wrong,' said Ella, delighted. 'I knew they were. I said the Academy was paying my income every quarter-day.'

'The Academy,' said Bessie. 'The Academy hasn't paid anybody since last June. It's that fool of an architect, his estimates were all wrong. But I do think the bank might wait a month or two, it's not as though *it* was short of money and worried to death by beasts and fools.'

'Oh, Bessie, so I haven't any money in the bank?'

'Goodness knows!' said Bessie. 'I know I haven't a penny. And it seems we can't start new classes till the workmen are out. But wait a moment.'

And she flew off to catch Groom, who had just come in, and to place him on the rug among a little court of students already prepared.

In the last year or two Groom had become reclusive. He fancied that people laughed at him in the streets. Guests now saw a tall, bent old man with an enormous nose, and shaggy white eyebrows, being guided among them almost like a blind man. His vague and sad glance was that of someone bewildered in a strange world.

But now Bessie would bring up her distinguished visitors for presentation. She would contrive to have usually at least two travelling Germans, an American, and a couple of others. And they would pay their compliments as to a very distinguished man. For they had no idea of Groom's real position. The controversies in which he had been maltreated, which seemed to him so disastrous, were carried on in scientific papers of very small circulation. Few people had read Beal's last letter, describing him as the eminent 'Professor Groom of the self-chartered Academy, who enjoys the unique distinction of having opposed every new development of research throughout the last twenty years. We do not say for one moment that the Professor is actuated by mere ignorance and mere prejudice, but it is necessary to choose between these alternatives.'

And in the admiration of pupils, the deference of Herr Doktor Von Ding, M. le Professeur Chose, Dean So-and-So from Missouri, the old war horse would revive a little; not, indeed, enough to neigh, to prance, but to speak a few words on the responsibilities of scientists to international peace and understanding. 'For they alone,' he would quote from some one of his old articles, 'are set above the conflicts of race and religion. They alone by the very nature of their work take the whole world for province and serve all nations, all sects, the whole of humanity. Yes.' And warmed a little by his own eloquence he would raise his head and lift his voice, 'To science alone with its unremitting and beneficent activity can we dare to look for that peace on earth, that brotherhood among men which . . .' and so on.

Tea was handed about by the maid, by Iris, the second daughter, beautiful and remote, wearing a marble look of boredom, and by Amanda.

Amanda, dressed in a white party frock, was always a centre of interest at these afternoon receptions. She would carry round plates of very thin bread and butter and offer them to the visitors, with the absorbed and grave air of a child trusted with a useful task.

Ella never greeted Amanda. She was afraid to be demonstrative;

afraid of that flashing harassed glance from Bessie, which meant, 'What is Ella going to do next? I must really deal with her.' She would place herself in the child's path, not too conspicuously, and wait. Amanda would come with her plate and hold it out, not looking at Ella, but keeping her eye on the bread and butter as if it might play her some trick and jump off on the floor.

But always, as if by instinct, or perhaps by acquaintance with Ella's skirts, she would look up, see Ella, and then glance round for some soft resting-place for the plate. Finally, she would put it on the floor and reach up her arms: 'Aunty Ella.' For she had learnt all the forms of family kindness, and always gave to aunts an embrace as well as a kiss. Ella would stoop down, scarcely able to trust her voice, and murmur, 'Dearest.' She felt the light careless touch of the thin arms, closing on her neck and instantly opening again, in a gesture almost mechanical, the quick brushing of lips; and then at once Amanda stooped quickly to rescue the important plate from danger, and balancing it with anxious arms, was passing to the next visitors.

Ella trembling in ecstasy and pain, conscious of tears rising in her eyes, would look down and try to hide herself behind some frock coat. She would think for the hundredth time, 'No, I can't bear it. It's dangerous, someone will notice. Amanda will notice something. Rose was right, it was mad of me to come at all. And why did I come?' She would ask herself in astonishment: 'What was my idea when I rushed to London like this? Nobody wants me here. I'm a perfect nuisance and anxiety to everybody. Of course, I hated the Villa. I shall never go back to the Villa. But why can't I go abroad again. I could go to Normandy and stay with Marion. Sooner or later I shall have to go back – why not now before some disaster happens. Before Amanda suspects something. She might easily overhear Bessie saying something to me, about taking care not to upset her, and then she would ask 'Why mustn't you upset me,' and I might easily lose my head and say, 'Amanda, do you know that you're not Bessie's little girl at all? You're my little girl, my own child.' Wouldn't that be dreadful?' Ella demanded of herself. 'Yes, a real disaster.'

In these reflections Ella had forgotten about her bill until, climbing the steps of the hotel, she saw the proprietor waiting behind the glass door. She turned at once and hurried away as fast as she could go, without actually running in an unladylike manner. So that she was back at Brent Square within twenty minutes.

Luckily Bessie had not yet left for her night duty. But she could only cry, as she hurried away, 'My dear, you may well ask about bills, but you're lucky, you can always go back to the Villa.'

'Oh, I can't. I can't go back to the Villa. I'd rather die.'

In fact Ella nearly did die. She crept back to her hotel and slipped up to her room by the back stairs. But she dared not come out again, she would not eat the food for which she could not pay, and in twenty-four hours she was ill with what was called influenza. A kind maid sent for the landlord, who sent for Bessie. Ella was taken to Brent Square in a cab and put to bed. Rose was summoned.

Bessie, during that twenty-four hours, had spent a night with Alice and a day with Muriel, who had refused Mr Paterson, but had done so, it seemed, under the delusion that No was the same thing as Yes. She complained to Rose, as she descended from the train at Paddington, 'Children are quite impossible nowadays. Everything you do is wrong. I thought I was safe in sending them to good schools, and now Iris says I've wasted her brains, and William wants to be a Roman Catholic, and Bertie tells everybody that scientific education is a fraud, and Muriel says I've ruined her life, that I brought her up in ignorance of everything that is most important for a girl to know. I can't understand what it all has to do with Tommy Paterson. I knew nothing about these ridiculous facts of life, as they call them now, when I married dear James, and I'm very glad.'

'*We* were taught our catechism,' said Rose, who thought that Bessie had neglected the religious education of her children. 'But of course one could not mention duty to a girl nowadays.'

'Catechism? She said I gave her nothing else. So now I'm to get her Tommy to propose again at once. And, meanwhile, if you please, I'm a bad mother and not fit to have daughters.'

Ella was ill for a week, and her sisters treated her with much anxious consideration. Amanda was brought to her bedside at least once a day, and when she proposed a plan for teaching the child music, no one gainsaid her. On the third day of her convalescence, her first downstairs, she waited eagerly for Amanda to come in from her walk, when she would suggest the first lesson.

Suddenly Bessie, in hat and cloak, burst into the room. 'Rose, I have to go.'

Rose, who was writing at the table, separated from Ella at the fire by the full length of the drawing-room, looked up and said, 'But where are you going?'

'Down to Muriel's. Her last letter was too frightening.'

'But I thought the young man had been—'

'Yes, to me, but he's not asked her again.'

'Offended, I suppose? These dashing young gentlemen of modern progress are extremely touchy, I've noticed.'

'I wish it were only that,' said Bessie. 'Offended boys are easy. No, I'm afraid that he's simply thought it over. But how can I tell Muriel, and she's sent me such a mad letter. Oh, I must fly, and I've to see Alice somehow before the train.'

'But Bessie, you promised to come to Paddington.'

'Good gracious!' Both glanced towards Ella. Bessie had forgotten Ella. 'But I can't wait until the eleven-fifty,' she cried. 'Suppose Muriel did something to herself.'

'Pooh!' said Rose. 'That's absurd.'

'The eleven-fifty,' said Ella, suspicious. 'Is Rose going home? But I'm not going. I won't, I won't go back.'

Rose crossed the room and sat down beside her. 'Ella, dear, you mustn't let yourself be so excited. The doctors say—'

'I won't go home.' Ella could see that Rose was alarmed; she was afraid that Ella would become hysterical. And Ella felt her power, she became more excited, she allowed herself to be more unreasonable. 'Even if I have lost my money I can work. I can char – Bessie, Bessie, come and tell her that she can't take me home.'

Bessie came quickly and impatiently to her side. 'It's all right, Ella. Rose will look after you. You've been ill, my dear. You don't seem to realize that you're not fit to be alone. Good gracious, it is half-past! I'll miss my train.'

Ella clutched at her hand. 'Don't let her take me. Oh, Bessie, you are kind, you understand what it means to me – to be here – you'll keep me. I don't mind where I sleep.'

'But, Ella, dearest, it's simply impossible.' Bessie, with an agonized glance at the clock, knelt down and kissed Ella.

'You're all the same,' said Ella. 'You treat me like a child, but I won't go home again, never, never.'

'Nobody treats you like a child,' said Rose. 'We all know you are the most gifted of us. But you are not strong and you easily overtire your nerves.'

'I am stronger than you, Rose, and wiser. I have been married and you haven't been married. I kept a man's home together, a poor man's home, and I've been a mother. I still am a mother, only you won't let me do my duty. I have to sit here and see my own child brought up in a strange house.'

'A strange house,' said Bessie. 'Well, really, Ella.'

'It is a strange house, without any God or any respect between parents and children. Rose is right, it's a bad house and James is not fit to be head of any house.'

'Yes, dearest.' Bessie was still patient. Like every mother, she had heard the most abominable things from her own children. The very violence of Ella's speech put her on guard of her temper. 'You're angry with me, and I know we don't seem very kind to you. It's a shame that I haven't any room for you, and that the Academy hasn't paid your dividends. But you know, my dear, that's only temporary. Next year it will pay twice over, and then you can do what you like.'

The door opened and Amanda came in. She was dressed in her blue sailor's coat and a sailor's hat. She walked reflectively across the room to Bessie. 'Mummie, dear, we saw a fire engine.'

'Kiss your Aunty Ella, darling.'

The rough sleeve of the sailor coat fell on Ella's neck, but Amanda continued to her mother, 'They weren't wearing their helmets. I suppose they were practising.'

'Why shouldn't I tell her?' said Ella, suddenly encircling Amanda in her arms. 'Yes, I'll tell her now, and she can come away with me. If you're ashamed I'll go to America. I can work for us both.'

Rose and Bessie both stared at their sister. Rose was almost as white as Bessie's natural colour. She could not find a word. Bessie said in an impatient and contemptuous voice, 'Very well, if you like. Only hurry up. I must go. I can't keep Muriel waiting at the station for an hour, not in her present state of mind, with trains going through.'

'Yes, I will tell her. Amanda, my darling child—' She stopped.

'Quick,' said Bessie, 'I haven't a moment.'

'Yes, Aunty,' the child looked at Ella with round eyes. She felt the tension and she was growing frightened.

But Ella could not speak. She perceived with all her nerves the wavering of Amanda's confidence, her child's peace of mind, and she understood how fragile it was. She pushed Amanda away and got up. 'No, I can't, not now. I'll go.' She rushed downstairs and entered Bessie's cab.

Bessie climbed in after her and intercepted protests from Rose, who had none of Bessie's quickness in family tactics. 'That's all right dear,' she said through the window. 'I'll take her with me to Paddington and go on by underground, you follow with the luggage, and bring her hat. She'll be in the waiting-room.'

And Ella patiently submitted to being left in the waiting-room, like a parcel to be called for. She was still horrified by that deed which she had so nearly committed. 'I mustn't see her again,' she said. 'Never again – Rose was right. Oh God has saved me from a crime – fearful, unforgivable.'

Bessie hastily kissed her. 'Of course you must see her again. Come up at Christmas. Goodbye, goodbye. I must run.' She rushed away determined still to catch that train which anyone else would have abandoned in despair.

CHAPTER 31

'Have you been asleep?'

Ella started and gave a faint cry. She gazed at Amanda as if in horror. What she had heard was a child's voice, and it had seemed to her for a moment that the child Amanda stood before her; the fragile, gentle, serious little girl whose thoughts were so mysterious, whose innocence at once brought her so near in affection and set her so far apart in understanding. She saw a pale, rather thick-set young woman whose dark-rimmed eyes, full of sophistication, seemed to look at her from an even greater distance.

'Were you asleep?' said Amanda. She knocked off her cigarette ash into the empty chamber pot: Rose's chamber pot.

'No. no, I was thinking. Are you well, dear? You don't look very well. Your eyes are quite dark underneath.'

'It's so stuffy, one can't sleep at night. And one feels so sleepy all day.'

'Have you seen poor Harry lately? Yes, we ought to go and see Harry.'

Amanda blew a cloud of smoke and answered in a drowsy tone, 'Do you think Uncle Venn was really devoted to Mrs Wilmot, or did he only make use of her?'

'My dear, he visited her almost every day.'

'She became a habit. Why didn't he marry her?'

'I told you – because of his consideration for – Rose.'

'So Aunty Rose dragged him downstairs in his nightshirt and let him die on the way home.'

'No, Amanda, we wrapped him in his dressing-gown, and Rose was very gentle with him. She was dreadfully unhappy, but what else could she do? How could she leave darling Papa to die in that woman's bed, and perhaps an inquest and an account in the papers. How would she have felt? But perhaps you don't understand.'

'Yes, I think so.' Amanda seemed to reflect a moment. Then she said, 'Aunt Rose's mind turned a great deal on beds, didn't it? On marriage beds and death beds.'

'What do you mean, dear?' said Ella with faint indignation. 'A bed is a bed. Of course, one feels more about a bed where children have been born, or where those you loved have died.'

'Yes, I'm sorry – I can' – Amanda gave an involuntary sigh, 'see that beds can be important. Yes, I daresay I might feel like that, too. Someday.' And going languidly to her desecrated room, heaped now to the ceiling, and layered with dust, she thought, 'I hope at least I shall have some feelings about something – some definite feeling. Even if I don't fall down on my knees in black silk, and break my heart for an old gentleman in his eighties.'

The parcel containing Nelly Raft's new-laundered underclothes had been lying for some days in Amanda's window-seat. She could not make up her mind whether or not to send a note with it; or what to write in the note. But the parcel accused her of escaping a difficulty, and seeing it again next morning, she took it downstairs with her and after breakfast drove with it to Ancombe.

The Rafts, a widow and three daughters, lived in a four-roomed cottage on the village street, but Amanda, not wishing to meet Mrs Raft, avoided the front door. She went into a wood-yard behind the cottage and looked over the fence. As she had expected on a Monday the garden was hung with wet clothes, and in a few minutes Nelly came out from the kitchen with a basket of washing. Amanda called to her over the fence: 'Miss Raft.'

Nelly bobbed down to look between the legs of a frilled pair of drawers, probably her mother's.

'Yes, Miss, and you're Miss Groom.'

'I brought a parcel for you.'

'Yes, Miss.' Nelly opened a gate in the fence. She was a plump young girl with a round face, blue eyes, a small cupid's mouth, as pretty as a doll, and with a doll's lack of expression, which, in a human face, can seem either insipid, or profound and aloof. At the moment Nelly's seemed insipid.

'It's the things you kindly lent me when I got wet.'

'Oh yes, Miss.' Nelly took the parcel with a nervous toss of her head, and blushed salmon-pink to her forehead.

'It was very good of you to lend me your nice things.'

'Yes, Miss Groom. Mr Dawbarn said you must have them.'

'That I *must* have them?'

'Yes, Miss Groom.'

'But I didn't ask for them. I'd no idea Mr Dawbarn would ask you for them.'

'That's all right, Miss Groom. I was very glad Mr Dawbarn should ask me. He's an old family friend.'

Nelly looked at Amanda with an air which might have been defiance or merely enquiry. She carried her round baby's chin always very high, probably, as Amanda reflected, because she was afraid of a double chin.

'But of course, Miss Groom, you know about Mr Dawbarn and me – everybody does, I'm sure. Why even to Queensport they do. They couldn't help it.'

'I was so sorry, Miss Raft.'

Nelly stepped back to leave the gateway free. 'Would you like to see the baby?'

'Oh, please!' Amanda, feeling a sense of lazy surprise, followed Nelly through an avenue of vests, pants, handkerchiefs, stockings, and drawers.

The perambulator stood under the kitchen window. Nelly lifted out the baby, a very small pale child, with a waxen texture to its skin which Amanda found unpleasant. She gazed at the baby and thought, 'No, I couldn't touch it.' The baby, nearly waked, screwed up its face in extraordinary contortions, and jerked its minute hands in the air as if agitated by clockwork.

'He's a boy.' said Nelly, 'just three months.'

'Oh, a lovely baby,' said Amanda, shocked by her repugnance.

'I don't show him to many,' said Nelly. 'Well, naturally. He don't go out of this garden, but seeing as you're such a friend of Mr Dawbarn's—'

Amanda thought vaguely, 'Is she playing some deep game, or is she only a simpleton,' and she said, 'It's very kind of you, such a sweet baby.'

The baby catching one finger in its own nose, pushed that feature out of shape and uttered a sharp cry. Nelly rocked it in her arms. 'I suppose you're engaged, Miss?'

Amanda hesitated, and the girl went on quickly, 'If it's private, you needn't tell me.'

Amanda was reflecting, 'Shall I feel disgusted by my own baby – it's not a nice thought. But one ought to face it.'

'I shouldn't ask, should I, Miss?' said Nelly. 'But don't hold back for me. I know Mr Dawbarn won't marry me now, not even if mother takes him up before the Bench. I'd be ashamed to have him forced to it. No. I couldn't have anything to do with him.'

'No, indeed,' said Amanda, in a vague tone. She gazed again at the baby.

'I know it used to be done in the villages,' said Nelly, suggesting in the last phrase not so much condescension towards old-fashioned country people, as a gentle grief for their lack of refinement. 'I suppose it's what they were accustomed to. But I wouldn't, no, I couldn't face a man if I knew he couldn't stomach me.'

A couple of excited sparrows dived chattering from behind the wet clothes almost between their feet, and then darted into the air with alarmed cries. The baby, dozing in Nelly's arms, started and clutched Nelly's cheek with its white claws. Amanda, fascinated by the creature's ruthless violence, said with conviction, 'You must have had an awfully hard time, Nelly.'

'It is hard, Miss.' Nelly carefully disengaged the baby's nails from her soft cheek. 'When you've got a baby and everyone knows you've no right to it. I didn't go out in the street for six months. I just couldn't. I think I should have died. But of course I have to go out now; you get used to everything.' Nelly's underlip began to shake, and tears appeared in her lashes.

'I'm frightfully sorry.' Amanda tried to comfort her. But the girl did not cry. The tears did not fall. And now her doll-like prettiness took on the marble firmness of a young woman of character. 'You can't do anything, Miss – it's not your fault,' she said. 'If Harry, Mr Dawbarn, likes you better. And of course you've brought him the Quarry. I couldn't blame him. And I'm not going to say he even promised me.'

'I'm glad to hear that.'

'No, he never promised me. I just bin silly. Oh, I'll get over it.' And to Amanda's surprise and admiration, she gave a prim little smile, 'You don't die of it. Only – I should like to get away from the village.'

'I can understand that.'

'I did try for a place, but they wouldn't have the baby. It makes it hard to get away, having the baby. Just when it's the baby makes you want to get away. But there—' she sighed.

'Shall I try and arrange something, Nelly?'

'I wish you would, Miss. You see, after Mr Dawbarn gets married, and being so close at the Quarry, well, you can see it mid be a bit awkward for me. *He* doesn't see, but then he's not me, he doesn't know how I'd be feeling. Well, of course, a man's got so much to think of, especially with a new farm.'

'I'll get you a place, Nelly, never fear.' Amanda took the girl's hand and then, on an impulse, stooped forward to kiss her. 'I do feel so sorry.' But Nelly did not understand the gesture. She remained at a polite distance and did not invite the kiss. She answered in her prim, gentle manner, 'I'm a good worker. Ask my mother. And clean. And nobody need be afraid for my character. You'd better tell them that, Miss. Truly, I'm not the one you might think. I've been brought up strict, and so I am strict. They can make any rules they like about followers or going out. I shan't mind if I never see a man again.'

'Why, it's Miss Groom!' Mrs Raft's voice, wheezing in eagerness, came from the kitchen window. A fat woman in spectacles, who had visibly been, twenty years before, the image of Nelly, but who was now, with her double chin, and fat cheeks, and red snub nose, a plain pug. 'They said you were here.' She bumped her shopping basket on the table, behind the window. 'And you're just the one I wanted to speak to.' She glared fiercely at Amanda through her little blue eyes; Nelly's eyes faded from periwinkle to bottle-glass. 'They tell me you're going to marry Harry Dawbarn, but what I tell you is that he ought to be marrying my Nelly here. And if he don't do her justice, I'll see justice done on him.'

'Oh, mother,' said Nelly, 'don't go on about it.'

'Yes, I am going on about it. I'm going into court about it, as you should do for yourself, if you had any proper pride.'

'I wonder you haven't more pride, mother, to drag me through all that muck before people.'

'Pride!' cried Mrs Raft, surging from the back door as if to come nearer to this source of evil. 'Don't talk to me of your pride. If you had any real pride in you you'd set about righting yourself and your family.'

Nelly hastily put back the baby in its pram, as if fearing that her mother might do it an injury. But when the baby at once began to scream, it was Mrs Raft who rocked the pram and said, 'Sh – sh, there, there; yes, why haven't you got a father, you may well ask.'

'Now, mother, you're not going on about Harry.'

'I didn't say Harry, I said a husband. There's better men than Harry. I should hope. You could make better out of a turnip with the finger and toe. Sh-sh, though indeed you've a right to cry.'

'I suppose you mean young Marten. You're always on at me about young Marten.'

'And so I should be. A nice, decent, clean-living boy that would take you tomorrow and thank you, and set you up in your own kitchen. And if you had any proper woman's sense you'd jump at him and the chance of a Christian home and lawful children, and your own proper lawful place in the world. Don't talk to me of the neighbours. They'll never say another word to you when you've got your ring and had your first in your own man's bed. They'll think all the better of you for making a good pudding in a cracked bowl.'

'Oh, Miss Groom, you must wonder at us. And it's not true about young Marten. He wouldn't take me except I go before the Court.'

'And why not?' cried Mrs Raft, quite enraged. 'Why should he have spoiled goods without a luck-penny. Not but he wouldn't have you sooner than another. But if he does want the Court-money, isn't that all to his credit and your good, you silly muffet. Don't it show his sense and management, and husband-like nature that God knows every woman might thank God for when she's wit enough to know that marriage is something more than feather beds and – well, I can't say it, though I should think I had every right in this present company.'

'Oh, mother, and before Miss Groom.'

'He knows what a pound a week means to a young family. Yes, and in decency, my girl, in washing and keeping things clean and proper so a woman can respect herself. It's all the difference, my lady, and you'll live to thank God for a mother that knows what's what in spite of your merikan films and your skule marms and their poetry – and ouldn't give way to your fala-di-das.'

Amanda caught Nelly's eyes fixed on her with deprecation or appeal, and came to her assistance. Indeed, Amanda felt strong personal sympathy with Nelly.

'I was wondering, Mrs Raft,' she said, 'if Nelly might like to leave Ancombe for a while, because I feel sure I could arrange something.'

'And whose idea is that – Mr Harry-Quarry-Dawbarn's or Miss Nelly Silly's?'

'It was mine, mother.'

'You can tell Harry Dawbarn from me, Miss Groom, that Nelly may be a silly lamb, but the old yowe Raft has got more than wool in her head. He may turn poor Nelly round his dirty finger, she was born meat for that sort's platter. But he can't turn me anyways. I'm going straight along to Court.'

'Oh, mother, you'll make me so ashamed, I'll go right away – indeed I can't bear it. No, I can't,' and she went, with her chin high and a movement of true dignity, into the kitchen. The dignity was not impaired by a certain dramatic quality which reminded Amanda of a film actress in a scene of proud renunciation.

But Mrs Raft did not approve of dignity in daughters. She pursued, exclaiming, 'And none of your Garbo airs can't stop me from my plain duty.'

'But really, Mrs Raft.' Amanda had followed to the rescue. 'Don't you think if I can find Nelly a good place out of Ancombe.'

'Ah, so that's it. A place. We've heard that one before. Going away from the only chance she's got of a real proper life to wash down the steps in some nasty London bed-and-breakfast house. Running away like a sheep with its tail on fire to put its head in a bush.'

'Oh mother.' Nelly turned to the sink and began to wash up dishes as if washing her hands of all this vulgarity.

'And of course you're encouraging her, Miss Groom. When it's Harry-don't-Marry's idea to get her out of Ancombe. Yes, that's it, I'll bet my burial money.'

'Really, Mrs Raft, I never dreamt—'

'You never dreamt and Nelly never thinks – so there's a pair of you then.'

'I can't have you go into Court, mother, no, I can't, and Miss Groom thinks the same. To have it all in the *Queensport News*.' And carefully she laid one washed plate upon another.

'You talk like a fule, Nelly. A fule from skule, for God knows *I* don't know what the skules put into you for all the money they cost. What with whim-whams from skule and the films, you girls are all bewitched. And what, may I ask, are you going to live on? With a baby to rear? This wonderful pride. It's a fine pride to starve your own baby and feed him on London blacks. It's a fine pride to go and hide yourself in some dirty hole when you might be a proper wife and mistress of your own home, and your own man, and face it out with the best lady in the England – for there's not one of 'em, not if she's a duchess, can have more than one husband and one set of lines. But I ont allow it. You may talk words but I'll act parsnips. I'll go for a summons today. I'll write to his lordship himself. Nothing like going to the top. The king's ears hear better than a beadle's belly; yes, I'll go to his lordship himself and tell him what a shame and disgrace it is to have such as Doggie Dawbarn taking up good land in Ancombe on the strength of his airings and fairings with some young ladies that ought to know better how to control their natural nature.'

'Oh, mother, I can't listen to such things. I'm sure Miss Groom could never know what you mean.'

'She knows well enough, and she knows what happened in the Tinker's piece up to Pinmouth Head, when Master Harry's car was standing there by the road two hours on Fair night – and I hope she's got him well tied down in writing or she might find herself where my Nelly is. But I suppose being a lady she's not so simple to take the crust with the crumb. It's only a frolic to her what mid have been death to a shame-faced, decent Christian girl like my Nelly that never thought but being a sweetheart was being a true lover, and being a true lover was being a wife, and being a wife was the same thing as being a mother, a girl that never learnt any nasty tricks to be anything but what God meant her. And so you see she's to be everybody's fule. No, not if I know it, Miss Groom.'

Amanda was already in retreat to the door. She even made an indignant face, though she felt less indignation than tedium. Nelly hastened to open the door for her. 'You must excuse mother, Miss Groom, it has been such a terrible let down for her after the struggle she had to bring us up.'

'Not to me,' cried Mrs Raft close behind. 'But I'll allow it's a let-down for Ancombe to have such as Harry Dawbarn come to the Quarry, and I'll say it to your face, Miss, however you may stare and sniff—'

Amanda did not want to stare or sniff. Her only desire was to go away from the hot little kitchen and the atmosphere of domestic feelings into some more peaceful air, and sleep. She was all at once so jaded that she feared she might yawn. Hastily she climbed into her car.

'She couldn't understand how I feel, Miss Groom, nor how you mid feel about these kind of things.' Nelly gave her melancholy little smile. 'She was one of the old-fashioned ones, never went to skule. But she's bin a good mother to us all; she means it all for the best.'

'I'm sure she does,' said Amanda, smiling at Nelly in a way which she felt to be stupid and even false. And she was only just in time in driving away. For at once she was seized with yawns. 'Oh dear,' she said, with tears in her eyes, 'I wish I didn't do that, it makes me feel so empty. Really, it's quite miserable. I shall cry in a moment. I don't seem to care about anything. Will that woman really take Harry into Court. I suppose she'll say it's my fault. But I don't really care. I don't really care about anything,' and once more she yawned, so cruelly, that her sigh was like a sob.

In fact Mrs Raft went to Queensport that same day, and Harry received a summons to attend the next petty sessions. This news he gave to Amanda two days later, in his own field, called Foxfallow, on the Ancombe road. He was harvesting his wheat in a great hurry, for fear of rain. Harry had decided to thrash direct from the stook, and to sacrifice his straw, and had brought together three waggons to carry the sheaves. Most of the neighbours were loading, and Harry himself was in charge of the machine. At three o'clock in the afternoon, when the two ladies from the Villa arrived, about a third of the work had been done. But the sky of the morning, the pale blue of a very hot day, had deepened and thickened. The heat was an oppression – and the sun itself, throwing down its glare on the stubble, seemed to flicker in the hot smells rising from the tractor, and the clouds of fine dust going up forty feet in the air from the shakers and riddles of the huge thresher. The very body of this machine, fresh-painted like all Okey's equipment, in lobster scarlet and prussian blue, seemed to gather up and insist upon the two presiding sensations of the moment, an intolerable heat, and the heavy threat of the opaque sky.

'Oh how lovely it is,' Ella cried every moment. 'How I love harvest. It makes all human worries seem so small, so petty. Before the plenty of God's bounty.'

Old Bobby, toiling with an enormous fork to remove the chaff from beneath the thresher, before it rose to the undercarriage and clogged the riddles, touched his bowler. Like most of the men present, he wore a bowler, considered in those parts to be the best protection against harvest dust, chaff, and awns. Ella gave a delighted response. She was always glad to be recognized in the fields; a greeting made her feel part of that productive and valuable world in which she had felt so often her worthlessness.

She waved to Harry, who, high up in the air, was feeding the drum. His gestures, in contrast with those of a serious pale young man who, with jerks like those of a clockwork toy, was cutting open the sheaves as they fell from the elevator canvas, were wild and loose. He seemed to be performing a barbaric dance of triumph on the bodies of the corn.

Ella at once became furiously energetic, and going up to the machine uttered cries of encouragement which were, however, quite inaudible in the noise.

Harry handed his fork to an assistant and climbed down by the wheel. But he disappeared at once under the elevator, where he examined the grain falling into the sacks.

'What beautiful weather for your harvest,' Ella cried. 'What shall we do – shall I go up there?'

Harry glanced round at the sky, which began, all round the horizon, to show a tawny or umber haze, very like the colour of the ripe wheat. 'We'll be lucky if that doesn't come down on us before evening, and if this old contraption holds together so long. She was stopped for an hour this morning, trust her.'

It was plain that Harry the master was not so resigned as formerly to the uncertainty of things. The glance of his blue eye from sky to tractor expressed a tragic indignation, heightened perhaps in dramatic effect by the negro-like blackness of the pits in which they rolled. Harry was extremely dirty, harvest dirty. His coffee-coloured cheeks were dabbled with sweat which darkened also the collarless shirt that clung to his body like a wet plaster.

'I bet she'll go back on us,' he said. 'She's just waiting to break something.'

'I thought Mr Okey had a new one,' said Amanda.

'So he has, but he keeps that for himself.' He let a handful of grain run into his palm, and squeezed it between finger and thumb. 'It's not too dry either.'

'I'll just go and get a fork,' said Ella, moving away towards Bobby, perhaps with some notion of assisting him. Amanda said to Harry, 'We're in the way.'

'No, Amanda, I've been wanting to see you. I've had no time to come along. Listen to that' – he started and looked angrily at the thresher – 'that's a new knock, but she's got so many knocks and wambles in her inside that you can't tell where the trouble is.'

'Have you got your new shed at Quarry?'

'You must come and see it. You never heard my bad news, Amanda, about Nelly.'

'I hope nothing has happened to poor Nelly.'

'It's not Nelly, it's the old woman. She's made Nelly take out a summons, for the baby – it will cost me a good fifteen shillings a week. That's the interest on a thousand pounds. And a thousand pounds would buy me a proper set of tools. I shouldn't have to depend on a domned old wreck like this, just when the bottom is falling out of the weather.'

'I shall be an expensive luxury, shan't I?'

'Ah!' Harry frowned at her.

'But at least I can help you now,' said Amanda hastily. 'I can go and load.'

'No, Amanda. Don't you be lifting up your arms, I've known two girls slip a baby that way.'

'Do you want my baby more than Nelly's?'

'It's due to it to take proper care,' said Harry austerely. 'I wouldn't have you lame yourself either.'

'Yes,' said Amanda, 'that thresher must be a worry with all that trouble going on inside. I'm not surprised you don't rush into matrimony.'

'I'm just the man for matrimony, as well you know,' said Harry. 'If only it wouldn't come on like this in harvest, when a dog hasn't time to turn himself round.'

'I'm sorry, Harry. I was only joking.'

'Joking,' said Harry with deep reproach. 'You may joke but it's no joke for me – I don't know how things could be awkwarder, and look at that sky. The weather may break this very day. Oh, dom the old octopus. Gee-orge.' With this yell uttered in tones of rage and agony, Harry dived from beneath the elevator and began to climb the thresher. At the same moment, tractor, and therefore elevator and thresher, stopped their roaring clatter. And suddenly distant voices, the jingling of harness, the creak of a wheel, the rustle of Bobby's fork among the draff, were heard – noises of such a different scale and quality that they spread peace over the field, and even the heat seemed less oppressive.

Amanda moved sleepily from the grey and dusty shade of the elevator into the bright sun. The stubbles pricked her ankles and tore her stockings as she went towards the nearest waggon. She was too sleepy to be amused by Harry's practicability of mind, but amusement dwelt with her as a possibility; she might smile when she was not so languid. Even her reflections seemed rather to occur to her than to be an activity in her brain. 'I suppose it ought to be quite pleasant, dawdling in this heat, and having a husband waiting for me, a good-natured husband that I could respect – I shall probably be very happy with Harry – as a kind of natural development. This don't care feeling is very likely the beginning of it. One only has to trust in the flesh, or nature, or the life force, whatever that is, and it will simply mould one into a wife – like dough. And first it makes the dough. Yes, I'm getting softer every day.'

And she felt so strong a wish to lie down by herself and doze, that when she returned to the Villa and heard Robin's voice echoing in the hall, where now every voice echoed on bare boards, she slipped up to her room by the back stairs. She did not want to be bothered by Robin. She had even forgotten that he was coming for the sale, and had preferred to arrive a day before. He had been writing to her lately in the old affectionate style, and now he would want to talk.

She took off her frock and lay down on the sofa. The door opened and Robin burst in. 'Hello, old girl, are you decent? It doesn't matter. How nice to see you. Oh God' – he sat down against her legs – '*how* nice it is, and I can stay a fortnight, and Kathy is fixed in her office, the boss can't do without her for a moment.'

'How is Kathy? Did she mind your coming?'

'No, hated it. She's very jealous of you.'

'That's rather silly, and a pity.'

'No, it's very sensible. She knows I'm not going back.'

'But Robin, you can't desert your new family, can you?'

'There isn't one. That was a yarn. The old trick – to fix me down and get me away from you. But I told you all about it in my letter. Don't you read my letters? No, don't apologize, why should you read them.'

'But I did – I just – I've been rather worried.' Amanda had in fact discounted all Robin's news about his quarrels with Kathy, his hatred of the office. She thought, 'Oh dear, this is going to be worse than I expected.'

'Never mind that,' said Robin impatiently. 'The *important* thing is, that I've been transferred to Exeter, and I'm going to do the estate business. No more Court work.'

'You'll enjoy that.'

'I'd better,' said Robin. 'I've even made an offer for a cottage, complete with ye old apple trees.'

Robin seemed thinner, much older, and much more erratic in mood. He gazed at Amanda with delight and cried, 'My hat, you look a picture – like a sunburnt Venus de Milo,' and then at once cried out, 'But oh, these last months! I wonder I didn't cut my throat – I suppose one gets so discouraged – that one hasn't the energy even to do the obvious sensible thing.'

'Yes, he's going to be difficult, poor Robin,' Amanda thought. And after supper, when a walk was proposed, she said, 'I do have to go down to the village, but it's only for half an hour, and it wouldn't amuse you.'

'But I'd love a walk, even down to the village – in the moon.'

'There's no moon and it's going to rain, and I'm taking the car, to Ancombe,' she looked at him significantly, 'to see if Harry's harvest is safely in.'

'*Harry's* harvest, I see.'

He frowned a moment, then became lively again. 'But why shouldn't I look at Harry's harvest, too?'

'Of course you must come. But we shall be caught. Where on earth is my mac?'

Robin, in his most excited mood, was chatting about his new adventure. 'Uncle Dick thinks I'm mad, but of course he would. He's all for a nice safe income.'

'It's rather important,' said Amanda.

And in the car, while Amanda drove to Ancombe, they had one of those discussions so pleasant to them both. Amanda urging the value of a secure income, because it left the mind free to consider problems more important than subsistence; Robin, demanding risk, danger, adventure. 'The important thing, Mandy, is the will to live, to act, to enjoy; without that the world will stop. Look at all those Polynesian tribes which died out when the missions stopped their dances.'

'The dances couldn't go on without the cult.'

'As you like – but the people died. They lost the will to carry on. And it's frightfully easy to lose. I know because I've lost it several times.'

'But you always enjoyed life, Robin – music, books, pictures.'

'Carrots in front of the donkey's nose.'

'That's nonsense.'

'That's what they were for this donkey, while he was a donkey, in that blasted mill.'

'But now you're out of the London mill.'

They had reached Quarry, and Amanda turned the car in at the gate of Harry's wheat field. It was growing dark and the sun was hidden in low cloud, but a bar of brilliant green light from the west illuminated the harvest field with a cold radiance like that of a neon lamp in which thirty or forty volunteers, resembling vigorous ghosts, were loading the waggons. All the boys and girls of the

village, as well as the young ladies from the Post Office and Colonel
Hicks from Kashmir Cottage, had come to save the crop. And all
were working with the utmost fury. The group round the machine
especially appeared like half-damned souls, labouring for their
salvation, in the very throat of limbo.

'You know, Mandy,' Robin was saying, and in the pale light his
anxious face seemed wasted by some mortal disease, 'I can hardly
believe that I'm clear at last, that I'll never see Kathy again. I'd
forgotten what it was like to be free. I'm like a pit pony brought up
during a strike.'

'Where shall we go?'

'I don't mind.' Robin's eyes were fixed on Amanda. 'But, Mandy,
when can you come and see our cottage?'

'Our cottage?'

'Why not, you'll have nothing to do here after the sale.'

'Yes, I'm afraid I may have.'

'You're not tied up with Harry Dawbarn?'

'I am rather. I'm sorry, Robin.'

'Oh, don't apologize; in fact, I might have guessed when you
stopped answering my letters.'

'I'm terribly sorry.'

'Oh, good heavens, it's quite in order. I deserve it, no one better.
You tried to pull me in, but I wouldn't jump. Very well, here I am,
left again. It's quite poetic.'

And he went on explaining with cheerful asperity that he had
always been like that; one of the fools who never got any cheese
because he was so careful to dodge the traps. 'I'm the wise guy who
starved himself to death for fear of indigestion.'

They were standing beside the great heap of straw at the tail of
the machine, now higher than itself, so that five men with forks
were throwing the wastage clear. It appeared that this expedient
was quicker than moving the machine forwards and readjusting
the driving bands. Old Bobby, toiling at the draff, was like a gnome
among gorges and crags of his own construction. His bowler now
carried in its brim a complete ring of chaff, resembling a large pie
crust. But still he was continually defeated by the drifts, and three
schoolgirls, every few moments, rushed to his help from their first
duty of bringing new sacks.

Rows of sacks standing against the straw heap were waiting to
be picked up and carried away to the Quarry barn, as soon as the
waggons should be free. But the waggons rolling like ships at sea

across the lands, were still travelling to and fro with their loads of sheaves, which now had to be brought from the farthest corner of the long field. And everyone, while he toiled himself at frantic speed, was continually shouting to the rest, 'Come on, there – hurry up!' Harry, waving his long arms, seemed the most frantic, so that Robin looked at him from time to time with surprise which changed gradually into disgust.

'All the same, it's a lot of fuss about a few pounds worth of corn.'

'It's more than that, and Harry's rather on his mettle for his first crop.'

'Oh, you needn't tell me. It's a bet. But look at that old lunatic if you please,' indicating Uncle Bob with a jerk of his chin. 'Why should he kill himself?'

'They're so afraid of the rain.'

But Robin's resentment against himself was becoming, as usual, a general bitterness against everybody and everything. He answered, 'Quite – it's a pious duty to beat the weather – or habit. Oh, I envy them, especially old Faithful. But you must admit that the spectacle of faith being victimized has its depressing side.'

The sun's edge had come below the clouds and threw out a yellow ray like an old-fashioned gas light which at once gave substance to the ghosts. They became figures of extremest solidity; in blue-black shadows outlined with fire. They were, as Robin remarked, 'like a lot of savages performing some juju rite before a fertility temple.' And it was true that the thresher in its gaudy red and blue, shaking as with rapidly beaten drums, had an exotic look, especially as the sun sank below the hedges and left the surface of the field in darkness, so that the waggons seemed to have run aground in a shallow brown sea, and the temple appeared to stand upon an island of tropical mud.

'The old witch doctor is as mad as the rest,' said Robin, looking at Colonel Hicks, who, in riding breeches, and an ancient polo shirt, was now feeding the elevator, 'taken in by his own racket.'

'It's rather nice, don't you think, that he does feel like that?'

'Oh, rather, it must be marvellous. All the same, it's rather a limited choice, don't you think, between being a blind ant among millions of blind ants, sweating your silly guts out to build a great useless mud heap for white ants to sweat in, or a free and independent voter who votes that mud is mud and refuses to breed more blind ants to make more mud heaps.'

'But, Robin, there's something between – '

'Yes, I'm between, that's where I fall down – oh, I know it's damn silly! But would you be a colonel in order to enjoy life, the tribal life?'

'I'm sure you'll like your new job.'

'Will you like your dung heaps and cooking pots – the sacramental vessels?'

'I don't know.'

'Rather unpleasant if you hated them – of course, I don't want to undermine your faith. Honestly, if I thought you could be happy as a tribal mammy, I'd push you on. But if I'm right, you're dithering already, and if so you'd better break it off quick. The independent voter can't change his spots without shooting out his brains, and unfortunately for you, you've got some brains.'

'Yes, but – I'm rather committed – the fact is, between ourselves, I've got a baby coming.'

'What? Never? But is it certain?'

'Quite.'

'And how on earth?' Robin kept staring at her with a face which astonishment made young and childish. 'I never dreamt that you would—'

'Neither did I – but, here I am.'

'Yes, there you are. My God, yes! Yes. I should think so. But what was the idea, or was it an accident?'

'No, I can't say it was an accident.'

'Then why? You didn't need to make sure of your farmer. Or was it religious, too, the real primitive touch? Are you one of the girls who react against weddings – who think any kind of official ceremony rather spoils the solemnity of being had?'

Two of the schoolgirls, rushing through the dusk with flying pigtails, as they dragged a pile of new sacks, almost ran into Robin's legs. They burst into loud giggles and circled round him, doubling themselves up in a dramatic show of mirth. But Robin and Amanda did not even notice this interruption.

'And you do take everything seriously – bloody seriously? Yes, I bet it's another of your religious quirks.'

'Oh, Robin, don't be angry with me. I don't even know if I'll like babies.'

'No, no.' He peered at her. 'So that's why – you wanted to commit yourself – you closed your eyes and took the big jump.'

'I don't know. Perhaps I just drifted over.'

'And you were right. By God, you were!' Robin had suddenly moved off at a new angle. 'Isn't that what I've always said – put yourself in a jam.'

'It's going to pour. Hadn't we better take cover?'

'Yes, but you women are lucky. You've got the biggest, finest kind of jam just waiting for you – you've only got to lie down and close your eyes and you're done for. You'll *have* to have the hell of a time whether you like it or not. You'll be right up against it – against everything, death, hell, and the Government.'

Suddenly the bulging clouds let fall sheets of tepid water. In a moment the stubble was shining with great pools. Robin and Amanda gazed up with astonishment at the crowd of figures, of every height and size, rushing towards them, some hastily putting on mackintoshes, others drawing sacks over their heads. 'Oh,' said Amanda, 'the tarpaulins.' She seized hold of the huge canvas sheet which now, dragged by twenty hands, was pulled over sacks and straw. For a moment Harry stood before her, shouting some directions. In his folded sack, with the corner standing out behind his blackened face, he resembled a Spanish monk. He turned suddenly to her and said, 'Is that you, Amanda? You shouldn't have been out so late. Come, go in under.' He pushed her beneath the edge of the tarpaulin.

'I hope you've saved most of the crop, Harry.'

'Ah, the rain beat us, coming on like that. And the sacks should have been covered. But dom it all, I haven't eyes all round me. Hi-hi,' he rushed away shouting at the tractor men to unhitch the driving band.

'Come under cover, Robin.' Amanda made room for the man, but he stood with the rain streaming down his face and soaking his thin tweeds, with the same bitter expression, as if relishing the knowledge that he looked ridiculous. 'Yes,' he said, 'you're lucky, you girls. You're born to be caught and racketeered – it's in your blood – and when you're caught you have to fight for your lives and so your lives are worth something, and you are worth something. Now if I'd had the luck to catch galloping consumption I might have been a poet, but if I went deliberately and caught it, I'd only be a lunatic or a masochist.'

'Come out of the rain, Robin, you'll be drowned.' She drew him under cover.

The two little girls, screaming with laughter inside their sacks, came diving among the straw and jerked down the edge of the tarpaulin, which at once poured a stream of water down Amanda's neck. She shivered and moved closer to Robin. 'You were in love with Kathy once?'

'Never. I was simply taking a chance.'

'Didn't you even expect to be happy?'

'Do you?' he asked in a gloomy, bitter tone.

'No, I don't think so.'

'I said it was all a religious thing.'

'I don't know. Perhaps—'

'Yes, by God, you women always manage to make a religion, if it's only out of two sticks and a po. It's your game – Aunt Rose was sirnply a household pope.'

'But Kathy – you can't say—'

'Kathy, *she's* the worst of the lot. She has the devil's religion.'

'Let's go Robin.'

'We couldn't be wetter than we are. And you ought to enjoy it, being damned uncomfortable around a family farm. That's real primitive religion, women's religion, the oldest in the world. You're starting at the bottom again. And Harry Dawbarn will be your household priest.'

'Let's go, Robin.'

'Now you're angry with me. I've upset you.'

'No, perhaps you're right.'

'Of course I'm right, but why shouldn't that upset you. And you're right, too, how right.' The young man seemed almost tearful in his anger and disappointment. 'You *ought* to follow your religion since you're lucky enough to bave one, to be born with one. It's your duty.'

'Let's go, Robin.'

'Yes, you get the car and I'll open the gate. No, I'll drive and you can open the gate. I don't understand those latches.'

Amanda, reflecting that Robin had chosen the drier task, ran to open the gate. As she pushed it back against the high bank, from which hawthorns poured down new fountains on her hat, Harry appeared beside her. In his peaked hood he seemed now, rather than a monk, the member of some secret society lurking in ambush.

'Amanda, Amanda, is that you there?' He roared as if, having been tuned for heroic events, he could not at once come down to the domestic scale. 'If the weather breaks we mid be married this week.'

'But isn't this only a thunder shower?'

'We're due for rain, the glass is going down, dom it, and the wireless says we're right into a depression. I'll warn 'em at the church.'

'But, Harry, you'd much better marry Nelly.'

'Nelly! Who said so?'

'Yes, you must marry Nelly. She'd make a far better wife for you, better for the farm, too.'

'Come, dearr,' said Harry, in a coaxing tone, 'you know you don't mean it.' He laid his hand on hers, which still gripped the top bars of the gate. 'What is it? Tell me. Have you got the idea I'm thinking too much of the money – why, I'd pay it to get you. But I know what it is – you think I'm making more of corn harvest than I ought. But, Amanda, you wouldn't have me make a fule of myself in my first year. And you know you're going to be the boss – yes, you'll be the mistress and no mistake. You'll turn me round your pretty fingers. Mother Raft has said so already, and she knows. Why, I know it myself, no one better.'

'Harry, please!'

The car had arrived and passed into the road. Amanda made a step beside it, Harry followed closely. 'Amanda, you don't mean it. But it's not a thing I want to sleep on. Indeed, I couldn't sleep.'

'Harry, I'm doing you a good turn. Marry Nelly and forget me.' She got into the car and was driven away. Robin said, 'Lucky chap all round. The weather has got him and he's got you, and you've got your own racket – the woman's racket – the biggest bloody swindle of the lot. Just to keep the old ant-heap going – the old squirrel-cage turning.'

'But he hasn't got me. I'm not going to marry him. I've just told him so.'

'Not going to?' Robin almost ran the car into the bank as he turned his face towards the girl. 'What's the idea?'

'I've changed my mind.'

'Don't talk nonsense. Excuse me, but you're being silly.'

'I know, but it struck me that you might be right.'

'What about?'

'This impulse – whatever it is – the woman's racket.'

'I said religion.'

'I don't mind about the names, but Harry is not a racketeer. And *should* I be a proper wife to him? Of course I shouldn't.'

'Now that *is* religion – it's almost mystical.'

'Oh, Robin, don't make things more difficult, and don't quarrel with me. I can't bear quarrelling.'

'But I've *got* to quarrel with you.' And then in a tone of surprise he asked, 'Do you mean to say that what I said made any difference?'

For a moment Amanda looked into a depth of modesty which was quite as dark as any bottomless pit.

CHAPTER 32

Iris and Bertie Groom, and Dorothy Pedley, all arrived next morning within an hour of each other. The first two had taken rooms in Queensport, but Dorothy was resolved on staying at the Villa. 'After all,' she said, 'it's all ours really, and it's going to stay ours. Dick says we can intervene at any time. And why should Amanda get anything? She's not even in the family.'

'She won't get the Queen Anne bureau, anyhow,' said Iris, who detested Dorothy and always defended Amanda, on principle, because Amanda was, in some measure, at a disadvantage.

'I *bought* the bureau,' said Dorothy.

'But did you pay anything for it?' said Iris in a voice which was at once soft and vindictive.

Dorothy moved away as if she had not heard. But she complained to Bertie and Ella of Iris's bad manners. 'It's not as if she were responsible for *everybody's* soul.'

And Bertie smiled as at a family joke. In fact, this phrase had been a favourite of Aunt Rose, and was for that very reason a family joke, especially with Iris.

Iris was a slender, pale, pretty little woman of forty-five, whose dark hair was turning grey, but in such a way that her looks were improved. She seemed still more appealing, gentle. In face she was like her grandfather Venn, and like her mother in build, but in character she was different from both. She was a born bachelor, and probably it was lucky for some man that she had not married. She was a born teacher, and should have been a head mistress if it had not been for a sharp, careless tongue and a certain lack of ambition. She loved books, luxury, good wine, clever girls, pretty frocks, and detested what she called poverty. She was also apt to quarrel with all authorities, all older people, and especially senior members of her own family. She had despised her father, and she had a special hatred for Rose, whom she called a sadistic old tyrant. She was a woman who treasured and improved her hatreds, and her quarrel with Rose dated from a famous battle, twenty years before, over the education of the younger girls, Muriel, Dorothy and Amanda. There was a nine-year gap between Iris and the next girl Dorothy, for a son born in '97 had died at three months. Thus at the outbreak of war, the three younger girls were still going to school, a cheap day school near Brent Square.

Iris had always protested against this place, and urged her own boarding school, Beltham, an enormous place, famous for its austerities and good instruction. Her parents answered that it was too expensive in their present distress. But in 1914 this objection was suddenly removed. The Government took over the Academy for a fuse factory, and gave Groom so good a salary as director of research that he was, for the first time in twenty years, well off. When Iris therefore renewed her demand that the girls should be properly educated, he warmly supported her. Groom, indeed, was not only a strong believer in education, but he tended to think that the more it approximated to the type of his own education, lectures and laboratory work in large, expensive buildings, remote from domestic interference, the better it must be.

Only Bessie opposed a change, because, as Iris declared, she was growing more possessive in her old age, or as others might have said, because, like most mothers, she was becoming more attached to her children, more absorbed in their interests, as their interests became more complicated.

And Bessie was at once convinced by the first Zeppelins, in 1915. She objected only to Beltham, and only because it was too far from London.

It was at this moment that Rose made her celebrated intervention. Rose had always hated girls' boarding schools of the public school type. And this issue with Bessie roused her most pugnacious feelings. It drew her, indeed, out of a certain apathy which had, for some years, seemed to threaten her with an old age of weariness and indifference. Thus in her sixties Rose had a rebirth of energy. She threw herself into the affairs of life with abandon, with violence. But to her family's surprise, her opinions had become much more old-fashioned, much narrower.

This event, so common but always surprising to families that suffer it, arose naturally from Rose's age. She was now too old to trouble about conciliating the enemy. She felt no doubt that she had nothing to expect from the world. She threw away discretion and used the frankness of her youth because, like that young girl, she was not afraid of anybody. She said aloud what she had felt for years, and called her opponents fools, rascals; the times shallow, self-seeking; its arts, cheap; its manners as vulgar as its ambitions.

As soon as she heard of Bessie's weakening towards girls' boarding schools, she hastened to town, and whereas ten years before, when Alice and Iris had been sent to Beltham, she had offered only a few reasoned objections, she now raged. She accused Bessie of wanting to ruin her girls. 'I don't know anything more detestable than Beltham – see what it has done for Alice and Iris. Alice, who can't do a single thing well, who can't even manage her servants, who drives her husband mad with her muddle, and Iris, a conceited selfish creature who thinks she knows everything and really knows nothing. Send the young ones to us at the Villa, my dear, they will be perfectly safe and I can get the most excellent governess.'

But Bessie had no intention of sending Amanda to the Villa. She was jealous of Rose with Amanda. She answered cheerfully, 'Thank you, my dear, but the girls may have to earn their living, and then Beltham will be a great advantage to them.'

'What for – a label? So you'd ruin your children to make them bad teachers, labelled Beltham. But the whole age is hypocrisy piled on hypocrisy.'

'Iris is a very good teacher.'

'Who thinks girls and boys should have exactly the same treatment, which is not even biologically true. A girl is not a boy, Bessie, you ought to know that better than I do. Continual turmoil and noise, in a great prison-like barrack, may be good for boys, but it is certainly not good for girls. I doubt if it is good for boys either, or for any human soul.'

Bessie put her off with a careless, 'I'm sorry, Rose, but it's all arranged – I've written to Beltham.'

The truth was that Rose was no longer taken seriously in Brent Square. The sudden appearance of this obstinate old spinster, thin and black as a kitchen poker, with her provincial cranks, affected these London people in the midst of the war which seemed to them, especially since the Zeppelins, so much more their war, as a stupidity, an impertinence. The anxious William, who had enlisted in the ranks, gazed at her with sad wonder; Iris, assisting at a Ministry, talked over her head, Bessie flying from committee to committee, child to child, looked through her, and Bertie, who had found in war at last a way of escape from his hated classroom, who was already a smart major in the smartest of regiments, curled his new moustache at her and drawled, 'Re-ally, Auntie – and how are they all at Queensport? I suppose they've hardly heard of the war down there?'

Even James Groom listened to her protests with a blank gaze which revealed the absence of his mind. For though James had been quietly put on one side by the young men of the research council, he was always anxious and perplexed; perpetually getting up in the night to make some important note, which, on the next day, found its way to some waste-paper basket.

But Rose was not to be put off her important duty, by indifference. No war was goung to make her acquiesce in what seemed to her needless folly and wickedness. She continued her attacks, 'You've no right, at least, to send Amanda to this school.'

'Excuse me,' said Bessie. 'I've every right, and I particularly want Amanda to have the *best* education.'

'You haven't even considered what a good education means.'

'I know that it's something every girl nowadays needs to get a job,' said Bessie, 'unless she's satisfied to be a kitchen maid. Things have moved on since Miss Simpson taught us the use of the globes in the library. Why, Rose, you can't realize how changed things are.'

'For the worse, and why? Because of these schools.'

'Oh stuff, my dear, a million things have changed, *everything's* changed, books, pictures, plays, politics, servants, even the food. And Mr Gladstone's been dead more than ten years. As for girls, they are quite a new sort of animal, right from the cradle.'

This argument only enraged Rose. For she felt its terrible force. She saw that the girls' boarding schools were in fact only one innovation in a world which was all new, all changed, and which never ceased changing. She seemed like a lost soul in some great house full of beautiful things, in which every kind of destruction was going on at a faster and faster rate. Thieves were going in and out, and no one was there to prevent them, storms were smashing the windows and no one would trouble to repair them, the roofs were leaking, ceilings were falling, magnificent pictures, beautiful hangings were rotting with mildew, and she, all alone, running desperately to close the shutters against a snowstorm drifting silently through the broken panes, would see at the same moment the roof of the chapel gently collapse inwards, and standing in dismay, would hear, from every side, above, below, from cellars, bedrooms, libraries, attics, the gnawing of a million hungry impatient rats.

But desperation made Rose only more determined. She hastened back to Ella. 'We must save Amanda from that sink at Beltham which has ruined Alice and Iris already.'

Unluckily Bessie had foreseen this move – she had written to Ella, and in all family battles Ella was with Bessie against Rose. She said at once, 'But Rose, don't you think perhaps that Amanda – in her – special position – ought to have the best qualifications?'

'I see Bessie has been at you,' said Rose.

'No – that is – she did write, but that isn't why I think – that perhaps—'

'Have you thought, Ella, that we – that you – are responsible for the child – for her very soul.'

'Oh, but Rose, Beltham makes a special point of religious training and music.'

'A soul,' said Rose, 'and a woman's soul, who may be a wife and mother, with responsibility for her own children.'

'Oh no, Rose.' Ella saw her responsibility stretching before her to all eternity, a long row of pale unhappy women who, for some reason, all looked angrily at her as if to say, 'See what you have done to me.' 'It's not me only,' Ella said, 'Bessie, too.'

'Yes, if anyone will have to answer to God for what they have done with their lives, it will be women, mothers who must answer not only for their own souls, but their children's,' cried Rose. 'And you are going to send Amanda to be brought up in a kind of prison or barrack, like a convict, under the influence of goodness knows whom.'

But though Ella could be frightened and even brought to tears though she was weak, she was also, like most timid people, extremely obstinate. So that Rose got nothing by unusual violence but an unusual crop of evasion. Ella promised to write and did not write; she was put on the telephone to talk to Bessie, and managed to say nothing decisive. In the end, the elder daughters joined in the conflict, and Iris especially hastened to her mother's support. She wrote to Rose one of her celebrated letters, which had done more than anything else to keep her poor and rather friendless. It was a masterpiece of sarcasm, the kind of letter only clever young people do write, and older ones burn. It had no effect on the enemy's morale. It only convinced Rose that Iris was a narrow and conceited fool, such as might be expected from her education, and provoked a family quarrel of such bitterness that for years Rose and Bessie did not meet.

There was no reconciliation even when, in 1920, after the slump, the Academy was closed for ever, utterly ruined by four years of war use. Rose did not, as formerly, come to the rescue. She asked James to make the Villa his home, but not Bessie; and James, of course, could not go alone. Neither did she offer to pay the school and college fees of the younger girls, as she had done for Bertie and William, after her father's death.

Rose, in her sixties, was perhaps almost as savage and bitter as Iris liked to think her; Iris having done more than anyone to make her so.

CHAPTER 33

Iris had been a happy young woman. The times between 1908, when she had gone to college, and about 1933, when the Nazis came into power, had suited her well. It was a period, first of feminine emancipation, and then of rational dialectics, which accorded well with her temperament. She was at home in it, just as her sister Muriel had been lost in it. Muriel, serious, intelligent but not quick, pretty in a milk-maid style, but rather too fat, and, above all, very shy, very loyal and rather passionate, had never understood how to deal with it, even with its jokes, which she took in earnest. Its clothes made her round figure and fat legs look absurd; its mockery wounded her to the soul, its confusion threw her into despair. And in the end, at a time when she was more than usually lonely and bewildered, she had been found dead in bed, with the room full of gas. The jury, by majority, had brought in accidental death. Only Iris was quite sure that Muriel had committed suicide, and she would say, wisely and coldly, 'Muriel never made up her mind to get what she didn't want or not to want what she couldn't get, and so she got nothing at all.'

But now it might be feared that Iris herself was demanding of changed times things she could not get. She was very bitter, for instance, against all the different dictators. 'Really all this nationalist rubbish gets on one's nerves,' she would say. 'One hardly dares to turn on the wireless, to open a newspaper.' Or, 'I don't mind their murdering each other so much if it wasn't for such silly reasons – all these parties and isms and propagandums make me tired.'

And since the renewal of interest in Victorian history and memoirs, in Trollope and Yonge, she had begun to nourish a special indignation against her mother. A regular hen, poor dear! whose only idea of life had been a baby every year. 'Perhaps it's not suprising that there were no brains over to give the children any reasonable guidance. She wrecked Muriel's life pretty effectively by throwing at her head every young man who came near the house, and she would have wrecked mine if I had ever wanted to be bothered with marriage. As for Bertie, she ruined any ambition he might have had by trying to ram Christianity down his throat with the usual results. In fact, her only success was Dorothy – I don't count William, who got away from her in time. Dorothy was all her own work, the pet. And she's a perfect Victorian lady, a snob, a ninny, a complete egotist and a parasite.'

Iris, in short, though she did not perceive it, was already old-fashioned. She belonged to the generation of 1890 which had naturally reacted against its Victorian parents, all the more vio-lently because of the strong and assured self-confidence of that age. And all Iris's virtues, her courage, her intellectual honesty, her chastity of soul, her love of freedom, were now objects of wonder or mild amusement, to young women of a new romantic age, suspicious of all that logic, moral or political, with which their own youth had been drenched. Iris called the younger generation reactionary, and much of her loathing for Dorothy was prompted by the latter's pose as a womanly woman, who took no interest in votes or politics.

Ella was rather afraid of all her nieces, but much preferred Dorothy to Iris. She could not overcome this fear even by reminding herself that Iris had always been Amanda's protector. She turned first pale and then red, when she kissed her, and could only say, 'My dear – how nice after all these years, and how pretty you look.'

Iris touched her cheek with her lips – Iris never kissed anyone – and said affectionately but softly and, as it were, dangerously, 'How are you Aunty, dear. What a shame to bother you. I heard Dorothy was coming, and I knew you would need protection. I suppose Dorothy took all the decent books, too, or have they gone into the dustbin?'

A few minutes later, seeing Dorothy with her aunt, examining the furniture in the hall, she approached and said, 'Did you *give* Dorothy the little walnut bureau, Aunty? It was rather a valuable piece, you know. The only first class thing in the house.'

Dorothy ignored her. 'Aunty, would you mind terribly if I camped out here tonight. I couldn't get into the hotel.'

'It's rather expensive and not even fashionable,' Iris said.

Ella, in a fluster, began to explain that there was no room fit for her; but Dorothy at once disclosed a plan. She would sleep in Ella's room and Ella in Rose's. 'Which really should be your room all the time, as it's the best. And it will be so much quieter for you during the sale. You can just retire there and be at peace.'

'Oh no, no – not Rose's room,' said Ella, suddenly alarmed. 'Not to sleep in.'

'Why, Aunty?' Dorothy's sharp eyes fixed themselves upon her.

'It's so – it hasn't any carpet.'

'That doesn't matter at night.'

'We'll bring the carpet back,' said Iris.

'The Turkish carpet, it's in the sale,' said Dorothy, who perhaps had her eyes on it. 'And that reminds me, Aunty, dear, what happened to Grandpapa's telescope?'

Ella did not seem to hear, she was still as it were stunned by the notion of being removed into Rose's room. But Iris answered her sister tartly:

'It's also in the sale, and Bertie is going to bid for it, aren't you, Bertie? He wants it for his flat at Clacton, to study the stars – bathing.'

Bertie smiled, made a little bow, and said nothing. He did not mean to be drawn into a family quarrel. He detested trouble. Bertie at fifty-three was growing very plump, with a polished bald head and a round red face. He had kept his military moustache, but now it seemed less soldierly than social; the decoration of a man who aims at a not too intellectual appearance. He was very smartly, rather loudly dressed, and smelt of scent. All his movements, his little bows to Aunt Ella, his smiles, his glances at Iris, had a certain air, not precisely false, but a little studied. It could be seen that Bertie admired himself as a man about town; yet not more seriously than a man about town should admire anything at all.

Bertie, in short, had taken after his grandfather. He was coarser, grosser in his pleasures; more vulgar perhaps in manner. He did not even pretend to that respect for art and literature which had given to Venn's hedonism a certain grace. Music, the only art which he still practised, he took as an indulgence. Where Venn had sought and found a woman of character and intelligence for his mistress, Bertie preferred to hunt in Piccadilly. On the other hand, Bertie was far more truly good-natured. Whether on account of his easy-going temper, his self-indulgence, or of some change in the spirit of the time, he was more friendly to all men, more affectionate, perhaps more loyal.

Ella still preferred him to all her other nephews and nieces. She knew that there was kind feeling behind his politeness; there was even respect, for he had always admired her playing. She turned to him now, eager to make Dorothy forget the project of moving her into Rose's room. The very notion of that room, of spending even one night among its shadows, filled her with terror. 'But Bertie,' she cried, 'of course you must have the telescope. It's in Amanda's study. I was keeping it.'

'Oh, but if Amanda wants it, I shouldn't dream—'

'Amanda seems to have grabbed everything of any value,' said Dorothy, 'but that's what one had to expect. Really, grandpapa's telescope – how I used to love it when he showed me Saturn and so on.'

'You don't need a telescope to see the main chance,' said Iris.

'No, it's for grandpapa's sake,' said Dorothy, whose lack of humour was an impenetrable armour. 'I did adore grandpapa. He was always so sweet to me and so generous. But Aunty, do you know, if you really want to change your room, you ought to do it at once, before the men come to arrange the last details. We can help you.'

'Aunty has no idea of changing her room,' said Iris. But Dorothy was already going upstairs. She called back, 'You won't need your bureau to be moved, will you, Aunty?'

'Shall I stop her, Aunty?' said Iris. 'Bertie, go and tell Dorothy that this is where she gets off.'

But Ella was horrified by the very proposal. 'No, please. After all, my room is so much more comfortable for a visitor.'

As for Bertie, he had quietly withdrawn himself out of earshot and was examining his grandfather's books. He was very anxious to find out if certain French editions de luxe, with illustrations, of Restiff de la Bretonne, La Fontaine and the Heptameron were still in the library. He had discovered them, as a boy, on a top shelf, and they remained with him as a pleasant, a rich memory, of his adolescence. Bertie began to feel the need of renewing that youth.

'Why do you submit to Dorothy, Aunty?' said Iris, turning a little pink. 'It's a damn shame the way she gets away with it. It's not fair.'

Iris had a strong hatred of oppression. On this subject alone she allowed herself to be angry. 'Dorothy is a menace,' she said. 'Shall I go and tell her off as she deserves. It's quite time somebody tackled her.'

'No, no, please Iris – I know you don't mean it, but—'

'But I do mean it – and as we're bound to fight, it might as well be now.'

Dorothy's voice was heard calling for Aunty, and Ella hastened to obey.

'What is so hopeless about these poor old things,' said Iris to Bertie, who was discovered seated on the top of the library ladder with a book on his lap, 'is that they can't stand up for themselves and won't let anyone else stand up for them. Why does Aunt Ella go on protesting that I love Dorothy and that Dorothy ought to love me, just because we are sisters. Everyone knows how I loathe that woman, and so I ought to loathe her, a social profiteer of the worst type.'

Bertie, musing over his book, murmured, 'They were great for family unity, the aunts.'

'Family hypocrisy – and how a weed like Dorothy has flourished on it. She used to wangle grandpapa as a little girl, and take his money out of his trousers pocket. Dorothy is a thoroughly Christian by-product – a love sucker, a hot-house parasite.'

'Auntie Rose smacked her, I remember, with some effect.' Bertie turned a page.

'And what howls there were. She ran to grandpapa at once. And Rose was ticked off. Grandpapa adored the female child. What have you got there, Bertie? It isn't philosophy, I suppose?'

'No, just a book I remember. I happened on it. We had good holidays here, Iris.'

'I didn't. I loathed my childhood. Half nag and half Sunday School. Thank God and Mrs Pankhurst I've been able to cut off on my own and have some freedom. It's a bloody world for women still, but one can hope for better things.'

Bertie descended the ladder. He had a little pile of books in his arms. 'I wonder where Aunty is.'

'Are you going to be a Dorothy, too?'

'No, I'll pay far more than she could get at a country sale, but I must have some memento of the dear old Villa.' He walked out with his treasures. He found Ella in her new quarters. She was standing in the very middle of the big room, which looked the bigger for the loss of its carpet and wardrobe, and she gazed at Bertie as he opened the door, with a strange look of confusion.

'Sorry, Aunty, I wanted to ask you about these books.'

'Oh, Bertie. I thought you were – papa. Come to see what I'm doing in his room.'

'There's just a few old French books.'

'Yes, take them, dear, take them.'

'Of course I must pay you.'

'No, no, take them, in memory of papa. He was so fond of you all. He was so kind, so generous, so loving, such a Christian gentleman. But you're not going—'

'Well, Aunty, I thought I might have another glance along the shelves.'

'Yes, yes, dear, take whatever you like, and you shall have the telescope. Papa would wish you to have them – I know you will love them for his sake. He was so kind, so gentle, no one was ever afraid of Papa.'

And standing once more alone, she continued to propitiate the ghosts of the dead and even their favourites. 'Dear, dear Papa, he was so fond of us, and of Dorothy, too. Dorothy was his pet, and she was a dear little girl. She used to come to him when he was having breakfast in bed to give him her good-morning kiss; often she used to jump in beside him. She was never afraid of him. Neither was I, I think. No, I'm sure I was not, and this was really his room, and Grandmama's. I don't know why it is called Rose's room. She did not even die here. It is Papa's room, darling Papa who never said an unkind word to anybody.'

But Ella was restless and uneasy. Even the embrace of her own armchair, with the broken springs, which Dorothy had kindly brought for her from her own room, did not give her as usual, by its peculiar lumps, a sense of comfort in the mind. She spent the day wandering unhappily from one empty or dishonoured bedroom to another, and when late at night, worn out and almost unable to stand, she ventured into the great bed, she became at once so wide awake that she was like one drugged. Her heart thumped, and it seemed that she could feel the blood rushing through her veins like something terrified; her head began to ache, her eyes to burn.

It had been raining all the evening, and now it began to blow. Clouds flew across the harvest moon, and as the Venetian blinds swayed and rattled, Jacob's ladders of livid bars ran up the walls on which shadowy figures, some small and agile, some enormous and clumsy, climbed and disappeared into the grey ceiling. When at last she dozed, these figures became familiar, she had known them all her life. Yet she could not name them and their movements were furtive. They kept their backs to her and hastened away, as if to escape through the ceiling before she could recognize them.

She started up with a cry, 'Stop, stop', and for a moment she thought that she was Rose. The great tester of the family bed hanging over her in the dim reflected light of the room, terrified her with this sensation of being in the body of her sister. It seemed to her half-awakened senses that it was impossible for her, Ella, to have ventured into such a place. Only Rose could be in that bed.

She sat up then, trembling, and fearful that her cry had been heard. At once she was surrounded by immensities, the great bed that stretched out to all sides, the walls of the room which had retreated to a great distance, and beyond that, empty rooms, the dusty corridor. And all these grey spaces answered her cry with a silence full of meaning. They seemed to say to her, 'We hear you but no one else can do so or wants to do so. No one in this house understands what you feel, or even what you say.'

Ella remembered her sister's cry, 'Oh, the loneliness!' and for a moment she looked into that loneliness as one might look into the vault of a tomb, from the open door. Then she quickly jumped out of bed and turned on the light. It was only three o'clock, but she dared not go back into the large bed. She sat in her chair in the farthest corner of the room, and read, dozed, with the light full on. So that when she waked up she found herself aching with cold, confused with horror.

It was past seven o'clock and a heavy shower was battering the windows. But voices were heard from the paddock. Cars drew up and harness jingled. The country people were arriving. Country people like sales, from curiosity, and to see their neighbours; and they come early to have first pick of the bargains.

There was a knock at Ella's door, and Polly put in her head. 'Young Mr Dawbarn, ma'am, would like to see you.'

'Polly, how can I, I'm not up.'

Ella was wearing a pink flannel dressing-gown with a kind of ruff at the neck.

'Oh dear, what can it be.' But Ella was already sure of good news, and now forgetting her undress, she gladly flew from the terrifying room and into the corridor. Harry was seen approaching the stairhead.

'Is that you, Harry? You'll excuse me – I was just going – I didn't expect.' She did not like to admit that she had been prepared to meet a gentleman in her dressing-gown.

Harry was dressed in his best Sunday suit, of dark blue with a pin stripe, a new mackintosh, and an almost new bowler with a string on the brim, a hunting bowler. His air was serious and anxious; it made Ella hold her breath with anticipation. He spoke slowly and deliberately.

'Well, Miss Ella, you know I'm bringing the cart to fetch your things to the Quarry.'

'Yes, Harry, tomorrow.'

It had been arranged that Ella, after the sale, was to lodge at the Quarry with her own furniture.

'I can't go today, Harry, because I have my nieces here.'

'No, Miss Ella, but I was wondering if I couldn't take some things for Amanda at the same time.'

'Why, of course, Harry.'

'And I was wondering what that little piano would go for. I mean the little one. Amanda'll want a piano. She has a right to one, being used to it all her life. Even my cowman's wife has a piano.'

'Why, that's very nice of you, Harry. Please take whatever you like.'

'But I'll pay you, Miss Ella – a piano like that is worth fifteen pounds, it mid go for sixteen.'

'And you want to buy it for the Quarry?'

'Well, Miss Ella, it's really the same thing, for Amanda or for the Quarry, as soon as she's Mrs Dawbarn, isn't it!'

At this oblique announcement, Ella gave a little cry of delight. 'Oh, but Harry, I didn't know.'

'It's been a settled thing these last three months,' said Harry in a tone of pained surprise, as if Ella were the defaulter.

'I'm so glad, so glad. It makes me very happy, Harry.'

'We just didn't think of telling you till we had a date fixed, and, of course, harvest came at an awkward time. I'm afraid Amanda has been put out a bit by me having to give so much time to harvest.'

'Of course not,' said Ella. 'Amanda is so fond of you.'

'I hope so,' said Harry, 'for I'm desperate about getting married as soon as ever we can. And I want to pick up the furnishing today.'

'A very good idea, Harry. Please take whatever you like – of course you shall have the piano. Amanda cannot play, I'm afraid, but perhaps if she has a daughter – well, it's quite exciting. Such a happy, such a delightful thing.'

'Shall we say fifteen pound ten, Miss Ella?'

'No, no, Harry, it will all be Amanda's, you know, so why pay? What does the money matter. No, I must give it to you. And you must take it away at once, before the sale begins. You've brought a cart, haven't you?'

'Yes, Miss Ella.'

'Come, then, fetch Bobby, get some men.'

Harry fetched two neighbours, and the three men began to move the piano. But as they did so Dorothy came down the stairs. 'Why, Aunty, I was just going to say that I was looking for a cheap piano. Triggie wants to make a present to the sergeants' mess.'

'I'm sorry, dear, but this piano is not for sale.'

'Oh yes, Aunty, excuse me. Put it down, would you?' with a sudden smile to the men. 'Yes, Aunty, here's the label, 115. Once it's in the catalogue, you know, it has to be sold, that's the law.'

Iris and Bertie, arriving from their hotel, approached, and Iris said, 'What is this law? Is Dorothy taking your piano, Aunty?'

'I was going to bid for it,' said Dorothy, 'and I was saying that it cannot be withdrawn from sale.'

'Why not,' said Iris. 'That's only Dorothy's nonsense, Aunty. Don't you believe a word she says.'

'Really, darling,' said Dorothy in a voice of gentle protest, 'that sounds rather rude. At least, it would – to anyone who didn't know that you were—'

'Were what?' Iris turned pink. Like many clever and lonely people, she had sensitive nerves and her offensive courage of imagination was much more vigorous than her physical ability to support a counter-attack. She was, indeed, quite unaccustomed, as a school mistress of high forms, to the brutal kinds of rudeness.

'I mean, you've had such awfully bad luck, really, right from the beginning. Never had a chance, but I didn't mean to upset you.'

'Oh please, please!' said Ella. She was horrified by this outbreak between the children.

'Thanks very much,' said Iris, in a trembling voice, 'I didn't know I'd had special bad luck.'

'Neither did I,' said Dorothy, who enjoyed the great superior force of one both insensitive and superbly confident of her own inability to feel. 'I always thought you were rather lucky, not having to worry about husbands and children and appearances and so on, and I'm sure you never complain about your life being spoilt, and being left on the shelf and so on.'

'Oh please, please!' cried Ella. 'What would your Aunty Rose think?'

'And why' – Iris was now almost incoherent – 'do you presume that I ever wanted to be off – what you call – the shelf?'

'No, exactly,' said Dorothy vaguely and indifferently. 'Why, that's what I always say myself. Why should you worry if people do pity you. Yes, Aunty, I really must have the piano. I'll give you two pounds for it now. It won't get ten shillings in the sale.' She walked over to the piano, struck two chords on it and began to play, very badly and loudly, the waltz 'Gold and Silver'.

'Bring it up to my room, men.'

Harry looked doubtfully at Ella, who seemed to nod her head, and he proceeded with his men to take the piano upstairs.

All this time Iris, turning from Ella to Bertie, was explaining in a hurried and confused manner that she had never wanted to be married, and that it was perfectly abominable that it should be supposed that she disliked the imputation of being an old maid. 'I don't mean the imputation, because it isn't an imputation, it's just a vulgar superstition, not that I expect Dorothy to understand that. But why should she, just because she *is* so dense, assume that—'

The poor woman's voice broke in despair at not being able to explain this complicated sense of the injustice of fate which had made her intelligent, celibate and sensitive, and exposed her, therefore, to suffer by the false standards and taunts of a despicable person.

'It's such a damned shame!' she cried.

'Oh dear, yes – I am so—' Ella muttered, distracted between horror at the quarrel and the piano disappearing upstairs. Suddenly she darted after the piano.

Fortunately Dorothy didn't notice this move. She was still exploiting her victory over Iris by strolling carelessly about, close to her, and examining chairs, wardrobes, without actually looking at her sister but still making it impossible for her to escape, under pain of seeming to run away. So that the beaten Iris, struggling with tears, and unable to speak for fear of breaking down, was obliged to stand in the middle of the hall, and submit to as much further torture as her conqueror chose to inflict. It seemed likely to be considerable.

Ella, therefore, was able to intercept the piano at the top of the stairs, where she accosted Harry with a most imperious and tragic air, the very look of Rose. 'Bring it to *my* room,' she said. 'I mean

Miss Venn's room, I'll keep it for you. No one,' she declared, as if denying the world, 'shall have this piano but you and Amanda.'

The piano was therefore conveyed into Rose's room. Ella, going in with it, locked the door and stayed on guard until the sale began.

Dorothy was much amused by Ella's desperate action. At the beginning of the sale she bought a cottage piano, one of the smuggled ones, with seven dumb notes and a broken pedal, for thirty shillings, saying that the sergeants' mess would be delighted with it, and could easily pay for repairs. This effort of her generosity put her in very good humour, and she remarked that poor dear Aunt Ella was not really to be blamed for her cranks. 'She's not responsible. Yes, I'm afraid we'll have to consider putting her away. I believe the county institutions are just wonderful nowadays, and so cheap.'

Ella indeed was in an excited condition. A desperate act always had a bad effect on her nerves. 'How dreadful,' she thought, 'that quarrel. Dorothy perhaps didn't mean to be unkind, but Iris was fearfully hurt. Rose always said that Bessie spoilt Dorothy, and perhaps she was right. Certainly Dorothy has certain faults – she is sometimes unkind, and she's always selfish. Her husband, they say, is not very happy, and she's not a very good mother either. Yes, I'm afraid she was spoilt, and Rose was right about Bessie.' And going to the door for the third or fourth time to see if the auctioneer had begun, and if Dorothy were safely occupied, she thought, or rather found, in her mind the reflection, 'Bessie is responsible even now for evil – just as Rose said. How fearful that is – a responsibility even after you are dead. Responsibility for living people – who may do all kinds of wrong.'

It was as though Rose's own voice had spoken in her mind. It startled Ella like a noise from the very air of the room. She looked nervously at the bed and, unlocking the door, went out into the passage.

The corridor was deserted. The auctioneer was in the dining-room below, whence one heard a practised voice chanting, 'How much for this fam-ily din-ner service – over two hundred pieces?'

'Responsibility for souls,' said Ella to herself, as if she had never understood the phrase before. 'Responsibility for Bertie and Dorothy and Iris and Amanda – for what they do and what they say.'

'This very magnificent service – ten pounds bid. Come, gentlemen and ladies – '

Ella found herself in Amanda's room, looking with surprise and embarrassment at Amanda and Robin, who were sitting at opposite ends of the sofa, both smoking and both wearing that utterly careworn appearance which is seen only in old people at funerals, and young ones after a night's debauch. Ella, seeing these grey faces and hollow, mournful eyes, thought with terror, 'What has happened – what have they been doing?'

'Oh Amanda,' she faltered, 'it's – I was looking for a blotter, your Aunt Rose's blotter – the morocco one. I'm so afraid—'

'Good morning, darling.' Amanda rose and kissed her mother. 'Have you had any breakfast?'

'Oh yes,' said Ella, looking at the tray on the floor and noticing that it held two dirty cups and two dirty plates. 'Yes, thank you – but I thought the blotter might be here. It's so important. Rose always used it for her private letters, to Bessie and Papa and all the nieces – and it was a present from Papa. She wouldn't like it to be – to go to strangers.'

'I'll come and see about it,' said Amanda.

'But I shouldn't like—' Ella glanced nervously at Robin.

'Never mind Robin, he'll be quite happy here.' Amanda drew her mother out of the room. 'Was it the red blotter?'

'Robin, he didn't sleep here?' said Ella.

'No, thank goodness. But he talked till two o'clock and came back again at eight. He's very depressed about his future.'

'But I thought his future was all settled.'

'He hates the office and he thinks of going on a farm. But I'm sure it wouldn't suit him at all. I don't think anything would suit him. All the small things are in the parlour – they'll be the last things sold.'

'Yes, Amanda, darling. Harry has told me about you and him. I am so glad. Oh, it's delightful. I'd been so afraid for you.' There was a short pause. Amanda pressed her mother's arm. She asked at last, 'What exactly did Harry tell you?'

'That you were going to be married. And he was anxious the wedding should be soon – as soon as possible. I think he's so right. I'm all against long engagements. Your Aunt Rose always said—'

'Do you think I'd make a good wife?' said Amanda.

This simple question caused in Ella a violent reaction of alarm, as if it had opened in herself large regions of doubt and anxiety. 'Yes. Oh, what do you mean?' she cried. 'You can learn housekeeping. Oh, what do you mean, Amanda?'

'I'm a little doubtful if it would be fair to Harry for me to be his wife.'

'But Harry wants you – he will be patient. Oh dear, I was afraid of something like this – that you'd grow hard like poor Iris – hard and cold. How can you refuse Harry now – perhaps your last chance. You're getting so neglectful of yourself – so indifferent. Don't you want to be happy? What are you afraid of? Hannah will do the cooking – and then there'll be babies – I hope. Oh, I'm quite sure.'

'Suppose I didn't find babies so exciting after all. I've known bored mothers and very bad mothers in consequence.'

'How can you say such a thing?' Ella, in her terror, cried out as if she had been struck. 'Oh, how could you be bored. But you don't understand. No, you can't understand – how can you? – what it's like to have a baby of your own, to feel that love, as if it were your whole self, your whole life.'

They had reached the hall where groups of sightseers and bargain hunters were wandering, all with the same look in their eyes, of anxiety and suspicion, as if they were, at that very moment, being defrauded or robbed of something. A large, red-faced woman swept Ella aside and, looking fiercely at her, exclaimed, 'Five shilling for five cups, and rubbish, too.'

Amanda took Ella's arm. 'Darling, hadn't we better go to your room, out of all this.'

But Ella, in her dismay, did not seem to understand what was going on. She gazed at the red-faced woman, at the greedy hunting wolves which had seized upon her home, with a blank face, and murmured, 'It's that school – it's that school – as Rose said, and I wouldn't believe her. That was the beginning of it.'

'That school!' Amanda was mildly surprised by this new distress.

'That school where you were all sent – Iris and Dorothy and poor Muriel and you – that nasty school where you had to cut up frogs and had no place of your own and weren't allowed even to have friends.'

Ella saw in the eye of her recollection a vast red barrack – or, rather, a range of barracks – echoing with the noise of boots and smelling of dust, ink, grease; and a peculiar scent to which she could put no name except that of school – a special sourness, like bad soup; a smell so revolting to her mind that she shook her head as if to deny the truth of her own memory.

'Oh, what a hideous place that was – those hordes of little girls rushing about among dusty railings, like animals, or big ones strolling along with their noses in the air. What did they call them, prefects? So self-righteous, so fearfully conceited and unloving, and to send a child there, with her gentle, tender soul. But I didn't know what I was doing, how could I know what schools were like? I had never even seen a school, and, yes, Rose knew. What did she say?' Ella clasped and unclasped her hands in apprehension.

'But dearest!' Amanda quite understood Ella's mind. She took her arm with an encouraging pressure. 'Aunt Rose was rather prejudiced against girls' schools. I loved my school, and as for not having friends, I had a mass of friends.'

'Worse than a barrack,' said Ella. 'Oh, I saw it, a great bare barrack, and not even allowed to speak to other girls in the passages, or walk arm-in-arm, and nowhere to go by yourself. Oh, your Aunt Rose was right.'

Amanda, mildly surprised by this explosion of anger, said, 'It's true we weren't allowed to schwärm —'

'Don't, please – that horrid word. But that's just like the whole horrid place. I really believe those school mistresses hated any real tenderness of heart.'

'But dearest, truly that's a little absurd. After all, girls between thirteen and eighteen are capable of the most frightful silliness. I know I was, and I'm very glad I wasn't encouraged.'

There was a silence. They were driven against the wall into the kitchen by the sudden end of the sale in the dining-room. The doors burst open before a mass of bidders who surged across the corridor into the drawing-room. The auctioneer, neatly dressed in a dark blue flannel suit which nicely found the mean between town smartness and country lack of pretension, was in the midst, and all heads were turned towards him. The effect was that of a revolutionary mob following, but also driving and constraining, some leader who might be expected to show them rich loot and terrified helpless victims.

Ella, indeed, appeared startled by this crowd, which paid no attention to her in her own house, or stared at her like part of the house furnishing. Amanda, taking her arm, drew her into the kitchen. 'Shall we have some tea, it's nearly twelve?'

'Yes, yes. Where's poor Polly? She must have some tea, too, in her own kitchen.' Ella had some surviving notions of the appropriate rights belonging to different functionaries in the domestic kingdom, now in dissolution.

'I loved Beltham,' Amanda repeated with some energy, as she put on a kettle. And she remembered with keen pleasure the long lines of glittering white counterpanes in the dormitories, the fresh cold breeze from open windows, the friendly intelligent faces of some of the mistresses, especially her history mistress, whom she had adored. Above all, the sense of a special kind of existence where everything was frank, easy, dependable, where life itself seemed to have a glittering clean aspect, a bright order and discipline, and to be pervaded everywhere by intelligence, by rules that could be understood in a moment, by ideas which were not only important, but simple and even prettily designed, like geometry. Amanda was quite startled by the reminder of that life. She thought for the first time, 'How happy I was there – I never was so happy', and at the same time she realized that this was a crisis in her life, one of those small turns which together make up the great curves of a life history. For the first time she had looked back and felt with conviction the happiness of her childhood. 'I suppose,' she thought, pouring out the tea into one of the cracked cups and a bowl, 'that I am really a little late. I ought to have begun to feel like that two years ago, when I was thirty. Iris looks upon me already as a very slow person, a regular provincial, and perhaps she's right.'

'Aunt Rose was rather behind the times,' she said to Ella, sitting down opposite her at the table and resting her cheek on her hand in a languid pose. 'She had no idea of progress.'

'Progress?' muttered Ella. 'But yes.' She looked round mournfully as if fearful that the revolutionary mob would burst in upon her. 'She was very strong for Mr Gladstone.'

'I'm very grateful to you and Aunt Bessie for insisting on Beltham,' said Amanda. 'Thank Heaven I did have a decent education. At least it's given me freedom, real freedom to earn.'

'Yes, that's what Bessie said – that her girls must be ready for the new world. But, of course, she got that idea from James. Because if she had not thought like that, and sent you all to school, there wouldn't have been a new world. I mean – and it needn't be a *better* world.'

'No, but here it is, whoever's idea it was and wherever the idea came from, if anywhere – I mean anywhere in reason.'

Through the open window, by way of the drawing-room window, the auctioneer's voice said something about a sofa, suitable for a courting couple. A country auctioneer usually begins to make jokes about midday, when his audience is beginning to feel jaded. There were a few laughs which showed however that the sale, on the whole, was being a success.

'Yes, where and why?' said Ella suddenly.

'What, dear?' Amanda, moodily sipping her tea, had forgotten the subject.

'Always new ideas. How Rose hated them.'

'Perhaps that was her fault.'

'Oh no, no, she felt so responsible. And the loneliness.' Ella gazed at Amanda with a frightened look. 'What fearful loneliness.'

What confused Ella was the notion, suggested by the mysterious operations of her own mind, that people composed a world by thinking it, that it was people like Bessie, not specially clever or wise, but energetic and reckless, who having acquired from somewhere or other, in her case from her husband and from young teachers and students, the idea of a 'new world', at once began to produce it. This was a very alarming idea to Ella, because it took from the idea of the new world its inevitability. It might, she saw, have been different; Amanda might, in short, have been brought up at the Villa and turned out quite a different person.

'It was Bessie and I sent Amanda to Beltham – and Bessie admitted that she had not been a good mother.' But at this reflection something terrifying, some dark and dangerous creature, moved in the depths of Ella's mind, so that she got up hastily from her chair and went towards her refuge on the second floor. 'Oh, but could we help it, with the bombs, and really if one's going to be responsible – besides Bessie was not herself at the end, she was so ill. It would be too cruel, if – oh, but it *is* cruel – the judgment.' Ella with faltering legs and white lips stood alone in the upper corridor. 'The judgment – the last day – so that's what – it means – what Bessie felt.'

When Bessie had had an operation for cancer in 1920 she nearly died on the table. Her heart was weak. But the operation, though not possible to be repeated, was declared a success. Two months later the doctors were not so confident. In three months they admitted that by a rare, almost unique accident, they had been too late. Bessie must die. They gave her a few weeks.

Ella and Rose came at once to town and took lodgings near Brent Square. It was as though some force outside themselves had issued a command, some hand in which all lay, had closed its fingers and drawn the three sisters together. Bessie herself seemed to recognize this compulsion, for she said only, 'So you've come up. I felt you might. It isn't really necessary, of course, I'm not going to die, these fools of doctors never know anything. They said I hadn't cancer, and then that it was too early to know what it was. Then they operated and said it was too late. You'll see that I'll outlive all of them.'

She was a strange colour. Her skin was like wrinkled tissue paper, blue-white; a pallor made startling by her black frocks. Since William's death she had given up her bright-coloured dresses and wore only black, cut in her own style, like a puritan dress, with narrow white lace at neck and cuffs. This severe dress did not accord with the feverish brilliance of her eyes, her impatient movements. She had never been so restless or so busy, gave parties, receptions almost every day, and spent the rest of her time writing letters, typing James's addresses, making appointments and paying visits.

The Academy was closed, but Bessie was confident that the Government would pay forty thousand pounds compensation for damages. She had organized an appeal from old students to the Government and the Press, demanding this sum.

At the end of this appeal one read the names of many dis-tinguished scientists, including Sir Walford Beal and Sir Henry

Dewes. When Rose remarked that they had been Groom's chief enemies, Bessie answered, 'That's why I asked them.'

'But have they changed their minds about James and the Academy?'

'I don't know,' said Bessie. 'I didn't ask, I just called and explained the facts that James was ruined if this horrible Government did not pay some compensation. And they signed at once. They were very nice. Sir Walford was quite charming, and of course when people saw his name they rushed in to sign. But people don't mind what they sign against governments. They all hate any government, and I don't blame them. It's so mean, it always takes a mean advantage. Oh, how I loathe it! To treat James like that, a man of seventy-eight.'

Bessie's appeal, in spite of its eminent names, had no effect. It was delivered privately, and no government pays any attention to private claims, not arranged for by statute.

But it had one valuable result. It attracted the attention of some of the younger generation of scientists, and especially of Sir Walford Beal's eldest son.

'Young Beal,' as Bessie called him, was a man of forty, completely bald on top of his head, but with very black hair at the sides. His long dark face had a solemn and even fanatical expression – he might have been taken for a Spanish dominican. He was an authority on enzymes but he was also the author of a book called 'Scientific Government', advocating world control by a committee of scientists, elected by the national parliaments, and empowered to direct world research and to organize world progress. He represented, in fact, a large group of the younger scientists who had held posts under Government during the war, and had been struck by the confusion and inefficiency of all Government departments, and also by the ignorance and mulish conservatism of private citizens in the face of the same Government departments.

He was not a Communist, but he had been to Russia, and he greatly admired the Communist rule. He would tell a story about a special train ordered to take some high official to a critical point. 'The station-master said it was impossible. But the train got there with ten minutes to spare. How did they do it? It was quite simple. They shot the station-master.' And then he would laugh heartily. Beal was not a cruel man. On the contrary, he was the most considerate and warmhearted of men – that is to say, in the presence of real people. If he had known that Russian station-master, or perhaps if he had known any Russian station-master, he would have been shocked and infuriated by that story which now gave him a fierce pleasure. He was a man, in short, of warm personal feelings but limited imagination, and a highly abstract mind.

Young Beal had refused to sign the petition. But Bessie ran him to ground at a friend's house and asked him to tea. He met Groom, and became at once his most devoted supporter. True, the old man would have been horrified by Beal's notions of progress; of a world designed as an enormous experimental and research camp for the breeding of bigger and healthier human robots, completely tame, clean and docile, under the control of their medical keepers, of committees of Beals. And Beal would have been contemptuous of the old man's naif anarchism. But Groom had never read Beal's books, he had never read any new books at all for many years. And Beal could not even grasp the antediluvian opinions of an old gentleman who spoke of Gladstone and Beaconsfield and Herbert Spencer.

To Beal, the only opinions worth attack were those of the last generation, including his own father. He thought little, therefore, of his father's attacks upon Groom's enormous errors, which, he considered, might not be so grave as Sir Walford supposed. Radium, for instance, was perhaps not so miraculous a healer as radiologists had claimed in the nineteen hundreds.

Groom's ideas, on the other hand, were utterly antique. One did not regard them as objects of criticism but of interest. They were like primitive monuments, surviving from a lost world.

Beal was bored with the teachers of his youth; he had explored and surpassed them. But Groom appeared to him as the mountain appeared to Wordsworth while he receded from it, like a mysterious monster, which grew every moment taller, darker; a giant from the past when there had been real giants; Darwin, Tyndal, Lister, Huxley, Faraday.

He visited Groom now with feelings of reverence and almost awe; perhaps the first true religious impression of his life. And when Groom, opening his big foolish preacher's mouth, now concealed by his fine white beard, pronounced his sixty-year-old platitudes about Science and Progress, he was moved as by the voice of a prophet.

He was enraged that this great man, this hero of the old wars against superstition and theology, should be thrown aside in his old age, and broken by the meanness of Government; and his rage took a special form. He felt that science itself was slighted in Groom's person. And so he raged to a purpose.

Beal was an excellent agitator. He was a fanatic, he was tireless; he was disinterested. He began at once to get up testimonials, appeals, to write to the papers, to lead deputations to the Home Office, to have questions asked in Parliament. He sent circulars, at his own expense, to all the leading men of science; he called on them morning, noon and night, until he found them in. And they were ready to sign almost anything he chose to write, in order to get rid of him.

The Government was of course, in a strong position. It knew that the Groom Academy, when taken over, had been bankrupt. But it made a false step – that is to say, the Under Secretary made a false step when his chief was absent at an election meeting. He cast doubts, in the House, on Groom's scientific standing, and declared that the Academy, at the beginning of the war, had been in a declining state. As Under Secretary, he had learnt enough to avoid the definite word bankrupt; but he was not yet wise enough to know the danger of giving any information at all to anybody about anything, except under extreme pressure. In this case, he had only to say that the matter was under consideration, and leave it there.

At once all Groom's old pupils rose up in defence of their own credentials. and swore that Groom was a genius and the Academy a centre of light. If its finances were bad, they declared, that was only because the Professor, in his lofty altruism, charged too little for fees, and reduced them for poor pupils. The Press now took up the cause with energy, and the Minister himself was obliged to act. Answering a question in the House, prompted by himself, he promised that the matter of the Groom Academy should be reviewed. It was then shelved. But Groom, having a stroke in the same week, was hastily offered a knighthood in the next birthday honours.

Bessie enjoyed the triumph only for a few days. Groom's illness had thrown extra work and anxiety upon her. He was taken to a country nursing home, where he made a slow recovery. But he demanded Bessie's presence every night, and she was obliged also to be in town on the affairs of the Academy and to keep open house for the girls, who would be returning for the Easter holidays. When the doctor advised her to rest, she asked him with her growing tartness to provide the time, by looking after a sick husband and seven children, all demanding special trouble. 'Perhaps,' she said, 'you would like to meet Alice today. She wants a new spring hat, and she can't make up her mind unless I'm there, and you might call about Dorothy's dance frock which hasn't been delivered.'

'I should let her dance frock go to the devil,' said the doctor.

'Should you?' said Bessie. 'But she needs it for tonight, and a certain young man is going to be there – just come on leave – whom she wants very much to please. Very much. It's a matter of life and death.'

'It will be your death then.'

'I suppose you think women are fools.' said Bessie, 'but that only shows you are one. You are certainly one if you don't know what a dance frock can mean to a girl of nineteen, going to meet a young man she likes. Yes, a perfect idiot.'

She was found a couple of days later lying on the hall floor in Brent Square, still clasping in her hands a sample of ribbon which she had been trying to match for this same frock. The doctor, called from the next street, had her carried upstairs and put to bed. He promised to bring a specialist next day, but to Rose and Ella, summoned from their lodgings, he gave little hope. 'She may last a day or two, she may go tonight, but you ought to warn the children that time is short.'

'Should we call Sir James?'

'No, no, not now. It would only upset him. Tomorrow, if she's still alive.'

Bessie was lying in her marriage bed, of Italian iron with brass knobs, in the style of 1880. The bedroom, high but narrow, was lighted by a fish tail gas jet over the dressing table, which threw a yellowish light, resembling a thin fog, over the counterpane and crumpled pillows; Bessie was propped high against the pillows. She was unable to lie down on account of the pain, which could not be drugged. Her heart was already failing.

But she was restless and talkative. She could not make up her mind whether the children should be summoned. 'Not James, he could not stand the journey. But I think the children might be told. Except Bertie, poor boy. He is always so tired after his work. And Alice has a cold. No, she mustn't be dragged out. But then she might be upset if I – if anything happened and she hadn't been told in time.'

'I think we should tell everyone,' said Rose.

'I see, the doctor thinks I mayn't last.'

'I think it would be wiser to tell them all.'

'Oh yes, Rose, if I can't last. Oh, I must see Alice again, there are things I must tell her, and Bertie, and Dorothy. I must hear about her dance.'

Rose went to the telephone. But no one answered from Muriel and Amanda's school, and Iris, at her country lodgings, was not on the telephone. Bertie, brought to the telephone after long delay, asked with a polite but reasonable voice, if the matter was urgent. 'I mean, is it a matter of minutes or hours.'

'She might last some hours or she might die at any minute.'

'Right,' said Bertie, and his tone expressed his feeling that Rose might have made that plain to begin with. 'I'll be along at once, as soon as the buses start.'

'But Bertie, that may be too late.'

There was no answer to this. Bertie had hung up the receiver.

Alice answered her call with cries of despair. 'But where can I get a taxi? What awful bad luck to happen now. Could you possibly send a taxi, I'm sure it's easier from there? Poor, darling Mum, do ask her, I'm sure she'll know of a place.'

The taxi company promised to send a cab as soon as they had one available. Rose then called up Dorothy, who was staying with the Pedleys, at their house near Hampstead.

The sleepy voice of Colonel Mark answered for her. When he understood that he was being asked to wake Dorothy, his voice became agitated. But she was very tired, she had gone to bed very late. 'Are you sure it is necessary to wake her?'

'Could I speak to her?'

'But she's asleep, you understand?'

'Tell her her Aunt Rose wants to speak to her at once.'

Dorothy was at last brought to the 'phone. Pedley's voice in the background was heard quaking apologies. He was plainly much alarmed by the state of the lady's temper. Dorothy at nineteen was one of those frank and boyish girls who establish themselves as good comrades in an hour or two, but being established suddenly reveal the caprices of a monkey and the spitefulness of a lap dog.

'Ye-s-s,' she said to Rose in a drawl of disgust.

'I'm sorry to give you bad news, my dear, but your mother is ill, very ill.'

'Oh, she'll see us all dead yet. Mum is fearfully tough, really.'

'The doctor says she may die at any moment. I was wondering how soon you could come.'

'I can't come tomorrow. I might manage the day after unless it's Thursday. Thursday is impossible.'

'Dorothy, she may not live till morning, you oughtn't to waste a moment.'

'I'd come if I could, but how can I get across London at this time? I can't ask poor Mark to get out the car.'

'I don't think you ought to grudge a little trouble, Dorothy.'

'Oh, my God, I suppose I ought to walk! All right, Aunt, I'll borrow a bicycle or something.'

'Dorothy, I'm sorry, but your mother has been good to you all. She gives you nothing but love.'

'That's what she's for, isn't it?' Dorothy banged down the receiver. Rose went back to the bedroom where Bessie received her with a cry: 'Is that Alice? No, of course not. She couldn't be here yet. Thank you, Rose, I'm afraid I'm a terrible nuisance. Do you think they will come?'

'They promised to come as soon as they can. Alice and Bertie and Dorothy.'

'I wonder were we right to call them up. Perhaps it won't be necessary. Doctors are so stupid. Is that the bell?' She listened hopefully and sighed. 'No, of course it couldn't be Bertie yet. I wonder will they come? Do you think they are coming, Rose?'

'They ought to. I told them quite plainly that there was no time to waste. But, of course, the difficulties may seem large to them. They might not understand the urgency.'

'You think I've spoilt them, Rose?'

'No, darling.'

'Yes, you've often said so. Of course you're quite right.' She held her breath as a car came down the street. The car passed and she said mournfully, 'I know I've been a bad mother. Oh dear, nobody knows that better than me!'

The others tried to reassure her. But Bessie as she grew weaker became more restless and troubled. She repeated that she '*must* see the children, she must *see* them', emphasizing the word as though she had never seen the children before, or seeing them now, under some new light, would discover in them some new extraordinary aspect. 'I must *see* them again, just once.'

'Dearest, they're coming as fast as they can.'

'But do you think so? Do you think they *will* come? Do you think they want to come?'

And this continued at intervals for more than two hours, until in the early morning she became suddenly calmer, patient, as if her hope was exhausted with her strength. She said in a gentle and resigned voice, 'It's my own fault if they don't come. I've made them selfish. Yes, I've been a failure.'

CHAPTER 36

'If Bessie was guilty, what am I?' Ella asked herself. She had reached Rose's room, seeking to escape the crowd which grew every moment more reckless and enterprising. For those who had failed to find what they wanted prowled into every corner with angry faces as if someone had defrauded them, as if it was impossible that a house containing such a mass of things should not have at least one specimen of what they needed. 'But Amanda can't be so unfeeling – so blind to her own nature.'

The door burst open, and two little black-coated, white-faced women dashed in, jostling each other in their haste to be first. Ella advanced on them in terror. 'Excuse me – this room is – private.'

'Private?' They stared at her in suspicion. Then one, the oldest and fiercest, squalled, 'Then why didn't you say so.' They flew out, simultaneously fearful of being left behind.

Ella, much alarmed before this indignation, quickly left the room and locked the door behind her. 'I must see Amanda – I must see Harry and explain how good she really is – that she's only uncertain of herself and a little shy.'

A mob was charging up the front stairs as if storming a palace. The auctioneer was coming to the bedrooms. Ella, afraid even to turn down the east passage towards Amanda's room, fled again to the ground floor and the kitchen, where she caught sight of Harry in the yard. She ran out to him.

'Oh Harry, have you seen Amanda? I'm sure you have only to explain that you don't expect her to know all about farming at once – not for a year or two.'

'Yes, I've seen her.' He paused. His expression told Ella nothing. 'I saw her just this minute.'

Harry was standing by a cart in which some large object stood, covered by a rick cloth. The cart, which was old and battered had upon its frame a new name board, of which the paint was startling in its brightness:

You've got the piano,' said Ella nervously.

'Yes, Miss Ella, thank you very much.' Harry approached the new name board, licked his forefinger, and picked off some dust. 'A lot of grit in your back avenue, Miss Ella.'

'And did you ask Amanda?'

'It's no go, Miss Ella, not for the present, anyhow,' in a tone of melancholy resignation to female fate.

'I'm sorry, Harry, but I'm sure it's only a little – shyness,' Ella hastened to reassure Harry.

'Oh yes, she'll come round, I know that,' Harry reassured Ella.

'If you're agreed – '

'Why, Miss Ella, it's as sure a thing as if we'd been married almost. Oh, she'll come round. She must come round. This is only an upset, over putting her off for harvest and Nelly Raft and what not.'

'About Nelly Raft?' Ella looked much alarmed.

'Yes, she says I ought to marry Nelly instead, that Nelly would suit me better. But all that, it's only an upset. It's natural. I'm not blaming her, Miss Ella, you mid say I asked for it. But I'm hoping she'll come round soon because we're going to be very busy at the Quarry in another week or so, and after the apples begin to fall.'

Harry made a gesture which seemed to describe the hopelessness of getting married after the beginning of the apple harvest. He then licked his forefinger again and made another experiment with the new boards, remarking, 'Ab, but I shouldn't touch it, should I, it's only scratching it.'

And as if answering a demand, Ella exclaimed, 'Oh, of course it will be all right, Harry. I'll see Amanda at once.'

'Thank you, Miss Ella, I don't want to worry you, but there it is. It's not that I couldn't wait a bit. It's things. Things keep pressing.'

He took off his hat and mounted the cart, where old Bobby was already sitting. They drove carefully through the yard gate, both glancing anxiously at the piano, as the cart rocked in the gutter.

Ella did not find Amanda for a long time. The invaders had now begun to disperse, and while the auctioneer was selling odd lots in the parlour, small bands roamed round the house, picking up bits of wood, broken frames, cracked scent bottles without their tops.

As Ella came into the parlour she saw a Queensport friend, a retired judge of exceedingly polite manners, in the act of thrusting his pen-knife into the back of an armchair, her grandfather's chair, fitted with high arms to hold a reading board. 'No,' he said to his wife, a little smart woman in black with whom Ella had co-operated many times in decorating the church for Easter. 'It's all right, it's mahogany, but I have my doubts,' prodding the bookcase, 'about those shelves.'

Both glanced round, but Ella, blushing, was already in flight. She pretended not to have recognized the couple. She felt ashamed as if she had caught these nice people without their clothes.

Amanda was found at last in the parlour, tying up bundles of books. She was covered with dust, and even the handkerchief knotted over her hair was black. She looked up at Ella and said, 'I was afraid they'd get mixed up again – these are for Iris. She's taken almost all the first editions, and Dorothy all the nice bindings.'

'I've just seen Harry – he was fetching the piano. Your piano.'

'Oh, it won't be mine, and besides, I can't play. De Retz, why didn't I read him while he was here?' Amanda scratched her nose irritably and left on it a long streak of dirt.

'Dear, I know perhaps Harry has been a little thoughtless in some ways. But don't you think you should be forgiving now? He loves you so much. And you mustn't be afraid of not loving him enough in return. I know sometimes girls do fear that. But you needn't do so – you needn't trouble about things which belong to – nature. Yes, God will look after you in that way, if you will only let Him.'

Amanda slapped down more books and said, 'Fhh, what dust! I'm quite sick of being filthy. Dearest, don't let's talk of Harry now – I'm so pestered and it's such a bore.' She got up to reach for the string on the table.

'Harry is not a boring subject.'

'No, Harry is a dear – I meant, getting married. Fhh,' she blew angrily and fanned the air as if to drive away the dust. 'It's such a – stuffy idea.'

There was a pause. Ella said mournfully, 'Yes, it's my fault – Rose warned me – but I wouldn't listen.'

'How could it be your fault?'

'If only your Aunt Bessie had not died. You never had a real home, and there was that terrible school.'

'Fhh!' Amanda looked round for scissors.

'Iris was the same – whenever one of her nice men friends was – attracted – she ran away.'

'Do you mean that I'm afraid of something – that I'm running away?' said Amanda, setting back on her haunches and looking up. Her dirty nose gave her an exasperated and reckless air.

'I can't help thinking—'

'But you don't understand.' Amanda looked at Ella with an enquiring gaze and then apparently came to a decision. 'I've got something to tell you.'

'Tell me. What?'

'You won't be shocked. Promise me. I can't think why you haven't guessed.'

'What is it – is it someone else – not Robin?'

'Oh well,' Amanda gazed at her, somewhat disappointed. 'I should have to tell you pretty soon, or you *would* guess. But I did hope you'd be rather pleased.'

'What about?' Ella seemed quite bewildered, but her bewilderment did not convince Amanda, who was accustomed to Ella's elusive manners.

'You do know,' she exclaimed, 'you have guessed, you must have. You know I used to be sick in the mornings – last month?'

'What do you mean? What can you mean?'

Amanda got up slowly, pressing her bundle of books against her stomach, and said in a careless manner, looking intently at Ella as if to see the effect. 'The real fact is – I *didn't* run away – at least from the most important thing – I'm going to have a baby.' She dropped her books on the table.

Ella exclaimed, 'But you don't mean – like Nelly Raft.'

'Just like poor Nelly, except, of course, that I had my eyes open. Are you terribly shocked, darling? Oh dear, I believe you are.'

'But – how can you be sure?'

'Oh, it's quite certain. I'm nearly three months gone. I'm really quite big. I can't imagine why no one has seen anything.'

Ella stood staring at Amanda as if at some monster suddenly emerged from the innocent box that had been Amanda.

'I – I can't believe it,' she muttered. 'I couldn't have dreamt – no, I—'

'But is it so terrible?'

'How could you – how could you bring yourself—'

'I thought you wanted me to go with Harry.'

'To go with Harry, without love, and without even knowing if you wanted to marry him?'

'But you yourself—'

'I?' Ella started back as if she had been hit. 'But how could you think that I – was the same. I loved your father – I wished only to be his wife.'

'Dearest, I didn't mean to hurt you. Just the other way. And you know it isn't necessary any more to take the conventional view. It's not such a disgrace, at least, for an unmarried girl. It's not as though I'd been deceiving a husband. Of course, I can understand that Aunt Rose would have some reason to be upset about me.'

'You don't know what you are talking about,' said Ella, turning away as if to fly. 'Your Aunt Rose – might have saved you – saved all this—' She made a gesture which seemed to include the empty and disgraced house, in a whole world of desolation. 'If we'd let her – if I hadn't been so obstinate – so blind and wicked.'

Amanda hurried after her. 'Dearest, don't be so upset – it's nothing very serious – you ought to be pleased. It's only a point of view.'

'And why – why,' Ella cried in amazement, 'when Harry *wants* to marry you?'

'I suppose – I don't love him. But really – I don't think I ever loved him.'

'And yet you – went with him?'

They were walking down the corridor; Amanda's arm was round Ella's waist.

'Yes, I suppose.' Amanda examined her own motives. 'I thought it would be an experience that I ought to have.'

'An experience – without love – and this poor baby. This poor child – without a father – without love.'

There was a silence broken by the auctioneer's voice above, now tired and impatient, heard against a sound of roving boots and tapping shoes.

'But widows love their children,' said Amanda.

'Widows love their husbands – their children were born in love – not like this – not as an – experiment.'

'Oh Lord!' said Amanda in a distressed voice, 'what can I say – and I promised to pack for Dorothy.'

Dorothy, having thoroughly explored Ella's room on the night before, had decided to join Bertie at his hotel, which would be more comfortable. And Bertie would pay the tips.

'No, you can't understand. It's my fault,' Ella muttered.

Amanda was gathering up the pile of Dorothy's leather bindings. She looked anxiously into her mother's small compressed features, full as always of a mysterious preoccupation, and said, 'But you mustn't worry about me – I'm not afraid – not the least bit.'

Ella looked severely at her daughter and said, 'There's only one thing to do – you must be married. You must take Harry. I insist.'

Amanda was astonished. It seemed to her that not Ella but Rose was speaking. Ella had never looked more like Rose.

'But if I don't love Harry?'

'You have to think of the child – your responsibility to the child – that's the important thing. Oh, I'm sure of it. The only thing now is to give your child a father – a real home. It's wicked not to do that. It's all you can do. And I can't let you – not do it at once. Oh, I've been too weak already.'

Amanda's surprise gave way to a look of bewilderment, as if after all she were not so confident of her refusal. She said nervously, 'But why the hurry?'

'Of course there's hurry – to put things right. And Harry must be told – he must give notice. You can't stay like this. Yes, you must call Harry back – telephone to him. Or shall I do so myself?'

'But I don't see.' Amanda's voice was childish and petulant. 'And I promised to pack for Dorothy – she's waiting—'

'You can pack for Dorothy afterwards.'

'Look out, here she is.'

Ella went out hastily and Amanda, witb a gloomy, perplexed air, received Dorothy's instructions for the proper folding of her cotton frocks.

CHAPTER 37

The sale was over by six o'clock, but for two hours afterwards local buyers were taking away heavy furniture. Dorothy, Bertie, and Robin, just before nine, resolved to give a picnic in the drawing-room. Iris, on the excuse of catching an early train, had escaped.

Bertie had found in the library a cigar box containing still four Henry Clays, and in the cellar, among a heap of old bottle jackets, a bottle of Heidsieck. He and Robin foraged for glasses and assembled three cups and a port glass without a foot. 'Here we are,' he cried, 'we can send the glass round – no heel taps. Where's Aunty and Amanda?'

'Must we have them?' said Dorothy, who was polishing a brooch, a heavy old cameo which she proposed to hang upon a chain begged from Ella's jewel box. She had found the cameo. Dorothy was good at finding things. Valuables of all kinds seemed to fly into her hands.

'Of course we must have them – it's a real family gathering,' said Bertie, 'and probably the last.' He was plainly shocked at the suggestion that the family should separate without some kind of ritual. 'Has anyone a notion where they are?'

'I saw them about an hour ago drinking tea and eating stale cake off a packing case in the back passage,' said Dorothy, 'and they're probably still there. It's extraordinary how those two live. They're always soaking tea together in some hole or corner. You'd think they were a couple of chars – and Amanda is much the dirtier of the two. Really, since Aunt Rose died, everything has gone completely to pieces.'

Bertie went out shouting, 'Amanda, Amanda', and returned in a short time with Ella from the kitchen. The old woman had a scared, owlish look, like one dragged suddenly from some dark cupboard into the light.

'But Aunty, darling,' Bertie was saying, 'of course we must drink your health – and you must play to us – to me.' He opened the big piano, which, though covered with dust, still stood at the end of the room, waiting to be taken away by its new owner. 'That will make it like a real family party – in the old style. Pour out, Robin, and give Aunty the first glass.'

Bertie was an accomplished celebrator. It was obvious at once to everyone that he understood thoroughly the art of putting people at their ease, making them feel gay, clever; making them drink, perhaps making them drunk. The very bend of his arm when he handed Ella the broken glass, was that of a master, who, moreover, delighted in his own mastery. A happy man so long as he was celebrating.

Amanda came in suddenly, looking blowsy and, one might say, crushed together as if she had been asleep somewhere in her clothes. She seemed annoyed to find Bertie giving Ella champagne.

But when Bertie, in the exercise of his art, took her by the arm and explained that this was a celebration, a farewell party, she could not protest, without seeming churlish. She accepted a cupful of champagne and, drinking it off, cried, 'Goodbye to the Villa.'

'Hsh!' said Bertie. 'Aunty is going to play.'

'But I can't – I can't. What shall I play?' Ella looked round at the family with a nervous and uncertain smile. Plainly she felt it a duty in the presence of Bertie's joviality to smile.

'All the favourites.' Bertie conducted her to the piano across the uncarpeted floor.

'"The Moonlight,"' cried Robin, who was restlessly jerking his thin legs about the room. 'The Moonlight, Aunty – certainly The Moonlight.'

'Do you really want The Moonlight?' Ella looked at them in doubt. But they answered in chorus, 'Please, The Moonlight.'

Ella hesitated. Obviously she thought that they were flattering her or perhaps laughing at her. 'But I could do something else.'

'No, no, The Moonlight,' cried Robin, coming up to the piano and speaking almost fiercely. 'Don't you see, Aunty, it's just what we *do* want for the last of the Villa.'

'Romance,' said Dorothy, confident of making the right comment.

Ella glanced at them. 'Romance,' she thought. 'What do they mean?' And she felt again an enormous loneliness, but could not tell whether it was her own or Rose's. 'Very well, children,' she murmured with resignation. 'But of course, I'm very out of practice – my fingers are getting so stiff.' She sighed.

But she drew herself up, her face became set and all at once she looked like a woman of power, of decision. She knew what she wanted to do and how to do it. And as she began to play the kind, indulgent smile of Bertie, even the polite airs of Dorothy, changed into looks of respect. Robin sat down squarely in front of his aunt, on a stool, and stared frowning at her, as if he hoped to look through her, to see how she worked and what she meant by the music. Only Amanda seemed inattentive. She sat apart by the window and looked out at the darkening lawn and the drive torn up by lorries and littered with old newspapers and broken straw. Once, it is true, her head was drawn downwards, one would have said that the girl was seized with a fit of weeping. But a glance from in front would have shown that she was suffering only from an enormous yawn.

Carts were still arriving, their tired horses straight from harvest fields; the iron-shod boots of field workers sounded on stairs and passages, and heavy objects were bumped on the floors. But in the drawing-room, emptied of everything except the grand piano and half a dozen gilt chairs, something of the old quality of the Villa seemed to return with the music, played with a sentiment of the old school, rich, confident, passionate, unashamed of its direct attack upon the primitive emotions.

In the dim light from the shadowed gardens and a cloudy sky, the bare unparquetted boards in the middle of the room seemed like a pale carpet, the shadows fell like curtains, the dark squares upon the walls, where pictures had hung, seemed like the ghosts of pictures, and the room itself enlarged by its emptiness had the full dignity of its classical proportions.

Ella was disappointed by her own performance. She had wanted to play very well, to do justice to this sonata which she and Rose had loved so much, but which was now almost a joke to their nieces. She felt while she played, 'You are lonely, too, no one understands you any more, not as we did.' And it seemed to her that the whole age of Bessie and Rose and her own youth, of love expecting sacrifice, even seeking it, of moonlight walks, of passionate dreams which contemplated nature itself as the grave and splendid cathedral of ideal devotion, had gone for ever. She alone, in that room, had the faintest notion of it. Only she knew that it was not in fact sentimental, but violent, bitter, tragic.

Bertie, turning over for the old lady, was enchanted. He smiled all the time as if he were tasting something sweet, and exclaimed, at the end, 'Wonderful, Aunty, I haven't heard anything like it for years. I don't know how it is, but I never seem to get time for concerts.'

'Neither do I,' said Dorothy. 'Really life is such a rush, it gets worse and worse. I have to be back in town somehow before three tomorrow afternoon. I've got to see Diana again this term. Diana is a darling, but sometimes I envy women who haven't got a family, they do get so much more time to do things.'

'And now some Schubert,' said Bertie.

Robin, clasping his nervous hands and rocking himself on his stool, was saying, 'Yes, yes, by Jove, it takes you there – right back.'

Ella looked round at them with her confused smile. Then she got up. 'No, I mustn't keep you. Thank you, darlings – thank you – this is a sad evening for us all. The last evening at the Villa. God bless you all, my dears, if your Aunt Rose could be here she would bless you, too.'

They came round her to say their good nights, which Dorothy performed most gracefully, from having the less feeling. Bertie and Robin then lighted the last cigars from the box, and with Dorothy, drove away to their hotel, a quite civilized modern hotel. Amanda had already disappeared.

Ella, on the excuse of shutting windows, did not go upstairs. She wandered through the rooms, and once returning to the piano played softly a few bars.

'Romantic,' she said, wondering at this word, thrown out by Dorothy; at Robin's concentrated gaze seeking to enter a world that he could not possibly understand. 'But no, life isn't words. And the music – it hasn't even words.' She touched the piano again as if seeking the soul of that past, distant already to herself. 'What does Amanda think I mean when I talk to her about – responsibility – for an unborn baby – for children. Bessie was not clever, but she knew – even from a child she understood – that it was a serious, important thing. She breathed it from the air. She couldn't escape from it – and in the end how fearfully it fell upon her.' Ella, sitting on the stool as on that hard bedroom chair in the bedroom at Brent Square, shivered in the recollection of her sister's deathbed.

'But Bessie was so ill.' Ella seemed to argue with an accuser. 'She was too hard on herself, as Rose said. Oh, I mustn't forget that. The times have been specially difficult for women, for wives and mothers. There have been so many changes, and James was always a difficulty – he influenced Amanda, too. Yes, James was a bad father. Rose admitted it – she had to – it was no good pretending any more, at that fearful time.'

Rose, indeed, seeing Bessie's despair, had said everything that might console her. 'Don't blame yourself too much, my darling. No one esteems James more than I do – he is a great man, with true nobility of mind. But greatness must have its faults, and then they are apt to be great faults. James had such force of confidence. I always feared for him on that side – the religious side – his prejudice against the Church. James had very deep faith, half his goodness is Christian in spirit, but he will not recognize it, and his influence has been all against the Church of Christ.'

But the dying woman, as if not only absorbed but surrounded by a conviction impenetrable to anyone else, by the judgment of death itself, answered only, 'I wasn't fit to be a wife and mother, and after I was married there was no time to learn.'

'You did far better than I should have done. No one could have done better. But James has made your work hard. As Papa always said, he is really an anarchist. He understands love but not duty, and without duty love is only a sentiment.'

'Everyone loves you, Bessie,' cried Ella. 'What shall we do without you?'

'Why are the children so unhappy?' Bessie asked, faintly and mournfully. 'Muriel is dreadfully unhappy, William was miserable before he was killed. Alice is frightened of everything, even Iris and poor little Amanda are not happy, they are so old for their age, so anxious and serious. What have I done to them?'

'It's not your fault.'

'But you don't know – you're not me, and I feel so afraid.'

The cold early light of an October day penetrating into the room was more like a quality of its own sadness and dinginess than an illumination. It seemed to come from the ceiling and the walls, the furniture, the faces and hands of the three sisters, like an essence of their quality; of the old cracked whitewash on the ceiling that had never seen the sky, of the flowered wallpaper, which, with its once gaudy colour and flamboyant pattern, seemed to brood in the resignation of some worn out belle; of the threadbare Axminster carpet, made to endure, but trodden at last into squalor and ugliness; of the battered mahogany chairs, chests and wardrobe, out of date, out of fashion, and seeming conscious of their fate, the worst corner of the cheapest junk shop; and for the three women with a profound sadness, a sorrow, which passing beyond grief, beyond tears, knew itself calmly, and took its bearings in this new world, by the light of its experience.

'Dearest Bessie, you needn't feel afraid, you of all people. God will know your heart, your true, loving heart.'

'Oh, I'm not afraid to die – death is too easy. If it were only that – if it were only hell.'

'My darling, don't.'

'Hell would be nothing, It's what I've done that can't be undone. God can't change that.'

'He can forgive – He can bring peace, in Christ's love.'

'But how can I forgive myself? Oh, how selfish I've been, how blind – just pleasing myself.'

'It pleased you to do good – you sacrificed yourself.'

'Yes, pleased me. I pleased myself and spoilt my children. I had no right to be a wife – I didn't know even what it meant.'

'That was my fault,' said Rose. 'I made you marry James, and pehaps I was wrong. It has lain heavily upon me. Perhaps I thought more of his happiness than of yours. Perhaps I sacrificed you.'

'William might have come back to the Church,' said Bessie, 'if he had not been killed. But what a dreadful struggle he had. You would have thought he didn't want to believe. And that girl whom he fell in love with, how wretched she made him. Oh my poor William, and he was such a dear little child, so friendly, so happy in himself. Why should the children have to suffer like that, and die in such agony of mind and body. Without hope, without any comfort. Was that my fault, too, Rose?'

Her voice became shrill, she was losing her self-command, which had been due perhaps to a passing freedom from pain. She cried out, 'Oh, why, why should he have suffered like that, by my fault? Because his mother was a fool.' She began to weep, struggling with the bedclothes, as if raging against their weight and confinement. 'No, it's too cruel, it's not fair. I can't bear it.'

Then her sisters tried to calm her. They, too, were weeping. 'Dearest, how can you blame yourself?' said Ella. She knelt beside the bed and tried to catch Bessie's struggling beating hands.

Bessie fell against Rose's shoulder, and she allowed Rose to draw her head to her breast.

'If anyone is to blame,' said Rose, 'it is I. You were too gentle, too unwary for such a life. And it has killed you at last. We've all used you and killed you – James, and your children, and I, too. And you should have been so happy, you had such powers of happiness. Forgive me, my darling.'

'Such happiness,' Bessie murmured, who probably had heard only this word. 'I didn't deserve – but God blessed me, so wonderfully, such great happiness.' She was almost unconscious, and though her lips moved again it was impossible to distinguish any word but happiness, breathed several times, as she died.

Alice arrived about an hour later. She was in such distress to find her mother dead that Ella was obliged to spend the next half hour comforting her. Bertie came after breakfast. He, too, was distressed, but more surprised. 'I'd no idea,' he said, 'that she was so ill. She seemed so full of go. Poor Mama, she had her troubles, but really I don't believe she would have been happy without something or somebody to worry her. She loved a real good old-fashioned fuss. Well, I suppose this means a bit of a family break-up.'

Bertie's regrets for his mother were mixed with a kind of satisfaction in the thought that the family were now disintegrating, that he would no longer be called upon to write birthday letters, to buy Christmas presents, or to go to meet young sisters at the station. But he was good-natured and competent. He arranged the funeral with efficiency, and said the right things to guests. He seemed, indeed, to have found his level as a man of that world which works, thinks, feels and amuses itself with a judgment nicely balanced between that of the pig and the fox.

Rose detested him, but was glad to find him easy to deal with. It was quickly arranged between them that Brent Square should be sold, and the money allotted to buying an annuity for his father, paying for Muriel's education, and investing for the other children a few hundred pounds each. She undertook, for her part, to complete Amanda's education and to see her established in life.

Groom, now Sir James, she took home to Florence Villa. The old man was wonderfully revived by his honour. He felt obviously that righteousness and science were once more established in heaven, and began to take a more optimistic view of the future of the world. When he died three years later, he was acknowledged by the papers, instructed by young Beal, as one of the famous men of

Victorian science. A statue was proposed for him in his native town, but after a little canvassing it was discovered that public feeling had not reached the necessary temperature to hatch a statue. It was warming, but Groom had died too soon. Three more years at least would have been needed to produce a statue. The committee, which under Beal's chairmanship had organized the subscription, decided finally on a plaque, with a head in bas-relief. This was duly put on the wall of the old Academy, now turned into the factory and sale room of a firm making patent medicines.

CHAPTER 39

'Are you still here?'

Ella, not at all startled by this interruption, looked up from the piano stool and saw Amanda. She was in her dressing-gown and her hair was taped, as for bed, but she had not put on her pyjamas. A cigarette jumped between her lips as she spoke.

'How bad she looks,' Ella thought. 'Corrupted, careless, defiant like a child that has done wrong and is afraid of being reproached. But how could I change her now?'

She got up and allowed Amanda to take her from the room. She thought, 'One can't go back with life – with children. Bessie felt that weight, even Rose. They lived with guilt – it was the air they breathed – the light of their path – they accepted it, it was in their souls. Yes, it was Rose's dignity – it was Bessie's power – to accept the guilt.'

'What have you been doing?' Amanda said. 'All these hours. It's nearly twelve.'

'Oh no. Yes, I see. But you should have gone to bed, darling.'

They had reached Amanda's room and the girl had sat down on her bed. She answered in a tone of drowsy reproach. 'I was too sleepy and the water was tepid. And I was waiting for you to say good night.'

'Polly went early. Aren't you cold?'

'No, frightfully hot.' She pushed her plait from her neck. It was true that her pale face shone with sweat; her eyelids seemed to be falling together with sullen weariness. But suddenly she stretched out her arms, so that her dressing-gown fell open, showing her full hanging breasts. 'Oh – oh – at last the sale's over. Let's have some tea. Tea – tea.'

She raised herself clumsily to her feet. 'The tea things are hidden in the housemaid's closet. Polly was guarding them from the invasion.'

'Hadn't you better put on your pyjamas?'

'There's no one to see – Polly went before supper.'

'Yes, yes, I forgot – we're alone.' Ella looked round with a startled air.

'Thank heaven we are! I was afraid Robin might stay here, but luckily there was no bed.' Arm in arm the two women walked along the passage, slowly and in silence. Each seemed to wait for some important decisive speech. The silence was apprehensive and critical. But as if by a simultaneous decision, both turned from it.

Amanda lit the gas ring in the housemaid's closet and made the tea. 'Where shall we go? Did anyone buy the old sofa?'

'I hope not. Granny was so particular about that sofa. It was specially made in London.'

The old sofa, of which the horse-hair stuffing was curling out from large tears in the cover, was found in the attic among ruined umbrellas, broken crockery, and the rubbish which no one would carry away.

'Heavens, how dusty!' said Amanda, opening windows. 'How sick I am of dust.'

They sat on the sofa to drink their tea, and Ella said, 'Bessie used to complain of the dust on her dance frocks, when she brought her partners here to flirt. She was afraid Papa or Rose would notice.'

'I didn't know Aunt Bessie minded what anybody said.'

'Oh yes, yes. At least she was afraid of – doing wrong. Very afraid. Of being undutiful – or disloyal. She asked a great deal of herself.'

'Thank God for a breeze,' said Amanda. The leaves of a horse chestnut, to be seen through the open window in front, by the attic light, were shaken suddenly with a loud metallic rattle.

'She had a very bad conscience when she died,' said Ella. 'She suffered very much. But I thought – Rose and I thought – that much had been asked of her.'

'All those babies,' said Amanda, bunching her shoulders and hollowing her chest as if to avoid a blow. 'What a life!' Suddenly she got up and went to the window. 'Poof, it's stifling! And what a glorious night outside.' She stepped out through the dormer upon the leads.

'Be careful, don't fall over.' Ella appeared beside her on the narrow walk which ran between roof and parapet, as it seemed, to a great distance upon either side. For though the night seemed clear the sky was overcast with thin cloud, and all distances were uncertain. There was, indeed, no horizon. The only clearly defined object was the chestnut tree with its enormous structure of leaves, picked out sharply by the attic light and resembling one of those centre pieces of Victorian silver work, enlarged a hundred times. This tree now stood perfectly still; the breeze had been a mere flaw of wind passing up the valley from the Longwater gap.

'Did she realize that her life had been rather wasted?' said Amanda.

'Oh no, no – she thanked God for her happiness. It was only that she thought – she hadn't deserved it.'

'Aunt Bessie was brought up to love that kind of life.'

'I always think perhaps – she was happy because – of her conscience.'

'You said it made her unhappy.'

'No, I meant it made her suffer – but one can suffer and have so much happiness. Perhaps people are meant to suffer – in order to have real happiness – the richness.'

There was a long silence. Amanda with her eyes fixed on the tree seemed to ponder. She frowned at the tree. But at last she made an impatient gesture of her shoulders. 'Alice, Muriel, Bertie, Dorothy, Iris – and look at me. But I suppose we're an average lot and Aunt Bessie had to be just herself.'

Again there was silence. A breeze shook the tree and Ella said, 'I suppose they will cut that tree down – it darkens the dining-room. Grandpapa planted it for the Great Exhibition.'

'Yes, it's too big – it's due to it to come down, as Harry would say.'

'Poor Harry!'

'Why is my hair coming out so freely? Does it always come out when one is in this state?'

'Darling, you must see that woman in Queensport.'

'She won't do any good. And what does it matter. But you think I ought to keep myself in repair – for a husband.'

There was again a critical silence. The moon which had been recognized only by a pale blue illumination behind the cloud became a little brighter, so that the tree was not so sharply defined. But the great stretch of landscape behind, woods, fields, the Longwater, darkly bright like lacquer; the hills and a triangle of the Atlantic seen between the cliffs at the mouth of the Longwater, though they seemed to take shape, were in fact vague in detail. The larger objects, impressive in bulk, had no edges. It was impossible to say where mountain became plain, the woods stopped, and the water began. A triangle of ocean, smaller than a finger-nail, suggested by its place, below cliffs, not an edge but a beginning, the foothills of the sea. All in fact was still background, only more complex and mysterious, to the minute distinction of the silver tree.

'You're determined on my taking Harry?' said Amanda. This was the first time either had referred to that scene when Ella had commanded Amanda to telephone to Harry.

'But you don't feel – that you ought to—'

'I'm afraid not. I don't think it would be fair to either of us.' Ella was silent, and Amanda said, 'Would you be very upset if I didn't?'

'Perhaps – I have no right – it's too late.'

'But, dearest, if I don't, you won't be sorry for me. You see, that's so unnecessary. I shall always get work. Professor Moss would still give me as much as I could do if I had six illegitimate babies.'

'Do you think I meant this to happen – that I sent you to the Fair on purpose?'

'No, of course not.'

'But perhaps I did secretly.'

'You mustn't imagine things.'

'I seem to have brought ruin to everything.'

'That's nonsense – come, you ought to be in bed.'

'Rose knew. She understood me. That I should do all kinds of evil. Yes, I sacrificed you, too – self-indulgence is so artful.'

'But you believe in love – you oughtn't to think it wrong. It isn't wrong,' said Amanda, 'it's only a nuisance.'

'But – but there is wickedness there, too.' Ella, hanging on Amanda's arm, as they turned from the window, spoke in a soft reflective voice. 'I remember – how wicked – how guilty I felt – even in loving. Perhaps I was glad to feel guilty – for his sake, or perhaps it was for the love's sake. Yes, I oughtn't to run away – I ought to admit the responsibility. Rose accepted her fate – such a hard and cruel fate.'

'But that wasn't your fault.'

'I was her fate.'

They were in the upper corridor, closely pressed together under the row of pale skylights.

'But you mustn't blame yourself – it was Aunt Rose gave you this feeling.'

'She had it, too – and Bessie – and she was quite right. One must have it – one must have a sense of conscience. Did I send you to Harry – to enjoy myself – in you?'

Amanda was tired. She said in a weary, patient voice, 'That's just a form of words.'

'That's what you thought. It shocked me very much. But now I think – it may be true – the evil will is so – fearfully cunning – you never know what it is aiming at. It walks in the dark. It made me kill Rose – it made me send you to the Fair – yes, and perhaps I wanted even to see you like this – like me when I—'

'But why not – I don't mind. I daresay it will be good for me.'

'Oh dear, you're tired to death – and it's so dangerous for you when you – I must put you to bed at once.'

Amanda was in fact exhausted and allowed herself to be put to bed. She wished to say something decisive, consoling, to remove Ella's obsession, but she could not think of any words at all. And looking at the old woman's obstinate countenance and large eyes, she thought, 'No, what's the good? People are what they are.'

'You must sleep, you must sleep – it's so important.'

'Good night, dearest, and don't worry about me.'

Ella kissed her suddenly and went out. Amanda, startled by this silent flight, put out her feet and wondered if she should follow. But she did not care to put her bare feet on the dusty floor, and again she was yawning. Her whole body and soul seemed to be one yawn. She fell back on the pillow and was at once so deeply asleep that when, in the full morning sun she found herself awake and looking at Robin, she had for the moment the feeling of being hung in space, or, rather, in nothingness.

Robin was dressed as for town. And as Amanda started up, blinking and clutching at her hair which was falling into her eyes, he said, 'I just walked in, all the doors seem to be open and most of the windows.'

'I hope you didn't wake Aunty – she is frightfully tired.'

'She's awake. I've just seen her wandering about downstairs with a tea cup in her hand.'

'But what time is it? Has she had breakfast?'

'Nearly ten o'clock.'

'My God, it's awful how I sleep – like an animal.' Amanda angrily crossed her arms as if to clutch herself together.

'Have you decided what you're going to do?' Robin spoke in the sharp voice which revealed embarrassment.

'I wrote to Moss on Tuesday, and he wired. The job's waiting.'

Robin got up and walked nervously about the room. At last he came up close to Amanda, fixed his eyes on her and said, 'Come with me now, never mind about the baby or the scandal or any other damn thing.'

'I must do this job.'

'So much the better. It will help. We'll be poor. You can do it anywhere, I suppose?'

'No, only in London. It will mean a lot of digging at the Museum.'

'Well, can't you get another job?'

'Couldn't you come to London?'

'I've just left London. It seems you prefer your job to me.'

'It's the dullest possible job, but I've taken it on now, and I can't very well let Moss down. It's for his big book.'

'Dammit,' said Robin, 'I *will* come to town, whenever you like.'

'Very well, then, as soon as I've got a flat for Aunty and myself.'

Robin was excited by his own bold stroke. 'But look here, Mandy' – he smiled as if inviting enthusiasm – 'that's the whole solution – Aunty.'

'I don't see.' Amanda scratched herself impatiently.

'Well, we'll each have our own room – we'd need that in any case.'

'I'll need a study.'

'And so shall I, and with Aunty as chaperone, it will be a perfectly ordinary household. You can slip away somewhere to have your baby. And there needn't be any fuss with the family.'

'I suppose it will work out like that in any case.'

'Yes, yes, but it's a *good* arrangement, the best possible. It solves all the problems. Don't you *see*, darling?' He plumped down beside Amanda on the bed and put his arm round her waist. 'We'll be together as much as we like, and yet you'll be able to get rid of me whenever you like. It's a marvellous plan.'

'And you of me. Yes, I think it's a good plan. I really do think so. The best possible.'

'And as for a job in London, Uncle Dick would have me back tomorrow.'

'Yes, I'm sure he would, if you'd like to go back.'

'You know, Mandy,' Robin jumped up again, 'I really believe that my principle trouble was simply Kathy – Kathy. It was Kathy who poisoned even the job. A woman like that gets on your brain – that is, I suppose, it's into your nerves. You know she's thinking of you all the time – she's nothing else to think of, and you know she's thinking all wrong. What *is* it, Mandy?' he stopped and looked with a little impatience at Amanda, who had gone to open the door.

'I was wondering if that was Aunty at the telephone? What does she want at the telephone? She went out and hurried downstairs to the hall, where Ella, in her pink wrapper, was calling in a shrill and unnatural voice, her telephone voice, 'Yes, at Mr Colley's. He will tell you all about it. Yes, thank you, officer. I'm so sorry to—'

'What *are* you doing?'

'Nothing. It was only – that nice Inspector at Queensport. I remembered about the cachets – that I got two kinds from Mr Colley, and that Rose took the strong ones. That is, I knew all the time – but I didn't know how important it was. Or did I?' Ella gazed at Amanda. 'Perhaps I was keeping it back on purpose.'

'It has no importance at all. You know the police don't really want to be bothered.'

'But they seem to be quite impressed – they're sending out a man on purpose – this afternoon. I seem to have told them just what *is* important.'

'Dearest, the whole thing was settled months ago. Have you slept at all?'

'Oh yes – no. The bed is so – strange. I never liked a strange bed. But I think – I could lie down now. I feel so relieved that I hit upon the right message at last. Do you think they will arrest me?'

'Of course not – they can't.'

'Yes, I shall lie down for a little. I must be fresh for the officer.' She kissed Amanda and said in a timid, anxious voice, 'I haven't said good morning, have I?'

'Yes, try to sleep.'

Ella went to her room. She said to herself, as she closed the door, 'What a relief. What a good idea it was to send them to Colley about the two sorts of cachets – yes, the only important thing now is to tell the officer the truth, the real truth, or I shall only make things worse. But I shall have to watch myself carefully. I'm so deceitful. Oh Rose, how right you were about my character, even when I was quite young you knew that I was slippery. That's what you used to say: "Ella, you're as slippery as an eel. No one can catch you or pin you down to anything. You're so full of lies and crookedness that you can't be honest even if you try."'

'Even if I try,' said Ella. 'How fearful it is to have such a character as that, to be such a miserable coward and liar, but now at last I shall tell the truth, the whole truth. Even if I can't find it out myself, I shall help the officers to do so. And then I shall go to my trial. Yes, I shall be glad to go.'

She reflected, 'But I must be fresh – I must sleep even a little sleep would clear my brain so much. I think I might really allow myself a cachet.'

The old woman, murmuring to herself, took out of Rose's washstand cupboard the box of sleeping cachets, broke one in a tooth-glass of water, and touched it with her lips. 'How I hate these things, how nasty they are – but perhaps it's not properly dissolved.'

She sat down beside the washstand and stirred the water with the handle of a tooth brush.

'I shall be glad if they hang me – glad. Oh, I am so tired of this mess – this muddle. Even if it's true – what the children say – that it's not really my fault – that it was Rose who made me weak and nervous – that she is driving me now – all the time – to my death. Yes, that is true – but it's not all the truth, it's only a little bit of the truth. And Rose was not revengeful. Never, never. She loved me dearly and she gave her life for us all, for me and Bessie and for Amanda. And in return how cruelly I treated her. Oh Rose, my darling, can I ever forget what you said that night when you died. The loneliness. Oh, what a fearful loneliness that was, to be hated for your sacrifice, your goodness. What agony you suffered then. What a wretched death. Yes, I drove you to that agony and death. My guilt is too fearful.' Ella shivered and her voice rose; she was speaking aloud: 'It's too heavy, I can't carry it alone – oh, to tell the truth – the whole truth for once.'

She was trembling with agitation, and said to herself, 'Oh dear, see what I've done – I've made myself excited. I'll never sleep, and I simply must be fresh for the officer. He's a special officer. It's so important to have a clear head. Did I put in a cachet – I can't remember. But it wouldn't do any harm to take two.'

She made up the draught and sipped it. 'How nasty it is, but I must be brave – for Rose's sake – yes, I must be clear.' She sat, glass in hand. 'I must make her see that I can be honest – that I shan't play any more cunning tricks. Yes, Rose, you'll see – I'll make them understand.'

She looked wondering at the glass. 'Did I put in the other cachet?'

When the detective sergeant arrived an hour later Ella was already past recovery. She had taken sleeping draught enough to kill four or five old ladies. The jury at the inquest brought in the verdict, 'Death due to an overdose of narcotic, taken on account of a disturbed mind.' A more merciful and probably more truthful verdict than the older form of 'temporary insanity'. The witnesses testified that Miss Venn had suffered from the delusion that she had been responsible, in some degree, for her sister's death.

The Venns and the Sants were much relieved by this death, which they felt had saved them much trouble. Robin alone was not so pleased.

He saw that he would have to make a new arrangement for his joint household with Amanda. At the funeral, when the cousins had only a few moments for private conversation, it was agreed that they could not, for the present, set up a flat together. It would be needlessly offensive to the relations. 'But there may be all sorts of other ways. Simply arranging to meet often. Or taking separate flats in the same block: that's often done. You can do anything in London. We'll soon get it fixed. I'll write. What's your new address? But it will come to the office.'

The address came in due course to the Sant office, where Ella's estate was administered. She had left no will, and the sale of the Villa, which went for very little, hardly met the bank debt. Amanda inherited nothing from her, and her legacy from Rose's estate was held up pending a family agreement.

Robin, seeing her lodging, a flat near Sloane Square, in his reference files, said often, 'I must write – no, I'll call,' but he was busy picking up the threads of his London work and he did not write or call.

Six weeks later, when he met Amanda by chance in the tube, he had not yet written. It was in the evening, when the workers came from the offices. The train was crowded, and at first glance he did not recognize Amanda. She was standing, squeezed between a young woman with a thin angular face, and thick highly-painted lips, and a young man, like a Red Indian, with a brown hat hung on the back of his head.

She was in black, but smart and neat with that special smartness of the responsible townswoman. Her body was stouter, but her face much thinner. This thinness had changed her greatly and spoilt the classical roundness and regularity of her features. It had brought out an unexpected likeness to Aunt Ella. Amanda's eyes seemed larger and more apprehensive. She was very pale, with the grey pallor of the town worker, exhausted in nerves, and her cheeks were hollow. Her tall, rather too square forehead showed that network of wrinkles which mark so many women of her age – horizontal from anxious reflections, vertical for concentration and responsibility.

Robin, as his eyes, looking for an office acquaintance with whom perhaps he might escape on Sunday for a day's golf, wandered over a mass of faces, with similar marks of tension and weariness, the men more oppressed, the women more apprehensive, noticed first the girl with the painted lips, and thought, 'A hot one, consumptive,' and then, 'That girl in black is a little like Amanda.'

Amanda turned her head, saw him, and without smiling, gazed at him. For a moment he hesitated. He felt a sudden reluctance from this unexpected meeting. He thought, 'Oh God, what shall I say? One can't make love here in a tube train. And I'm too tired. What I really want is a cocktail.'

Then he pushed towards her, almost knocking off the Red Indian's hat. 'Amanda.' He seized her hands. 'Sorry, sir.'

The Red Indian saved his hat but did not move his long yellowish mask of a face. Robin might have been a passing breeze.

'How marvellous to meet you,' said Robin.

'How are you, Robin?'

'Existing, vegetating, assimilating. And terribly busy.'

'I heard from Iris you were back with Kathy.'

'Well, not exactly back. We inhabit the same house. And are very tactful. It's just an additional nuisance. It would almost be better if we were back.'

There was silence between them. The pretty girl, who, on a close view, had on her forehead exactly the same lines as Amanda, only more faint, gazed, at one foot's range, straight past Robin's chin; the Red Indian, whose elbow just avoided Amanda's hat, stared past her ear into some illimitable distance of the imagination. Both were visibly hearing every word of the conversation and ignoring it, at the same time. The cold mask of the pretty, worn young girl seemed to say, 'Go on. I've got my manners.' The time and workworn face of the man was full of discreet apology. He averted his eyes a fraction, as if to beg, 'Consider me as not here.'

'I hadn't your address – not at first. And none of the family seemed to know where you were.'

'I'm rather avoiding the family just now.'

'Yes, of course.' But he was embarrassed. 'Disappointing price for the Villa.'

'It was very inconvenient for servants.'

'And you didn't even get the farm.' With a tone of apology, like one who pretends to regret an indiscretion, he added, 'No news of Dawbarn?'

'Oh yes, Nelly Raft is looking after his dairy – I think she's living in.'

'Do you mind very much?'

'I'm very glad – for both of them.'

'He's got some cheek, Dawbarn. He worries us all the time for new byres, new gates, a bay window on the house, new everything.'

'Yes, but he'll make the place pay – you'll get your rent.'

And again there was silence. Amanda's hand, gloved in its grey kid, grasping the ring in the coach roof, was pressed by Robin's tan glove; their bodies were crushed together by the silent crowd which, like them, swayed and jerked with the movement of the carriage, whirling them through the tunnel between office and home. From time to time their eyes met, and turned aside. But not before they had seen in each other's glances the same pondering enquiry, which had always attracted them to a point of common interest, and then held them there, apart.

'I must see you, Amanda. Why shouldn't I come home with you tonight?'

'I'm afraid I'll be busy. I've just started on this new job and I'm rather behind.'

'The new job that bores you so much?'

'I have to earn, you know – and I've got to save. If only for education.'

'Why, I suppose we had that, too – at great expense to our parents. And look at us.'

The pretty girl had turned to stone in her resolve to pay no attention to this interruption of her private thoughts. The Red Indian cast down his eyes and raised his brows in a profounder melancholy, as if saying, 'All that goes without saying.'

'What's happened to us, Amanda? I want to cry.'

Amanda did not answer this, but her patient expression seemed to approve. 'Yes, do if you like. I shall understand.'

Robin glanced round at the sad, self-absorbed faces. 'Look at us,' he said, hardly troubling to modify his voice, which certainly reached the pretty girl and the Red Indian. 'All waiting for something, some resurrection, some miracle of the Lord. And miracles don't happen any more, they've been abolished, they're unscientific.'

'We're only rather tired,' said Amanda, consoling him.

'This is your station, isn't it?'

'So it is.' She held out her hand. But Robin followed her on to the platform and drew her aside against the wall. 'We aren't going to say goodbye like that.'

'No, we must meet. You must come and see me when this rush is over.'

'Yes, I must. But what's the good of saying it, I shan't. I like my friends very much, but I don't go to see them, and I love you, but I shall never see you either.'

'Everyone is so busy,' said Amanda.

'What should we do if I came – talk, and talk is so nice at the time, so depressing afterwards. No, we'd better not meet. You remind me that I'm hopeless. Goodbye, Amanda.'

He suddenly took her in his arms and they kissed. It was, however, only an experiment. Their lips did not give anything but merely asked a question.

Ten minutes later Amanda stood in her flat. She had two rooms at the top of a high Victorian house, broken into flats. The rooms were small but well furnished with her own pieces from Florence Villa. They looked out upon the winter trees of a square.

These rooms were austerely neat. Even the supper, on a tray, laid out upon a side table, as Amanda had brought it up from below, the plates with their china covers, the small coloured napkin, had a monastic severity. They belonged in character with their owner, with the smart but austere lines of her hat, coat, even of her expression. No one could have recognized in Amanda the blowsy and discouraged girl of the Villa's last days. Nor could he have discovered the scholar of a year before, charming but sleepy. She was visibly a woman of the world, at grips with its lonely and mortal necessity.

The desk was heaped with files, docketed and ordered. Amanda, having finished her supper in a very few minutes and removed the tray, now, with its dirty plates, an obscene spectacle, outside the door, opened her portfolio. It was full of the notes made during the day, statistics, schedules. She arranged them methodically on her blotter. She had work to do, and her gestures as well as her face showed preparation for a long and troublesome task. She knew that when she had begun it she would continue at an even pace till it was finished. She had a woman's power of monotonous work. But she was very tired, even more tired than usual, and so she hesitated to begin.

She sat down, meaning to smoke a cigarette, but remembered that she had foresworn smoking till her baby was born. So she remained with bent head, not reflecting but allowing the sense of time to fall upon her, existing in a feeling that seemed not her own, since it was without will or desire. And this feeling was one of pity and emptiness; not self-pity, but a universal pity as for all the loss, the frustration, the waste, in the world, and the emptiness was the shell of this pity. It lodged in a vacuum, without object, without will or hope or love. It was merely a vast still grief.

At last Amanda lifted her hands and put them on her waist. She was growing big. She said to herself, 'But do miracles happen? It will be interesting to see.'

She got up and went to her desk. She was not going to let herself off the work, only because it was a bore.

SUGGESTIONS FOR FURTHER READING

Adam International Review, nos. 212–13: Joyce Cary special issue 1950. Includes 'The Novelist at work: a conversation between Joyce Cary and Lord David Cecil', on Cary's technique.

Allen, Walter, *Joyce Cary* (London: Longmans, 1953). Writers and Their Work, no. 41. Highly useful short early account and criticism.

Adams, Hazard, *Joyce Cary's trilogies: pursuit of the particular real* (Tallahassee: University Presses of Florida, 1983).

Bishop, Alan, *Gentleman rider: a life of Joyce Cary* (London: Michael Joseph, 1988). With bibliography and notes containing references to reviews, newspaper articles, interviews and broadcasts.

Bloom, Robert, *The indeterminate world: a study of the novels of Joyce Cary* (Philadelphia: University of Pennsylvania Press, 1962).

Christian, Edward, *Joyce Cary's creative imagination* (New York: Peter Lang, 1988).

Cook, Cornelia, *Joyce Cary: liberal principles* (London: Vision Press, 1981).

Echeruo, Michael, *Joyce Cary and the novel of Africa* (London: Longman, 1973).

Echeruo, Michael, *Joyce Cary and the dimensions of order* (London: Macmillan, 1979).

Fisher, Barbara, *The House as a symbol: Joyce Cary and 'The Turkish House'* (Amsterdam: Rodopi, 1986).

Fisher, Barbara, *Joyce Cary: the writer and his theme* (Gerrards Cross: Colin Smythe, 1980).

Fisher, Barbara (ed.), *Joyce Cary remembered: in letters and interviews by his family and others* (Gerrards Cross: Colin Smythe, 1988).

Foster, Malcolm, *Joyce Cary: a biography* (London: Michael Joseph, 1969).

Gardner, Helen, 'The Novels of Joyce Cary'. *Essays and Studies*', new series, vol. XXVIII, pp. 76–93 (London: John Murray, 1975).

Hoffmann, Charles G., *Joyce Cary: the comedy of freedom* (Pittsburgh University Press, 1964).

Hall, Dennis, *Joyce Cary: a reappraisal* (London: Macmillan, 1983).

Mahood, M. M., *Joyce Cary's Africa* (London: Methuen, 1964).

Modern Fiction Studies. Joyce Cary Special Issue, Autumn, 1963.

Raskin, Jonah, *The Mythology of imperialism: Rudyard Kipling, Joseph Conrad, E. M. Forster, D. H. Lawrence and Joyce Cary* (New York: Dell, 1971).

Starkie, Enid, 'Joyce Cary, a portrait' (Tredegar Memorial Lecture, Royal Society of Literature). *Essays by Divers Hands*, new series, vol. XXXII, pp. 125–44 (Oxford University Press, 1963).

Wright, Andrew, *Joyce Cary: a preface to his novels* (London: Chatto and Windus, 1958).

WOMEN'S WRITING IN EVERYMAN

A SELECTION

Female Playwrights of the Restoration
FIVE COMEDIES
Rediscovered literary treasures in a unique selection **£5.99**

The Secret Self
SHORT STORIES BY WOMEN
'A superb collection' *Guardian* **£4.99**

Short Stories
KATHERINE MANSFIELD
An excellent selection displaying the remarkable range of Mansfield's talent **£3.99**

Women Romantic Poets 1780-1830: An Anthology
Hidden talent from the Romantic era rediscovered **£5.99**

Selected Poems
ELIZABETH BARRETT BROWNING
A major contribution to our appreciation of this inspiring and innovative poet **£5.99**

Frankenstein
MARY SHELLEY
A masterpiece of Gothic terror in its original 1818 version **£3.99**

The Life of Charlotte Brontë
ELIZABETH GASKELL
A moving and perceptive tribute by one writer to another **£4.99**

Vindication of the Rights of Woman and The Subjection of Women
MARY WOLLSTONECRAFT
AND J. S. MILL
Two pioneering works of early feminist thought **£4.99**

The Pastor's Wife
ELIZABETH VON ARNIM
A funny and accomplished novel by the author of *Elizabeth and Her German Garden* **£5.99**

£6.99

AVAILABILITY

All books are available from your local bookshop or direct from **Littlehampton Book Services Cash Sales, 14 Eldon Way, Lineside Estate, Littlehampton, West Sussex BN17 7HE.** PRICES ARE SUBJECT TO CHANGE.

To order any of the books, please enclose a cheque (in £ sterling) made payable to Littlehampton Book Services, or phone your order through with credit card details (Access, Visa or Mastercard) on 0903 721596 (24 hour answering service) stating card number and expiry date. Please add £1.25 for package and postage to the total value of your order.

In the USA, for further information and a complete catalogue call 1-800-526-2778.

SHORT STORY COLLECTIONS
IN EVERYMAN

A SELECTION

The Secret Self 1:
Short Stories by Women
'A superb collection' *Guardian* **£4.99**

Selected Short Stories
and Poems
THOMAS HARDY
The best of Hardy's Wessex in a
unique selection **£4.99**

The Best of
Sherlock Holmes
ARTHUR CONAN DOYLE
All the favourite adventures in one
volume **£4.99**

Great Tales of Detection
Nineteen Stories
Chosen by Dorothy L. Sayers **£3.99**

Short Stories
KATHERINE MANSFIELD
A selection displaying the remarkable range of Mansfield's writing
£3.99

Selected Stories
RUDYARD KIPLING
Includes stories chosen to reveal the
'other' Kipling **£4.50**

The Strange Case of
Dr Jekyll and Mr Hyde
and Other Stories
R. L. STEVENSON
An exciting selection of gripping
tales from a master of suspense **£3.99**

The Day of Silence and
Other Stories
GEORGE GISSING
Gissing's finest stories, available for
the first time in one volume **£4.99**

Selected Tales
HENRY JAMES
Stories portraying the tensions
between private life and the outside
world **£5.99**

£4.99

AVAILABILITY
All books are available from your local bookshop or direct from
**Littlehampton Book Services Cash Sales, 14 Eldon Way, Lineside Estate,
Littlehampton, West Sussex BN17 7HE.** PRICES ARE SUBJECT TO CHANGE.

To order any of the books, please enclose a cheque (in £ sterling) made payable to
Littlehampton Book Services, or phone your order through with credit card details (Access,
Visa or Mastercard) on 0903 721596 (24 hour answering service) stating card number and
expiry date. Please add £1.25 for package and postage to the total value of your order.

In the USA, for further information and a complete catalogue call 1-800-526-2778.

CLASSIC FICTION IN EVERYMAN

A SELECTION

Frankenstein
MARY SHELLEY
A masterpiece of Gothic terror in its original 1818 version **£3.99**

Dracula
BRAM STOKER
One of the best known horror stories in the world **£3.99**

The Diary of A Nobody
GEORGE AND WEEDON GROSSMITH
A hilarious account of suburban life in Edwardian London **£4.99**

Some Experiences and Further Experiences of an Irish R. M.
SOMERVILLE AND ROSS
Gems of comic exuberance and improvisation **£4.50**

Three Men in a Boat
JEROME K. JEROME
English humour at its best **£2.99**

Twenty Thousand Leagues under the Sea
JULES VERNE
Scientific fact combines with fantasy in this prophetic tale of underwater adventure **£4.99**

The Best of Father Brown
G. K. CHESTERTON
An irresistible selection of crime stories – unique to Everyman **£4.99**

The Collected Raffles
E. W. HORNUNG
Dashing exploits from the most glamorous figure in crime fiction **£4.99**

£5.99